COMMON CORE BRIEF REVIEW 2015

Algebra 1

William Caroscio / Irene "Sam" Jovell

PEARSON

Authors

William Caroscio taught mathematics for 33 years. This experience included junior high s[...] high school, undergraduate, and graduate college teaching experience. After retirement fr[...] the classroom Bill has worked for 10 years as a mathematics consultant providing training[...] focused on integrating the use of technology in mathematics instruction. Bill is Past Presid[...] the Association of Mathematics Teachers of New York State and Past President of New Y[...] State Association of Mathematics Supervisors. He is a national contract instructor for the [...] (Teachers Teaching with Technology) program. Bill conducts sessions and workshops at t[...] local, state, and national levels. During his career he has served as an item writer for the [...] New York State Education Department assessment committees, as a member of the Commissioner's Committee on the New Mathematics Standards, and the Geometry Comm[...] writing sample tasks for the new state standards. Bill is a member of NCTM, AMTNYS, NYSAMS, MAA, and NYSMATYC.

Irene "Sam" Jovell is presently a Senior Mathematics Specialist for the Questar III BOCE[...] Albany NY. She provides professional development for teachers and administrators, K–12,[...] emphasis on mathematical literacy, curriculum design, assessment development, and effec[...] teaching practices. She previously taught at Niskayuna High School, Union University, an[...] served the New York State Education Department by participating on new standards an[...] ment development committees. Mrs. Jovell is a past president of both the Association of[...] Teacher of NYS and the New York State Mathematics Supervisors. She has been a spea[...] the local, state, and national levels and has authored texts on Algebra and Pre-Calculus. [...]

Reviewer

Michael Green
Mathematics Editor, Writer, and Reviewer
Chicago, Illinois

Acknowledgments appear on p. A-1, which constitutes an extension of this copyright page.

ISBN-13: 978-0-13-331777-0
ISBN-10:   0-13-331777-3

PEARSON

TABLE OF CONTENTS

Chapter 1   Real Numbers and Algebraic Expressions

		Common Core State Standards	MP
1.1	Set Theory. 2	N.Q.2 N.Q.3 8.SP.4	
1.2	Names for Real Numbers 6	N.RN.3	MP6
1.3	The Real Number Line 10	N.Q.2	MP5
1.4	Properties of Exponents 13	A.APR.6	
1.5	Radical Expressions and Order of Operations. 18	N.RN.3	
1.6	The Pythagorean Theorem 26	A.CED.1 8.G.7	MP7
1.7	Arithmetic and Geometric Sequences. 30	F.BF.2 F.IF.3	MP7
1.8	Dimensional Analysis 35	N.Q.1 N.Q.3	MP4
1.9	Variables and Variable Expressions 38	A.CED.1 F.BF.1.a	MP1

Chapter 2   Functions

Chapter 3   Linear Equations and Inequalities in One Variable

Chapter 4 Linear Equations and Inequalities in Two Variables

Chapter 5 Exponential Functions and Applications

Chapter 6 Transformations in the Plane

Chapter 9 Statistics

INTRODUCTION

This book has been written for you, a high school student enrolled in a Common Core Algebra 1 mathematics course. You can use it as a tool for understanding the process and the content of the Common Core Algebra Curriculum.

The Common Core standards identify the mathematical knowledge, skills, and behaviors that students should acquire during high school, so when they graduate they will be mathematically ready to enter college or a career. The knowledge and skills for each course are defined in the **Standards for Mathematical Content,** while the **Standards for Mathematical Practice** describe the processes and behaviors that lead a student toward well-developed problem-solving skills and mathematical proficiency.

The **Standards for Mathematical Practice** can be found in their entirety at:

http://www.corestandards.org/Math/Practice

An overview of each of the eight Mathematical Practices is below.

1. Make sense of problems and persevere in solving them.
2. Reason abstractly and quantitatively.
3. Construct viable arguments and critique the reasoning of others.
4. Model with mathematics.
5. Use appropriate tools strategically.
6. Attend to precision.
7. Look for and make use of structure.
8. Look for and express regularity in repeated reasoning.

Throughout the Brief Review, look for the (MP) symbol to show that you should apply the indicated Practice(s) to the problem situation.

The **Standards for Mathematical Content** for Algebra I are presented in the Brief Review first as a "snap-shot" at the start of each chapter's section, but again in the back of the book. There the content standard is stated completely and tracked to its chapter and section location in the Brief Review.

Structure of the Brief Review

Included in the front of the book are brief diagnostic tests for each chapter. These tests will allow you to measure your level of understanding of the content and concentrate on the specific concepts according to your needs.

Each lesson in this book
- addresses specific content standards of the Algebra I Curriculum.
- includes definitions, formulas, and examples with complete explanations.
- provides practice exercises at the end of every lesson to check for understanding.

At the end of each chapter, review exercises entitled *Preparing for the Assessment* address the entire content of the chapter and include both short and extended response questions.

INTRODUCTION

Calculator Solutions

Graphing calculator solutions are offered throughout the text as an alternative problem-solving method.

Glossary

A complete glossary of terms is included in the back of this book. It offers a complete definition of the term, with examples as appropriate.

Problem Solving Strategies

The Brief Review models lots of problems that might appear on an Algebra 1 assessment. These problems are either short-response questions, usually graded at 1 or 2 points with no partial credit, or an extended response question, graded with a rubric, which would assign points based on the quality of the work shown.

Based on the **Standards of Mathematical Practice,** here are problem-solving strategies that should be used throughout the Brief Review.

Problem Solving Strategies

Strategies for Short-Response Questions

- Carefully read each question before answering to be sure that you know what is being asked. MP 1

- Think about the concept of the problem and what you have been taught. MP 7

- Immediately cross out choices that you know cannot be correct. MP 2

- Work backwards from the choices. MP 2

- Use guess-and-check or trial-and-error. MP 5

- Try to estimate the answer when appropriate. This may help you eliminate some choices. MP 2

- Draw a diagram, table, or picture, or write an equation. MP 4

- Look for patterns. MP 8

- Use your calculator for square roots, decimals, percents, and fractions. MP 5

- Before choosing a final answer make sure it is labeled with correct units. MP 6

- Before choosing a final answer, check to see that it is reasonable. MP 2

- Check each choice against the wording of the question, just as you would check the solution in the problem. MP 1

- Don't give up, THINK! MP 1

While many short-response questions are multiple choice with one correct choice, other common short-response questions may be fill-in-the-blank or multiple choice with many correct choices. In the three short-response questions that follow, examine how the problem solving strategies have been used.

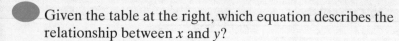

● Given the table at the right, which equation describes the relationship between x and y?

x	0	1	2	3	4
y	−1	1	3	5	7

(1) $y = 2x$ (2) $y = x - 1$ (3) $y = 2x - 1$ (4) $y = 2x + 1$

Strategies: Use concept and what you know; trial-and-error; elimination.

You know the equation is in $y = mx + b$ form and that "b" is the y-intercept $(0, -1)$, so $b = -1$. **Eliminate** choices 1 and 4.

Try choice (2): $y = x - 1$.
When $x = 1$, it is clear that
$y = x - 1$ will not produce
the given table.

x	0	1	2	3	4
y	$0 - 1 = -1$	$1 - 1 = 0$			

Now you complete the work to determine the correct answer.

Try choice (3): $y = 2x - 1$. Fill
in the table at the right.

x	0	1	2	3	4
y					

The answer is _____.   *[See page xviii for the answer.]*

● The math club presently has 25 members. It has set a goal to increase membership by 5 members each year.

Determine a recursive formula for $f(n)$, the number of members the math club has as a goal for membership in n years.

If $f(1) =$ ⬚ , then $f(n) =$ ⬚ , for $n >$ ⬚

From the choices below, place the letter of the expression needed to complete each of the blanks in the above statement.

A. 0   B. 1   C. 2   D. 5   E. 10   F. 25   G. $f(1) + 5$ H. $f(n) + 25$

J. $f(n - 1) + 5$ K. $f(n - 1) + 25$ L. $f(n + 1) + 5$ M. $f(n + 1) + 25$

Strategies: Build a table, look for a pattern, eliminate choices.

Table starts at 25 in the first year and increases by 5.

The table gives a huge clue for the value of year 1 and also eliminates choices H; K; and M, since those functions are increasing by 25

Year	1	2	3	4
Members	25	30	35	40

The answer is _____; _____; and _____   *[See page xviii for the answer.]*

Which of the 5 equations shown below are equivalent to
$30 - 10x = \frac{1}{3}(x - 3)$?
Circle all the choices that apply.

A. $5(6 - 2x) = \frac{1}{3}(x - 3)$

B. $90 - 30x = x - 3$

C. $30 - 2x = \frac{1}{3}x - 3$

D. $-31 = -\frac{31}{3}x$

E. $x = -3$

Strategies: Use substitution to check solutions, use the properties of equality.

Choice E is a possible solution of the given equation. Do a check.

$$30 - 10x = \frac{1}{3}(x - 3) \quad \rightarrow \quad 30 - 10(-3) = \frac{1}{3}((-3) - 3)$$

$$30 + 30 = \frac{1}{3}(-6)$$

$$60 = -2 \qquad \text{False statement.}$$
$$\text{Not equivalent.}$$

Choice A's right expression is the same as the right expression of the given equation. How are the left expressions related? Does $5(6 - 2x) = 30 - 10x$? Distributive Law. Equivalent!

There are two more correct choices in B, C, and D. Can you find the remaining two equivalent equations?

The correct choices are __A__; _____; and _____

[See page xviii for the answer.]

PROBLEM SOLVING STRATEGIES

Strategies for Extended-Response Questions

You will find many of the same strategies used for short-response questions, but these extended-response strategies also stress good communication skills, as your work will be graded by others who have to understand what you have written.

- Carefully read each question before answering to be sure that you know what is being asked. MP 1

- Think about the concept of the problem and what you have been taught. MP 7

- Represent your variables at the start of each solution, so relationships are clearly understood. MP 4

- Draw a diagram, table, or picture, or write an equation. MP 4

- When asked to justify, make sure your evidence is both verbal and numerical, and clearly supports your conclusions. MP 4

- You need to show work. No work…No credit! MP 1

- If a solution includes measurements, label your answer with the proper unit of measure, such as inches, centimeters, hours, or miles per hour. MP 6

- If you are using a calculator, estimate your answers to make sure your calculator answer is reasonable. Be sure to explain your work in detail, including those steps you performed on the calculator. MP 2

- If a question has multiple parts, do all parts. Even if you can not do the first part, you can still get partial credit for any appropriate work shown in the other parts. MP 1

- Use guess-and-check or trial-and-error. Show trials both right and wrong. MP 5

- Use your calculator for square roots, decimals, percents, and fractions. MP 5

- Don't give up, THINK! MP 1

Extended-response questions are graded with a rubric. The rubric awards credit based on the correctness of the work shown. For the practice problems that follow, you will award credit to two students' solutions using the accompanying rubric.

Model Rubric

Credit	The Work Shown ...
No	is blank; is totally incorrect; lacks understanding of the problem's concept.
Little	is incomplete; has multiple calculation errors; indicates some understanding of the problem's concept.
Most	is conceptually complete but not correct; contains calculation errors; lacks unit or labels; has a weak justification.
Full	is conceptually complete and correct; includes representing variables; has all required labels; has viable justifications.

Put the rubic to work to show model solutions at each credit level.

> Jane has saved $40 to buy a new dress. She sees a $52 dress on sale for 25% off. The state sales tax is 8%. Can Jane afford to buy the sale dress? Justify your answer.

Credit	Work shown to solve Jane's problem...	Why the Credit?
No	No, because $52 is more than $40.	No understanding of concept.
Little	Yes, because 0.75 ($52) = $39	Incomplete sales tax not calculated.
Most	No, because 0.75 ($52) = $39 and sales tax would be more than a dollar.	Justification weak since the exact cost with sales tax not found.
Full	No, because 0.75 ($52) = $39. Then need sales tax, so 1.08 ($39) = $42.12 $42.12 > $40.00	Complete and correct Label with $ Good justification

The next three problems show two student solutions, but no scores are given. At the end of each problem, you will be asked to score each students solution using the Model Rubric.

PROBLEM SOLVING STRATEGIES

Mary and Amy had 20 yards of material with which to make costumes. Mary used three times the amount of material that Amy used. Two yards of material were not used. How many yards did Amy use for her costume?

Student 1's solution

Let x represent the amount Amy used.
Then $3x$ represents the amount Mary used.
$$3x + x + 2 = 20$$
$$4x = 22$$
$$x = 5.5$$

Student 2's solution

Mary ☐☐☐
Amy ☐ 20 } yds
Not used 2 yds

$$4☐ + 2 = 20$$
$$4☐ = 18$$
$$☐ = 4.5 \text{ yds}$$

Imagine that you are the scorer. Study the scoring key, award appropriate credits to each student, and give reasons for the score you gave.

My score for student 1 _____

My reason(s) _____
_____

My score for student 2 _____

My reason(s) _____

[See page xviii for the answers.]

Here's another problem, with two more students' work for you to score. The two-way table shows the number of students who take a science or mathematics course at the local high school.

	Science	No Science
Math	14	22
No Math	6	8

Given that you take a science course, what is the relative frequency of those students who take no math class?

Student 1's solution

A total of 20 students take a science course so the 6 science students that do not take a math class represent
$$\frac{6}{20} = \frac{30}{100} = 30\%$$

Student 2's solution

6 students take no math

My score for student 1 _____

My reason(s) _____
_____

My score for student 2 _____

My reason(s) _____

[See page xviii for the answers.]

Here's the last problem for you to score:

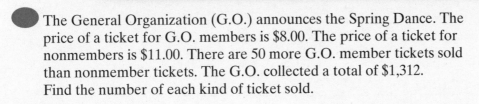 The General Organization (G.O.) announces the Spring Dance. The price of a ticket for G.O. members is $8.00. The price of a ticket for nonmembers is $11.00. There are 50 more G.O. member tickets sold than nonmember tickets. The G.O. collected a total of $1,312. Find the number of each kind of ticket sold.

Student 1's solution

$$x + y = 50$$
$$8x + 11y = 1,312$$

$$8x + 8y = 400$$
$$8x + 11y = 1,312$$
$$3y = 912$$
$$y = 304$$

Student 2's solution

Let x = nonmembers
then $y = x + 50$ members
$$8(x + 50) + 11x = 1,312$$

$$8(x + 50) + 11x = 1,312$$
$$8x + 400 + 11x = 1,312$$
$$19x = 912$$
$$x = 48 \text{ nonmembers}$$
and $y = 98$ members

My score for student 1 _____

My reason(s) _____

_____

My score for student 2 _____

My reason(s) _____

_____

[See page xviii for the answers.]

ANSWERS

Short-Response Questions

Table Problem	(3)
Math Club Problem: Insert	(F, J, B)
Equivalent Equations Problem: Circle	(A, B, D)

Extended-Response Questions

Your scores for the Extended-response questions should be the same as those shown below. The exact words that you used in writing the reasons for your scores might be a little different than the words used in the reasons below.

Costume Problem

Score for Student 1: Most Credit
Reason(s) for Score: appropriate method shown but incorrect answer found

Score for Student 2: Full Credit
Reason(s) for Score: correct answer and appropriate method shown

Two-Way Table Problem

Score for Student 1: Full Credit
Reason(s) for Score: correct answer and appropriate method shown

Score for Student 2: Little Credit
Reason(s) for Score: is incomplete

Spring Dance Problem

Score for Student 1: Little Credit
Reason(s) for Score: no definition of variables; incorrect relationship between variables; wrong and incomplete answer

Score for Student 2: Full Credit
Reason(s) for Score: defined variables; substitution shown and calculations are correct with answers defined

A Tool of Mathematics—Graphing Calculators

The use of a graphing calculator in mathematics instruction provides the user with a new set of algorithms for solving problems. This technology tool also provides a new set of challenges. If not used properly, incorrect results can inappropriately be attributed to a calculator solution. **Consider solution methods that can be implemented on a graphing calculator throughout this text. Often these solutions will lead to an insight that would otherwise be overlooked.** A real advantage of many graphing calculators is that the tools described in the CCSS Mathematical Practice #5 are included in one handheld device. This offers students a single platform with the power envisioned by the authors of the standards. In the material that follows, and throughout this book, a number of different methods from three popular graphing calculators will be shown. Whichever tool you choose, become aware of its features in order to maximize its potential.

> **The Common Core State Standards Mathematical Practice #5.**
>
> Use appropriate tools strategically. This practice includes the statement, *"…These tools might include pencil and paper, concrete models, a ruler, a protractor, a calculator, a spreadsheet, a computer algebra system, a statistical package, or dynamic geometry software. …"*

Numeration

The large screen displays on graphing calculators allow the user to see both the problem and the answer on the screen at the same time. In the accompanying figures, we see that both a rational answer and a decimal answer can be displayed. These figures are from three different calculators, however the results are very similar. You should make sure you are able to display both forms of an answer on your calculator of choice. When you enter an operation without first entering a value, the calculator will perform the operation on the previous answer.

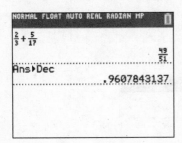 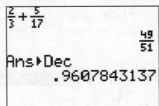 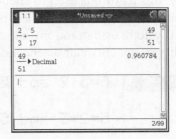

Some calculators are able to display the results of calculations with very large numbers. Others will display the result in **scientific notation.** In the following figures, we see one result is written in standard form and the other is written in scientific notation. The result in scientific notation is the same as $6.050760407 \times 10^{12}$ the symbol E represents multiplying by 10 and the number following the symbol is the exponent.

USING A CALCULATOR

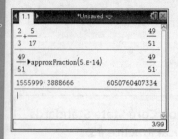 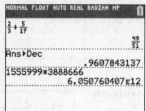 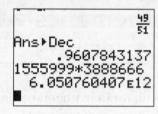

Evaluating Algebraic Expressions

Expressions can be evaluated using the STO→ command. For example, the expression $a^2 - ab$ can be evaluated when a and b take on specific values. Notice that multiple statements can be combined on one command line by using a colon between the commands. **CAUTION:** Make sure to press the multiplication key between the a and b in the expression as some calculators allow for variables with multiple characters. To ensure the correct calculation, place a times sign between variables.

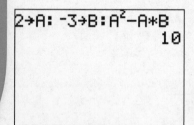  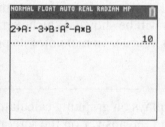

Informal Logic

Logical statements can be investigated using the [TEST] feature of some calculators. Other calculators allow you to simply type the statement and a result is reported. Notice that some calculators report a *one* for *true* and a *zero* for *false* while others actually print the words *true* and *false*. In the second set of figures below, this feature is used to check the validity of algebraic expressions. Although the particular calculators used here do not contain a computer algebra system, using random, carefully chosen values for the variables, the validity of equality can be checked.

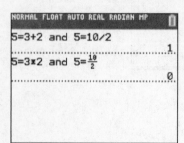 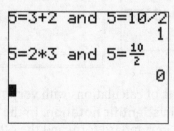 

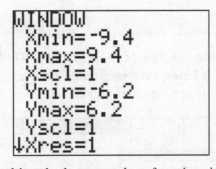

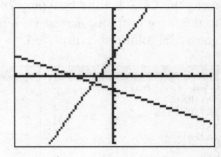

Friendly Window

When using a graphing calculator, it is important to have graphical representations displayed accurately. Perpendicular lines should look perpendicular; circles should look like circles, and so on. With most graphing calculators, this can be accomplished by setting a "friendly window". The figure at the right shows the graph of the lines $y = 2x + 3$ and $y = -\frac{1}{2}x - 2$ graphed in the default window.

Due to the number of pixels on the screen, a friendly window for this calculator is shown, and the graph is displayed using the new window. Note that the graphs of the lines now appear perpendicular. This window establishes a "nice" value for Δx, and also takes the screen aspect ratio into account. When this calculator graphs a function, it creates a table of values beginning with x-min and ending with x-max. These values are incremented by $\Delta x = \dfrac{x_{\max} - x_{\min}}{94}$. Therefore, when the numerator is a multiple of 94, the increment of x will be "nice". In the case shown $\Delta x = .2$. By maintaining a ratio of approximately $\frac{3}{2}$ for x to y, the screen is "squared," which will result in perpendicular lines looking perpendicular, etc. If students are to interpret graphical information visually, it is important that they can set windows that take into account these two important ideas: "nice" Δx, and square window. The calculator features under the **ZOOM** key, namely **ZDecimal** and **ZSquare**, can accomplish these same results. However, by setting the window manually, the user will better understand the numerical features of the calculator he or she is using. Whichever graphing calculator you choose to use, it will be helpful to determine the appropriate setting for establishing a "friendly window."

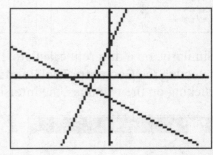

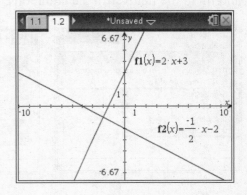

Some calculators have a default window that is friendly, as the one shown in the figure at the right. Notice also that both the graph of the line and its equation are shown on the screen at the same time. In some cases, the color of the line can be changed, and the graph of the line and its equation will be displayed in the same color. This helps make a connection between the graphical and analytical representations for the same line.

Solving Systems of Equations

Solutions to systems of linear equations can be implemented in a variety of ways when using technology. By providing students with multiple solution methods, they are able to choose which works best for them. Consider the equations $y = x + 1$ and $y = -\frac{1}{2}x + 3$. By graphing these equations and using the **CALC** feature by typing **2nd[CALC]**, select **Intersect**. Now respond to the three prompts; *first curve, second curve,* and *guess.* After entering a guess, the solutions is displayed.

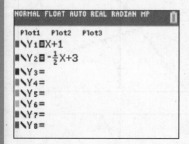 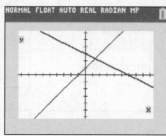 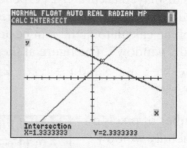

Similarly, on a different calculator, the equations can be graphed. Then selecting the **Geometry Tool Points & Lines, Intersection Point(s)** and clicking on the two lines, the intersection point is displayed.

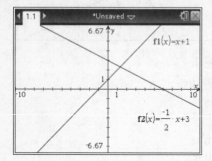 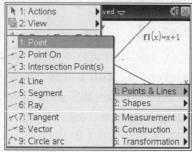 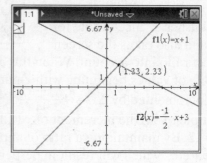

This particular calculator has a built in system solver. It can be accessed by pressing **MENU Algebra>Solve System of Linear Equations**. Respond to the dialogue boxes giving the number of equations and the variables. Press **[OK]** and fill in the fields with the equations, then press **ENTER**.

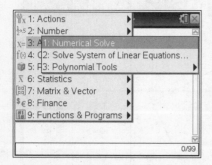 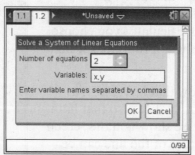 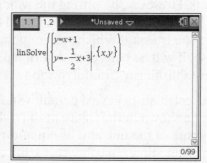

Notice the results using this method are displayed in rational form.

The use of technology allows the implementation of a **matrix** solution for linear systems. We will solve the matrix equation $AX = B$ by multiplying both sides by the inverse of matrix A. Namely, $A^{-1}AX = A^{-1}B$ which results in the solution matrix. In the series of screens below, the matrix editor can be entered by pressing **ALPHA ZOOM** and selecting the number of rows and columns. The cells of the matrix are filled in and the matrix is stored. It must be stored in a matrix location with is accessed by pressing **2nd[MATRX].** Here the coefficient matrix is stored in A and the constant matrix is stored in B.

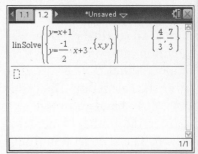

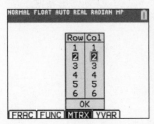
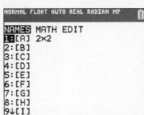
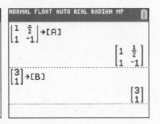

The matrix multiplication is performed and the result is displayed. The result can be converted to rational form by pressing **MATH ▶Frac**.

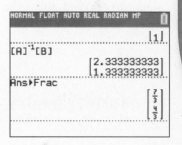

In more sophisticated calculators, the matrix editor is accessed by pressing **MENU** Matrix & Vector>Create>Matrix. Fill in the fields in the dialogue box and enter the values. This calculator allows the matrix to be stored immediately in variable a.

A template for entering matrices can also be used by selecting the appropriate template, as shown on the first screen below. Enter the constant matrix and perform the matrix multiplication as follows:

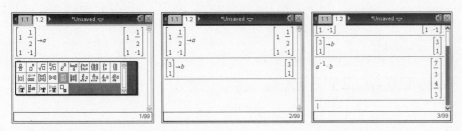

USING A CALCULATOR

Solving Inequalities

Similar to solving a system of equations graphically, a system of inequalities can be solved using the calculator. The system $y < -\frac{1}{2}x + 3$ and $y \geq x + 1$ is entered into the Y= menu as shown. The style icon in front of the y_1 and y_2 is changed to the appropriate **shade above** or **shade below** icon. As seen in the figure, the regions where the shaded areas intersect is the solution set.

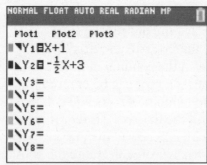

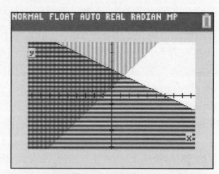

It is important when using the calculator solution to state whether the line is part of the solution or not. Some calculators do not allow the line to be drawn as "dashed" when the boundary is not included.

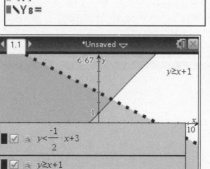

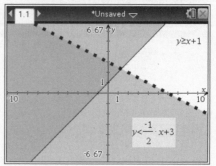

Some newer calculators allow for the inequalities to be entered in mathematical form and the boundaries are graphed properly. Make sure you know which the case is for the calculator you are using.

Quadratics

When solving quadratic equations, a graphical solution is easily implemented using the calculator. The equation is entered in Y= and graphed by pressing GRAPH. The CALC menu is used by pressing **2nd[CALC]** zero. Each root is found separately by entering a **left bound**, **right bound**, and a **guess**. The screens for this procedure are shown in the sequence below.

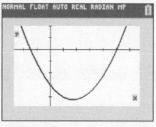

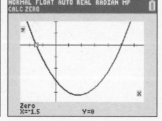

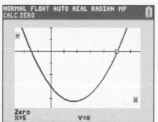

Here again, newer technology tools make this process much smoother. Simply graphing the function and tracing along the curve, the critical points are identified.

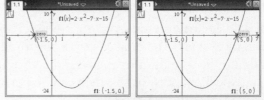

The **nature of the roots** of a quadratic can also be determined by looking at its graph. Here three quadratics are graphed.

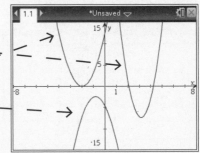

- one has two real roots, crosses the x-axis twice,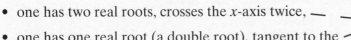
- one has one real root (a double root), tangent to the x-axis,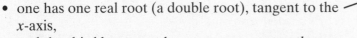
- and the third has no real roots, never crosses the 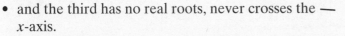 x-axis.

When trying to factor quadratic expressions, the graph can be helpful. For example, when factoring $3x^2 + x - 24$ it would be helpful to know the roots of the parabola. The roots can be found as described above. Then, knowing the roots, the factors can be determined algebraically.

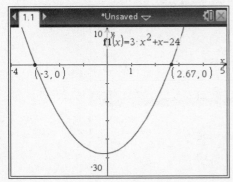

$$x = -3 \qquad\qquad x = 2\tfrac{2}{3} = \tfrac{8}{3}$$
$$x + 3 = 0 \qquad\qquad 3x = 8$$
$$\qquad\qquad\qquad\quad 3x - 8 = 0$$
$$(x + 3)(3x - 8) = 3x^2 + x - 24$$

A calculator can be useful in creating a table of values when graphing by a traditional paper and pencil method. Enter the equation in the **Y=** menu. Then the values are entered into **2nd[TBLSET]**. Finally, type **2nd[TABLE]** to display the table of values. By using the calculator in this way, it is often possible to eliminate careless mistakes in creating a table of values.

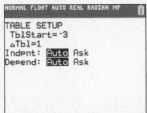

In this figure, we see the graph of the same function and the table in a split screen at the same time. Once the function is graphed on this calculator, pressing **CTRL-T** splits the screen and displays the table. There are real advantages to having both the graph and the table displayed at the same time when students need to see the connection between the two representations.

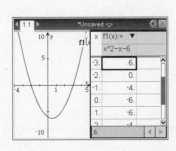

USING A CALCULATOR

Statistics

Statistical data can be entered from the home screen by using the **{}** keys and listing the data as a set. The data can then be stored in a list. The data can also be entered into the list editor by pressing the **STAT** key and selecting Edit. One variable statistical analysis for this data can be performed by pressing **STAT** then selecting **CALC** and 1-Var Stats.

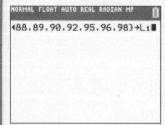

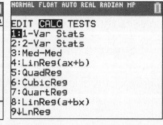

The results are displayed. The down arrow in front of Q_1 in the last line informs the user that there is more information to be shown. Pressing the down arrow key reveals the remainder of the information.

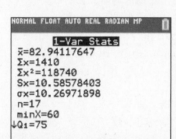

A graphical representation of the data set that includes the five statistical summary: Min, Q_1, Median, Q_3, and Max is called a **box plot**.

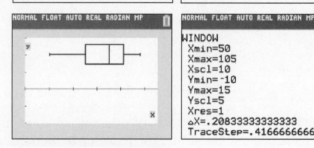

A second plot can be added to show a histogram of this data. These graphs can be displayed together as shown. If desired, the graphs could be displayed individually also.

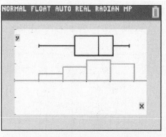

Some calculators allow you to use names for variables. Here we see the list is stored in *grades*.

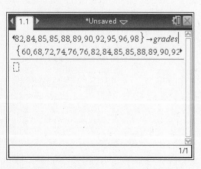

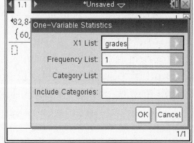

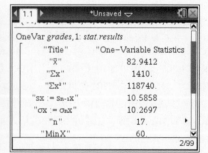

This particular calculator includes more statistics in this analysis than the previous one. Again, it takes more than one screen to display all the information. Some of the information contained in these screens is beyond the scope of this book, while others will be discussed in detail in the material that follows.

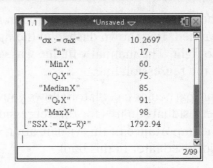

This calculator allows both the data and graph to be displayed. If desired, they can be displayed separately.

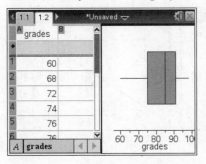
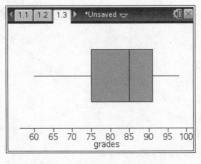

As before, a histogram can be drawn, and, in this case, the labels are placed on the appropriate axes. Notice that because this calculator displays more information, it is much easier to interpret this graph than the one drawn on the previous calculator.

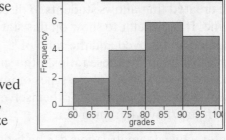

If the set of scores we have been using were the scores received in a math test and we want ot compare them to a second set, let's say in science, a **scatter diagram** can be used to visualize these two sets of data.

The science scores are entered in a second list and the scatter plot is graphed. Notice that this calculator allows you to label the axes appropriately and shows the "name" of each ordered pair.

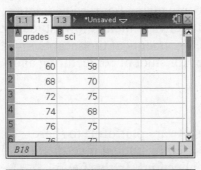
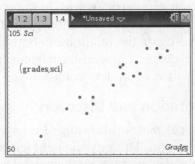

A line can be added to this scatter plot and then manipulated until it best fits the data. Once you are satisfied with the fit, you can have the calculator display the equation of the line.

This manually drawn line of best fit can be compared to the least squares regression line by performing a **linear regression** analysis.

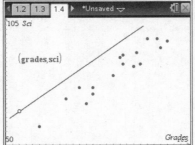
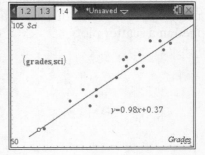

The regression equation is stored in $f1(x)$ and graphed. It is shown dashed in the figure to the right. The manually fit line was very close to the regression line.

This particular calculator allows you to show the residual squares for this regression line. The importance of this visualization will be addressed later in this book.

Interactive Geometry

Many graphing calculators also include software for drawing interactive geometric figures. This platform is not only for use in the geometry class, but is very useful in algebra as well. It can be used as a tool for investigation and discovery of important relationships.

Using the construction features of the geometry software, a drawing can be created that allows students to discover the slope relationship for a line. It is difficult to show on this static page, but this line can be grabbed and moved and the ratio of $\frac{rise}{run}$ and $\frac{run}{rise}$ remain constant. However, only one of these ratios is the same as the slope of the line that has been measured. These types of investigation allow students to discover the mathematics for themselves. It is the mathematics they discover that they will remember.

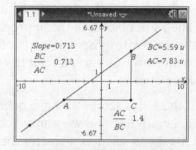

The interactive geometry tools can be used to discover relationships between geometric figures. In the accompanying figure, a geometric construction in an interactive geometry environment allows students to investigate the relationship between segments of the secants. This provides a powerful environment for student conjecturing and verification of student conjectures.

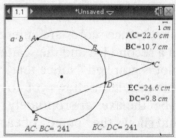

Integration and Discovery

Some calculators allow the different software platforms to share information. This environment lends itself to student investigation and the discovery of mathematical connections. In this figure, the measures of the radii of a circle and its area are collected and graphed in a scatter plot.

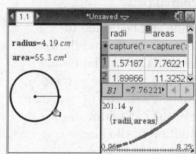

A quadratic function is then fit to the scatter plot. In this case $f(x) = 3.1x^2 + .14x - .44$. This leads to a discussion about what this function represents and how accurate an approximation it is. In this case $f(x)$ is an approximation for the area function with x representing the radius. $f(x) = 3.1x^2 + .14x - .44 \approx 3.1x^2$ which is a very good approximation for $A = \pi r^2$.

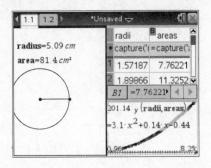

Multiple Representations

People learn in different ways. The ability to approach problems from multiple perspectives provides a powerful tool for investigation. Technology provides a platform where you can approach problems from multiple perspectives. As you work through this text, challenge yourself to ask how the problem could be approached from a different perspective. Try to approach problems from numeric, algebraic, and graphical perspectives.

A Final Word About Technology

Some parents, teachers and mathematicians are concerned that the use of the graphing calculator can inhibit computational skills and the development of algebraic skills. These concerns are not supported by the research. Algebraic thinking is not necessarily dependent upon computational competency. When technology tools are used appropriately, they can help develop both computational and algebraic skills.

It would be wonderful if all our students had a strong number sense and strong arithmetic skills, including mastery of fractions and decimals. The unfortunate fact is that many start secondary school without those skills and understandings. Fortunately this situation no longer needs to prevent learners from continued mathematical study. Available technology tools can provide the necessary arithmetic assistance to enable mathematical investigation, analysis, and augmentation for learning algebraic concepts. Often, this can also provide the motivation for improving missing competencies.

Name _____ Date _____

Diagnostic Test 1: Chapter 1

Real Numbers and Algebraic Expressions

Choose the numeral preceding the word or expression that best completes the statement or answers the question.

1 Evaluate: $-x^2 + 5x^0 + 3x^{-2}$ for $x = -1$.

   (1) 9   **(3)** 1

   (2) 7   **(4)** -3

2 Let $P = \{x \mid x$ is a multiple of 2$\}$ and $Q = \{x \mid x$ is a multiple of 3$\}$. What is $P \cap Q$?

   (1) $\{x \mid x$ is a multiple of 2$\}$

   (2) $\{x \mid x$ is an integer$\}$

   (3) $\{x \mid x$ is a multiple of 6$\}$

   (4) $\{x \mid x$ is a multiple of 3$\}$

3 If n is a number, write the expression that represents "6 less than the product of n and 5".

   (1) $6 < 5n$ **(3)** $5n - 6$

   (2) $5n < 6$ **(4)** $6 - 5n$

4 Which expression names an integer?

   (1) $\dfrac{2}{6}$ **(3)** $0.\overline{3}$

   (2) $\dfrac{-6}{2}$ **(4)** 0.333

5 The top of a 12-foot ladder leaning against a vertical wall touches a point 12 feet up the wall. How far from the wall is the base of the ladder?

   (1) 11 feet   **(3)** 5 feet

   (2) 14 feet   **(4)** 9 feet

6 Which equation, in recursive form, can be used to find the next number in the sequence: 16, 8, 4, 2, …?

   (1) $a_n = 2a_{(n-1)}$ **(3)** $a_n = 16(\frac{1}{2}n)$

   (2) $a_n = \frac{1}{2}a_{(n-1)}$ **(4)** $a_n = 16(\frac{1}{2})^{n-1}$

7 If $9^x \cdot 3^5 = 3$, find the value of x.

   (1) -2 **(3)** -4

   (2) 2   **(4)** 4

Questions 8–10 will be graded using the model rubric from Problem Solving Strategies. Points for your solution are based on the amount of credit awarded your work:

   NO = 0 ; LITTLE = 1; MOST = 2; FULL = 3

8 Show all work and simplify:

$$(-2)^3 - 30 \div [3(4 - 9) + (\tfrac{1}{3})^{-2}]$$

9 Simplify to an expression with only positive exponents.

$$\frac{-6x^5y^{-2}}{3x^{-4}y^6}$$

10 The tennis court is 1.75 miles from your house. You are walking toward the courts at 2.5 mph and after 6 minutes your pal picks you up in her car. Driving at the neighborhood speed limit of 30 mph, how many minutes did it take to get to the tennis court?

Diagnostic Test 2: Chapter 2

Functions

For 1–7, choose the numeral preceding the word or expression that best completes the statement or answers the question.

1 If $g(x) = 3x - 5$, find the value of $g(-2)$.

(1) 1   **(3)** 4

(2) −1   **(4)** −11

2 Which of the following does **not** define a function?

(1)

x	2	3	4	5	6
y	2	2	2	2	2

(2)

x	2	2	2	2	2
y	2	3	4	5	6

(3)

x	2	3	4	5	6
y	3	4	5	6	7

(4)

x	−2	−1	0	1	2
y	3	1	0	1	3

3 You pay a math tutor a retainer fee of $100 and then $20 per hour for each hour of tutoring. Write a function, c(t) for the cost of t hours of tutoring.

(1) $c(t) = 100t$ **(3)** $c(t) = 20t + 100$

(2) $c(t) = 20t$ **(4)** $c(t) = 100$

4 In what interval does the graph shown represent a constant function?

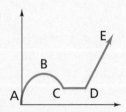

(1) [A, B]   **(3)** [C, D]

(2) [B, C]   **(4)** [D, E]

5 Given $h(x) = x^2 + 3$. If the domain of $h(x)$ is $\{-1, 0, 1\}$, then the range is

(1) {−3, 4, 3}   **(3)** {0, 4}

(2) {−4, 0, 4}   **(4)** {3, 4}

6 What does a vertical line test determine?

(1) A graph's end behavior

(2) If a graph is a function

(3) Where a graph is increasing

(4) The graph's domain

7 Water is poured into a vase at a constant rate. The graph below shows the water's depth (d) over time (t). Based on the graph, what is the shape of the vase?

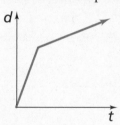

(1)   **(3)**

(2)   **(4)**

Name _____ Date _____

Diagnostic Test 2: Chapter 2 *continued*

Questions 8–10 will be graded using the model rubric from Problem Solving Strategies. Points for your solution are based on the amount of credit awarded your work:

NO = 0; LITTLE = 1; MOST = 2; FULL = 3

8 Bill and Sam had an 8-mile bike race. Based on the graph below, write a description of the race.

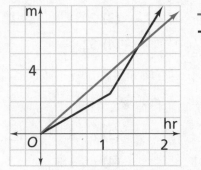

— Bill
— Sam

9 Complete the table of values for the function defined below.

$$f(x) = \begin{cases} x - 2, & [-5, 0) \\ 3 - x^2, & [0, 5] \\ 4, & (5, \infty) \end{cases}$$

x	10	5	0	−4
y	(a)	(b)	(c)	(d)

10 Fill in the missing parts of the function defined by the graph below.

$$f(x) = \begin{cases} x + 1, & \underline{\quad(a)\quad} \\ \underline{\quad(b)\quad}, & (0, 3] \\ -2x + 8, & \underline{\quad(c)\quad} \end{cases}$$

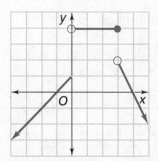

Name _____ Date _____

Diagnostic Test 3: Chapter 3

Linear Equations and Inequalities in One Variable

Choose the numeral preceding the word or expression that best completes the statement or answers the question.

1 If $a = b$, then $a + 3 = b + 3$, illustrates which property?

(1) reflexive property of $=$

(2) addition property of $=$

(3) subtraction property of $=$

(4) multiplicative property of $=$

2 Solve for x in terms of y and p: $5x + y = p^2 - px$

(1) $\dfrac{p^2 - px - y}{5}$ **(3)** $\dfrac{p^2 - y}{5 + p}$

(2) $\dfrac{p^2 + px + y}{5}$ **(4)** $\dfrac{p^2 + y}{5 - p}$

3 What is the solution set of $5 \le 4 - x < 8$?

(1) $(-4, -1)$ **(3)** $[-4, -1)$

(2) $[-4, -1]$ **(4)** $(-4, -1]$

4 Solve for t: $-3(t + 2) = 6 - 3t$

(1) 0   **(3)** {Reals}

(2) -12 **(4)** $\varnothing$

5 Which graph represents the solution set of the inequality $42 > -3x$?

(1)
$$\xleftarrow{\quad\overset{\oplus}{\underset{-14}{\mid}}\quad\underset{0}{\mid}\quad}$$
    -28 -14 0

(2)
    -28 -14 0

(3)
    0 14 28

(4)
    0 14 28

6 The sixth term of an arithmetic sequence is 10. If the common difference is -2, what is the value of the first term?

(1) 0   **(3)** 20

(2) 2   **(4)** 32

7 Solve for c.
$$\frac{c + 4}{12} = \frac{c + 2}{10}$$

(1) $c = 1$ **(3)** $c = 8$

(2) $c = -1$ **(4)** $c = -8$

Questions 8–10 will be graded using the model rubric from Problem Solving Strategies. Points for your solution are based on the amount of credit awarded your work:

NO = 0; LITTLE = 1; MOST = 2; FULL = 3

8 Jim and Susan mow lawns. The day they earned \$65 together, the ratio Susan's time mowing to Jim's time mowing was 8:5. Showing all work and models, determine Susan's part of the money earned?

9 Joe earns \$300 per week plus a 10% commission on his weekly sales. Showing all work and models, determine what his sales per week must be if he wants his weekly earnings to be at least \$500.

10 Justify the steps of the equation's solution.

$$
\begin{aligned}
5 - 2y &= 4 - 5(y + 1) \qquad &\text{property} \\
5 - 2y &= 4 - 5y - 5 \qquad &\rule{2cm}{0.4pt} \\
5 - 2y &= -1 - 5y \qquad &\rule{2cm}{0.4pt} \\
3y &= -6 \qquad &\rule{2cm}{0.4pt} \\
y &= -2 \qquad &\rule{2cm}{0.4pt}
\end{aligned}
$$

Name _____ Date _____

Diagnostic Test 4: Chapter 4

Linear Equations and Inequalities in Two Variables

Choose the numeral preceding the word or expression that best completes the statement or answers the question.

1 The slope of the line passing through the points (3, −2) and (7, 2) is

- **(1)** 0.
- **(2)** 1.
- **(3)** undefined.
- **(4)** −1.

2 Which best describes the slope of the line whose equation is $y = -3$?

- **(1)** positive
- **(2)** negative
- **(3)** zero
- **(4)** no

3 Write the equation of a line parallel to $y = 3x - 5$ and containing the point (0, −8).

- **(1)** $y = 3x - 3$
- **(2)** $y = 3x - 8$
- **(3)** $y = -\frac{1}{3}x - 3$
- **(4)** $y = -\frac{1}{3}x - 3$

4 Which best describes the solution of the system: $2x + y = 4$ and $8x = 16 - 4y$?

- **(1)** no points
- **(2)** infinitely many points
- **(3)** 1 point
- **(4)** parallel

5 Which point is in the solution of: $x - y < 2$?

- **(1)** (0, 0)
- **(2)** (0, −2)
- **(3)** (2, 0)
- **(4)** (2, −2)

6 What is the slope of a line perpendicular to $y = 4x + 3$?

- **(1)** 4
- **(2)** −4
- **(3)** $\frac{1}{4}$
- **(4)** $-\frac{1}{4}$

7 The equation $y = |x - 2| + 5$ is which translation of the absolute value function?

- **(1)** left two, up five
- **(2)** right two, down five
- **(3)** left two, down five
- **(4)** right two, up five

Questions 8–10 will be graded using the model rubric from Problem Solving Strategies. Points for your solution are based on the amount of credit awarded your work:

NO = 0; LITTLE = 1; MOST = 2; FULL = 3

8 Showing all work, write an equation of a line between (4, −5) and (−4, −1). Express the equation in standard form.

9 There are 352 students in the Senior class. Show work and models used to find the number of women in the Senior class if there are 40 more women than half the number of the men.

10 A rectangular garden is designed to be built next to a barn, so that the barn acts as the fourth side of the garden's fence. The remaining three sides must be fenced using between 50 and 100 feet of wire. The design requires that the length of the garden must be more than twice its width.

Write a set of inequalities that represent the constraints for the garden's design and find a possible set of garden dimensions.

Name _____ Date _____

Diagnostic Test 5: Chapter 5

Exponential Functions

Choose the numeral preceding the word or expression that best completes the statement or answers the question.

1 If $a \neq 0$ and $y = a^x$, what value of x will result in a value of 1 for y?

  (1) $x = 1$ **(3)** $x = 0$

  (2) $x = -1$ **(4)** $x = a$

2 The function $y = a(b^x)$ will represent exponential growth when

  (1) $a < 0$ and $b > 1$.

  (2) $a < 0$ and $b < 1$.

  (3) $a > 0$ and $b > 1$.

  (4) $a > 0$ and $b < 1$.

3 The graphs of every exponential function of the form $y = k^x$ have a point in common. What is that point?

  (1) $(1, 1)$ **(3)** $(1, 0)$

  (2) $(0, 1)$ **(4)** $(0, 0)$

4 Which is **not** an exponential function?

  (1) $y = 2(3)^x$ **(3)** $y = 5, 7, 9, 11, \ldots$

  (2) $y = 2, 4, 8, 16, \ldots$ **(4)** $y = (\frac{1}{4})^{x-1}$

5 Which exponential function exhibits negative end behavior?

  (1) $f(x) = -(0.5)^x$ **(3)** $f(x) = (5)^x$

  (2) $f(x) = (0.5)^x$ **(4)** $f(x) = x^5$

6 A geometric sequence has a first term of 300 and an explicit function rule $h(x) = 300(0.1)^{x-1}$. For what value(s) is x defined?

  (1) $x = 0$ **(3)** $x > 1$

  (2) $x > 0$ **(4)** $x \geq 1$

7 Suppose a city's population is 36,000 people today and its projected yearly growth is $1\frac{1}{2}$%. At this projected growth rate, what will be the city's approximate population be in 10 years?

  (1) 42,000   **(3)** 37,000

  (2) 40,000   **(4)** 146,000

Questions 8–10 will be graded using the model rubric from Problem Solving Strategies. Points for your solution are based on the amount of credit awarded your work:

  NO = 0; LITTLE = 1; MOST = 2; FULL = 3

8 You have 500 grams of a certain substance whose half-life is two days. Write an explicit function to define this decay. Be sure to clearly define variables.

9 You have 500 grams of a certain substance whose half-life is two days. Write recursive function to define this decay. Be sure to clearly define variables and function constraints.

10 New cars lose value at a rate of 18.5% of their initial cost as soon as you take ownership. 10 years ago, your car cost $45,000 new. Find the approximate value of the car today being sure to show the function used.

Name _____ Date _____

Diagnostic Test 6: Chapter 6

Transformations in the Plane

For 1–7, choose the numeral preceding the word or expression that best completes the statement or answers the question.

1 A function $y = x$ is translated up 6 units. What are the x and y intercepts of the new function?

(1) $(6, 0)$ and $(0, 6)$ **(3)** $(6, 0)$ and $(0, -6)$

(2) $(-6, 0)$ and $(0, 6)$ **(4)** $(6, 0)$ and $(0, -6)$

2 The graph of $f(x) = |x|$ is shown. Which is the graph of $g(x) = -|x - 3| - 2$?

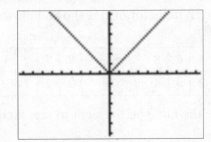

(1) 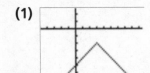   **(3)**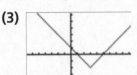

(2) 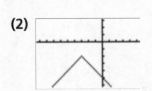   **(4)**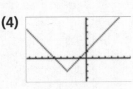

3 If $r(x)$ represents the rate that a car is traveling in x minutes, in miles per minute, then $f(x)$, the function that represents the car's rate in miles per hour, would be represented as

(1) $f(x) = r(x) + 60$

(2) $f(x) = \frac{r(x)}{60}$

(3) $f(x) = 60r(x)$

(4) $f(x) = r(x + 60)$

4 The transformation of $y = (5)^x$ to $y = (5)^{-x} - 2$ could be described as

(1) reflection over the x-axis; translation down 2 units.

(2) reflection over the x-axis; translation up 2 units.

(3) reflection over the y-axis; translation down 2 units.

(4) reflection over the y-axis; translation up 2 units.

5 The point (x, y) is on the graph of $y = x^2$. Which point is on the graph of $y = (x + 2)^2 - 5$?

(1) $(x + 2, y - 5)$

(2) $(x - 2, y + 5)$

(3) $(x + 2, y + 5)$

(4) $(x - 2, y - 5)$

6 The point $P(2, -5)$ is on the graph of $f(x)$ and then $f(x)$ is transformed to $g(x) = f(\frac{1}{2}x) + 1$. What are the new coordinates of P?

(1) $(1, -2)$ **(3)** $(1, -4)$

(2) $(4, -2)$ **(4)** $(4, -4)$

Name _____ Date _____

Diagnostic Test 6: Chapter 6 *continued*

7 Below, the upper table of values represents points of $f(x) = (2)^x$.

x	−1	0	1	2	3
f(x)	$\frac{1}{2}$	1	2	4	8

x	−1	0	1	2	3
f(x)	$\frac{1}{4}$	$\frac{1}{2}$	1	2	4

The lower table of values represents a transformation of $f(x)$ to $g(x)$. Which is NOT a representation of $g(x)$?

(1) $g(x) = \frac{1}{2}(2)^x$ **(3)** $g(x) = (2)^{\frac{x}{2}}$

(2) $g(x) = (2)^{x-1}$ **(4)** $g(x) = \frac{f(x)}{2}$

Questions 8–10 will be graded using the model rubric from Problem Solving Strategies. Points for your solution are based on the amount of credit awarded your work:

NO = 0; LITTLE = 1; MOST = 2; FULL = 3

8 You are working with an isotope that has a half-life of 1 hour. After 5 hours of work, there are 25 grams of the isotope left. Write an equation that can be used to find the initial amount of the isotope. How many grams were in the initial amount? (Hint…Write equation for now, then do a transformation to the initial time.)

9 The graph shown is a transformation of $y = x^2$ after a reflection over the x-axis, a vertical stretch, and both a horizontal and vertical translation. Write this graph's function rule, then use it to confirm that the point (6, 1) is on the graph.

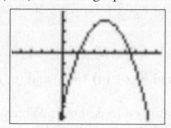

10 The function table for $h(x)$ is shown below on the left.

x	0	2	4	6	8		x	?	?	?	?	?
h(x)	4	0	2	0	4		g(x)	?	?	?	?	?

Complete the table on the right to represent $g(x) = h(2x)$.

Diagnostic Test 7: Chapter 7

Polynomials and Factoring

Choose the numeral preceding the word or expression that best completes the statement or answers the question.

1 Subract $c^2 - c + 2$ from $6 - 3c + 2c^2$.

    (1) $c^2 - 4c + 4$ **(3)** $c^2 - 2c + 4$

    (2) $-c^2 + 4c - 4$ **(4)** $-c^2 + 2c - 4$

2 Factor the expression $4x^2 - 36$.

    (1) $4(x - 3)(x + 3)$ **(3)** $(x - 6)(x + 6)$

    (2) $(4x - 9)(4x + 9)$ **(4)** $(4x - 9)(x + 4)$

3 Which is NOT a possible value for n that makes $n^2 + n - 12$ a factorable trinomial?

    (1) 11   **(3)** -4

    (2) -13 **(4)** 1

4 Simplify $(c - d)^2$.

    (1) $c^2 - d^2$ **(3)** $c^2 - d^2$

    (2) $c^2 - 2cd + d^2$ **(4)** $c^2 + 2cd + d^2$

5 Find the product $(y + 8)(y - 1)$.

    (1) $y^2 + 9y - 9$ **(3)** $y^2 - 7y - 8$

    (2) $y^2 + 7y - 8$ **(4)** $y^2 + 9y - 8$

6 What are the factors of $6x^2 + 25x - 9$?

    (1) $(x - 9)(6x + 1)$ **(3)** $(2x - 9)(3x + 1)$

    (2) $(x - 3)(6x + 3)$ **(4)** $(2x + 9)(3x - 1)$

7 For what value of n is $x^2 - 6x + n$ a perfect square trinomial?

    (1) 36   **(3)** 9

    (2) -36 **(4)** -9

Questions 8–10 will be graded using the model rubric from Problem Solving Strategies. Points for your solution are based on the amount of credit awarded your work:

    NO = 0; LITTLE = 1; MOST = 2; FULL = 3

8 Write a polynomial in standard form that represents the volume of a rectangular prism with length of $3x + 2$; width of $x - 1$; and height of $3 - 2x$.

9 Simplify: $(x - 3)^2 - (2x - 1)(2x + 1)$

10 Solve: $-2b(b - 5) - (b - 3b^2) = b^2 + 18$.

Name _____ Date _____

Diagnostic Test 8: Chapter 8

Quadratic Equations and Functions

Choose the numeral preceding the word or expression that best completes the statement or answers the question.

1 If the roots of a quadratic equation are $x = 2$ and $x = 5$, which of the following are possible factors of the quadratic?

(1) $(x + 2)$ and $(x + 5)$

(2) $(x - 2)$ and $(x - 5)$

(3) $(x + 2)$ and $(x - 5)$

(4) $(x - 2)$ and $(x + 5)$

2 What are the roots of $f(x) = 2x^2 - 3x - 1$?

(1) 1 and $\frac{1}{2}$

(2) -1 and $-\frac{1}{2}$

(3) $\frac{3}{4} \pm \frac{\sqrt{17}}{4}$

(4) $\frac{3}{4} \pm \frac{\sqrt{-17}}{4}$

3 A quadratic function's graph has an axis of symmetry at $x = -2$. If the point $(1, 4)$ is on the graph, what other point must be on the graph?

(1) $(-2, 4)$

(2) $(-5, 4)$

(3) $(3, 4)$

(4) $(-4, 4)$

4 Which of the following does not have a maximum?

(1) $y = x^2 + 3x + 5$

(2) $y = -4x^2 - 3x - 7$

(3) $y = 5x + 7 - 3x^2$

(4) $y = -x^2$

5 Which of the following are the coordinates of the vertex of the parabola whose equation is $y = x^2 - 4x + 5$?

(1) $(0, 0)$

(2) $(1, 2)$

(3) $(2, 1)$

(4) $(-4, 5)$

6 A parabola has a vertex of $(-3, 4)$ and passes through the point $(6, -5)$. Which is a possible equation for the parabola?

(1) $y = (x - 6)^2 - 5$

(2) $y = -(x - 6)^2 - 5$

(3) $y = (x - 3)^2 + 4$

(4) $y = -(x - 3)^2 + 4$

7 For which equation will the graph of $y = -x^2 + 2$ and the line intersect in two points?

(1) $y = -2x + 3$

(2) $y = 2$

(3) $y = 5$

(4) $y = 0$

Questions 8–10 will be graded using the model rubric from Problem Solving Strategies. Points for your solution are based on the amount of credit awarded your work:

NO $= 0$; LITTLE $= 1$; MOST $= 2$; FULL $= 3$

8 A farmer's rectangular pen is enclosed with 200 feet of fencing. What is the area function of the pen in Vertex form? What is the maximum area of the pen?

9 Compare the *average rate of change* for both functions in the interval $[0, 3]$.
$g(x) = -x^2 - 5x + 3$ and $h(x) = -8x + 10$

10 Describe the transformations on $f(x) = x^2$ represented by the function $g(x) = -2(x + 4)^2 - 3$.

Name _____ Date _____

Diagnostic Test 9: Chapter 9

Statistics

Choose the numeral preceding the word or expression that best completes the statement or answers the question.

1   A data set consists of ages. The mean of the data set is 24 years old with a standard deviation of 2 years. Which statement is **not** true?

   (1) The mean is a measure of central tendency.

   (2) The standard deviation is a measure of variability.

   (3) About 50% of the data are between ages 22 and 26.

   (4) About 68% of the data are between ages 22 and 26.

2   When the data were plotted, the shape of the distribution was not symmetric and skewed right. Which statement is true?

   (1) the mean and median are equal

   (2) the standard deviation equals the IQR

   (3) the mean is less than the median

   (4) the mean is greater than median

3   Which distribution would not be described as symmetric and bell-shaped?

   (1) scores on ACT/SAT exam

   (2) people's heights

   (3) salaries of employees at a large bank

   (4) men's shoe sizes

4   A set of data has a mean of 70. If 5 is added to each value in the set, what will the new mean will be?

   (1) less then 70

   (2) 75

   (3) 70

   (4) The new mean cannot be determined.

5   The correlation coefficient between two variables is 0.987. Which statement is **not** necessarily true?

   (1) There is positive correlation between the variables.

   (2) The slope of the regression line is positive.

   (3) The shape of the data is linear.

   (4) There is a high chance of causation between the variables.

6   The best graphical representation for bivariate data would be a

   (1) histogram.   **(3)** bar graph.

   (2) box plot.   **(4)** scatter plot.

Name _____ Date _____

Diagnostic Test 9: Chapter 9 *continued*

7 What type of correlation is shown in the graph below?

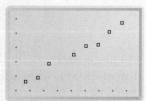

(1) negative   **(3)** positive

(2) no correlation   **(4)** scatter plot

8 Jessie wants a 90% average for the quarter in Statistics. So far she has earned scores of 85, 83, 90, and 97 on four of the five exams. Can she get her 90% for the quarter? Justify your answer.

9 The two-way table shows the results of a survey taken at the Quick Bite Café.

	Dogs	No Dogs
Burgers	64	12
No Burgers	15	9

According to the Quick Bite survey, find the percent of customers who:

a Only like hot dogs, but also eat burgers.

b Do not like burgers, and do not like dogs.

c Like burgers.

10 The table below shows the stopping distance (in feet) at certain speeds (in miles per hour).

Stopping Distances							
Speed (mph)	10	20	30	40	50	60	70
Distance (ft)	27	63	99	164	218	275	320

Use the data to determine:

a An equation to model stopping distance.

b The stopping distance at 100 mph.

c Discuss the model's variability.

1 Real Numbers and Algebraic Expressions

1.1 Set Theory

N.Q.2
N.Q.3
8.SP.4

The word **set** is used to describe a group of objects such as a set of dishes, a set of golf clubs, and so on. In mathematics, the word *set* indicates a group of objects, usually numbers, in which each object is an **element,** or **member,** of the set.

Note

The notation $5 \in N$ means that 5 is an element of the set N.

The elements, or members, of a set are listed in braces with a comma after each member except the last. A letter can represent the name of a set. For example, the set of numbers from 1 through 5 can be written $T = \{1, 2, 3, 4, 5\}$. You can also use set notation to indicate a set of numbers. For example,

$N = \{x \mid x \text{ is a counting number}\}$ is read as "The set N includes all of the values of x such that x is a counting number."

The number of elements of a set can be **finite** or **infinite.** If a large finite set has a recognizable pattern, it can be listed by using dots to imply the missing elements. So the set of whole numbers from 1–100 can be written as $S = \{1, 2, 3, 4, \ldots, 100\}$.

If the set is infinite, you can use dots to show that it continues without end. The set of counting numbers can be written as $N = \{1, 2, 3, 4, \ldots\}$.

If a set has no elements, open braces $\{ \ \}$ or the Greek letter ϕ is used, and the set is called the **null** or **empty** set. A **subset** of a given set can contain any element or all elements of the given set, including the null set and the given set itself. The symbol for subset is $\subset$.

EXAMPLE 1 Listing subsets of a set

1 List all the possible subsets from the set of toppings for ice cream {sprinkles, nuts, cherry}. How many possible subsets are there?

■ SOLUTION

{ }, {sprinkles}, {nuts}, {cherry}, {sprinkles, nuts}, {sprinkles, cherry}, {nuts, cherry}, {sprinkles, nuts, cherry}. Therefore there are 8 possible subsets.

The **complement** of a subset consists of all the elements from the original set that are not included in the subset. If A is the given subset, then the complement of A is written A'.

EXAMPLE 2 Finding the complement of a given set

2 Given set $X = \{\text{the set of whole numbers from 1–10}\}$, set $Y = \{1, 2, 3, 4, 5\}$, and $Y \subset X$, find the complement of set Y.

■ SOLUTION

$Y' = \{6, 7, 8, 9, 10\}$

The **union** of two or more sets is the set of all elements in the given sets. The symbol for the union of two or more sets is ∪.

EXAMPLES 3 and 4   **Finding the union of two or more sets**

 3 If $A = \{1, 2, 3\}$ and $B = \{4, 5, 6\}$, what is $A \cup B$?

■ SOLUTION

$A \cup B = \{1, 2, 3, 4, 5, 6\}$

4 If $P = \{a, g, h, k, m, u\}$ and $Q = \{a, f, h, m\}$, what is $P \cup Q$?

■ SOLUTION

$P \cup Q = \{a, g, f, h, k, m, u\}$

Venn diagrams are used to show relationships between and among sets. Venn diagrams consist of circles within a rectangle. The rectangle is used to show all of the elements, or the **universal** set, and the circles are used to show subsets of the total set.

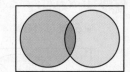

Each circle represents part of the given set. The diagram illustrates the overlapping or **intersection** of the sets. When two or more sets have common elements, they are intersecting sets. The symbol for set intersection is ∩.

EXAMPLE 5   **Using Venn diagrams to solve problems**

 5 Some ninth grade students take algebra or Earth science or both algebra and Earth science. How many students are studying algebra? How many are studying Earth science? How many are studying both?

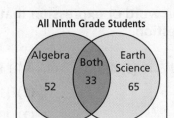

■ SOLUTION

Students studying algebra   (52)+ 33 = 85 ← **circle labeled Algebra**

Students studying Earth science   (65)+ 33 = 98 ← **circle labeled Earth Science**

Students studying both   33 ← **overlapping circles**

The diagram below illustrates the ninth grade students studying Latin and those studying French. Because none of them study both languages, the sets have no common elements. If sets have no elements in common, they are **disjoint** sets.

Note

The intersection of 2 or more disjoint sets is the null set.

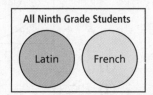

6 Draw a Venn diagram to illustrate the intersection of the set of even numbers and the set of odd numbers.

■ SOLUTION

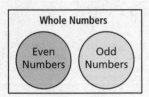

$\{x \mid x \text{ is an even number}\} \cap \{x \mid x \text{ is an odd number}\} = \{\ \}$

7 If $R = \{1, 2, 3, 4, 5, 6, 7, 8, 9, 10\}$ and $S = \{3, 5, 7, 9\}$, draw a Venn diagram to illustrate $R \cap S$.

■ SOLUTION

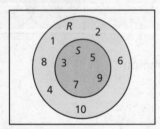

Because $S \subset R$, $R \cap S = S$.

Practice

Choose the numeral preceding the word or expression that best completes the statement or answers the question.

In Exercises 1–2, let $A = \{1, 2\}$ and $B = \{3, 4\}$.

1 $A \cap B = ?$

(1) $\{1, 2\}$ (3) $\{3, 4\}$

(2) $\{\ \}$ (4) $\{1, 2, 3, 4\}$

2 $A \cup B = ?$

(1) $\{1, 2\}$ (3) $\{3, 4\}$

(2) $\{\ \}$ (4) $\{1, 2, 3, 4\}$

In Exercises 3–5, use the following diagram.

3 Set $X = ?$

(1) $\{1, 5, 7\}$ (3) $\{2, 3, 4, 6, 8\}$

(2) $\{3, 6, 8\}$ (4) $\{1, 3, 5, 6, 7, 8\}$

4 $X \cap Y = ?$

(1) $\{1, 5, 7\}$ (3) $\{2, 3, 4, 6, 8\}$

(2) $\{3, 6, 8\}$ (4) $\{1, 3, 5, 6, 7, 8\}$

5 $X \cup Y = ?$

(1) $\{1, 2, 3, 4, 5, 6, 7, 8\}$

(2) ϕ

(3) $\{1, 3, 5, 6, 7, 8\}$

(4) $\{3, 6, 8\}$

6 The diagram below illustrates:

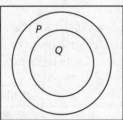

(1) $P \cup Q$ (3) $P \cap Q$

(2) $P \subset Q$ (4) $Q \subset P$

4

In Exercises 7–12, find the union and intersection of each of the following sets.

Let $A = \{1, 4, 7\}$, $B = \{4, 6, 8\}$, $C = \{1, 6, 7\}$, and $D = \{x \mid x$ is a positive odd integer $\leq 7\}$.

7 A and B

8 B and C

9 C and D

10 A and C

11 B and D

12 A and D

13 In a gym class of 20 students, 14 students like basketball, 18 like baseball, and 12 like both. Use a Venn diagram to show how many students like both basketball and baseball.

In Exercises 14–15, use the given information.

Let $P = \{x \mid x$ is a multiple of 2; $0 \leq x \leq 12\}$ and $Q = \{x \mid x$ is a multiple of 3; $0 \leq x \leq 15\}$.

14 Draw a Venn diagram to show $P \cap Q$.

15 Is $12 \in P \cap Q$? Explain.

In Exercises 16–17, use the given information.

Let $X = \{1, 2, 3, 4, 5, 6, 7, 8, 9, 10, 11, 12\}$ and $Y = \{x \mid x$ is a multiple of 5; $x \leq 20\}$.

16 Draw a Venn diagram to show $X \cap Y$.

17 Is $Y \subset X$? Explain.

In Exercises 18–20, use the given information.

Let $A = \{0, 3, 6, 9, 12\}$ and $B = \{0, 2, 4, 6, 8\}$.

18 Find $A \cup B$.

19 Find $A \cap B$.

20 Draw a Venn diagram to represent sets A and B.

21 If set $Q = \{$letters a through $m\}$, find Q'.

22 Refer to the Venn diagram below.

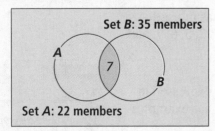

How many members are in set A or set B but not both?

23 In a high school of 1,200 students, 900 students passed the first mathematics test, 700 students passed the second mathematics test, and 500 students passed both mathematics tests. How many students failed to pass either test? Use a Venn diagram to solve and show your work.

In Exercises 24–27, use the Venn diagram. How many members are in the specified set(s)?

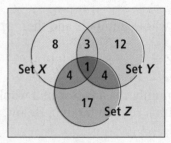

24 in set X but no other set

25 in set X, set Y, and set Z

26 in set Y or set Z but not set X

27 in set X or set Y but not set Z

In Exercises 28–29, solve the following problems. Clearly show all necessary work.

28 In a group of 47 students, 42 students are studying Earth science, algebra, or both subjects and 24 students are studying both subjects. How many students are studying one subject but not both? How many students are studying neither? Use a Venn diagram to solve.

29 In a class of 550 students, students may take all, none, or a combination of courses as follows. Draw a Venn diagram to find how many students are not in any of these courses.

Mathematics	280
Science	200
Technology	230
Mathematics and Technology	110
Science and Technology	100
Mathematics and Science	80
Mathematics, Science, and Technology	20

1.2 Names for Real Numbers

N.RN.3

The set of **natural numbers,** or **counting numbers,** consists of the numbers that you use when you count.

$$N = \{1, 2, 3, 4, 5, 6 \ldots\} \text{ or } N = \{x \mid x \text{ is a counting number}\}$$

When 0 is an element, the new set is the set of **whole numbers.**

$$W = \{0, 1, 2, 3, 4, 5, 6 \ldots\} \text{ or } W = \{x \mid x \text{ is a whole number}\}$$

The set of whole numbers and their **opposites** is called the set of **integers.**

$$Z = \{\ldots, -3, -2, -1, 0, 1, 2, 3 \ldots\} \text{ or } Z = \{x \mid x \text{ is an integer}\}$$

A natural number is a **factor** of a whole number if it divides the whole number with a remainder of 0. Below, the first number is **divisible** by the second.

$18 \div 6 = 3\text{R}0 \quad \rightarrow \quad 6$ is a factor of 18. $\quad \rightarrow \quad 18$ is divisible by 6.

$18 \div 7 = 2\text{R}4 \quad \rightarrow \quad 7$ is *not* a factor of 18. $\quad \rightarrow \quad 18$ is not divisible by 7.

The following are some commonly used *divisibility tests.*

Divisibility Tests

A number is divisible by

2 if its last digit is 0, 2, 4, 6, or 8;
3 if the sum of its digits is divisible by 3;
4 if the number formed by the last two digits is divisible by 4;
5 if the last digit is 0 or 5;
8 if the number formed by the last three digits is divisible by 8;
9 if the sum of its digits is divisible by 9;
10 if the last digit is 0.

A **prime number** is a natural number greater than 1 that has exactly two factors, 1 and the number itself. The first eight prime numbers are 2, 3, 5, 7, 11, 13, 17, and 19.

A **composite number** is a natural number greater than 1 that has more than two factors. For example, the number 18 has six factors in all: 1, 2, 3, 6, 9, and 18. So the number 18 is composite.

The set of **rational numbers** consists of all numbers that can be expressed in the form $\frac{a}{b}$, where a and b are integers and b $\neq$ 0. The following are examples of rational numbers.

$$\frac{9}{14} \qquad -5 = \frac{-5}{1} \qquad 2\frac{1}{7} = \frac{15}{7} \qquad 0.71 = \frac{71}{100} \qquad 0.\overline{83} = \frac{83}{99}$$

Note

The number 246 is divisible by

2 since its last digit is 6 and
3 since $2 + 4 + 6 = 12$, and 12 is divisible by 3.

The number 246 is *not* divisible by

4 since 46 is not divisible by 4;
5 since its last digit is not 0 or 5;
8 since 246 is not divisible by 8;
9 since $2 + 4 + 6 = 12$ and 12 is not divisible by 9;
10 since its last digit is not 0.

Note

Recall these symbols.
= is equal to
$\neq$ is not equal to

Expressions that name the same number are **equivalent expressions.** To write a fraction that is equivalent to a given fraction, you can multiply or divide the fraction by 1. That is, you can multiply by a fraction with the same numerator and denominator.

EXAMPLES 1 and 2   **Writing equivalent fractions**

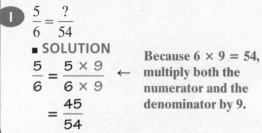

Replace each ___?___ with the number that makes the fractions equivalent.

1 $\dfrac{5}{6} = \dfrac{?}{54}$

■ **SOLUTION**

$\dfrac{5}{6} = \dfrac{5 \times 9}{6 \times 9}$ ← Because $6 \times 9 = 54$, multiply both the numerator and the denominator by 9.

$= \dfrac{45}{54}$

2 $\dfrac{24}{40} = \dfrac{?}{10}$

■ **SOLUTION**

$\dfrac{24}{40} = \dfrac{24 \div 4}{40 \div 4}$ ← Because $40 \div 4 = 10$, divide both the numerator and the denominator by 4.

$= \dfrac{6}{10}$

The expression $0.\overline{83}$ is an example of a *repeating decimal.* The bar over 83 shows that this block of digits repeats without end. That is, $0.\overline{83} = 0.838383\ldots$. Any rational number can be expressed in equivalent form either as a repeating decimal or as a *terminating decimal.*

> **Note**
> The fraction bar is a division symbol.
> $\dfrac{a}{b} = a \div b \rightarrow b\overline{)a}$

EXAMPLES 3 and 4   **Writing a fraction as a decimal**

3 Write $\dfrac{5}{8}$ as a terminating decimal.

■ **SOLUTION**

$\begin{array}{r} 0.625 \\ 8\overline{)5.000} \\ -48 \\ \hline 20 \\ -16 \\ \hline 40 \\ -40 \\ \hline 0 \end{array}$ ← The division *terminates.*

Therefore, $\frac{5}{8} = 0.625$.

4 Write $\dfrac{2}{3}$ as a repeating decimal.

■ **SOLUTION**

$\begin{array}{r} 0.666\cdots \\ 3\overline{)2.000} \\ -18 \\ \hline 20 \\ -18 \\ \hline 20 \\ -18 \\ \hline 2\cdots \end{array}$ ← The 6 *repeats.*

Therefore, $\frac{2}{3} = 0.666\ldots = 0.\overline{6}$.

Any repeating or terminating decimal can be written as a fraction. A fraction is in **lowest terms** if the greatest common factor (GCF) of its numerator and denominator is 1.

$\dfrac{a}{b}$ ← **numerator**
   ← **denominator**

EXAMPLES 5 and 6   **Writing a terminating or repeating decimal as a fraction**

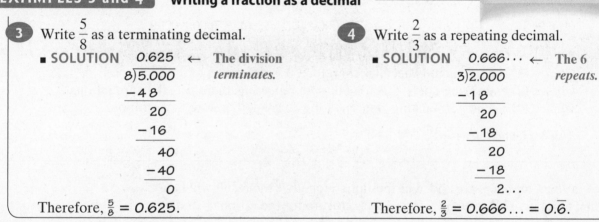

5 Write 0.28 as a fraction in lowest terms.

■ **SOLUTION** $0.28 = \dfrac{28}{100} = \dfrac{28 \div 4}{100 \div 4} = \dfrac{7}{25}$ ← The GCF of 28 and 100 is 4.

6 Write $0.\overline{45}$ as a fraction in lowest terms.

■ **SOLUTION**

$100 \times 0.\overline{45} = 45.454545\ldots$ ← **Multiply by 100.**
$-\ 1 \times 0.\overline{45} = -0.454545\ldots$ ← **Subtract the original number.**
$\overline{99 \times 0.\overline{45} = 45}$

$\dfrac{99 \times 0.\overline{45}}{99} = \dfrac{45}{99}$ ← **Divide by 99.**

$0.\overline{45} = \dfrac{45 \div 9}{99 \div 9} = \dfrac{5}{11}$ ← **Write in lowest terms.**

Therefore, $0.\overline{45} = \dfrac{5}{11}$.

> **Note**
> If only one digit repeats, multiply by 10, then subtract, and then divide by 9.
>
> If three digits repeat, multiply by 1,000, then subtract, and then divide by 999.

Some decimals do not terminate or repeat. If we try to find the square root of a nonperfect square, we will get only an approximation. Square roots of numbers that are not perfect squares are examples of **irrational numbers.**

The resulting root will be a **nonterminating, nonrepeating decimal.** These decimals make up the set of **irrational numbers.**

Some examples of irrational numbers are:

a) $0.01011011101111\ldots$

b) $\pi = 3.14159\ldots$

c) $\sqrt{3} = 1.732\ldots$

The **rational numbers** and the **irrational numbers** together make up the set of **real numbers.** The diagram at the right shows how the real numbers and its subsets are related.

Real Numbers

Rational Numbers

Integers

Whole Numbers

Natural Numbers

Irrational Numbers

 EXAMPLE 7   **Recognizing irrational numbers**

7   Which of the following is an irrational number?

(1) 5.209   **(2)** $5.2\overline{09}$ **(3)** 5.209090909...   **(4)** 5.2090090009...

■ **SOLUTION**

Choice **(1)** is a terminating decimal; therefore, it is rational.
Choice **(2)** and **(3)** are nonterminating but are repeating; therefore, they are rational.
Choice **(4)** is a nonterminating, nonrepeating decimal; therefore, it is irrational.

The correct choice is **(4)**.

If two rational numbers are added or multiplied together the result will be a rational number. This result is referred to as **closure** for the rationals under addition and multiplication.

Show the sum of two rational numbers is rational. If x and y are two rational numbers then they can be written $x = \frac{a}{b}$ and $y = \frac{c}{d}$ where a, b, c, and $d \in$ integers and $b \neq 0$ and $d \neq 0$. Therefore, $x + y = \frac{a}{b} + \frac{c}{d} = \frac{ad + cb}{bd}$. This result is a rational expression.

EXAMPLE 8   **Finding that the sum of a rational and an irrational is irrational**

Consider the irrational number $x = .14114111411114111114\ldots$ and the rational number $y = \frac{2}{3} = .666666666\ldots$ Their sum would be .807807780777807777... which is a non-repeating non-terminating decimal and therefore an irrational number.

Choose the numeral preceding the word or expression that best completes the statement or answers the question.

1 Which expression does *not* name an integer?

(1) −9   **(2)** 0   **(3)** $\frac{3}{15}$ **(4)** $\frac{8}{2}$

2 Which expression represents an irrational number?

(1) 0.040404 . . .   **(3)** 0.7070070007 . . .

(2) $1.\overline{01001}$ **(4)** $\sqrt{2} - \sqrt{2}$

3 Which number is *not* a whole number?

(1) 3   **(2)** 0   **(3)** −5   **(4)** $\frac{12}{2}$

4 $0.\overline{381}$ can be written as which fraction?

(1) $\frac{127}{333}$ **(2)** $\frac{381}{10,000}$ **(3)** $\frac{19}{15}$ **(4)** $\frac{3}{10}$

5 Which of the following is a true statement?

(1) −3 is a whole number.

(2) $\sqrt{9}$ is an irrational number.

(3) 0 is a natural number.

(4) $\frac{1}{3}$ is a rational number.

In Exercises 6–9, write each fraction as a decimal.

6 $\frac{94}{100}$ **7** $\frac{17}{20}$

8 $\frac{1}{3}$ **9** $\frac{2}{9}$

In Exercises 10–13, write each decimal as a fraction in lowest terms.

10 0.72   **11** 0.102

12 $0.4\overline{3}$ **13** $0.\overline{43}$

In Exercises 14–17, show that each expression represents a rational number.

14 $4\frac{1}{8}$ **15** 0.42

16 0.222 . . .   **17** 0

In Exercises 18–23, give an example to illustrate the type of number described and explain your answer.

18 a whole number that is not a natural number

19 a real number that is not rational

20 a rational number that is not an integer

21 two whole numbers that are neither prime nor composite

22 two composite numbers that are relatively prime

23 two nonequivalent expressions that use the same numbers; like $\frac{1}{4}$ and 1.4

1.3 The Real Number Line

Recall that the set of rational numbers and the set of irrational numbers make up the set of real numbers.

There is a *one-to-one correspondence* between the set of real numbers and the points on a **number line.**

The point that corresponds to a real number is called the **graph of the number.** The number line below shows the graphs of $-2\frac{3}{4}$, -1.6, $\sqrt{2}$, 2, and π.

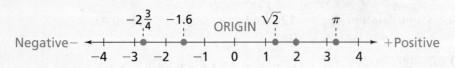

You can use a number line to *compare* numbers. Given real numbers a and b, exactly one of the following is true.

a is less than b		a is equal to b		a is greater than b
$a < b$	or	$a = b$	or	$a > b$

> **Note**
> If $a < b$ or $a > b$, then $a \neq b$ (a is not equal to b). Also, if $a < b$ or $a = b$, then $a \le b$ (a is less than or equal to b) and if $a > b$ or $a = b$, then $a \ge b$ (a is greater than or equal to b).

EXAMPLE 1 Using a number line to compare

1 Replace __?__ with <, >, or = to make a true statement: 1 __?__ −3

■ **SOLUTION**

Draw a number line like the one at the right.
The graph of 1 is to the right of the graph of −3.
Therefore, **1 > −3.**

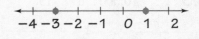

To order a set of fractions, you may need to write equivalent fractions using the least common denominator. The **least common denominator,** or **LCD,** of a set of fractions is the least common multiple (LCM) of all the denominators.

You can use a calculator to check the order a set of numbers that includes both fractions and decimals.

> **Note**
> $a < b < c$ means that "a is less than b and b is less than c" or "b is between a and c."

EXAMPLE 2 Ordering fractions and decimals

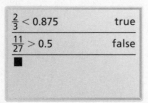

Most current technology tools offer a test menu for testing the order of numbers.

When subsets of the real numbers contain all the numbers in a particular range of values the interval can be represented in different ways.

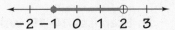

Here the numbers greater than or equal to −1 and less than 2 are represented graphically on a number line. This set of numbers can be described using the inequality $−1 \leq x < 2$.

A second representation is *interval notation.* This notation represents an interval as a pair of numbers with brackets or parentheses. In this case, the notation is $[−1, 2)$. The numbers are the endpoints of the interval. Brackets and/or parentheses show whether the endpoints are included (bracket) or excluded (parenthesis).

EXAMPLES 3 through 6	Using interval notation

Represent the following graphs using inequalities and interval notation.

3

■ SOLUTION $[0,3]$ or $0 \leq x \leq 3$

4

■ SOLUTION $(−\infty,1]$ or $x \leq 1$

5

■ SOLUTION $(−2,1]$ or $−2 < x \leq 1$

6

■ SOLUTION $(−2,3)$ or $−2 < x < 3$

Choose the numeral preceding the word or expression that best completes the statement or answers the question.

1 Which number is not greater than -5?

  (1) $-5\frac{1}{2}$ **(2)** $-\frac{5}{2}$ **(3)** 0 **(4)** $5\frac{1}{2}$

2 Which statement is true?

  (1) $\frac{1}{4} < \frac{1}{3}$ **(3)** $-\frac{1}{4} > \frac{1}{3}$

  (2) $-\frac{1}{2} > -\frac{1}{4}$ **(4)** $\frac{1}{2} < -\frac{1}{3}$

3 Which number is between -2.5 and $-2\frac{3}{5}$?

  (1) $-2\frac{2}{5}$ **(3)** $-2.\overline{5}$

  (2) $-2.\overline{3}$ **(4)** 0

In Exercises 4–13, replace each ___?___ with <, >, or = to make a true statement.

4 -100 ___?___ 4 **5** -2 ___?___ -35

6 6.01 ___?___ -6.1 **7** -8.98 ___?___ -8.94

8 $\frac{7}{12}$ ___?___ $\frac{11}{18}$ **9** $1\frac{1}{5}$ ___?___ $1\frac{1}{6}$

10 $-2\frac{3}{4}$ ___?___ $-2\frac{7}{8}$ **11** $2\frac{5}{11}$ ___?___ 2.45

12 -0.23 ___?___ $-\frac{2}{9}$ **13** $\frac{14}{25}$ ___?___ $0.5\overline{6}$

In Exercises 14–19, write each set of numbers in order from least to greatest.

14 $\frac{9}{5}, \frac{5}{3}, \frac{17}{10}$ **15** $-\frac{5}{6}, -\frac{13}{15}, -\frac{8}{9}$

16 $-3, 7, -10, 0, -5, 1, -2$

17 $-1.1, -1.01, -1.101, -0.1001$

18 $\frac{1}{20}, 0.5, \frac{2}{5}, \frac{5}{9}, 0.505$

19 $-\frac{9}{2}, -4.3, -4\frac{1}{3}, 4.\overline{3}, -4\frac{3}{100}$

Write each of the following intervals as an inequality and in interval notation.

20

21

22

Graph the following intervals.

23 $[-1, 2)$

24 $[-1, 4]$

1.4 Properties of Exponents

 A.APR.6

The exponential expression a^n is read as "a to the nth power." In this expression, a is the **base** and n is the **exponent**. The number represented by a^n is called *the nth power of a.*

When n is a positive integer, you can interpret a^n as follows.

$$a^n = \underbrace{a \cdot a \cdot a \cdot \ldots \cdot a}_{n \text{ factors}}$$

Note

Notice that you can add exponents only when the bases are the same.

Now observe how this interpretation can help you simplify products such as the following.

$p^5 \cdot p^3 = (p \cdot p \cdot p \cdot p \cdot p) \cdot (p \cdot p \cdot p) = p^8$ ← Notice that $5 + 3 = 8$.

$(q^2)^3 = (q^2)(q^2)(q^2) = (q \cdot q) \cdot (q \cdot q) \cdot (q \cdot q) = q^6$ ← Notice that $2 \cdot 3 = 6$.

$(rs)^4 = (r \cdot s)(r \cdot s)(r \cdot s)(r \cdot s) = (r \cdot r \cdot r \cdot r)(s \cdot s \cdot s \cdot s) = r^4 s^4$

These examples are generalized in the following properties of exponents.

Multiplication Properties of Exponents

Let m and n represent integers and a and b represent nonzero real numbers.

Product of Powers Property	**Power of a Power Property**	**Power of a Product Property**
$a^m \cdot a^n = a^{m+n}$	$(a^m)^n = a^{mn}$	$(ab)^m = a^m b^m$

You can use the multiplication properties of exponents to simplify the following exponential expressions.

EXAMPLES 1 through 7   Using the multiplication properties of exponents

Simplify each expression. Write answers using positive exponents.

1 $2^3 \cdot 2^4$ ■ SOLUTION $2^3 \cdot 2^4 = 2^{3+4} = 2^7 = 128$

2 $(n^3)^3$ ■ SOLUTION $(n^3)^3 = n^{3 \cdot 3} = n^9$

3 $(-2x)^3$ ■ SOLUTION $(-2x)^3 = (-2)^3 x^3 = -8x^3$

4 $(yz^4)^2$ ■ SOLUTION $(yz^4)^2 = (y^1 z^4)^2 = (y^1)^2 (z^4)^2 = y^{1 \cdot 2} z^{4 \cdot 2} = y^2 z^8$

5 $(pq)^3 \cdot (pq)^5$ ■ SOLUTION $(pq)^3 \cdot (pq)^5 = (pq)^{3+5} = (pq)^8 = p^8 q^8$

6 $(-3s^3 t^2)^4$ ■ SOLUTION $(-3s^3 t^2)^4 = (-3)^4 (s^3)^4 (t^2)^4 = 81 s^{3 \cdot 4} t^{2 \cdot 4} = 81 s^{12} t^8$

7 $(df)^2 (gh)^5$ ■ SOLUTION $(df)^2 (gh)^5 = d^2 f^2 g^5 h^5$

Notice that in order to apply the product property of exponents, you add exponents when you are multiplying powers of like bases. In some numerical expressions, however, you can apply this property if the given bases are not alike but can be changed to like bases.

EXAMPLE 8   Applying the product property of exponents to a numerical expression

8 Which is equivalent to $3^5 \cdot 9^4$?

   (1) 3^{11} (2) 3^{13} (3) 27^9 (4) 27^{20}

   ■ SOLUTION

   The bases of the factors are not alike; however, 9 can be written as an exponent with a base of 3. $9 = 3^2$

   Rewrite the expression, substituting 3^2 for 9. $3^5 \cdot 9^4 = 3^5 \cdot (3^2)^4 = 3^5 \cdot 3^8 = 3^{13}$

   The correct choice is (2).

When you understand the multiplication properties of exponents, you can multiply terms by using the following procedure.

Multiplying Terms

Step 1 Multiply the coefficients, using the rules for multiplying signed numbers.

Step 2 Multiply the variable factors, using the multiplication properties of exponents.

Step 3 Write the product of the results from Steps 1 and 2.

EXAMPLES 9 and 10   Multiplying terms

Simplify each expression. Write answers using positive exponents.

9 $(3a^2)(5a^4)$

   ■ SOLUTION

   $(3a^2)(5a^4)$
   $= 3 \cdot 5 \cdot a^2 \cdot a^4$
   $= 15 \cdot a^2 \cdot a^4$
   $= 15 \cdot a^{2+4}$
   $= 15a^6$

10 $(2rs^3)(5r^3s)^2$

   ■ SOLUTION

   $(2rs^3)(5r^3s)^2$
   $= (2r^1s^3)(5^1r^3s^1)^2$
   $= (2r^1s^3)(5^2r^6s^2)$
   $= 2 \cdot 5^2 \cdot r^1 \cdot r^6 \cdot s^3 \cdot s^2$
   $= 50 \cdot r^{1+6} \cdot s^{3+2}$
   $= 50r^7s^5$

Now examine these quotients involving exponents.

$$\frac{x^9}{x^2} = \frac{\overset{1}{\cancel{x}} \cdot \overset{1}{\cancel{x}} \cdot x \cdot x \cdot x \cdot x \cdot x \cdot x \cdot x}{\underset{1}{\cancel{x}} \cdot \underset{1}{\cancel{x}}} = \frac{x^7}{1} = x^7 \quad \leftarrow \text{ Notice that } 9 - 2 = 7.$$

$$\left(\frac{v}{w}\right)^5 = \frac{v}{w} \cdot \frac{v}{w} \cdot \frac{v}{w} \cdot \frac{v}{w} \cdot \frac{v}{w} = \frac{v \cdot v \cdot v \cdot v \cdot v}{w \cdot w \cdot w \cdot w \cdot w} = \frac{v^5}{w^5}$$

Note

A quotient involving exponents is also called a **ratio of powers.**

The results of the divisions on the preceding page are generalized in the following properties of exponents.

Division Properties of Exponents

Let m and n represent integers and a and b represent nonzero real numbers.

Quotient of Powers Property

$$\frac{a^m}{a^n} = a^{m-n}$$

Power of a Quotient Property

$$\left(\frac{a}{b}\right)^m = \frac{a^m}{b^m}$$

You can now divide terms by using the following procedure.

Dividing Terms

Step 1 Divide the coefficients, using the rules for dividing signed numbers.

Step 2 Divide the variable factors, using the division properties of exponents.

Step 3 Write the product or quotient of the results from Steps 1 and 2.

EXAMPLES 11 through 14   Dividing terms

Simplify each expression. Write each answer using positive exponents.

11 $\dfrac{5^6}{5^3}$ ■ SOLUTION $\dfrac{5^6}{5^3} = 5^{6-3} = 5^3$

12 $\left(\dfrac{2}{z^3}\right)^2$ ■ SOLUTION $\left(\dfrac{2}{z^3}\right)^2 = \dfrac{2^2}{(z^3)^2} = \dfrac{4}{z^6}$

13 $\dfrac{6r^8}{3r^2}$ ■ SOLUTION $\dfrac{6r^8}{3r^2} = 2r^{8-2} = 2r^6$

14 $\dfrac{32m^5n^3}{2^3m^4n^2}$ ■ SOLUTION $\dfrac{32m^5n^3}{2^3m^4n^2} = \dfrac{2^5m^5n^3}{2^3m^4n^2} = 2^{5-3}m^{5-4}n^{3-2} = 2^2m^1n^1 = 4mn$

The division property of exponents is used to develop rules for an exponent of zero and negative exponents. It is known that any nonzero number divided by itself is one. Therefore the following must be true.

$$1 \Leftarrow \frac{25}{25} = \frac{5^2}{5^2} = 5^{2-2} = 5^0$$
$$\therefore 5^0 = 1$$

In a similar fashion

$$\frac{25}{125} = \frac{25 \div 25}{125 \div 25} = \frac{1}{5}$$

and

$$\frac{25}{125} = \frac{5^2}{5^3} = 5^{2-3} = 5^{-1}$$

$$\left.\begin{array}{c} \end{array}\right\} \quad \therefore \frac{1}{5} = 5^{-1}$$

Zero and Negative Exponents

In general then:

$$n^0 = 1; n \neq 0$$

and

$$\frac{1}{n^k} = n^{-k}; n \neq 0$$

EXAMPLES 15 through 18 Using zero and negative exponents

Simplify the following expressions. Write each answer with only positive exponents.

15 $\dfrac{a^5k^{-2}z^0}{a^3k^3}$

■ SOLUTION

$\dfrac{a^2}{k^5}$

16 $\left(\dfrac{r^{-3}t^5}{r^{-7}t^8}\right)^0$

■ SOLUTION

1

17 $2^3 \cdot 5^6 \cdot 2^{-3} \cdot 5^{-5}$

■ SOLUTION

5

18 $\left(\dfrac{w^2d^{-3}}{w^{-5}}\right)^{-1}$

■ SOLUTION

$\dfrac{d^3}{w^7}$

Practice

Choose the numeral preceding the word or expression that best completes the statement or answers the question.

1 Which is equivalent to r^4s^8?

  (1) $(rs)^{12}$ **(3)** $(rs^2)^4$

  (2) $(r^4s^4)^2$ **(4)** $r^4 + s^4 + s^4$

2 Which expression is equivalent to $\dfrac{4^{12}}{2^6}$?

  (1) 2^6 **(3)** 4^8

  (2) 2^4 **(4)** 2^{18}

3 Which is not equivalent to $(-w)^2$?

  (1) $-w^2$ **(3)** w^2

  (2) $w \cdot w$ **(4)** $(-w)(-w)$

4 Which is the product of pr^3 and p^2q^2r?

  (1) $p^3q^2r^4$ **(3)** $p^3q^2r^3$

  (2) $p^5q^2r^4$ **(4)** $\dfrac{r^2}{pq^2}$

5 If $a = -2$ and $b = 3$, find the value of $\dfrac{a^2b^3}{a^3b^2}$.

  (1) $-\dfrac{3}{2}$ **(3)** $-\dfrac{2}{3}$

  (2) $\dfrac{3}{2}$ **(4)** $\dfrac{2}{3}$

6 Which is the quotient of $18gh^3k^5$ and $20g^6hk^3$?

  (1) $\dfrac{10g^5}{9h^2k^2}$ **(3)** $\dfrac{9h^2k^2}{10g^5}$

  (2) $\dfrac{9g^5h^2}{10k^2}$ **(4)** $\dfrac{10h^2k^2}{9g^5}$

7 If $g^x \cdot g^3 = g^{12}$, find x.

  (1) $x = 4$ **(3)** $x = 36$

  (2) $x = 15$ **(4)** $x = 9$

In Exercises 8–10, simplify each expression.

8 $3^3 \cdot 3^2$ **9** $\dfrac{5^4}{5^7}$ **10** $\left(-\dfrac{1}{2}\right)^3$

In Exercises 11–18, simplify each expression. Write answers using positive exponents.

11 $(-5r^2s^2)(-3r^2s)$ **12** $(-3a^3b^2c)^3$

13 $\dfrac{p^6q^{10}}{p^3q^8}$ **14** $\left(\dfrac{3a}{7b}\right)^2$

16

15 $\left(\dfrac{-2ab}{c}\right)^2$

16 $\left(\dfrac{c^3d^3}{c^2}\right)^3$

17 $\dfrac{(3y^2)(2y^3)}{3y^4}$

18 $\dfrac{(9x^2y)(3x^3y^2)}{-27x^5y}$

19 The planet Earth is approximated by a sphere with a radius of 6.4×10^6 meters. Use the formula $S = 4\pi r^2$ to approximate the surface area of the Earth.

20 The national debt was approximately 8.5 trillion dollars in August of 2006. At that time, the population of the United States was 300 million. If the debt were divided equally among all of the people in the United States, how much would each person owe?

In Exercises 21–37, simplify each expression. Write each answer using positive exponents.

21 $b^{-4} \cdot b^{-3} \cdot b^5$

22 $(m^{-3}n^4)^{-4}$

23 $2^3 \cdot 7^4 \cdot 2^{-3} \cdot 7^{-4}$

24 $\dfrac{15c^8d^3}{-3c^{10}d^{-2}}$

25 $\left(\dfrac{-2x^3y^{-3}}{x^2y^5}\right)^3$

26 $\left(\dfrac{s^3t^{-5}}{s^{-1}t^{-4}}\right)^2$

27 $(4g^3h^3)^{-4}(-2gh)^3$

28 $\dfrac{r^3s^{-1}}{r^2s^6}$

29 $\left(\dfrac{a^{-2}b^{-1}}{a^{-5}b^3}\right)^{-3}$

30 $a^3 \cdot a^3 \cdot a^3$

31 $(-4m^3)^2$

32 $(7x^2y^3)(-2xy)$

33 $(a^2b^3)^{-1}(a^2b^3)$

34 $\dfrac{25a^2b^3}{5a}$

35 $\dfrac{4p^2q^{-2}}{16p^{-3}q}$

36 $\left(\dfrac{-3x^2y^3}{4x^4}\right)^{-2}$

37 $\left(\dfrac{2m^3}{3mn^{-2}}\right)^{-3}$

In Exercises 38–43, find the value of x that makes each statement true. Assume that no base is equal to zero.

38 $r^x \cdot r^2 = r^6$

39 $(r^x)^2 = r^6$

40 $r^x \cdot r^2 = 1$

41 $(r^x)^2 = 1$

42 $\dfrac{r^2}{r^x} = r^6$

43 $\left(\dfrac{r}{r^x}\right)^2 = r^6$

In Exercises 44–45, solve the problem. Clearly show all necessary work.

44 Are -5^2 and $(-5)^2$ equivalent expressions? Explain your answer.

45 Given that m and n are integers and x is a nonzero real number, is it true that $(x^m)^n = (x^n)^m$? Justify your answer.

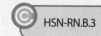
1.5 Radical Expressions and Order of Operations

Recall that when solving equations like $x^2 = 144$, $x = \pm 12$. However, when asked to evaluate or simplify a radical, we will consider only the positive or **principal square root.**

The square root $\sqrt{}$ symbol is also called a **radical sign.** An expression that involves a radical sign is called a **radical expression.** The expression under the radical is called the **radicand.**

$$^{\text{radical}}\sqrt{16}_{\text{radicand}} = 4_{\text{root}}$$

You can simplify some radical expressions by using the definition of square root.

$$\sqrt{144} = 12 \text{ because } 12 \cdot 12 = 12^2 = 144.$$
$$\sqrt{\frac{1}{9}} = \frac{1}{3} \text{ because } \frac{1}{3} \cdot \frac{1}{3} = \left(\frac{1}{3}\right)^2 = \frac{1}{9}.$$

To simplify other radical expressions, you may need to apply one of the following properties of square roots.

Properties of Square Roots

Let a and b represent real numbers.

Product Property

If $a \geq 0$ and $b \geq 0$,

then $\sqrt{ab} = \sqrt{a} \cdot \sqrt{b}$.

Quotient Property

If $a \geq 0$ and $b > 0$,

then $\sqrt{\dfrac{a}{b}} = \dfrac{\sqrt{a}}{\sqrt{b}}$.

EXAMPLES 1 through 4

Using the properties of square roots to simplify rational square roots

Simplify each expression.

1 $\sqrt{1600}$

■ SOLUTION

$$\begin{aligned}
\sqrt{1600} &= \sqrt{16 \cdot 100} \\
&= \sqrt{16} \cdot \sqrt{100} \\
&= 4 \cdot 10 \\
&= 40
\end{aligned}$$

2 $\sqrt{\dfrac{81}{64}}$

■ SOLUTION

$$\begin{aligned}
\sqrt{\frac{81}{64}} &= \frac{\sqrt{81}}{\sqrt{64}} \\
&= \frac{9}{8}
\end{aligned}$$

3 $\sqrt{2916}$

■ SOLUTION

$$\begin{aligned}
\sqrt{2916} &= \sqrt{36 \cdot 81} \\
&= \sqrt{36} \cdot \sqrt{81} \\
&= 6 \cdot 9 \\
&= 54
\end{aligned}$$

4 $\sqrt{\dfrac{16}{144}}$

■ SOLUTION

$$\begin{aligned}
\sqrt{\frac{16}{144}} &= \frac{\sqrt{16}}{\sqrt{144}} \\
&= \frac{4}{12} \text{ or } \frac{1}{3}
\end{aligned}$$

When the square root of a number is rational, the number is a **perfect square**. In the set of whole numbers, the perfect squares less than or equal to 100 are 1, 4, 9, 16, 25, 36, 49, 64, 81, and 100. Most whole numbers are not perfect squares and do not have rational square roots. These non-perfect squares have *irrational* square roots.

This means that their decimal representation are nonterminating, nonrepeating decimals. Therefore, you cannot write exact decimal values. However, it is possible to find an *approximation*.

You can use a calculator to find an approximation by entering the number and then pressing the  or  key. Thus $\sqrt{5} \approx 2.236067978$. You press the √ key and then the number on a graphing calculator to approximate a root.

EXAMPLE 5   Locating square roots between consecutive integers

5 Between which two consecutive integers is $\sqrt{42}$?

■ **SOLUTION 1**

$\sqrt{36} < \sqrt{42} < \sqrt{49}$ ← 42 is between the
$6 < \sqrt{42} < 7$ perfect-square
                          integers 36 and 49.

Therefore, $\sqrt{42}$ is between 6 and 7.

■ **SOLUTION 2**

You can also use a calculator to find an approximation of a radical expression.

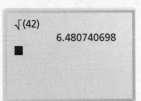

Therefore, $\sqrt{42}$ is between 6 and 7.

Some radical expressions containing non-perfect squares can also be simplified.

A radical expression is in simplest form if:

- the radicand contains no perfect-square factors other than 1;
- the radicand contains no fractions; and
- no denominator contains a radical.

To find the simplest form of an irrational square root, you can use the product and quotient properties of square roots.

Note

When you simplify a non-perfect square, your answer will still contain a square root.

Using the product and quotient properties of square roots to simplify irrational square roots

Simplify each expression.

6 $\sqrt{72}$

■ SOLUTION
$$\sqrt{72} = \sqrt{36 \cdot 2}$$
$$= \sqrt{36} \cdot \sqrt{2} \quad \leftarrow \sqrt{ab} = \sqrt{a} \cdot \sqrt{b}$$
$$= 6\sqrt{2}$$

7 $\sqrt{48}$

■ SOLUTION
$$\sqrt{48} = \sqrt{2 \cdot 2 \cdot 2 \cdot 2 \cdot 3} \quad \leftarrow \text{If at first you}$$
$$= \sqrt{2^2 \cdot 2^2 \cdot 3} \qquad \text{cannot identify}$$
$$= \sqrt{2^2} \cdot \sqrt{2^2} \cdot \sqrt{3} \qquad \text{a perfect-}$$
$$= 2 \cdot 2 \cdot \sqrt{3} \qquad \text{square factor,}$$
$$= 4\sqrt{3} \qquad \text{write the prime factors.}$$

8 $\sqrt{\dfrac{5}{49}}$

■ SOLUTION
$$\sqrt{\frac{5}{49}} = \frac{\sqrt{5}}{\sqrt{49}} \quad \leftarrow \sqrt{\frac{a}{b}} = \frac{\sqrt{a}}{\sqrt{b}}$$
$$= \frac{\sqrt{5}}{7}, \text{ or } \frac{1}{7}\sqrt{5}$$

9 $\sqrt{\dfrac{8}{25}}$

■ SOLUTION
$$\sqrt{\frac{8}{25}} = \frac{\sqrt{8}}{\sqrt{25}}$$
$$= \frac{\sqrt{8}}{5}$$
$$= \frac{\sqrt{4 \cdot 2}}{5}$$
$$= \frac{\sqrt{4} \cdot \sqrt{2}}{5}$$
$$= \frac{2\sqrt{2}}{5}, \text{ or } \frac{2}{5}\sqrt{2}$$

You also use the product and quotient properties of square roots when multiplying and dividing with radical expressions.

Using properties of square roots to simplify products and quotients

10 Simplify each expression.
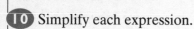
$$\sqrt{15} \cdot \sqrt{6}$$

■ SOLUTION
$$\sqrt{15} \cdot \sqrt{6} = \sqrt{15 \cdot 6}$$
$$= \sqrt{90}$$
$$= \sqrt{9 \cdot 10}$$
$$= \sqrt{9} \cdot \sqrt{10}$$
$$= 3\sqrt{10}$$

11 $\dfrac{\sqrt{128}}{\sqrt{8}}$

■ SOLUTION
$$\frac{\sqrt{128}}{\sqrt{8}} = \sqrt{\frac{128}{8}}$$
$$= \sqrt{16}$$
$$= 4$$

In a simplified radical expression, no denominator contains a radical. So if an expression has a radical in the denominator, and if that radical is not a perfect square, then you must *rationalize the denominator*. You do this by multiplying both numerator and denominator by the radical in the denominator.

EXAMPLES 12 and 13   **Rationalizing the denominator**

Simplify each expression.

12 $\sqrt{\dfrac{4}{3}}$

■ SOLUTION

$$\sqrt{\dfrac{4}{3}} = \dfrac{\sqrt{4}}{\sqrt{3}}$$

$$= \dfrac{2}{\sqrt{3}}$$

$$= \dfrac{2}{\sqrt{3}} \cdot \dfrac{\sqrt{3}}{\sqrt{3}} \qquad \leftarrow \textbf{Multiply by } \dfrac{\sqrt{3}}{\sqrt{3}} = \textbf{1.}$$

$$= \dfrac{2 \cdot \sqrt{3}}{\sqrt{3} \cdot \sqrt{3}}$$

$$= \dfrac{2\sqrt{3}}{3}, or \dfrac{2}{3}\sqrt{3}$$

13 $\dfrac{5\sqrt{10}}{4\sqrt{6}}$

■ SOLUTION

$$\dfrac{5\sqrt{10}}{4\sqrt{6}} = \dfrac{5\sqrt{10}}{4\sqrt{6}} \cdot \dfrac{\sqrt{6}}{\sqrt{6}}$$

$$= \dfrac{5\sqrt{60}}{4\sqrt{36}}$$

$$= \dfrac{5\sqrt{4 \cdot 15}}{4 \cdot 6}$$

$$= \dfrac{10\sqrt{15}}{24}$$

$$= \dfrac{5\sqrt{15}}{12}$$

Radical expressions with exactly the same radicand are called **like radicals**.

Examples of like radicals	Examples of unlike radicals
$\sqrt{2}$ and $5\sqrt{2}$	$2\sqrt{3}$ and $2\sqrt{5}$

You add and subtract radical expressions in much the same way that you add and subtract variable expressions. That is, you can use the Distributive Property to combine like radicals.

EXAMPLES 14 and 15   **Adding and subtracting radical expressions**

Simplify each expression.

14 $3\sqrt{7} - \sqrt{7}$

■ SOLUTION

$$3\sqrt{7} - \sqrt{7}$$
$$= 3\sqrt{7} - 1\sqrt{7}$$
$$= (3 - 1)\sqrt{7}$$
$$= 2\sqrt{7}$$

15 $\sqrt{8} + \sqrt{50}$

■ SOLUTION

$$\sqrt{8} + \sqrt{50}$$
$$= \sqrt{4 \cdot 2} + \sqrt{25 \cdot 2} \qquad \leftarrow \textbf{Rewrite unlike radicals.}$$
$$= 2\sqrt{2} + 5\sqrt{2} \qquad \leftarrow \textbf{Simplify.}$$
$$= (2 + 5)\sqrt{2} \qquad \leftarrow \textbf{Apply the Distributive Property.}$$
$$= 7\sqrt{2} \qquad \leftarrow \textbf{Add.}$$

To simplify certain radical expressions, you must use the Distributive Property.

EXAMPLES 16 and 17 **Using the Distributive Property to simplify a product involving radical expressions**

Simplify each expression.

16 $\sqrt{2}(10 + 4\sqrt{7})$

■ SOLUTION

$$\sqrt{2}(10 + 4\sqrt{7}) = \sqrt{2} \cdot 10 + \sqrt{2} \cdot 4\sqrt{7}$$
$$= 10\sqrt{2} + 4\sqrt{2 \cdot 7}$$
$$= 10\sqrt{2} + 4\sqrt{14}$$

17 $\sqrt{3}(\sqrt{12} + 2\sqrt{15})$

■ SOLUTION

$$\sqrt{3}(\sqrt{12} + 2\sqrt{15}) = \sqrt{3} \cdot \sqrt{12} + \sqrt{3} \cdot 2\sqrt{15}$$
$$= \sqrt{3 \cdot 12} + 2\sqrt{3 \cdot 15}$$
$$= \sqrt{36} + 2\sqrt{45}$$
$$= 6 + 2\sqrt{5 \cdot 9}$$
$$= 6 + 6\sqrt{5}$$

Examples 14 through 17 provide evidence that the sum and difference of two irrational numbers is irrational. This is not true for multiplication and division. Consider $\sqrt{2} \cdot \sqrt{8} = \sqrt{16} = 4$ and $\dfrac{\sqrt{2}}{\sqrt{8}} = \dfrac{1}{\sqrt{4}} = \dfrac{1}{2}$. Here the product of two irrationals is rational and the quotient of two irrationals is rational.

In the case of the sum, difference, product, and quotient of a rational and an irrational number the result will be irrational. In the cases of multiplication and division the rational numbers must be nonzero.

EXAMPLES 18 through 21 **Using operations with real numbers**

18 $3 + \pi = 3 + 3.14159\ldots = 6.14159\ldots$

19 $5.14114111411114\ldots - 2.125 = 3.0161411141111\ldots$

20 $5 \cdot 3\sqrt{2} = 15\sqrt{2}$

21 $\dfrac{6\sqrt{14}}{3\sqrt{21}} = \dfrac{2\sqrt{2}}{\sqrt{3}} \cdot \dfrac{\sqrt{3}}{\sqrt{3}} = \dfrac{2\sqrt{6}}{3} = \dfrac{2}{3}\sqrt{6}$

For any real number a, finding the value of a^3 is called **cubing** the number.

$3^3 = 27 \quad \rightarrow \quad$ three cubed is equal to 27 $\quad \rightarrow \quad$ The cube of 3 is 27.

$(-3)^3 = -27 \quad \rightarrow \quad$ negative three cubed is equal to negative 27 $\quad \rightarrow \quad$ The cube of -3 is -27.

If $a^3 = b$ then a is called the **cube root** of b. The symbol $\sqrt[3]{}$ indicates a cube root. As seen above, the result of cubing a negative number is negative. Therefore taking the cube root of a negative number results in a real number answer.

Rational numbers such as 8, -64, and $\frac{8}{27}$ are called **perfect cubes** because their cube roots are rational numbers. $\sqrt[3]{8} = 2$, $\sqrt[3]{-64} = -4$, and $\sqrt[3]{\frac{8}{27}} = \frac{2}{3}$.

EXAMPLES 22 and 23 **Simplifying radical expressions**

Simplify the radical expressions.

22 $2\sqrt[3]{54}$

- **SOLUTION**

$$2\sqrt[3]{54} = 2\sqrt[3]{27 \cdot 2} = 6\sqrt[3]{2}$$

23 $\dfrac{3\sqrt[3]{12}}{5\sqrt[3]{3}}$

- **SOLUTION**

$$\frac{3\sqrt[3]{12}}{5\sqrt[3]{3}} \cdot \frac{\sqrt[3]{9}}{\sqrt[3]{9}} = \frac{3\sqrt[3]{108}}{5\sqrt[3]{27}} = \frac{3\sqrt[3]{27 \cdot 4}}{5\sqrt[3]{27}} = \frac{3\sqrt[3]{4}}{5}$$

Many expressions involve two or more operations. When simplifying such expressions, it is important to perform the operations in the following order.

Order of Operations

1. Perform any operations(s) within grouping symbols.
2. Simplify all powers.
3. Multiply and divide in order from left to right.
4. Add and subtract in order from left to right.

Note

Grouping symbols
Parentheses ()
brackets []
braces { }
fraction bar —
absolute-value bars | |
radical sign $\sqrt{}$

EXAMPLES 24 and 25 **Applying the order of operations**

Simplify each expression.

24 $11 - 3 \cdot 8$

- **SOLUTION**

$11 - 3 \cdot 8$ ← **Multiply first.**
$11 - 24$ ← **Then subtract.**
-13

25 $3(5 + 4^2) \div 7 - 7$

- **SOLUTION**

$3(5 + 4^2) \div 7 - 7$ ← **Simplify 4^2.**
$3(5 + 16) \div 7 - 7$ ← **Add within the parentheses.**
$3(21) \div 7 - 7$ ← **Multiply 3(21).**
$63 \div 7 - 7$ ← **Divide 63 ÷ 7.**
$9 - 7$ ← **Subtract.**
2

Practice

Choose the numeral preceding the word or expression that best completes the statement or answers the question.

1 Which expression is equivalent to 3^{-4}?
  (1) $3(-4)$ **(2)** $\dfrac{1}{3^4}$ **(3)** $|3^4|$ **(4)** $\dfrac{1}{3 \cdot 4}$

2 Between which two consecutive integers does $-\sqrt{20}$ lie?
  (1) 4 and 5   **(3)** -5 and -3
  (2) -5 and -4 **(4)** -21 and -19

3 To simplify $15 + 5(12 \div 4)$, first calculate
  (1) $15 + 5$.   **(3)** $12 \div 4$.
  (2) $5(12)$.   **(4)** $5 \div 4$.

4 Which set of numbers has been placed in order from least to greatest?
  (1) $-\sqrt{7.2}, -2.\overline{7}, -2\frac{1}{7}$
  (2) $-2\frac{1}{7}, -2.\overline{7}, -\sqrt{7.2}$
  (3) $-2.\overline{7}, -\sqrt{7.2}, -2\frac{1}{7}$
  (4) $-2.\overline{7}, -2\frac{1}{7}, -\sqrt{7.2}$

5 Which statement is false?
  (1) $\sqrt{5} \cdot \sqrt{6} = \sqrt{30}$
  (2) $\sqrt{5} + \sqrt{6} = \sqrt{11}$
  (3) $(\sqrt{5})^2 = 5$
  (4) $\sqrt{5^2} = 5$

6 Which expression is in simplest form?
  (1) $\sqrt{12}$ **(3)** $\sqrt{19}$
  (2) $\sqrt{\dfrac{1}{3}}$ **(4)** $\dfrac{2}{\sqrt{5}}$

7 Which shows the expression $\sqrt{250}$ in simplest form?
  (1) $125\sqrt{2}$ **(3)** $5\sqrt{10}$
  (2) $25\sqrt{10}$ **(4)** $5\sqrt{5}$

8 Which expression is equivalent to $2\sqrt{72} - \sqrt{2}$?
  (1) $2\sqrt{70}$ **(3)** $11\sqrt{2}$
  (2) $71\sqrt{2}$ **(4)** 12

In Exercises 9–41, simplify each expression.

9 11^2 **10** 2^7 **11** 5^0 **12** 9^1

13 $\sqrt{324}$ **14** $\sqrt{1089}$ **15** $\sqrt{40,000}$

16 $\sqrt{\dfrac{1}{36}}$ **17** $\sqrt{\dfrac{169}{25}}$ **18** $\sqrt{\dfrac{441}{10,000}}$

19 $\sqrt{\dfrac{10}{9}}$ **20** $\sqrt{\dfrac{12}{49}}$ **21** $\sqrt{\dfrac{50}{81}}$

22 $\sqrt{8} \cdot \sqrt{32}$ **23** $\sqrt{5} \cdot \sqrt{30}$

24 $\dfrac{\sqrt{120}}{\sqrt{15}}$ **25** $\dfrac{\sqrt{8}}{\sqrt{50}}$

26 $6\sqrt{11} - 2\sqrt{11}$ **27** $-8\sqrt{15} + 9\sqrt{15}$

28 $3\sqrt{2} + \sqrt{8}$ **29** $4\sqrt{3} - \sqrt{12}$

30 $\sqrt{75} - \sqrt{48}$ **31** $2\sqrt{20} + \sqrt{45}$

32 $\sqrt{2}(\sqrt{2} + \sqrt{3})$

33 $\sqrt{3}(\sqrt{6} - \sqrt{5})$

34 $\sqrt{5}(3\sqrt{5} - 2\sqrt{2})$

35 $2\sqrt{3}(7\sqrt{2} - \sqrt{6})$

36 $(\sqrt{2} + 1)(\sqrt{2} - 3)$

37 $(\sqrt{5} + 2)(2\sqrt{5} - 2)$

38 $(2\sqrt{3} + 3)(2\sqrt{3} - 3)$

39 $(2\sqrt{5} + 3)^2$

40 $\sqrt{27} - \sqrt{24} - \sqrt{54} + \sqrt{48}$

41 $2\sqrt{75} + 4\sqrt{12} - 2\sqrt{18}$

In Exercises 42–44, use a calculator to approximate to the nearest hundredth.

42 $\sqrt{3}$ **43** $-\sqrt{24}$ **44** $-\sqrt{4.9}$

45 Which of the following is (are) not real numbers?

   (1) The square of a negative number

   (2) The cube root of a negative number

   (3) The square root of a negative number

   (4) The cube of a negative number

46 List the operations in the order they should be performed for the given expression.

   ◯◯◯◯ ◯ ◯

$$3^2 - 2(5 + 4) + 8 \div 2$$

47 Which of the following is a perfect cube?

   (1) 3

   (2) 0.125

   (3) 25

   (4) 100

48 What is the square root of the cube root of 64?

49 What is the cube root of the square root of 729?

50 The result of a calculation carried out on a calculator is shown in the accompanying figure. What do you know about the value of n?

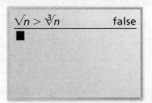

51 Using a calculator verify which of the following is true.

   (1) $\sqrt{8} = 2\sqrt{2}$

   (2) $\sqrt[3]{64} = \sqrt{16}$

   (3) $\sqrt{8} \approx 2.828$

   (4) $\sqrt{\dfrac{25}{36}} = \dfrac{5}{6}$

1.6 The Pythagorean Theorem

A.CED.1
8.G.B.7

The figure shown is a right triangle with sides a, b, and c. The side opposite the right angle, called the **hypotenuse,** is the longest side. Each of the sides, a and b, that form the right angle, is called a **leg** of the right triangle.

You can use the Pythagorean Theorem to find an unknown side length of a right triangle.

The Pythagorean Theorem

In any right triangle, the sum of the squares of the lengths of the legs is equal to the square of the length of the hypotenuse. That is, $a^2 + b^2 = c^2$.

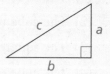

EXAMPLES 1 and 2 — Finding lengths of sides in a right triangle using the Pythagorean Theorem

Find the unknown to the nearest hundredth.

1 Find n in the right triangle below.

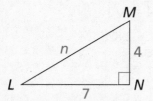

■ **SOLUTION**

The unknown n is the length of the hypotenuse.

$$n^2 = 7^2 + 4^2$$
$$n^2 = 65$$
$$n = \pm\sqrt{65} \approx \pm 8.06$$
$$n = \sqrt{65} \text{ units, or about 8.06 units}$$

2 Find z in the right triangle below.

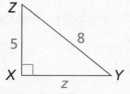

■ **SOLUTION**

The unknown z is the length of a leg.

$$8^2 = z^2 + 5^2$$
$$39 = z^2$$
$$z = \pm\sqrt{39} \approx \pm 6.24$$
$$z = \sqrt{39} \text{ units, or about 6.24 units}$$

If the lengths of all three sides of a right triangle are counting numbers, they form a **Pythagorean Triple.** The following are some examples of side lengths that form Pythagorean Triples.

a) 3, 4, 5   b) 5, 12, 13   c) 8, 15, 17   d) 7, 24, 25

EXAMPLE 3 — Using Pythagorean Triples ratios

3 Find the hypotenuse of a right triangle whose legs are 60 and 144.

■ **SOLUTION**

$$\frac{60}{144} = \frac{12(5)}{12(12)} = \frac{5}{12} \qquad \text{60 and 144 are in the ratio of 5 to 12.}$$

Therefore, the hypotenuse = 12(13) or 156.

The Converse of the Pythagorean Theorem

If a, b, and c are the lengths of the sides of a triangle such that $a^2 + b^2 = c^2$, then the triangle is a right triangle with hypotenuse of length c.

Since the hypotenuse is always the longest side of a right triangle, you can use the Converse of the Pythagorean Theorem to find out if a triangle is a right triangle.

EXAMPLE 4 Determining if three positive numbers can represent the sides of a right triangle

 Can 5, 12, and 14 represent the sides of a right triangle?

■ **SOLUTION**

Since the hypotenuse of a right triangle must be the longest side, check to see if $5^2 + 12^2$ equals 14^2.

$$5^2 + 12^2 = 169 \qquad 14^2 = 196$$

Since $169 \neq 196$, these numbers *cannot represent the sides of a right triangle.*

The next example shows how you can use the Pythagorean Theorem to solve problems.

EXAMPLE 5 Solving problems involving the Pythagorean Theorem

 A ladder is placed against the side of a building. To climb the ladder safely, the ladder must be placed against the building at a height that is three times the distance from the foot of the ladder to the base of the building. To the nearest tenth of a foot, how far from the base of a building should the foot of a 24-foot ladder be placed to match safety recommendations?

■ **SOLUTION**

Step 1 Draw a sketch. Let x represent the distance from the foot of the ladder to the base of the building.

Step 2 Use the Pythagorean Theorem to solve for x.

$$x^2 + (3x)^2 = 24^2$$
$$10x^2 = 576$$
$$x^2 = 57.6$$
$$x \approx 7.6$$

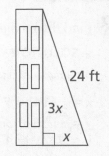

The foot of the ladder should be placed about 7.6 feet from the base of the building.

To apply the Pythagorean Theorem, you must know the lengths of two sides of a right triangle. However, if you are only given the length of one side of a right triangle, you can find the other side by knowing the values of its complementary angles.

Certain right triangles have special properties that make it easier to find the length of a side. You can use formulas based on these special properties to find the leg and hypotenuse of triangles with angle measures 45°-45°-90° and 30°-60°-90°.

An isosceles right triangle with each base angle of 45°
is called a 45°-45°-90° triangle. Since both of its base
angles are congruent, both of its legs are also congruent.

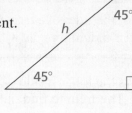

Let each leg = s.
Then $h^2 = s^2 + s^2$
$h^2 = 2s^2$
$\sqrt{h^2} = \sqrt{2s^2}$
$h = s\sqrt{2}$

In a 45°-45°-90° triangle, the length of the hypotenuse is the length of the
leg times $\sqrt{2}$. **hypotenuse = leg • $\sqrt{2}$; $h = s • \sqrt{2}$**

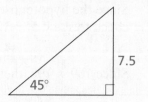

Note

If you know the
hypotenuse, solving for
s gives $s = \frac{1}{2}h\sqrt{2}$.

EXAMPLE 6   Finding lengths in a 45°-45°-90° triangle

6 Find the length of the hypotenuse of the given right triangle
with side length 7.5.

■ **SOLUTION**
Since $h = s\sqrt{2}$, then $h = 7.5\sqrt{2} \approx 10.6$.

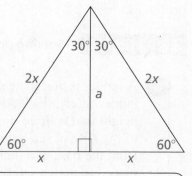

An easy way to work with a 30°-60°-90° right triangle is to make it a part
of an equilateral triangle with sides $2x$ and altitude a. The altitude a
bisects the vertex angle and the base. Therefore, the side opposite the
30° angle = $\frac{1}{2}(2x) = x$.
The length of the hypotenuse is two times the length of the side opposite
the 30° angle (the shorter side). Therefore, $h = 2x$.

The length of the side opposite the 60° angle (the longer side) is $\sqrt{3}$
times the length of the side opposite the 30° angle. Therefore, $a = x\sqrt{3}$.

EXAMPLE 7   Finding lengths in a 30°-60°-90° triangle

7 Find the missing lengths in the given right triangle with hypotenuse 14 units.

■ **SOLUTION**
x = length of shorter leg = $\frac{1}{2}h$
$x = \frac{1}{2}(14) = 7$
y = length of longer leg = length of shorter leg $\sqrt{3}$
$y = 7\sqrt{3} \approx 12.1$ units

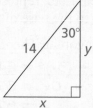

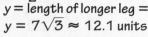

Special Right Triangles

45°-45°-90° Triangles
The hypotenuse of a 45°-45°-90° triangle with side length s and
hypotenuse h is given by $h = \sqrt{2}s$.

30°-60°-90° Triangles
The side opposite the 30° angle (the shorter side) = $\frac{1}{2}$ hypotenuse, or the
hypotenuse = 2 times the shorter leg. The side opposite the 60° angle is $\frac{1}{2}$
hypotenuse times $\sqrt{3}$, or the longer leg = shorter leg times $\sqrt{3}$.

Practice

Choose the numeral preceding the word or expression that best completes the statement or answers the question.

1 Which of the following is the measure of the side of a square whose diagonal is 14?

(1) 7 **(2)** $7\sqrt{2}$ **(3)** 14 **(4)** $7\sqrt{3}$

2 What is the length of a diagonal of a square whose sides are 5 units long?

(1) 5 **(3)** $5\sqrt{3}$
(2) $5\sqrt{2}$ **(4)** 50

3 Which three lengths cannot represent the sides of a right triangle?

(1) 6, 8, and 10

(2) 5, 12, and 13

(3) 3, 4, and 7

(4) 7, 24, and 25

4 Find the altitude of an equilateral triangle with side length 9 to the nearest tenth.

(1) 9 **(3)** 6.4
(2) 4.5 **(4)** 7.8

5 Find the perimeter of a right triangle whose leg lengths are 5 and 12 units.

(1) 40 **(2)** 34 **(3)** 30 **(4)** 17

6 Which represents x in this right triangle?

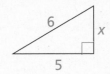

(1) $6 - 5$

(2) $6^2 - 5^2$

(3) $\sqrt{6^2 - 5^2}$

(4) $\sqrt{6^2 + 5^2}$

In Exercises 7–9, *ABC* is a right triangle with hypotenuse of length *c* and legs of lengths *a* and *b*. Find the unknown length exactly and rounded to the nearest tenth as necessary.

7 $a = 10$ and $b = 12$

8 $a = 12$ and $c = 13$

9 $a = 5\sqrt{3}$ and $c = 10\sqrt{3}$

In Exercises 10–13, find the missing value to solve the problem.

10 A garden is in the shape of a right triangle. One leg of the triangle is 6 feet long and the hypotenuse is 12 feet long. To the nearest tenth of a foot, how long is the third side?

11 In an isosceles right triangle, the length of the hypotenuse is 10 units. How long is each leg? Give an exact answer.

12 In a right triangle, the acute angles measure 30° and 60°. The shortest side is 6 ft long. Find the lengths of the other sides, as necessary to the nearest tenth of a foot as necessary.

13 In a rhombus, the sides are 14 in. long. Two intersecting sides form a 60° angle. What is the length of each diagonal? What is the area of the rhombus? Give exact answers.

In Exercises 14–17, find the value of the variable(s). Give exact answers.

14

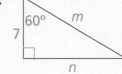

15

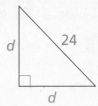

16

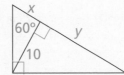

17

29

1.7 | Arithmetic and Geometric Sequences

 F.BF.2
F.IF.3

A number pattern is called an **arithmetic sequence** when each **term** of the sequence differs by a fixed number, called the **common difference**.

EXAMPLES 1 and 2 | **Finding the common difference of a sequence**

Find the common difference and determine the next three terms of the sequence.

1 $-9, -4, 1, 6, \ldots$

■ SOLUTION

To find the common difference, find the difference between consecutive terms.

$$-4 - (-9) = 5$$
$$1 - (-4) = 5$$
$$6 - 1 = 5$$

The common difference is 5.

Add 5 to the fourth term to find the fifth term, add 5 to the fifth term to find the sixth, and so on. So the next three terms of the sequence are **11, 16, 21.**

2 $11, 4, -3, -10$

■ SOLUTION

To find the common difference, find the difference between consecutive terms.

$$4 - 11 = -7$$
$$-3 - 4 = -7$$
$$-10 - (-3) = -7$$

The common difference is -7.

Add -7 to the fourth term to find the fifth term, add -7 to the fifth term to find the sixth, and so on. So the next three terms of the sequence are $-17, -24, -31.$

a_1 represents the first term of a sequence, a_2 the second term, a_3 the third, and so on to the nth term a_n. You can find any term of an arithmetic sequence by using the common difference d and the first term a_1 of the sequence.

In the sequence $6, 10, 14, 18, \ldots$, the first term a_1 is 6 and each consecutive term is found by the formula $a_n = 6 + (n-1)4$ where n represents the number of the term in the sequence.

The nth Term of an Arithmetic Sequence

The nth term in an arithmetic sequence a_n, where a_1 is the first term and d is the common difference, is

$$a_n = a_1 + (n-1)d$$

EXAMPLES 3 and 4 | **Finding the terms of an arithmetic sequence**

3 Find the 9th term of the sequence $29, 26, 23, \ldots.$

■ SOLUTION

$a_n = a_1 + (n-1)d$
$a_9 = 29 + (9-1)(-3)$ ← $a_1 = 29$ and $d = -3.$
$a_9 = 29 + (-24)$
$a_9 = 5$

4 A sequence is given by $a_n = 8 + (n-1)3.$ Find a_4.

■ SOLUTION

$a_n = 8 + (n-1)3$
$a_4 = 8 + (4-1)3$
$a_4 = 8 + 9$
$a_4 = 17$

You can also find the equation that represents the *n*th term of an arithmetic sequence. Once you have found this equation you can find the value of any term of the sequence.

EXAMPLE 5   **Finding the equation for the *n*th term of an arithmetic sequence**

5 Write the equation that represents the *n*th term of the sequence
12, 17, 22, 27, . . .

■ SOLUTION

Step 1

Identify a_1.

$a_1 = 12$

Step 2

Find *d*.

$17 - 12 = 5, 22 - 17 = 5, 27 - 22 = 5$

$d = 5$

Step 3

Use the formula $a_n = a_1 + (n - 1)d$ to write the equation for the *n*th term.

$a_n = 12 + (n - 1)5$

Another type of number sequence is a **geometric sequence.** The quotient is constant between consecutive terms of a geometric sequence and is called the **common ratio *r*.** You can find the common ratio by dividing any term of the sequence by the preceding term.

EXAMPLES 6 and 7   **Finding the common ratio of a geometric sequence**

Find the common ratio and the next two terms of each of the following geometric sequences.

 4, 12, 36, . . .

■ SOLUTION

Find the common ratio

$$\frac{12}{4} = 3$$

The common ratio is 3.
The next two terms are $36(3) = 108$ and $108(3) = 324$.

 9, 3, 1, . . .

■ SOLUTION

Find the common ratio

$$\frac{3}{9} = \frac{1}{3}$$

The common ratio is $\frac{1}{3}$.

The next two terms are $1\left(\frac{1}{3}\right) = \frac{1}{3}$ and $\frac{1}{3}\left(\frac{1}{3}\right) = \frac{1}{9}$.

The *n*th Term of a Geometric Sequence

The *n*th term in a geometric sequence a_n, where a_1 is the first term and *r* is the common ratio, is

$$a_n = a_1 r^{n-1}$$

EXAMPLES 8 and 9 Finding the terms of a geometric sequence

8 Find the 6th term of the sequence
7, 14, 28, …

■ SOLUTION

$a_n = a_1 r^{n-1}$ ← $n = 6$.

$a_6 = a_1 r^{6-1}$ ← $a_1 = 7$ and $r = 2$.

  $= 7(2)^{6-1}$

  $= 7(2)^5$

  $= 224$

The 6th term of the sequence is **224**.

9 Find the 8th term of the sequence
4, 20, 100, …

■ SOLUTION

$a_n = a_1 r^{n-1}$

$a_8 = a_1 r^{8-1}$

  $= 4(5)^{8-1}$

  $= 4(5)^7$

  $= 312,500$

The 8th term of the sequence is **312,500**.

A **recursive formula** gives a rule for computing any term of a sequence (except the first) from the preceding terms.

The sequence $-\dfrac{1}{2}, 0, \dfrac{1}{2}, 1, \dfrac{3}{2}, 2, \dfrac{5}{2}, \dots$ has a recursive formula $a_n = a_{n-1} + \dfrac{1}{2}$.

EXAMPLE 10 Using a special sequence

10 A famous sequence known as the Fibonacci sequence has the following recursive formula. Write the first eight terms of the sequence.
$a_1 = 1$, $a_2 = 1$, and for $n \geq 3$, $a_n = a_{n-1} + a_{n-2}$

■ SOLUTION

$1, 1, 2, 3, 5, 8, 13, 21, \dots$

You can write an equation for the *n*th term of a given geometric sequence by determining the value of the common ratio, *r*.

EXAMPLE 11 Finding the equation for the *n*th term of a geometric sequence

11 Write an equation for the *n*th term of the sequence 10, 7.5, 5.625, …

■ SOLUTION

Step 1

Identify a_1.

$a_1 = 10$

Step 2

Find the common ratio, *r*.

$$\frac{7.5}{10} = \frac{5.625}{7.5} = \frac{3}{4}$$

Step 3

Use the equation $a_n = a_1 r^{n-1}$ to write the equation for the *n*th term.

$$a_n = 10\left(\frac{3}{4}\right)^{n-1}$$

You can also use geometric sequences to solve real-world problems.

EXAMPLE 12   **Using geometric sequences to solve real-world problems**

12 In February 2006, about 65 thousand homes were sold in northeastern United States. If the number of home sales increases by about 3.5% each year, write an equation for the total number of homes sold a_n in terms of the year.

■ **SOLUTION**

Let $a_1 = 65$. Then $a_n = 65(1.035)^{n-1}$

EXAMPLE 13   **Determining a truth value**

13 If m, n, p represents an arithmetic sequence then $2^m, 2^n, 2^p$ will represent a geometric sequence.

■ **SOLUTION**

True. Since $n = m + d$ and $p = m + 2d$ the second sequence becomes $2^m, 2^{m+d}, 2^{m+2d}$. Using properties of exponents, this results in $2^m, 2^m \cdot 2^d, 2^m \cdot 2^{2d} \Rightarrow 2^m, 2^m \cdot 2^d, 2^m \cdot (2^d)^2$ which is geometric with a common ratio of 2^d.

Practice

Choose the numeral preceding the word or expression that best completes the statement or answers the question

1 Which set of numbers extends the pattern 27, 9, 3, 1, ...

(1) 3, 9, 27

(2) $\dfrac{1}{3}, \dfrac{1}{9}, \dfrac{1}{27}$

(3) $3, \dfrac{1}{3}, \dfrac{1}{27}$

(4) $\dfrac{1}{3}, \dfrac{1}{12}, \dfrac{1}{36}$

2 Which equation can be used to find the next number in the pattern 4, 8, 16, 32, 64, ...

(1) $a_n = 4^{n-1}$

(2) $a_n = 4(2n)$

(3) $a_n = 4(2)^{n-1}$

(4) $a_n = 4(n^2)$

3 What is the 8th term of the sequence 48, 24, 12, 6, ...?

(1) 0.375

(2) 0.75

(3) 0.25

(4) 1.5

4 What is 7th term of the sequence $a_n = -9 + (n-1)0.5$?

(1) −6.5

(2) −6

(3) −7

(4) −5.5

In Exercises 5–8, determine whether each sequence is arithmetic or geometric.

5 −6, 0, 6, 12, ...

6 2, 6, 18, 54, ...

7 $4, 2, 1, \dfrac{1}{2}, ...$

8 13, 6, −1, −8, ...

In Exercises 9–12, find the 7th and 10th term of each sequence.

9 $a_n = 2 + (n-1)3$

10 $a_n = -5 + (n-1)7$

11 $a_n = 9 + (n-1)(-6)$

12 $a_n = 0.5 + (n-1)3$

In Exercises 13–16, find the 3rd and 5th term of each sequence.

13 $5(3)^{n-1}$

14 $-2(5)^{n-1}$

15 $5(-3)^{n-1}$

16 $-5(3)^{n-1}$

In Exercises 17–20, find the common difference in each sequence and then find the next two terms in each sequence.

17 $-5, -10, -15, \ldots$

18 $0.7, 1.4, 2.1, \ldots$

19 $12, 8, 4, 0, \ldots$

20 $0.5, 0.25, 0, \ldots$

In Exercises 21–24, find the common ratio in each sequence and then find the next two terms.

21 $18, 9, 4.5, \ldots$ **22** $2, 12, 72, \ldots$

23 $9, -36, 144, \ldots$ **24** $9, 12, 16, \ldots$

In Exercises 25–32, write an equation for the *n*th term of the sequence.

25 $7, 14, 21, 28, \ldots$

26 $3, 9, 27, 81, \ldots$

27 $-252, -42, -7, -\dfrac{7}{6}, \ldots$

28 $5, 2, -1, -4, \ldots$

29 $4, 9, 14, 19, \ldots$

30 $3, 12, 48, 192, \ldots$

31 $-8, -4, -2, -1, \ldots$

32 $10, 8, 6, 4, \ldots$

Determine the first five terms of each of the following sequences.

33 $a_1 = 3, a_n = 2a_{n-1} - 1$

34 $a_1 = 2, a_n = \dfrac{1}{2} a_{n-1}$

35 $k_1 = 1, k_2 = 3, k_n = 2k_{n-2} + k_{n-1}$

36 Toppings for burgers at Fast Fred's are {pickle, onions, mustard, ketchup} List the subsets of toppings for burgers.

37 Shemeka's MEMUSIC player contains 80 songs. How many different playlists can she create?

(1) 80^1 **(3)** 2^{80}

(2) 80^2 **(4)** $2^{80}-1$

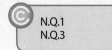
1.8 Dimensional Analysis

Often it is necessary to convert within the same system. To change a given measurement from one unit of measure to another, you can use a process called **dimensional analysis.** This process involves multiplying the given measurement by a conversion factor. A **conversions factor** is a ratio of two measurements that is equal to 1.

For example: 12 in. = 1 ft, so $\dfrac{12 \text{ in.}}{1 \text{ ft}} = 1$.

Since the conversion factor is equal to 1, the value of the measurement does not change when multiplying by the factor of one.

EXAMPLES 1 and 2   **Using dimensional analysis to convert measurements**

1 Use dimensional analysis to convert 15 quarts to gallons.

■ SOLUTION

$$15 \text{ qts} = \frac{15 \text{ qts}}{1} \cdot \frac{1 \text{ gal}}{4 \text{ qts}} = \frac{15 \text{ qts} \cdot 1 \text{ gal}}{1 \cdot 4 \text{ qts}} = \frac{15}{4} \text{ gal} = 3\frac{3}{4} \text{ gal}$$

2 How many kilometers are in 20000 meters?

■ SOLUTION

$$20000 \text{ m} = \frac{20000 \text{ m}}{1} \cdot \frac{1 \text{ km}}{1000 \text{ m}} = 20 \text{ km}$$

Measurements are only approximations. If you try to measure a paper clip with a ruler that is celebrated in $\dfrac{1}{4}$ inches, it will not be as precise as measuring the paper clip with a ruler calibrated in millimeters.

Precision in measurement is how exact the measurement is. When comparing measurements, the one that uses the smallest unit of measure is the more precise measurement. When **problem solving,** the precision of measurements places limitations on the problem. In stating a solution **the answer cannot be more precise that the smallest measure in the problem.**

Dimensional analysis can also be used as a form of check of your answer. When solving problems, carry the units throughout and if the answer results in the correct unit you can be confident that the process you followed was correct.

If Janielle runs 4 mph for $\dfrac{1}{2}$ an hour how far has she run? If we multiply her speed by the length of time she ran the result would be $4\dfrac{\text{mi}}{\text{hr}} \cdot \dfrac{1}{2} \text{ hr} = \dfrac{4 \text{ mi} \cdot 1 \text{ hr}}{1 \text{ hr} \cdot 2} = 2$ mi. By carrying the units throughout the solution the dimensional analysis results in an answer of miles which is the correct unit. We were trying to determine a distance.

As another example, what if Danny runs 3 miles in 25 minutes and he wants to know how fast he ran? By mistake he multiplies these two values together: 3 miles(25 minutes) = 75 mile minutes. However, he was looking for his speed and mile minutes is not a unit of measure for speed. This is a clue to Danny that he performed the wrong operation. The correct solution would be:

$3 \text{ mi} \div 27 \text{ min} = 3 \text{ mi} \cdot \dfrac{1}{27 \text{ min}} = \dfrac{3 \text{ mi}}{27 \text{ min}} = \dfrac{1}{9}$ mile per minute. Now the unit
of the answer is a unit of speed so Danny can be confident that this solution is
correct.

EXAMPLE 3   **Converting units**

 3 Convert Danny's speed of $\dfrac{1 \text{ mi}}{9 \text{ min}}$ to miles per hour.

■ SOLUTION

$$\dfrac{1 \text{ mi}}{9 \text{ min}} \cdot \dfrac{60 \text{ min}}{1 \text{ hr}} = \dfrac{20 \text{ mi}}{3 \text{ hr}} = 6\dfrac{2}{3} \text{ mph}$$

EXAMPLE 4   **Using Dimensional Analysis to Determine Appropriate Units for the Answer.**

 4 If you spend a dollar every second how long will it take you to spend one
million dollars?

■ SOLUTION

It is obvious that it would take one million seconds but how long is that?
What unit of time would make sense in this problem situation?
$\dfrac{1,000,000 \text{ dollars}}{1} \cdot \dfrac{1 \text{ sec}}{1 \text{ dollar}} \cdot \dfrac{1 \text{ min}}{60 \text{ sec}} \cdot \dfrac{1 \text{ hr}}{60 \text{ min}} \cdot \dfrac{1 \text{ day}}{24 \text{ hr}}$. Performing the indicated
operations the result is $11.574 \text{ days} \approx 11.6 \text{ days}$.

Practice

1 How many milligrams are equal to 0.5 g?

  (1) 0.005   **(3)** 5000

  (2) 500   **(4)** 5

2 Which unit is most appropriate when
measuring the length of a pencil?

  (1) cm   **(3)** L

  (2) m   **(4)** g

3 Which unit would provide the most precise
measurement?

  (1) inches   **(3)** feet

  (2) centimeters   **(4)** meters

**Convert each of the following to the
indicated unit.**

4 340 in. = ? ft.

5 23 qt = ? gal

6 $5\dfrac{1}{2}$ qt = ? pt

7 5 km = ? m

8 6,000 ft = ? mi

9 355 ml = ? L

**Choose the more precise measurement in
each of the following.**

10 15 in. or $11\dfrac{3}{4}$ in.

11 23 L or 35 ml

12 6 months or 2 years

13 10 cm or 100 mm

14 2 qt or 32 oz

15 50 g or 50 mg

Write the given measurement in the specified unit of measure. Give your answer to the nearest tenth of a unit as necessary.

16 340 in.; yards

17 640 yd; feet

18 245 ft; yard

19 2.5 mi; feet

20 7392 ft.; mi

21 2816 yd; mi

Use the following information to answer 22–24.

You are riding your bike on a 3 mile trail. A sign says you have completed 1500 ft.

22 What part of the ride have you completed as a percentage?

23 How many feet do you have left to bike?

24 Approximately how many miles do you have left to bike?

25 What is the final unit for the calculation below?

$$\frac{20 \text{ mi}}{1 \text{ hr}} \cdot \frac{1 \text{ hr}}{60 \text{ min}} \cdot \frac{1 \text{ min}}{60 \text{ sec}}$$

26 Write an expression to determine the number of seconds in one year.

27 John says that 1 yard is equal to three feet so to convert 1760 yards to feet you would perform the following calculation: 1760 yd $\cdot \frac{1 \text{ yd}}{3 \text{ ft}}$. Is he correct? How do you know?

28 Spending a dollar every second, how long would it take to spend one billion dollars? What is the best unit for your answer? Why?

1.9 Variables and Variable Expressions

 A.CED.1
F.BF.1.a

A **variable** is a letter that represents a number. An expression that contains at least one variable is called a **variable expression** or an **algebraic expression.** A variable expression has one or more *terms.* A **term** is a number, a variable, or a product of numbers and variables.

$$\text{variable expression} \rightarrow 7x^2y + \tfrac{1}{2}xy + x - 5$$

4 terms

When working with variable expressions, you often use the following basic principle.

Substitution Principle

If $a = b$, then a may be replaced by b in any expression.

The set of numbers that a variable may represent is called the **replacement set,** or **domain,** of the variable. Each number in the replacement set is a **value** of the variable. To **evaluate a variable expression,** you replace each variable with one of its values and simplify the numerical expression that results.

Note

A product involving a variable is often written without an operation symbol or parentheses.
$m \cdot n$ is written mn.
$3 \cdot x$ is written $3x$.

EXAMPLES 1 through 3   Evaluating variable expressions

Evaluate each expression for $x = 10$ and $y = -7$.

1 $3x - 4y$ ■ **SOLUTION**

$$3x - 4y$$
$$3(10) - 4(-7) \quad \leftarrow \text{ Replace } x \text{ with 10 and } y \text{ with } -7.$$
$$30 - (-28) \quad \leftarrow \text{ Multiply first.}$$
$$30 + 28 \quad \leftarrow \text{ Rewrite the subtraction as an addition.}$$
$$58 \quad \leftarrow \text{ Add.}$$

2 $(x + y)^2$ ■ **SOLUTION**

$$(x + y)^2$$
$$(10 + [-7])^2 \quad \leftarrow \text{ Replace } x \text{ with 10 and } y \text{ with } -7.$$
$$3^2 \quad \leftarrow \text{ Add inside the parentheses first.}$$
$$9 \quad \leftarrow \text{ Simplify the power.}$$

3 $5xy^2$ ■ **SOLUTION**

$$5xy^2$$
$$5(10)(-7)^2 \quad \leftarrow \text{ Replace } x \text{ with 10 and } y \text{ with } -7.$$
$$5(10)(49) \quad \leftarrow \text{ Simplify the power first.}$$
$$2{,}450 \quad \leftarrow \text{ Multiply.}$$

To **simplify a variable expression,** you must perform as many of the indicated operations as possible. The Distributive Property is frequently used to do this.

EXAMPLE 4   **Simplifying an indicated multiplication**

④ Simplify $-4(k - 6)$.

■ **SOLUTION**

$$-4(k - 6)$$
$$-4(k + [-6]) \qquad \leftarrow \text{Rewrite the subtraction as addition.}$$
$$(-4) \cdot k + (-4) \cdot (-6) \qquad \leftarrow \text{Apply the Distributive Property.}$$
$$-4k + 24 \qquad \leftarrow \text{Simplify each term.}$$

In a variable expression, **like terms** are terms that have exactly the same variable part. The numerical part of a term that contains variables is the **coefficient,** or **numerical coefficient,** of the term. The Distributive Property allows you to simplify an expression by adding the coefficients of like terms. This process is called *combining like terms.*

Note

Examples of Like Terms
$4n$ and $-6n$
pq and $2pq$
1 and -5

Examples of Unlike Terms
$4n$ and $-6n^2$
pq and $2pr$
x and -5

EXAMPLES 5 and 6   **Combining like terms**

⑤ Simplify $-5w - 9 + w$.

■ **SOLUTION**

$$-5w - 9 + w$$
$$[-5w + w] - 9 \qquad \leftarrow \text{Change the order. Group like terms.}$$
$$[-5w + 1w] - 9 \qquad \leftarrow \text{Rewrite } w \text{ as } 1w.$$
$$-4w - 9 \qquad \leftarrow \text{Combine like terms by adding the coefficients of } w.$$

⑥ Simplify $6c^2 - 8c - 4c^2 - 2c$.

■ **SOLUTION**

$$6c^2 - 8c - 4c^2 - 2c$$
$$6c^2 + (-8c) + (-4c^2) + (-2c) \qquad \leftarrow \text{Write the subtractions as additions.}$$
$$[6c^2 + (-4c^2)] + [(-8c) + (-2c)] \qquad \leftarrow \text{Change the order. Group like terms.}$$
$$2c^2 + [-10c] \qquad \leftarrow \text{Add the coefficients of } c^2 \text{ and of } c.$$
$$2c^2 - 10c$$

It often is helpful to use a numerical or variable expression to represent a real-life situation. To do this, you must be able to translate words and phrases into symbols. The following table shows some common translations.

English Phrase	Mathematical Expression
m plus n, the sum of m and n, m increased by n, n more than m	$m + n$
m minus n, the difference when n is subtracted from m, m decreased by n, n less than m, n fewer than m	$m - n$
m times n, the product of m and n	$mn, m \times n, m \cdot n, (m)(n)$
m divided by n, the quotient when m is divided by n	$m \div n, \frac{m}{n}$

Write each phrase as a variable expression.

7 five less than a number s

■ SOLUTION $s - 5$

8 three times a number z, increased by 4

■ SOLUTION $3z + 4$

9 seven times the sum of a number p and 25

■ SOLUTION $7(p + 25)$

10 the square of a number a, divided by nine

■ SOLUTION $a^2 \div 9$, or $\dfrac{a^2}{9}$

You may also be asked to translate an algebraic expression into words.

EXAMPLES 11 through 13   Translating algebraic expressions into English phrases

Note

Translations may vary.

Translate the algebraic expressions into English phrases.

11 $2x + 3y$

12 $-4(a + b)$

13 $\dfrac{a}{b} - c$

■ SOLUTION

the sum of twice a number and 3 times a different number

■ SOLUTION

-4 times the sum of a and b

■ SOLUTION

c subtracted from the quotient of a and b

Translating word phrases into arithmetic and algebraic expressions can be helpful when setting up and solving application problems.

EXAMPLES 14 and 15   Using variable expressions in problems

Note

even numbers:
$\dots, -4, -2, 0, 2, 4, \dots$
odd numbers:
$\dots, -5, -3, -1, 1, 3, \dots$
Both differ by 2.

14 Let y represent an odd number. What are the next two odd numbers?

■ SOLUTION

$y + 2$ and $y + 4$

15 Sam started hiking on a trail at 6:00 A.M. His sister Lisa began hiking the same trail at 8:00 A.M. Sam has now been hiking for h hours. Which expression represents the number of hours that Lisa has been hiking?

(1) $h + 2$ **(2)** $h - 2$ **(3)** $h + 8$ **(4)** $h - 6$

■ SOLUTION

Lisa started two hours after Sam, so she has been hiking two fewer hours. *Two fewer than a number h* is translated into symbols as $h - 2$.

The correct choice is (2).

Explaining the meaning of variable expressions.

Simplify the following expressions. Write each answer with only positive exponents.

16 If Raul has *d* dimes and *n* nickels, explain the meaning of the expression .10*d* + .05*n*.

■ SOLUTION

The expression .10*d* + .05*n* represents the value of the coins Raul has.

17 Fernando weighs *F* pounds and Luis weighs *L* pounds. Explain the meaning of $F + L$ and $F - L$.

■ SOLUTION

$F + L$ represents their total weight and
$F - L$ represents how much more Fernando weighs than Luis.

Note

If this result is negative then Luis weighed more than Fernando.

EXAMPLE 18 **Writing an expression based upon a table**

18 The value of *n* in the following table is based upon the value of *m*. Express the missing value for *n* in terms of *z*.

m	1	2	3	4	*z*
n	3	5	7	9	?

■ SOLUTION

? = 2*z* + 1

EXAMPLE 19 **Finding a counterexample**

19 Carlos says the word *total* in a verbal statement is a clue to use the operation of addition. Give an example of a statement that includes the word total where addition is not used.

■ SOLUTION

Pens cost $3.25 apiece. If you are going to purchase 5 pens what is the total cost?

Practice

Choose the numeral preceding the word or expression that best completes the statement or answers the question.

1 Which expression results from substituting 5 for m and -6 for n in $-3m - 9n$?

  (1) $-3(-6) - 9(5)$ **(3)** $-3(-6) - 9(-6)$
  (2) $-3(5) - 9(5)$ **(4)** $-3(5) - 9(-6)$

2 Which number is the value of $\dfrac{k - p}{p - k}$ for $k = -6$ and $p = 6$?

  (1) -12 **(2)** -1 **(3)** 0 **(4)** 1

3 If $a = -2$, then $3a^2 - 4a + 6$ equals

  (1) 2 **(2)** 5 **(3)** 10 **(4)** 26

4 Which are a pair of like terms?

  (1) $5x$ and $7y$ **(3)** $5x$ and $7x$
  (2) $5x$ and $7x^2$ **(4)** $-5x$ and $-5y$

5 Which expression is not equivalent to $-5n + 9 - 2n$?

  (1) $-5n - 2n + 9$ **(3)** $-5n + 2n - 9$
  (2) $9 - 5n - 2n$ **(4)** $9 + (-5n - 2n)$

6 Which expression represents the phrase "a number x less a number y"?

  (1) $x < y$ **(3)** $x - y$
  (2) $y - x$ **(4)** $y < x$

7 If $d + 2$ is an even integer, which is the next greater even integer?

  (1) d **(2)** $d + 3$ **(3)** $d + 4$ **(4)** $2d$

8 For which value of z is the following true?

$$z < \sqrt{z + 1} < 1$$

  (1) -1 **(2)** 1 **(3)** 2 **(4)** 3

In Exercises 9–13, evaluate each expression for the given value(s) of the variable(s).

9 $3s - 5$; $s = -5$

10 $q^2 + 9q$; $q = -3$

11 $\dfrac{j + k}{2}$; $j = 5$ and $k = 6$

12 $rs - r$; $r = 2$ and $s = -3$

13 $3a^2 - 4b$; $a = -2$ and $b = 0$

In Exercises 14–21, simplify each expression.

14 $2(a + b)$ **15** $-5(r - s)$

16 $8(6 - p)$ **17** $-3(x + 12)$

18 $(c + 5)(6)$ **19** $(v - 7)(-11)$

20 $-6n + 20n$ **21** $3t - (-15t)$

In Exercises 22–27, write each phrase as a variable expression.

22 eight more than a number t

23 a number c decreased by seventeen

24 the quotient when the square root of a number n is divided by two

25 twice the sum of a number y and nine

26 twelve less than the product of a number m and its opposite

27 the quotient when the sum of a number a and a number b is divided by their product

In Exercises 28–30, translate the algebraic expressions into English phrases.

28 $(abc)^3$ **29** $\sqrt{\dfrac{3a^2}{5b^4}}$ **30** $(7 - 2x)(-3y)$

In Exercises 31–33, solve the following problems. Clearly show all necessary work.

31 If $-2n - 4$ represents an even integer, write an expression to represent the next lesser even integer.

32 If n is an integer, which of the following expressions represents an odd integer? Show your work.

$$n - 2, n - 1, n, 2n + 1, 2n + 2$$

33 Mel began studying at 6:45 P.M., and Tim began at 6:15 P.M. Let m represent the number of minutes Mel has been studying. Write an expression to represent the number of minutes Tim has been studying.

Preparing for the Assessment

Choose the numeral preceding the word or expression that best completes the statement or answers the question.

1 Which statement represents the relationship between the set of integers and the set of rational numbers?

(1) All integers are rational numbers.

(2) All rational numbers are integers.

(3) Some integers are rational numbers and others are not.

(4) No numbers are in both sets.

2 Evaluate the expression $-|x + y|$ for $x = 3$ and $y = -10$.

(1) 13   **(3)** 7

(2) -13 **(4)** -7

3 Which is a true statement about sets A and B?

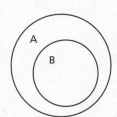

(1) $A \cap B$ **(3)** $A \subset B$

(2) $B \subset A$ **(4)** $A \cup B$

4 If $a \neq 0$ and the product of x and $-a$ is 1, then

(1) $x = 1$.   **(3)** $x = 1 + a$.

(2) $x = a$.   **(4)** $x = -\dfrac{1}{a}$.

5 Which expression is not equivalent to $-\dfrac{1}{2}(3 + 2)$?

(1) $(3 + 2)(-0.5)$ **(3)** $-\dfrac{1}{2}(3) + 2$

(2) $-\dfrac{3 + 2}{2}$ **(4)** $-\dfrac{5}{2}$

6 If a, b, and z are positive numbers, simplify the expression $\sqrt{az} \cdot \sqrt{bz}$.

(1) $\sqrt{abz}$

(2) $z\sqrt{ab}$

(3) $z\sqrt{a + b}$

(4) $z^2\sqrt{ab}$

7 For which value of x is $\sqrt{3x - 5}$ a real number?

(1) 1   **(2)** 0   **(3)** 2   **(4)** -1

8 Simplify: $\sqrt[3]{\dfrac{64}{54}}$

(1) $\dfrac{4}{\sqrt[3]{54}}$ **(3)** $\dfrac{4\sqrt[3]{2}}{3}$

(2) $\dfrac{4}{\sqrt[3]{2}}$ **(4)** $\dfrac{2}{3}\sqrt[3]{4}$

9 Approximate $\sqrt{93}$ to the nearest thousandth.

(1) 9.644   **(3)** 0.964

(2) 9.643   **(4)** 0.963

10 Find the value $-\sqrt{225}$.

(1) 15   **(3)** 15(−15)

(2) ± 15 **(4)** -15

11 Which of the following is irrational?

(1) $\sqrt{\dfrac{9}{25}}$

(2) $-\sqrt{625}$

(3) $\sqrt{\dfrac{200}{50}}$

(4) $\sqrt{0.90}$

12 Which expression is equivalent to $\sqrt{27} + \sqrt{48}$?

(1) $7\sqrt{3}$ (3) $5\sqrt{3}$

(2) $\sqrt{75}$ (4) $7\sqrt{6}$

13 Compare the values $16\sqrt{2}$ and $\dfrac{16\sqrt{8}}{2}$. Which statement is true?

(1) The value of $16\sqrt{2}$ is greater than $\dfrac{16\sqrt{8}}{2}$.

(2) The value of $\dfrac{16\sqrt{8}}{2}$ is greater than $16\sqrt{2}$.

(3) The two values are equal.

(4) Nothing can be determined.

14 What is $\sqrt[3]{8} \cdot \sqrt[3]{32}$ simplified?

(1) $3\sqrt[3]{256}$ (3) 16

(2) $4\sqrt[3]{4}$ (4) $4\sqrt[3]{8}$

In Exercises 15–17, simplify each expression.

15 $(-4)^3$

(1) -12 (3) 64

(2) -64 (4) 12

16 7^0

(1) 1 (3) 7

(2) 0 (4) $\dfrac{1}{7}$

17 $-12.8 + 17$

(1) -29.8 (3) 29.8

(2) 4.2 (4) -4.2

18 Ari bought twelve CDs that each cost d dollars. Write an expression to represent the total cost in dollars of the CDs.

(1) $12 + d$ (3) $12d$

(2) $\dfrac{d}{12}$ (4) $12 + d + 100$

19 Given that $a = 3b$, simplify $a - 3b$.

(1) $6b$ (3) $3 - ab$

(2) $3ab$ (4) 0

20 If $z = -2$, what is the value of the square of z divided by the sum of twice z and 3?

(1) $-\dfrac{4}{3}$ (3) $\dfrac{4}{7}$

(2) -4 (4) 4

21 If $2n - 1$ represents an odd integer, which of the following expressions represents the next greater odd integer?

(1) $2n + 2$ (3) $2n$

(2) $2n - 3$ (4) $2n + 1$

In Exercises 22–29, simplify. Write each in simplest radical form.

22 $\sqrt{784}$

23 $\sqrt{\dfrac{121}{400}}$

24 $\sqrt{108}$

25 $\sqrt[3]{\dfrac{1}{6}}$ $\dfrac{1}{6}\sqrt[3]{36}$

26 $\sqrt{32} + \sqrt{50}$

27 $5\sqrt{12} - \sqrt{3}$

28 $\sqrt{10}(\sqrt{2} - \sqrt{10})$

29 $(\sqrt{3} + 1)^2$

In Exercises 30–32, evaluate each expression for the given values of the variable.

30 $g(h + 9)^2$; $g = -10$ and $h = 8$

(1) $-2,890$

(2) $5,041$

(3) 8

(4) -64

31 xy^2z; $x = -4$, $y = -1$, and $z = 5$

(1) 20 (3) -20

(2) -80 (4) 100

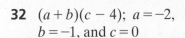

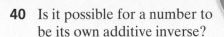

32 $(a+b)(c-4)$; $a=-2$, $b=-1$, and $c=0$

(1) 4   **(3)** -4

(2) 12   **(4)** 0

In Exercises 33–37, solve the following problems. Clearly show all necessary work.

33 Evaluate $5m+7n-1$ for $m=8$ and $n=-2$.

34 The employees of a company contributed d dollars to charity. The company matched the contribution with an equal amount, and the result was then shared equally among c charities. Write an expression to represent the dollar amount received by each charity.

35 Which has the greater value: $3r^2s$ when $r=-2$ and $s=4$, or $3r^2s$ when $r=2$ and $s=-4$?

36 Which of these is irrational? Explain.

$$\sqrt{64},\ \sqrt{\frac{1}{64}},\ \sqrt{6.4}$$

37 Are any of the following three expressions equivalent? Explain your reasoning.

$$|-2-3|,\ |-2|-|3|,\ -|2-3|$$

In Exercises 38–40, solve the following problems. Clearly explain your reasoning and show all necessary work.

38 Draw a Venn diagram to show the relationship between the sets $A=\{2, 3, 7, 8, 10, 11, 15\}$ and $B=\{1, 2, 6, 7, 11, 12, 15, 18\}$, given that the universal set is $U=\{x\mid x$ is a whole number less than or equal to 20}.

39 Draw a Venn diagram that shows the relationship between the set of whole numbers W and the set of integers Z, given the universal set as the set of all real numbers.

40 Is it possible for a number to be its own additive inverse?

41 Which expression is not a perfect square?

(1) $\sqrt{10}$ **(3)** $\sqrt{.01}$

(2) $\sqrt{100}$ **(4)** $\sqrt{\frac{9}{16}}$

42 Evaluate $\sqrt[3]{\frac{27}{8}}$

(1) 1.837   **(3)** 1.5

(2) $\frac{9}{4}$ **(4)** $\frac{3}{2}$

43 Which of the following is (are) true?

(1) $\sqrt{25}\le\sqrt[3]{125}$ **(3)** $\sqrt{36}>\sqrt[3]{216}$

(2) $\sqrt{16}<\sqrt[3]{27}$ **(4)** $\sqrt[3]{8}=\sqrt{4}$

44 What are the first five terms of the sequence whose recursive definition is: $n_1=20$, $n_{k+1}=n_k+3$

(1) 0, 3, 6, 9, 12

(2) 23, 26, 29, 32, 35

(3) 20, 23, 26, 29, 32

(4) $k, k+3, k+6, k+9, k+12$

45 Which of the following is a recursive formula for the sequence 1, 2, 2, 4, 8, 16, …

(1) $a_1=1, a_n=a_{n-2}\cdot a_{n-1}$

(2) $a_1=1, a_2=2, a_{n+1}=a_{n-2}\cdot a_{n-1}$

(3) $a_1=1, a_2=1, a_n=a_{n-2}\cdot a_{n-1}$

(4) $a_1=1, a_2=2, a_n=a_{n-2}\cdot a_{n-1}$

46 If m is a rational number and n is a rational number then mn is

(1) an integer   **(3)** rational

(2) positive   **(4)** negative

47 Which of the following numbers is irrational?

(1) $\sqrt[3]{\frac{1}{8}}$ **(3)** $\sqrt{49}$

(2) $.17171717\ldots$ **(4)** $\sqrt{8}$

48 If the length of the side of a square is 5 in. what is not true about the length of its diagonal?

(1) It is real.

(2) It is larger than 5 in.

(3) It is rational.

(4) It is not an integer.

49 For what values of x are the $\sqrt{x}$ & $\sqrt[3]{x}$ both real?

(1) an integer   **(3)** rational

(2) positive   **(4)** negative

50 The sum of a rational number and an irrational number is

(1) Rational   **(3)** Irrational

(2) an integer   **(4)** undefined

51 Justify the fact that $5^0 = 1$.

52 Write the first six terms of the sequence defined as: $a_1 = 2$, $a_2 = 4$, $a_n = a_{n-1} + a_{n-2}$.

53 The short leg of a right triangle is represented by w and the hypotenuse is represented by $w + 2$. Represent the long leg in terms of w.

54 Convert $\frac{1}{4}$ mile to yards.

55 Each large pizza can feed three teenage boys. How many pizzas would be needed to feed the Southside football team which is made up of 55 teenage boys?

56 The average teenager watches 5.5 hours of TV each day. How many hours would the average teenager have watched when they turn 20 years old? Which of the following could be used to determine how many days of TV had been watched? (Teenager means age 13–19.)

(1) 7 yrs $\cdot$ 5.5 hours

(2) 7 yrs $\cdot \dfrac{365 \text{ days}}{1 \text{ yr}} \cdot \dfrac{5.5 \text{ hours}}{1 \text{ day}} \cdot \dfrac{24 \text{ hours}}{1 \text{ day}}$

(3) 7 yrs $\cdot \dfrac{365 \text{ days}}{1 \text{ yr}} \cdot \dfrac{5.5 \text{ hours}}{1 \text{ day}}$

(4) 7 yrs $\cdot \dfrac{365 \text{ days}}{1 \text{ yr}} \cdot \dfrac{5.5 \text{ hours}}{1 \text{ day}} \cdot \dfrac{1 \text{ day}}{24 \text{ hours}}$

57 Angelica has a marbles and Felipe has f marbles. Explain in words $a > f$.

58 A = {dime, nickel, quarter} and B = {penny, half-dollar, dollar}. Determine $A \cap B$.

59 Express the numbers represented in the accompanying figure using interval notation.

60 Jose is riding his bike at the rate of r mph and he does so for 1.5 hours. What does the expression $r \cdot t$ represent?

61 Express $\dfrac{2^5 \cdot 3^{-1}}{3^0 \cdot 2^3}$ as an expression with only positive exponents.

62 M = {0, 1, 2, 3, 4, 5, 6, 7, 8, 9} and N = {−2, −1, 0, 1, 2}. Determine $M \cup N$.

2 Functions

2.1 Relations and Functions

A.CED.A.1
8.F.A.1
F.IF.A.1-2-3-4
F.BF.A.1

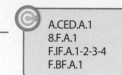

A student earns $4.50 per hour as a baby sitter. She is paid for a whole number of hours of work and works up to 6 hours at a time. The sitter can represent the relationship between time worked and money earned in a table, a list, an equation or rule, or a graph.

hours h	1	2	3	4	5	6
wage w	$4.50	$9.00	$13.50	$18.00	$22.50	$27.00

$$\{(1, 4.50), (2, 9.00), (3, 13.50), (4, 18.00), (5, 22.50), (6, 27.00)\}$$
$$w = 4.5h$$

The relationship between hours worked and wages is an example of a *function*. A **function** is a relationship in which every member of one set, the **domain,** is assigned exactly one member of a second set, the **range.** Members of the range of a function are also called **values of a function.** If the function is defined by an equation, you *evaluate the function* to find its values.

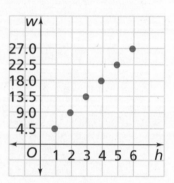

EXAMPLES 1 and 2   Recognizing functions

1 Which list does not represent a function?

    (1) $\{(1, 2), (3, 4), (5, 7), (7, 5)\}$ **(3)** $\{(0, -3), (-2, 0), (7.5, 8.9), (-0.002, -0.002)\}$

    (2) $\{(-2, 4), (0, 0), (1, 1), (2, 4)\}$ **(4)** $\{(1, 1), (4, 2), (9, 3), (4, -2), (49, 7), (100, 10)\}$

■ SOLUTION

In choice (4), 4 is paired with 2 and with -2. So the list in choice **(4)** does not represent a function.

domain 4 ⟶ 2 range / −2

2 If domain members are represented by x and range members are represented by y, which does not represent a function?

    (1) $y = 3x - 5$ **(2)** $y^2 = x$ **(3)** $y = x^2 - 5$ **(4)** $y = |x|$

■ SOLUTION

In choice (2), $x = 9$ gives $y^2 = 9$. Both 3 and -3 satisfy $y^2 = 9$. The equation in choice **(2)** does not represent a function.

A **relation** is any correspondence between two sets, the **domain** and **range,** without requiring that each domain member be assigned only one range member. These *mapping diagrams* show the difference between a function and a relation.

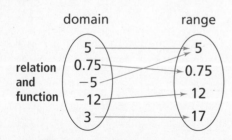

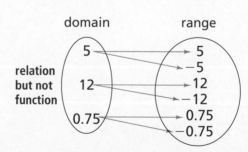

The domain and range of a function can be given using a list, interval notation, or a written description. You find the domain of a function by identifying all of the possible independent values of the function. You find the range of a function by identifying all of the possible dependent values of the function.

EXAMPLES 3 and 4   **Finding the domain and range of a function**

Find the domain and range of each function.

3 $\{(1, 5), (2, 10), (3, 15), (4, 20), (5, 25), (6, 30)\}$

■ **SOLUTION**

domain: first members in the ordered pairs
range: second members in the ordered pairs

domain: $\{1, 2, 3, 4, 5, 6\}$
range: $\{5, 10, 15, 20, 25, 30\}$

4 $y = x^2 + 2$

■ **SOLUTION**

For any real number x, $x^2 \geq 0$.
Thus, $x^2 + 2$ is always 2 or more.

domain: all real numbers
range: all real numbers 2 or more

The *vertical-line test* can help you determine whether a graph represents a function. If the graph does represent a function, you can use the graph to find the domain and range. The graph at the right does not represent a function because it does not pass the vertical-line test.

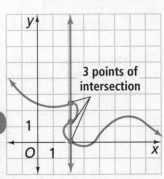

3 points of intersection

Vertical-Line Test

If every vertical line that intersects a graph does so in exactly one point, then the graph represents a function.

EXAMPLES 5 and 6   **Using graphs and the vertical-line test**

Does the graph represent a function? If it does, what are the domain and range?

5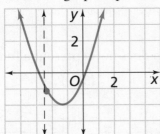

■ **SOLUTION**

Every vertical line intersects the graph in exactly one point. The graph represents a function.

Domain: all real numbers, $\{x \mid x \in \mathcal{R}\}$, $(-\infty, \infty)$
Range: all real numbers -2 or more,
$$\{y \mid y \geq -2\}, [-2, \infty)$$

6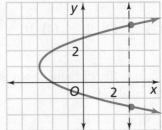

■ **SOLUTION**

Every vertical line with x-coordinate more than -3 intersects the graph in two points. For example, the line $x = 3$ intersects the graph in two points.

The graph does not represent a function.

You can use what you know to recognize relations and functions given in different representations, such as a list, a table, a graph, or an equation.

EXAMPLE 7 **Recognizing a relation from different representations**

7 Which represents a relation that is not a function?

(1) {(0, 0), (0, 7), (6, 6), (6, −6)}   (3) $y = -3.5x + 7$

(2)

domain	range
−3	0
5	10
7	−5.4

(4)

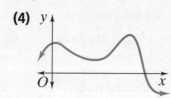

■ SOLUTION

In choice (1), the domain values 0 and 6 are each assigned two range values. The list in choice (1) is a relation but not a function. The correct choice is (1).

Practice

Choose the numeral preceding the word or expression that best completes the statement or answers the question.

1 Which is a relation but not a function?

(1) {(−2, 3), (−1, 1), (0, 7), (2, 3), (3, 2)}

(2) {(2, 3), (3, 4), (5, 7), (1, 2), (9, 9)}

(3) {(−2, 4), (2, 3), (5, 6), (−2, 6)}

(4) {(−1, −1), (−2, −2), (−3, −3), (4, 4)}

2 Given $y = 3x + 1$ and $x = 3$, find y.

(1) 1   (2) 3   (3) 9   (4) 10

3 If {−3, −1, 1, 2, 3} is the domain, what is the range of $y = x^2 - x$?

(1) {−3, −1, 1, 2}

(2) {0, 2, 6, 12}

(3) {1, 4, 9}

(4) {−3, −2, −1, 1}

4 A graph passes the vertical-line test if a vertical line that intersects the graph intersects it at

(1) exactly one point.

(2) two points.

(3) more than one point.

(4) two or more points.

5 Which graph does not represent a function?

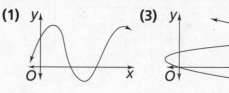

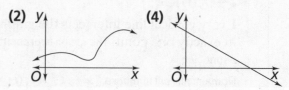

6 Which equation represents the verbal description of this function?

To change length f in feet to length I in inches, multiply f by 12.

(1) $f = 12I$ **(3)** $I = 12f$

(2) $I = \dfrac{12}{f}$ **(4)** $f = \dfrac{12}{I}$

7 The values of the independent variable for a function are also known as the

(1) values.   **(3)** range.

(2) domain.   **(4)** coordinates.

8 Given the function rule $g(x) = 2x - 1$, what is the value of $g(3)$?

(1) 3   **(3)** 5

(2) 9   **(4)** 10

9 $A = \{(1, 4), (4, 7), (3, 7), (5, 9), (9, 2)\}$. Which of the following statements is **not** true?

(1) The domain of A is $\{1, 4, 3, 5, 7, 9\}$.

(2) A is a function.

(3) The range of A is $\{4, 7, 9, 2\}$.

(4) A is a relation.

10 Which of the following lines has an undefined slope?

(1) a line containing the points $(3, -4)$ and $(-4, 3)$

(2) a line containing the points $(2, 1)$ and $(-2, -3)$

(3) a horizontal line through the point $(3, 4)$

(4) a vertical line through the point $(-1, 5)$

In Exercises 11–15, write a formula for the relation described and give its domain and range.

11 To convert a length in inches i to centimeters c, multiply by 2.54.

12 The Coach USA Center seats 3200 fans. Tickets sell for \$9. The number of seats sold s determines the gross take G.

13 Your grade G on a test worth 80 points is the number of points you earned e divided by 0.8.

14 The points you earn p in basketball is 2 times the number of field goals f you make.

15 The area A of a square is the length of its side s multiplied by itself.

In Exercises 16–20, graph the function by using a table of values and state its domain and range.

16 $y = 2x - 1$

17 $f(x) = |x| - 1$

18 $y = -5x + 7$

19 $4x + 3y = 12$

20 y is the sum of 3 times x and 4.

21 When an object is dropped from the roof of a house its distance (in feet) above the ground is given by the function $d(t) = -16t^2 + 50$ where t is in seconds. What is the average rate of change in the distance in the first 1.5 seconds?

22 Betty rode her bike at 6 miles per hour starting from a location that was 2 miles from her home. Which graph best represents her travels? *d* represents distance from home and *t* is time in hours since she started riding.

(1)

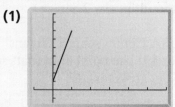

(2)

(3)

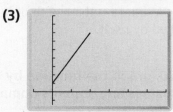

(4)

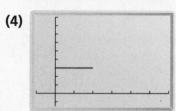

23 The table shows the number of two types of trees (in hundreds) in a forest reserve for five different years.

Year	2000	2004	2008	2010	2012
Spruce	53	63	73	83	93
Pine	85	80	75	70	65

Using words from the list below complete the following statement.

The average rate of change would be negative for _____ trees over this period of time. From 2010 to 2012 the average rate of change for Spruce trees was _____. The decline of Pine trees seems to be occurring at a _____ rate.

		1000 trees	500 trees per year	−500 trees per year
Spruce	constant	1000 trees	500 trees per year	−500 trees per year
Pine	variable	10 trees	5 trees per year	−5 trees per year

24 The slope of a line is $\frac{3}{2}$.

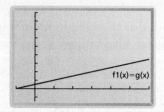

The accompanying figure shows the graph of a function. The table contains data that has been collected.

Variable 1	2	4	6	8	10
Variable 2	2	3	4	5	6

Which of these situations has the smallest rate of change: A line with slope of $\frac{3}{2}$? The function shown in the graph? The data shown in the table? Find each rate and compare.

25 Which of the following representations describe a function?

(1) a, b, c, d   **(3)** b, d

(2) a, b, d   **(4)** none

a {(1, 0), (2, 2), (3, 2), (5, 5)}

b

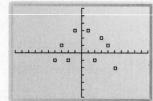

c

x	2	3	2	7
y	2	4	5	2

d

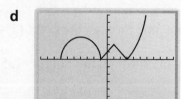

26 The *vertical line* test is a geometric way of testing what feature of a function?

Function Notation

F.IF.2

Functions often express the idea of one variable depending upon the other. The amount of a tip depends upon the amount of the total bill. The cost of a sundae depends upon the number of toppings. The number of gloves sold depends upon the time of year.

Therefore a function can also be thought of as a rule that takes a numerical **input** and assigns exactly one result as **output.**

This idea can be thought of as a function machine. For each input into the machine there is one and only one output.

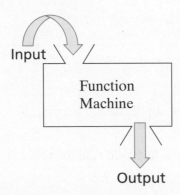

Function notation is used to represent the output of a function in terms of its input. Consider the example of the amount of a 20% tip being a function of the cost of a meal. This could be expressed as

Tip = function of Cost = 0.20(cost)

This is expressed as Tip = f (cost) = 0.20(cost) or $f(c) = 0.20c$ where c represents the cost of the meal. The f stands for the function and not for a number. If the cost of the meal were $24.00 then

$$f(24) = 0.20(24) = 4.80 = \text{Tip}$$

This expression would be read as "f of 24 equals 4.80". There is nothing unique about the letter f you may choose any appropriate letter to name a function.

Function Notation

In the expression $f(x)$

- f is the name of the function

- x is an element from the function's domain (input)

- $f(x)$ is an element in the range (output) of the function

The symbol $f(x)$ is read as **the value of the function f at x.**

To evaluate a function $f(x)$ for a particular value of x the value is substituted into the equation to obtain a result. Given $f(x) = 3x + 5$ the value $f(4)$ is determined by substituting 4 into the function wherever there is an x. $f(4) = 3(4) + 5 = 12 + 5 = 17$. Thus $f(4) = 17$.

1 The area of a circle is a function of its radius. Write a function for the area of a circle and evaluate it for a circle whose diameter is 7.

■ **SOLUTION**

$$A(r) = \pi r^2 \rightarrow A\left(\frac{7}{2}\right) = \pi\left(\frac{7}{2}\right)^2 = \frac{49\pi}{4} \approx 38.485$$

2 Total cost is a function of price and sales tax. If a skateboard costs $108.95 and the sales tax rate is 7.5%, write the total cost as a function of price and determine the total cost for this skateboard.

■ **SOLUTION**

$$c(p) = p + 0.075p = 1.075p = 1.075(108.95) = \$117.12$$

n	$g(n)$
0	1
1	3
2	5
3	7
4	9
5	11

Tables can also be used to represent functions by listing particular input and output pairs.

The accompanying table lists values for n and $g(n)$. A function rule for this table could be "twice a number increased by one".

Use the table above for n and $g(n)$ to determine each value.

3 $g(3)$

4 $g(-5)$

5 $-g(8)$

■ **SOLUTION**

$g(3) = 2(3) + 1 = 7$

■ **SOLUTION**

$g(-5) = 2(-5) + 1 = -9$

■ **SOLUTION**

$-g(8) = -(2(8) + 1) = -17$

There is no restriction to just numerical values when evaluating functions. If $f(x) = 3x^2 - 2x + 1$, then to determine $f(z)$ replace each occurrence of x with the variable z. The result would be $f(z) = 3z^2 - 2z + 1$. Likewise $f(\blacklozenge)$ would be $3\blacklozenge^2 - 2\blacklozenge + 1$.

Some functions are defined as a discrete set of points. For example, a particular country reports its population each year as shown in the accompanying table. As can be seen the graph of this function is a set of discrete points.

The domain could be defined using set and interval notation: $\{ t \mid t \in \text{integers and } 0 \le t \le 6 \}$

Population of Magali t years after 1990	
t years	Population in millions
0	64.28
1	68.25
2	71.10
3	72.79
4	74.58
5	76.65
6	78.61

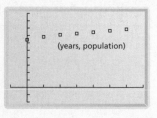
(years, population)

1 If $f(x) = 3x + 5$, determine $f(3)$.

In exercises 2 & 3, fill in the blank and simplify

2 $g(x) = 2x - 7$

    (1) $g(1) = 2(\square) - 7$

    (2) $g(-3) = 2(\square) - 7$

    (3) $g(z) = 2(\square) - 7$

    (4) $g(a + b) = 2(\square) - 7$

3 $h(x) = 4 - 3x$

    (1) $h(-1) = 4 - 3(\square)$

    (2) $h(2) = 4 - 3(\square)$

    (3) $h(\blacklozenge) = 4 - 3(\square)$

    (4) $h(n - 1) = 4 - 3(\square)$

4 Express the perimeter P of a square as a function of the length s of one of its sides.

5 A car is traveling at 60 mph. Express the distance d in miles traveled by the car as a function of the time t traveled in hours.

6 A worker earns \$14 an hour for regular time and time and a half for overtime. Overtime is hours worked over 40 hours. The weekly earnings for this worker is given by the function
$$W(h) = \begin{cases} 14h & , 0 < h \le 40 \\ 21(h - 40) + 560, & h > 40 \end{cases}$$
where h is the number of hours worked during the week.
Determine each of the following.

    (1) $W(25)$ **(3)** $W(55)$

    (2) $W(40)$ **(4)** $W(-3)$

7 A function is defined by the table shown. Determine the value of each of the following.

n	$Z(n)$
2	15
3	22
4	4
5	25
6	30
10	35
12	40

    (1) $Z(3) = ?$

    (2) $Z(?) = 30$

    (3) $Z(?) = 4$

    (4) $Z(12) = ?$

8 The cost of manufacturing widgets is given by the function $\text{Cost}(n) = 5.5\sqrt{n} + 0.125n + 1250$ where n represents the number of widgets. Determine each of the following.

    (1) $\text{Cost}(100)$

    (2) $\text{Cost}(500)$

    (3) $\text{Cost}(875)$

    (4) $\text{Cost}(900.5)$

9 The function $v(t)$ represents the volume in liters of a balloon when the temperature is t degrees Celsius. Suppose $v(35) = 2.75$.

    (1) What are the units of the 35 and the 2.75?

    (2) What is the volume of this balloon at 35°C?

10 The total cost of dinner at Sam's Pasta House includes the cost of the meal, sales tax of 7.5% on the meal, and a 20% tip. Write a function c for the total cost of dinner in terms of m the meal costs.

Piecewise Defined Functions

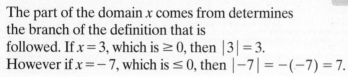

F-IF.2
F-IF.7b

Some functions are defined in pieces by putting restrictions on their domain. The absolute value function can be defined in two pieces.

$$|x| = \begin{cases} x, x \ge 0 \\ -x, x < 0 \end{cases}$$

The part of the domain x comes from determines the branch of the definition that is followed. If $x = 3$, which is ≥ 0, then $|3| = 3$. However if $x = -7$, which is ≤ 0, then $|-7| = -(-7) = 7$.

The function $f1(x) = \begin{cases} x + 2, x \ge 0 \\ x - 3, x < 0 \end{cases}$ can be

graphed as shown in the accompanying diagram. Note the closed circle indicating that the point $(0, 2)$ is included and the open circle indicating that the point $(0, -3)$ is not included in the graph of this function. Because this function has two parts whenever $x \ge 0$ follow the line $y = x + 2$ and whenevery $x \le 0$ follow the line $y = x - 3$.

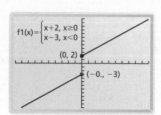

Some functions take on a particular value over an interval of its domain. For a while, United States first class postage rates were $.46 per ounce with a $.20 increase for each additional ounce. The graph of this function is shown in the figure. Values on the horizontal axis represent the weight of the item and values on the vertical axis represent the cost of postage. This type of function is called a **step function**.

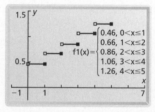

Note

This step function can be represented using interval notation

$$f1(x) = \begin{cases} 0.46, (0, 1] \\ 0.66, (1, 2] \\ 0.86, (2, 3] \\ 1.06, (3, 4] \\ 1.26, (4, 5] \end{cases}$$

EXAMPLE 1   **Graphing piecewise functions**

Graph the function defined as $g(x) = \begin{cases} x + 2, x \le -1 \\ x^2, -1 < x \le 2 \\ 2, x > 2 \end{cases}$

and complete the function table.

x	g(x)
−3	
−1	
−0.5	
1.5	
2	
4	
5	

■ **SOLUTION**

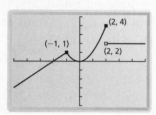

x	g(x)
−3	−3 + 2 = −1
−1	−1 + 2 = 1
−0.5	$(−0.5)^2 = 0.25$
1.5	$(1.5)^2 = 2.25$
2	$2^2 = 4$
4	2
5	2

1 Use the accompanying graph to complete the table below.

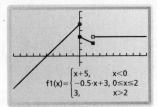

$$f1(x) = \begin{cases} x+5, & x<0 \\ -0.5 \cdot x+3, & 0 \le x \le 2 \\ 3, & x>2 \end{cases}$$

x	F(x)
−4	
1	
	2
0	
	5

2 Sketch the function

$$h(x) = \begin{cases} -x, & x \le -2 \\ x, & -2 < x < 2 \\ 3, & x \ge 2 \end{cases}$$

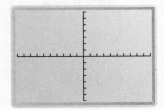

3 Write an algebraic expression for the function shown in the graph.

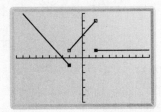

4 The graph of $f(x)$ is shown. Determine each of the following.

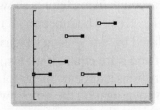

(1) $f(0.5)$

(2) $f(1.75)$

(3) $f(3)$

(4) $f(2)$

5 Which story is best represented by the graph shown?

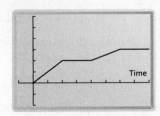

(1) Johnny runs up a steep hill and then runs on level ground until he reaches another hill and runs up it to level ground.

(2) Water is flowing into a tub at a constant rate and then turned off for a period of time. The water is again turned on at a lesser rate and turned off when it reaches 3 ft.

(3) Joan turns on the oven and the temperature increases until the oven is hot enough to bake her cookies.

(4) A car traveling at a constant rate moves up the side of a hill with two level sections and two steep sections.

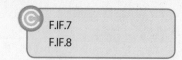

F.IF.7
F.IF.8

Given the functions $f(x) = \frac{x^2}{x}$ and $g(x) = x$, are these functions equal? The accompanying figures show these two functions graphed as $f1(x)$. The function $f(x)$ can algebraically be simplified by $\frac{x^2}{x} = \frac{x(x)}{x} = x$, which might seem to indicate that f and g are equal. If we inspect the graphs of these functions it appears the graphs are the same. However by investigating the graphs we can see that the point $(0, 0)$ is on the graph of $f1(x) = f(x)$ and not on the graph of $f1(x) = g(x)$. In the case of $f1(x) = f(x)$ the point $(0, 0)$ is the y-intercept but when $f1(x) = g(x)$ the function is undefined for $x = 0$. Therefore 0 is in the domain of $f(x)$ and **not** in the domain of $g(x)$. This implies that these two functions do not contain the same points and therefore are not equal.

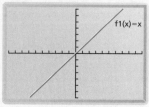
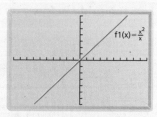
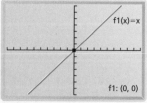
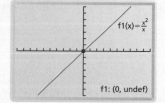

Equal Functions

Two functions $f(x)$ and $g(x)$ are equal if and only if

- The domain of f is equal to the domain of g, **and**

- For any element in the domain, $f(x)$ is equal to $g(x)$.

Function Behavior

It is helpful when describing a graph of a polynomial, or when trying to graph the polynomial, to have an idea of the behavior of the function. There are a number of aspects of the curve's shape that would be helpful. Features such as **intercepts,** over which interval(s) the function is **increasing** or **decreasing,** intervals where the function is **positive** or **negative, turning points,** and **end behavior** are features to be considered.

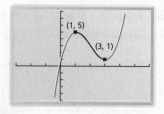

> **Note**
>
> "Polynomial" means many terms.

The graph of the function in the accompanying figure has two turning points. The point $(1, 5)$ is called a relative maximum and the point $(3, 1)$ is called a relative minimum. The function is increasing to the left of the point $(1, 5)$ and to the right of the point $(3, 1)$. These portions of the graph are blue. Between the turning point the function is decreasing.

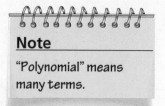

Increasing and Decreasing Functions

- If, when looking at a graph of a function, the y values are increasing as the x values increase, the function is said to be **increasing.**

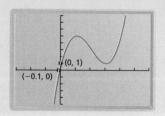

- If, when looking at a graph of a function, the y values are decreasing as the x values increase, the function is said to be **decreasing.**

The function on the previous page has an *x*-intercept at (0.1, 0) and a *y*-intercept at (0, 1). To the left of the *x*-intercept the function is below the *x*-axis or negative, and to the right of the *x*-intercept the function is above the *x*-axis or positive.

EXAMPLE 1   **Describing function behavior**

The graph of $y = 3x + 3$ is shown. When is this function increasing or decreasing and when is it positive or negative?

■ **SOLUTION**

This function is always increasing over the domain of all real numbers.

It is negative if $x < -1$ and positive if $x > -1$.

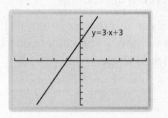

Consider the graphs below of polynomials with even degree and a leading coefficient that is positive or negative.

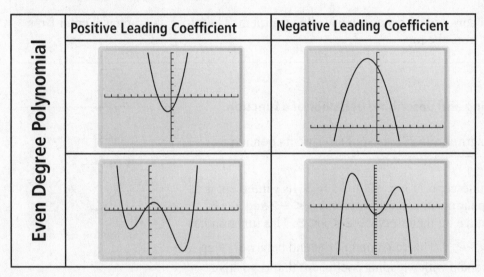

Compare the graphs above with the graphs below, which illustrate odd degree polynomials with a leading coefficient that is positive or negative.

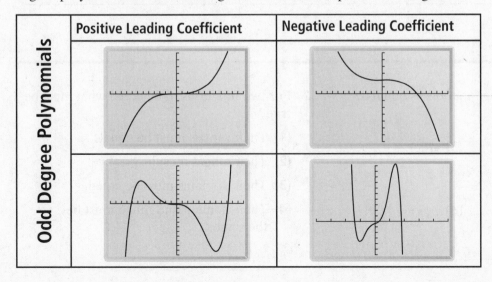

Notice that even degree polynomials either open up on both ends or open down on both ends. That is, their graphs enter and leave the graph window from the top or bottom.

Odd degree polynomials have ends that move off in opposite directions. If the graph entered from the bottom it leaves through the top and if it entered from the top it leave from the bottom.

All even degree polynomials have end behavior like quadratics and all odd degree polynomials have end behavior like cubics or linear functions with a nonzero slope.

EXAMPLE 2   Describing end behavior

Describe the end behavior of the function $g(x) = 2x^7 - 5x^6 + 2x^4 - 3x^3 + 3x + 11$ without graphing the function.

■ SOLUTION

This function is odd powered with a positive leading coeffient. Therefore its graph will enter from the bottom and exit from the top.

EXAMPLE 3   Graphing and describing behavior of a function

Use a calculator to graph $y = x^2 - x - 6$. Describe its behavior.

■ SOLUTION

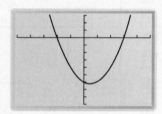

This function has x intercepts at $x = -2$ and $x = 3$. Its y intercept is at $y = -6$. The function is positive on the intervals $x < -2$ and $x > 3$. The function is negative on the interval $-2 < x < 3$. This function has a turning point at $\left(\frac{1}{2}, -\frac{25}{4}\right)$. This function has the end behavior of an even degreed polynomial with a leading coefficient that is positive. It is decreasing on the interval $-\infty < x < \frac{1}{2}$ and increasing on the interval $\frac{1}{2} < x < \infty$.

Practice

1 Which of the following functions is equal to the function $h(x) = x$?

(1) $g(x) = \dfrac{x^3}{x^2}$

(3) $d(x) = \dfrac{1}{x}$

(2) $k(x) = \begin{cases} \dfrac{x^3}{x^2}, x \neq 0 \\ 0, x = 0 \end{cases}$

(4) $n(x) = |x|$

2 For two functions to be equal what must be true?

(1) Their ranges must be equal.

(2) Their ranges must be positive.

(3) Their domains must be equal.

(4) Their domain and range must be the same.

3 Which function is equal to $f(x) = \sqrt{(-x)^2}$

(1) $k(x) = -\sqrt{x^2}$ (3) $n(x) = x^2$

(2) $m(x) = \sqrt{x}$ (4) $r(x) = |x|$

4 If $s(x) = t(x)$ and $x = \blacklozenge$ with $s(\blacklozenge) = \clubsuit$, then

(1) $t(x) = x$ (3) $t(\blacklozenge) = \clubsuit$

(2) $t(\clubsuit) = \blacklozenge$ (4) $\blacklozenge = \clubsuit$

5 Which graph represents an even powered function with a negative leading coefficient?

(1)
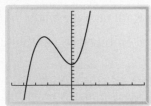

(2)
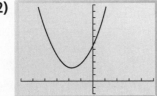

(3)
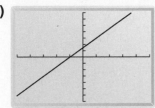

(4)
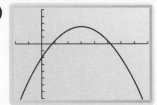

6 The function shown in the accompanying graph is negative over which interval?

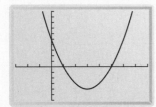

(1) $1 < x < 5$ (3) $-\infty < x < 3$

(2) $-\infty < x < 1$ (4) $0 < x < 5$

7 Complete the table using the accompanying graph.

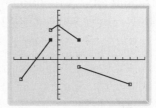

x	−3	−1			10
y			6	4	

8 This graph shows the height of a baseball in feet as a function of time in seconds.

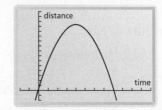

(1) What would the y intercept represent?

(2) What would the coordinates of the turning point represent?

(3) Approximately when did the ball hit the ground?

9 Aidan uses a graphing calculator to graph the function $f(x) = -3x^3 - 2x^2 + 7x + 5$ and the following graph is produced. Grace says that the result is not correct. How did she know?

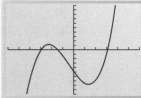

10 The values in the accompanying table represent points on a function.

(1) What are the coordinates of the x intercept?

(2) What are the coordinates of the y intercept?

(3) Is this function increasing or decreasing?

(4) Can you write a rule for this function?

x	h(x)
−3	−4
−1	0
0	2
2	6
$\frac{5}{2}$	7

11 The accompanying graph shows the number of hours of daylight each month (0 = Jan.) for a particular city. A function which approximates these values is also shown.

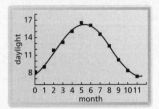

(1) For what months is the length of daylight increasing?

(2) Which month has the longest amount of daylight?

(3) What is the approximate rate of change from July to Nov.?

(4) Bob has solar landscape lights which require 12 hours to recharge. What are the best months to operate these landscape lights based upon recharging time?

12 The accompanying graph shows the results of a 100 yard race between Joe, Raul, and Bob. Based upon this graph, answer the following questions. Time is measured in seconds.

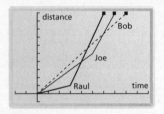

(1) Who won the race?

(2) When did Raul take the lead?

(3) When were Bob and Joe at the same spot?

(4) How much longer did it take Bob to run the race than Raul?

When appropriate, choose the numeral preceding the word or expression that best completes the statement or answers the question.

1 The cost for producing delphs is $1.25 per delph plus a $375 set up charge. Write a function, $c(d)$ for the cost of producing d delphs.

2 The function $g(h)$ represents the grade a student earns on a test after studying for h hours. Explain the meaning of the following statements.

(1) $g(4)$

(2) $g(h) = 85$

(3) $g(3) < g(5)$

3 If $f(x) = -3x - 5$ which of the following are (is) true?

(1) $f(3) = -14$ **(3)** $f(3) > f(0)$

(2) $f(4) = 7$ **(4)** $f(0) = 0$

4 A school kept track of the number of students who owned cell phones starting in 2010. The information is shown in the table. Based upon this information, the graph of this function would be:

Year after 2010 = n	Number of students in hundreds = f(n)
0	0.4
1	0.8
2	1.8
3	3

(1) A line

(2) A parabola

(3) A set of points

(4) A piecewise graph

5 Using the table from #4, what is the meaning of the expression $f(2) = 1.8$?

6 The cost of a taxi ride is $1.50 per mile up to 5 miles. Each additional mile, or part thereof, is an additional $1.75. If the ride is over 12 miles, each mile over 12 costs an additional $2.00. Explain the similarities and differences between the following representations for this function?

(1)

$$c(m) = \begin{cases} 1.50m, 0 \le m \le 5 \\ 1.50m + 1.75(m-5), 5 < m \le 12 \\ 1.50m + 1.75(m-5) + 2.00(m-12), 12 < m \end{cases}$$

(2)

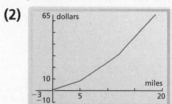

(3)

Miles	3	6	9	12	15	18
Cost	4.50	10.75	20.50	30.25	46.00	61.75

7 The distance, in feet, above the ground of an object thrown vertically up into the air can be determined by the function $s(t) = -16t^2 + 56t + 3$, where t is measured in seconds.

(1) What is $s(3)$?

(2) What does $s(0)$ represent?

(3) This object reaches its maximum height in $1\frac{3}{4}$ seconds. What is its maximum hieght?

(4) Given the graph of $f2(x)$ as shown complete the function table given.

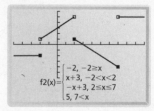

x	-3	-1		2		7	15
y			3		0		

8 Which of the following functions are (is) equal to $f(x) = x$?

(1) $g(x) = \dfrac{3x}{3}$

(2) $h(x) = \dfrac{3x^2}{3x}$

(3) $k(x) = 3x - 2x$

(4) $m(x) = x^2 - x$

9 Over which interval is the function in the graph decreasing?

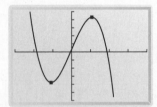

(1) $x < -1$

(2) $x > 1$

(3) $-1 < x < 1$

(4) $x < -1$ and $x > 1$

10 If a function is of even degree with a leading coefficient that is positive, the end behavior of the function is like what letter of the alphabet?

11 Over what interval(s) is $g(x) \geq f(x)$?

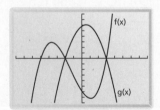

(1) $-\infty \leq x \leq \infty$ **(3)** $x \leq -2$ and $x \geq 3$

(2) $-2 \leq x \leq 3$ **(4)** $-8 \leq x \leq 8$

12 $z(x)$ is a function that opens up and $v(x)$ is a function which opens down. Which region is shaded in the accompanying graph?

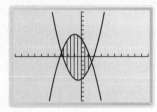

(1) $z(x) = v(x)$

(2) $z(x) < v(x)$

(3) $z(x) > v(x)$

(4) $z(x) \neq v(x)$

13 The accompanying graph shows three graphs representing the amount of a $200 investment over a 20 year span. The dashed graph is for an investment earning 5%. The dotted curve is for an investment earning 8% and the solid graph is for an investment earning 12%. Approximately how long does it take each investment to double?

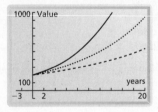

14 State the "Vertical Line Test."

64

3 Linear Equations and Inequalities in One Variable

Mathematician in the Spotlight

Paul Erdős

Born in Hungary, Paul Erdős was famous for elegant proofs of difficult and often previously-considered unsolvable mathematical problems, many in the area of numbers theory. Today, an "Erdős number" is used to describe a mathematician's publishing relationship to Erdős.

Erdős' devotion to mathematics meant that he never married, owned no property, and didn't hold a job because it would limit his ability to focus on mathematical problems. Instead he traveled from one place to another. He would knock on a fellow mathematician's door and ask, "is your mind open?" indicating that he was interested in doing mathematical work. His money was quickly given away, either to charity or as prizes to those who solved the difficult mathematical problems he gave them.

3.1 Solving Linear Equations in One Variable

A.CED.1
A.CED.3
A.REI.1
A.REI.3

An **equation** is a statement that sets two mathematical expressions equal.

When both sides of an equation are numerical expressions, the equation is a closed statement. This means the equation can be assigned a truth value.

$$6 + 4 = 10 \quad true \qquad 7 - 2 = 6 \quad false$$

If an equation is neither true nor false, the equation is an **open sentence**. When variables are present in an equation, the **solution** is unknown. The set of numbers that you use to represent the variable(s) is called the **replacement set**. The **solution set** consists of all the value(s) for the variable from the replacement set makes the equation a **true statement**.

EXAMPLES 1 and 2 — Finding the solution of an equation from a replacement set

1 Find the solution set of the equation $x + 4 = 13$, given the replacement set $\{5, 6, 7, 8, 9\}$.

■ **SOLUTION**

Substitute the values from the replacement set for x into the equation.

Let $x = 5$; is $5 + 4 = 13$?   *No*

Let $x = 6$; is $6 + 4 = 13$?   *No*

Let $x = 7$; is $7 + 4 = 13$?   *No*

Let $x = 8$; is $8 + 4 = 13$?   *No*

Let $x = 9$; is $9 + 4 = 13$?   *Yes*

Therefore, {9} is the solution set or solution for $x + 4 = 13$.

2 Find the solution set of the equation $3x - 6 = 12$, given the replacement set $\{5, 6, 7, 11, 13\}$.

■ **SOLUTION**

Substitute the values from the replacement set into the equation.

Let $x = 5$; is $3(5) - 6 = 12$?   *No*

Let $x = 6$; is $3(6) - 6 = 12$?   *Yes*

Let $x = 7$; is $3(7) - 6 = 12$?   *No*

Let $x = 11$; is $3(11) - 6 = 12$?   *No*

Let $x = 13$; is $3(13) - 6 = 12$?   *No*

Therefore, {6} is the solution set or solution for $3x - 6 = 12$.

If you multiply all of the terms of the equation in example 1 by 2, will $2x + 8 = 26$ still have a solution of $x = 9$?

Does $2(9) + 8 = 26$? Yes; $18 + 8 = 26$.

Equations that have the same solution set are called **equivalent equations.**
In general, solving an equation is a process of writing a set of equivalent
equations until you *isolate* the variable on one side. To find these equivalent
equations, you must apply the following *properties of equality.*

Properties of Equality

Let a, b, and c represent real numbers.

Reflexive Property	$a = a$
Symmetric Property	If $a = b$, then $b = a$.
Transitive Property	If $a = b$ and $b = c$, then $a = c$.
Addition Property	If $a = b$, then $a + c = b + c$.
Subtraction Property	If $a = b$, then $a - c = b - c$.
Multiplication Property	If $a = b$, then $ac = bc$.
Division Property	If $a = b$ and $c \neq 0$, then $\dfrac{a}{c} = \dfrac{b}{c}$.

To determine which property of equality to apply, you use *inverse operations.*
Addition can "undo" subtraction, and subtraction can "undo" addition.
Addition and subtraction are considered inverse operations. By similar
reasoning, multiplication and division are inverse operations.

EXAMPLES 3 through 6   **Solving equations by using one property of equality**

Solve each equation.

3 $n - 6 = 9$

■ SOLUTION

Use the addition property of equality.

$$n - 6 = 9$$
$$n - 6 + 6 = 9 + 6 \quad \leftarrow \begin{array}{l}\textit{To isolate } n, \\ \textit{add } 6 \textit{ to each} \\ \textit{side.}\end{array}$$
$$n = 15$$

Check: $n - 6 = 9 \rightarrow 15 - 6 = 9$ ✔

4 $y + 12 = 5$

■ SOLUTION

Use the subtraction property of equality.

$$y + 12 = 5$$
$$y + 12 - 12 = 5 - 12 \quad \leftarrow \begin{array}{l}\textit{To isolate } y, \\ \textit{subtract } 12 \textit{ from} \\ \textit{each side.}\end{array}$$
$$y = -7$$

Check: $y + 12 = 5 \rightarrow -7 + 12 = 5$ ✔

5 $\dfrac{x}{-4} = 8$

■ SOLUTION

Use the multiplication property of equality.

$$\dfrac{x}{-4} = 8$$
$$-4\left(\dfrac{x}{-4}\right) = -4(8) \quad \leftarrow \begin{array}{l}\textit{To isolate } x, \\ \textit{multiply each} \\ \textit{side by } -4.\end{array}$$
$$x = -32$$

Check: $\dfrac{x}{-4} = 8 \rightarrow \dfrac{-32}{-4} = 8$ ✔

6 $-35 = -5r$

■ SOLUTION

Use the division property of equality.

$$-35 = -5r$$
$$\dfrac{-35}{-5} = \dfrac{-5r}{-5} \quad \leftarrow \begin{array}{l}\textit{To isolate } r, \\ \textit{divide each} \\ \textit{side by } -5.\end{array}$$
$$7 = r$$

Check: $-35 = -5r \rightarrow -35 = -5(7)$ ✔

You may need to apply more than one property of equality to solve an equation.

Solving equations by using two properties of equality

EXAMPLES 7 and 8

Solve each equation. *Justify each step with its property*

 7 $\quad 4z + 28 = 5$

■ SOLUTION

$$4z + 28 = 5$$
$$4z + 28 - 28 = 5 - 28 \quad \leftarrow \text{subt prop of } =$$
$$4z = -23$$
$$\frac{4z}{4} = \frac{-23}{4} \quad \leftarrow \text{div prop of } =$$
$$z = -5.75$$

Check: $4z + 28 = 5$
$$\rightarrow 4(-5.75) + 28 = 5 \checkmark$$

8 $\quad 6 = -4 - k$

■ SOLUTION

$$6 = -4 - k$$
$$6 + 4 = -4 - k + 4 \quad \leftarrow \text{add prop of } =$$
$$10 = -k$$
$$(-1)10 = (-1)(-k) \quad \leftarrow \text{mult prop of } =$$
$$-10 = k \quad \text{(recall that } -k = -1k)$$

Check: $6 = -4 - k$
$$\rightarrow 6 = -4 - (-10) \checkmark$$

> **Note**
> If the variable is negative, such as $-x$, $-y$..., then you can multiply both sides of the equation by -1 to make the variable positive. The variable in the solution of an equation must always be positive.

Sometimes the first step in solving an equation is using the distributive property to simplify one or both sides.

EXAMPLE 9   Using the distributive property before solving

9 Solve $-3(m + 3) = 16$.   *Justify each step with its property*

■ SOLUTION

$$-3(m + 3) = 16$$
$$-3m - 9 = 16 \quad \leftarrow \text{Distributive property}$$
$$-3m - 9 + 9 = 16 + 9 \quad \leftarrow \text{Addition property of equality}$$
$$-3m = 25$$
$$\frac{-3m}{-3} = \frac{25}{-3} \quad \leftarrow \text{Division property of equality}$$
$$m = -\frac{25}{3}$$

Check: $-3(m + 3) = 16 \rightarrow -3\left(-\frac{25}{3} + 3\right) = 16 \checkmark$

> **Note**
> To check a solution, substitute it for the variable in the original equation. If the resulting statement is true, you have found a solution.

You must combine all like terms on one or both sides of an equation before solving an equation.

EXAMPLE 10   Combining like terms before solving

 10 Solve $99 - 4s - 6s = -1$.   *Justify each step with its property*

■ SOLUTION

$$99 - 4s - 6s = -1 \quad \leftarrow -4s \text{ and } -6s \text{ are like terms}$$
$$99 - 10s = -1$$
$$99 - 10s - 99 = -1 - 99 \quad \leftarrow \text{Subtraction property of equality}$$
$$-10s = -100$$
$$\frac{-10s}{-10} = \frac{-100}{-10} \quad \leftarrow \text{Division property of equality}$$
$$s = 10 \qquad \textbf{Check:} \ 99 - 4s - 6s = -1 \rightarrow 99 - 4(10) - 6(10) = -1 \checkmark$$

Sometimes there are variable terms on both sides of an equation.

EXAMPLE 11 **Solving equations with variable terms on both sides**

 Solve $-5 - \frac{1}{2}g = 4 + \frac{1}{4}g$. **Justify each step with its property**

- **SOLUTION**

$$-5 - \tfrac{1}{2}g = 4 + \tfrac{1}{4}g$$

$$-5 - \tfrac{1}{2}g + \tfrac{1}{2}g = 4 + \tfrac{1}{4}g + \tfrac{1}{2}g \quad \leftarrow \textbf{Addition property of equality}$$

$$-5 = 4 + \tfrac{3}{4}g$$

$$-5 - 4 = 4 + \tfrac{3}{4}g - 4 \quad \leftarrow \textbf{Subtraction property of equality}$$

$$-9 = \tfrac{3}{4}g$$

$$\tfrac{4}{3}(-9) = \tfrac{4}{3}(\tfrac{3}{4}g) \quad \leftarrow \textbf{Multiplication property of equality}$$

$$-12 = g \qquad \textbf{Check: } -5 - \tfrac{1}{2}g = 4 + \tfrac{1}{4}g \rightarrow -5 - \tfrac{1}{2}(-12) = 4 + \tfrac{1}{4}(-12)✔$$

Note

If the variable term is isolated and the coefficient is a fraction, multiply both sides of the equation by the reciprocal of the fraction.

Some equations are true for all values of the variable. An equation like this is called an **identity,** and its solution set is the set of all real numbers. Other equations are true for no value of the variable, and they have no solution. No solution is represented symbolically by { } or $\varnothing$.

EXAMPLES 12 and 13 **Solving equations that are identities or that have no solution**

Solve each equation and justify.

 $-7t + 9 = 1 - 7t$

- **SOLUTION**

$$-7t + 9 = 1 - 7t$$
$$-7t + 9 + 7t = 1 - 7t + 7t \leftarrow \textbf{add prop of =}$$
$$9 = 1$$

The equation $9 = 1$ is a false statement. The equation has no solution. The solution set is { } or $\varnothing$.

13 $3(q + 5) = 3q + 15$

- **SOLUTION**

$$3(q + 5) = 3q + 15$$
$$3q + 15 = 3q + 15 \leftarrow \textbf{distributive property}$$

The equation $3q + 15 = 3q + 15$ is true for any value of q, so it is an identity. The solution set is the set of all real numbers.

EXAMPLE 14 **Justifying a solution. A solution to the give equation is shown. Justify each step of the solution with an Algebraic Property.**

- **SOLUTION**

14 $2x - \frac{1}{3}(x + 3) = 3x + 7$	**Given**	**Given**
$2x - \frac{1}{3}x - 1 = 3x + 7$	_____	$\leftarrow$ **Distributive property**
$\frac{5}{3}x - 1 = 3x + 7$	_____	$\leftarrow$ **Add like terms**
$-1 = \frac{4}{3}x + 7$	_____	$\leftarrow$ **Subtraction property of Equality**
$-8 = \frac{4}{3}x$	_____	$\leftarrow$ **Subtraction property of Equality**
$-6 = x$	_____	$\leftarrow$ **Multiplication property of Equality**

Practice

Choose the numeral preceding the word or expression that best completes the statement or answers the question.

1 Which is a solution to $\dfrac{2a-1}{3} = 7$?

  (1) $5\dfrac{1}{3}$ **(2)** 11   **(3)** 12   **(4)** 21

2 In which equation is it possible to isolate the variable by first subtracting 3 from each side and then multiplying each side by 4?

  (1) $4x + 3 = 7$ **(3)** $4x - 3 = 7$

  (2) $\dfrac{1}{4}x + 3 = 7$ **(4)** $\dfrac{1}{4}x - 3 = 7$

3 Which equations are equivalent?

      I. $6(m + 5) = -6$
     II. $4 + 2(m + 3) = 28$
    III. $\dfrac{m}{4} = -2.25$

  (1) I and II   **(3)** II and III

  (2) I and III   **(4)** none of these

In Exercises 4–17, solve each equation. Check your solution(s). If there is no solution, so state.

4 $b - 13 = 24$ **5** $j + 8 = 7$

6 $-x + 12 = -9$ **7** $10 = 3 - m$

8 $\dfrac{d}{5} = -20$ **9** $-45 = -3h$

10 $14 = -\dfrac{2}{3}k$ **11** $4z + 5 = -25$

12 $4(z + 5) = -25$ **13** $0.4(s + 4) = 4.8$

14 $\dfrac{1}{4}(p + 8) = 12$ **15** $n + 9n + 7 = -41$

16 $6g + 1 = -3g - 8$ **17** $1 + 2(y + 4) = 29$

In Exercises 18–20, solve and justify each step of your solution with an Algebraic Property.

18 $5 = 6h + 5(h - 5)$

19 $4(x - 1) - 2x = 2x - 4$

20 $6(q - 4) - 3(q - 2) = 12$

In Exercises 21–22, solve the problem. Clearly show all necessary work.

21 Sean says that the equation $s + 3 = s - 3$ has no solution. Is Sean's statement correct? Explain your answer.

22 Daneesha says that the equation $3t = -3t$ has no solution. Is Daneesha's statement correct? Explain your answer.

3.2 Problems Involving Linear Equations in One Variable

A.CED.1
N-Q.2
F.BF.2

Just as you can translate verbal phrases into mathematical expressions, you can translate English sentences into mathematical statements. This means that you can use an equation to model and solve a problem.

In general, before solving a problem you should assign a variable to the unknown and translate the problem into a mathematical equation. After you have solved the equation for the variable, use that value to answer the question asked. To check whether the solution is correct, apply the problem statement to the solution and check to see if your solution makes mathematic sense in the problem context.

EXAMPLES 1 through 3   Using equations and formulas to model and solve problems

1   Wendy has 14 coins. Some are quarters and some are nickels. The total value of the coins is \$1.70. How many quarters does Wendy have?

■ SOLUTION

Let q represent the number of quarters. Then $14 - q$ is the number of nickels.

Step 1 Translate the words into an equation.

value of quarters in cents	plus	value of nickels in cents	is	170 cents
↓	↓	↓	↓	↓
$25q$	$+$	$5(14 - q)$	$=$	170

Step 2 Solve the equation.

$$25q + 5(14 - q) = 170$$
$$20q + 70 = 170$$
$$20q = 100$$
$$q = 5$$

Wendy has five quarters.

2   The sum of three consecutive integers is 99. Find the three integers.

■ SOLUTION

Step 1 Assign the variable and write the equation.

$x = $ 1st integer,
$x + 1 = $ 2nd integer,
$x + 2 = $ 3rd integer.

So, $x + (x + 1) + (x + 2) = 99$
      or $3x + 3 = 99$

Step 2 Solve the equation.

$$3x + 3 = 99$$
$$3x = 96$$
$$x = 32$$

Therefore, the three integers are $x = 32$,
$x + 1 = 33$,
$x + 2 = 34$.

Note

Consecutive integers always increase by 1, so if x represents an integer, then x + 1 represents the next consecutive integer.

3   Mr. Redbird is driving at an average speed of 60 miles per hour. How far can he drive in 4.5 hours?

■ SOLUTION

Step 1 Apply the formula $d = rt$, where d represents distance, r represents rate, and t represents time.

d	$=$	r	×	t
↓		↓		↓
d	$=$	60	×	4.5

Step 2 Solve the equation.

$$d = 60 \times 4.5$$
$$d = 270$$

Mr. Redbird can drive 270 miles in 4.5 hours.

EXAMPLE 4   **Using the Arithmetic Sequence formula**

④ The first term of an arithmetic sequence is 12 while its tenth term is 57. Find the common difference, d, and then write the sequence's first 5 terms.

■ **SOLUTION**

Step 1 Apply the formula for the nth term of an arithmetic sequence. $a_n = a_1 + (n-1)d$
Step 1 Substitute for the values known. $n = 10$, $a_1 = 12$ and $a_{10} = 57$ $57 = 12 + (10-1)d$
Step 1 Solve for d. $57 = 12 + 9d$
   $45 = 9d$
   $5 = 9d$

The first 5 terms of the sequence are 12, 17, 22, 27, 32.

It is always important to check to make sure that your solution makes sense in the context of the problem.

EXAMPLE 5   **Making Sense**

⑤ Explain why each of the following solutions does not make sense in the problem's context.
   a. $x = 31\frac{3}{4}$ when x = 1st consecutive integer.
   b. $w = -7$ when w = the width of a rectangle.

■ **SOLUTION**

   a. an integer is a positive or negative whole number.
   b. the width of a rectangle is a measure of distance, which must be positive.

Practice

Choose the numeral preceding the word or expression that best completes the statement or answers the question.

1 The total value of some nickels and dimes is \$2.20. There are 36 coins in all. Which equation gives the number of dimes, d?

   (1) $10d + 5d = 220$

   (2) $10d + 5(d - 36) = 220$

   (3) $10d + 5(36 - d) = 220$

   (4) $10d + 5(36 - d) = 2.20$

2 If the number represented by $x - 5$ is an odd integer, which expression represents the next greatest odd integer?

   (1) $x - 7$

   (2) $x - 4$

   (3) $x - 3$

   (4) $x - 6$

3 Half of the money collected for a show was donated to charity. Tickets for a show cost \$100 per pair. The charity collected \$3500. How many tickets were sold?

   (1) 140

   (2) 700

   (3) 350

   (4) 70

4 Find four consecutive integers whose sum is 138.

    (1) 68, 69, 70, 71

    (2) 38, 39, 40, 41

    (3) 33, 34, 35, 36

    (4) 35, 36, 37, 38

In Exercises 5–7, solve the problem.

5 Complementary angles have a sum of 90°. The sum of the measure of an angle and 5 times its complement is 298°. What is the measure of the angle?

6 A train traveling at the rate of 90 miles per hour (mi/hr) leaves New York City. Two hours later, another train traveling at the rate of 120 mi/hr also leaves New York City on a parallel track. How long will it take the faster train to catch up to the slower train?

7 Five times a number n is three less than twice n. Find n.

In Exercises 8 and 9, use the Arithmetic sequence formula to solve the problems.

8 The fifth term of an arithmetic sequence is 0. If the common difference is -3, what is the value of the first term?

9 24.5 is the nth term in an arithmetic sequence whose first term is 7 and the common difference is 3.5. What is the value of n?

Use the following problem for Exercises 10 to 12.

A computer programmer charges $30 for an initial consultation and $35 per hour for programming.

10 Write a formula for her total charge, c, for h hours of work.

11 If you were charged $184 for work done by the programmer, how long did she work?

12 Explain how your solution makes sense in the problem's context.

3.3 Special Concept Equations

A.CED.1
A.CED.4
A.REI.1
A.REI.3

In your middle school mathematics classes, you studied ratios, proportions, and percents. These types of problems are solved using equations.

Ratios are used to compare quantities. While a ratio is usually expressed in lowest terms, many equivalent ratios can be formed by multiplying the given ratio by 1.

EXAMPLES 1 and 2   **Writing equivalent ratios.**

1 The ratio of freshmen to sophomores is 6 to 5. Write 3 ratios that are equivalent to 6 : 5.

- **SOLUTION**

The ratio $6 : 5$ can be expressed as the fraction $\frac{6}{5}$. Multiplying $\frac{6}{5}$ by 1 produces an equivalent fraction. Any nonzero number divided by itself is equal to 1, so there are infinitely many equivalents.

$\frac{6}{5} \cdot \frac{7}{7} = \frac{42}{35}$; $\frac{6}{5} \cdot \frac{5}{5} = \frac{30}{25}$; $\frac{6}{5} \cdot \frac{2}{2} = \frac{12}{10}$;   so $6 : 5 = 12 : 10 = 25 : 30 = 42 : 35$ all equivalent ratios.

2 The ratio of freshmen to sophomores is 6 to 5. If there are a total of 495 freshmen and sophomores in the school, how many are in each class?

- **SOLUTION**

We need to find the ratio equivalent to $6 : 5$ whose terms add to 495.

Let $x =$ the missing factor.   Multiplying by 1, $\frac{6}{5} \cdot \frac{x}{x} = \frac{6x}{5x}$ represents **any** fraction equivalent to $\frac{6}{5}$.

Let $6x =$ the number of freshmen.   Write the equation, $6x + 5x = 495$
Let $5x =$ the number of sophomores.   Solve, $11x = 495$
                                                                $x = 45$

Remember that x represents a factor needed to determine the number of freshmen and sophomores.

$6x = 6(45) =$ the number of freshmen $= 270$.
$5x = 5(45) =$ the number of sophomores $= 225$.

A **continued ratio,** or **extended ratio,** relates more than two numbers.

EXAMPLE 3   **Using continued ratios to solve problems**

3 The measures of the angles of a triangle are related by the ratio $2 : 3 : 4$. Find the measure of each angle.

- **SOLUTION**

The ratio $2 : 3 : 4$ is equivalent to $2x : 3x : 4x$. $2x + 3x + 4x = 180$ ← **The sum of the**
Write an equation using $2x, 3x,$ and $4x$ to $9x = 180$ **measures of the**
represent the measures of the angles. $x = 20$ **angles is 180°.**

The measures of the angles are $2(20°), 3(20°),$ and $4(20°),$ or $40°, 60°,$ and $80°$.

74

Visual models can help in solving word problems.

EXAMPLE 4 Drawing a visual model

4   Draw a model to visualize Example 3.

■ SOLUTION

$\angle 1 = \square\square$

$\angle 2 = \square\square\square$ $\left.\phantom{\begin{matrix}a\\b\\c\end{matrix}}\right\}$ $= 180° \Rightarrow$ $9\,\square = 180°$

$\angle 3 = \square\square\square\square$ $1\,\square = 20°$

$\angle 1 = 40°\ \angle 2 = 60°\ \angle 3 = 80°$

Proportions are used to solve many problems. A proportion is a statement that two ratios are equal. The terms of the proportion have a special relationship called the *cross products property*.

Cross Products Property of Proportions

For real numbers a, b, c, and d, where $b \neq 0$ and $d \neq 0$, if $\frac{a}{b} = \frac{c}{d}$, then $ad = bc$.

EXAMPLE 5 Using cross products to solve a proportion

5   Solve $\dfrac{r}{8.5} = \dfrac{3}{4}$.

■ SOLUTION

$\dfrac{r}{8.5} = \dfrac{3}{4}$

$r(4) = (8.5)(3)$ ← **Write the cross products.**

$4r = 25.5$ ← **Simplify each side.**

$r = 6.375$ ← **Divide each side by 4.**

You can use a proportion to solve problems involving ratios.

EXAMPLE 6 Using a proportion to solve problems

6   The scale of a map is 1 inch : 24 miles. What map distance represents 75 miles?

■ SOLUTION

Step 1 Write a proportion.

map distance in inches → $\dfrac{1}{24}$ $= \dfrac{n}{75}$ ← **Let n represent**
actual distance in miles →   **the unknown map distance.**

The map distance is 3.125 inches, or $3\frac{1}{8}$ inches.

Step 2 Solve the proportion.

$\dfrac{1}{24} = \dfrac{n}{75}$

$1 \cdot 75 = 24 \cdot n$ ← **Write the cross products.**

$3.125 = n$ ← **Divide each side by 24.**

You can use a percent equation to solve real-life problems.

7 Carlos works at a computer store. He earns a 4% commission on all of his sales. What amount must he sell to earn a commission of $200?

■ **SOLUTION**

$200 is 4% of what amount? → $200 = 0.04n → n = $200 ÷ 0.04 = $5000

Carlos must sell $5000 worth of goods to earn a $200 commission.

8 Jane and Susan go to dinner. The cost of the dinner is $45.60 and they leave a 15% tip. What is the total cost of the dinner, including the tip?

■ **SOLUTION**

Step 1 What is 15% of $45.60? → n = 0.15($45.60) → n = $6.84

Step 2 Add the tip to the price of the dinner. $6.84 + $45.60 = $52.44

The total cost of the dinner is $52.44.

9 Carlos purchases a sweater on sale for 30% off. The original price of the sweater is $54. How much does Carlos spend on the sweater?

■ **SOLUTION**

Step 1 What is 30% of $54? → x = 0.30($54) → x = $16.20

Step 2 Subtract the discount from the original price. $54 − $16.20 = $37.80

The purchase price of the sweater is $37.80.

Visual models can help in solving word problems.

EXAMPLE 10   Using a visual model

10 Draw a model to visualize Example 9.

■ **SOLUTION**

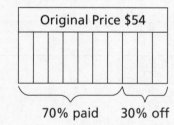

Original Price $54 $54(0.70) = $37.80

70% paid   30% off

A **percent of change** is the percent something increases or decreases from an original amount.

$$\begin{matrix}\text{percent of} \\ \text{increase}\end{matrix} = \frac{\text{new amount} - \text{original amount}}{\text{original amount}} \qquad \begin{matrix}\text{percent of} \\ \text{decrease}\end{matrix} = \frac{\text{original amount} - \text{new amount}}{\text{original amount}}$$

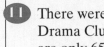 **EXAMPLES 11 and 12** **Solving problems involving percent of change**

11 There were 75 members of the Drama Club last year, but there are only 65 members this year. What is the percent of decrease?

■ SOLUTION

Let p represent the percent of decrease.

$$p = \frac{75 - 65}{75} \quad \leftarrow \quad \frac{\text{original} - \text{new}}{\text{original}}$$

$$p = \frac{10}{75} = 0.13333\ldots = 13\frac{1}{3}\%$$

The percent of decrease is $13\frac{1}{3}\%$.

12 Sam's employer has promised him a 20% pay increase. He presently earns $15 per hour. What will be his new hourly pay after the increase?

■ SOLUTION

Let n represent the new hourly pay.

$$20\% = \frac{n - 15}{15} \quad \leftarrow \quad \frac{\text{new} - \text{original}}{\text{original}}$$

$$15(20\%) = n - 15$$
$$3 = n - 15$$

Sam's new pay will be $18 per hour.

A **literal equation** is an equation that contains two or more variables. You can use the properties of equality to solve for one variable *in terms of* the others. The set of real numbers is represented symbolically by { R }.

 EXAMPLE 13 **Solving a literal equation for one of its variables**

13 Given that $2a + b = c$, which equation expresses a in terms of b and c?

(1) $a = -\frac{1}{2}b + c$ (2) $a = -\frac{1}{2}b - c$ (3) $a = -\frac{1}{2}(b + c)$ (4) $a = \frac{1}{2}(c - b)$

■ SOLUTION

$$2a + b = c$$
$$2a = c - b \qquad \leftarrow \text{ Subtraction property of equality}$$
$$a = \frac{c - b}{2} = \frac{1}{2}(c - b) \leftarrow \text{ Division property of equality}$$

The correct choice is (4).

A **formula** is a literal equation in which each variable represents a specific quantity. The formula describes the relationship between the quantities. Often a formula is given in one form and you need to *transform* it to an equivalent form.

EXAMPLE 14 — **Transforming formulas**

14 The formula $F = \frac{9}{5}C + 32$ gives the temperature F in degrees Fahrenheit in terms of a given temperature C in degrees Celsius. Write a formula for C in terms of F.

- **SOLUTION**

$$F = \frac{9}{5}C + 32$$

$$F - 32 = \frac{9}{5}C \qquad \leftarrow \text{ Subtraction property of equality}$$

$$\frac{5}{9}(F - 32) = C, \text{ or } C = \frac{5}{9}(F - 32) \leftarrow \text{ Multiplication property of equality}$$

Practice

Choose the numeral preceding the word or expression that best completes the statement or answers the question.

1 If $2c - d = c - 2d$, then $c =$

(1) 0   (2) 1   (3) d (4) $-d$

2 There were 420 students in the senior class last year. This year's senior class has 378 students. Which statement is false?

(1) The percent of decrease in the size of the class is 10%.

(2) This year there are 10% fewer students in the senior class than there were last year.

(3) The size of the senior class increased by 10% from last year to this year.

(4) This year's class is 90% of the size of last year's class.

3 The scale of a map is 1 in. : 50 mi. How many miles correspond to a map distance of 3.25 in.?

(1) 150 mi   (3) 62.5 mi

(2) 162.5 mi   (4) 200 mi

4 Solve the proportion $\frac{54}{8} = \frac{r}{6}$.

(1) 72   (2) 40.5   (3) 324   (4) 48

In Exercises 5–6, find the percent of change from the first quantity to the second. Describe it as a percent of increase or decrease.

5 16 pounds   **6** $13.98
   20 pounds $9.32

In Exercises 7–8, solve each proportion.

7 $\frac{m}{2} = \frac{56}{16}$ **8** $\frac{51}{21} = \frac{z}{7}$

In exercises 9–12, solve each equation for the given variable.

9 $a + b = c$; b **10** $2(p - q) = r$; p

11 $xy = z$; y **12** $I = prt$; p

In Exercises 13–17, solve the problem. Clearly show all necessary work.   **MP**

13 The marked price of a CD is $12.75. In addition, there is a state sales tax of 4% of the price. What is the total cost of the CD?

14 A retailer buys T-shirts from a supplier for $6 each and sells each T-shirt for $13.50. What is the percent of increase in the price?

15 Tamara buys a $23 blouse on sale for 20% off. How much did Tamara spend on the blouse?

16 A food inspector weighs 50 cans of soup taken at random from a shipment of 3,000 cans. She finds that 4 out of the 50 cans are underweight. Based on this sample, how many cans in the shipment can the inspector expect to be underweight?

17 At the first City Run, 125 walkers wore red shirts and the 50 joggers wore blue shirts. This year 1,400 people are expected to walk or jog. The run organizers have found that they can use the numbers from the first run to order the correct number of red and blue shirts. How many of each color should they order for this years run?

Solve each equation for the given variable then justify each step in your solution with the algebraic property used.

18 $2p - q = r; \ p$ **19** $r = \dfrac{d}{t}; \ t$

In exercises 20–22 draw a visual model like the one used in Example 10.

20 for example 13

21 for example 15

22 for example 17

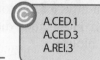
3.4 Solving Linear Inequalities in One Variable

An **inequality** is a statement that consists of two mathematical expressions joined by an inequality symbol. The expressions are called the **sides of the inequality.** Just as with equations, both sides of an inequality may be numerical expressions. In such a case, the inequality is a closed statement and can be assigned a truth value.

$$5 + (-9) < 0 \quad true \qquad\qquad 5 + (-9) > 0 \quad false$$

When at least one side of an inequality is a variable expression, the inequality is an open statement. To solve the inequality, you must find its solution set. When the replacement set of the variable is the set of all real numbers, the inequality may have infinitely many solutions. For example, given the inequality $x < 3$, each of the following replacements for x results in a true statement.

$$-17 < 3 \qquad -5.4 < 3 \qquad 0 < 3 \qquad \frac{1}{2} < 3 \qquad 2.999 < 3$$

In fact, any number to the left of 3 on a number line is a solution to $x < 3$. Clearly it would be impossible to list all these solutions. For this reason, a number line is used to draw the *graph of the inequality*. The **graph of an inequality** consists of the graph of all its solutions.

Remember that interval notation is a good way to represent inequalities.

> **Note**
>
> Inequality Symbols
>
> $<$ is less than
> $\leq$ is less than or equal to
> $>$ is greater than
> $\geq$ is greater than or equal to
> $\neq$ is not equal to

EXAMPLES 1 through 5   **Graphing an inequality**

Graph each inequality on a number line. Represent the inequality in interval notation.

1 $x < 3$ ■ **SOLUTION**   Graph all real numbers to the left of 3.

$(-\infty, 3)$

     −2 −1   0   1   2   3   4   5   6   7

Use an open dot to indicate that 3 is *not* a solution.

2 $x > 3$ ■ **SOLUTION**   Graph all real numbers to the right of 3.

$(3, \infty)$

     −2 −1   0   1   2   3   4   5   6   7

3 $x \leq 3$ ■ **SOLUTION**   Graph 3 and all real numbers to its left.

$(-\infty, 3]$

     −2 −1   0   1   2   3   4   5   6   7

Use a closed dot to indicate that 3 *is* a solution.

4 $x \geq 3$ ■ **SOLUTION**   Graph 3 and all real numbers to its right.

$[3, \infty)$

     −2 −1   0   1   2   3   4   5   6   7

5 $x \neq 3$ ■ **SOLUTION**   Graph all real numbers except 3.

$(-\infty, 3)$ and $(3, \infty)$

     −2 −1   0   1   2   3   4   5   6   7

Inequalities that have the same solution set are called **equivalent inequalities.** Solving an inequality is a process of writing equivalent inequalities until you isolate the variable. To do this, you apply the following *properties of inequality*.

Properties of Inequality

Let a, b, and c represent real numbers.

Addition Property of Inequality

If $a < b$, then $a + c < b + c$.
If $a > b$, then $a + c > b + c$.

Subtraction Property of Inequality

If $a < b$, then $a - c < b - c$.
If $a > b$, then $a - c > b - c$.

Multiplication Property of Inequality

If $a < b$ and $c > 0$, then $ac < bc$.
If $a < b$ and $c < 0$, then $ac > bc$.

If $a > b$ and $c > 0$, then $ac > bc$.
If $a > b$ and $c < 0$, then $ac < bc$.

Division Property of Inequality

If $a < b$ and $c > 0$, then $\dfrac{a}{c} < \dfrac{b}{c}$.

If $a < b$ and $c < 0$, then $\dfrac{a}{c} > \dfrac{b}{c}$.

If $a > b$ and $c > 0$, then $\dfrac{a}{c} > \dfrac{b}{c}$.

If $a > b$ and $c < 0$, then $\dfrac{a}{c} < \dfrac{b}{c}$.

Transitive Property of Inequality

If $a < b$ and $b < c$, then $a < c$.
If $a > b$ and $b > c$, then $a > c$.

> **Note**
> For each property of inequality, a true statement also results if $<$ is replaced by $\leq$ and if $>$ is replaced by $\geq$.

Summary: Adding or subtracting the same number on each side of an inequality preserves the order of the inequality.

EXAMPLES 6 and 7 — Solving inequalities by using addition or subtraction

> **Note**
> If a is greater than b, it is also true that b is less than a. So $a > b$ is equivalent to $b < a$.

Solve each inequality and graph the solution on a number line.

6 $b + 7 \leq 4$

■ SOLUTION

$b + 7 \leq 4$
$b + 7 - 7 \leq 4 - 7$ ← Subtraction property of $\neq$
$b \leq -3$

All numbers less than or equal to -3 are solutions.

-6 -5 -4 -3 -2 -1 0 1

7 $-5 < n - 3$

■ SOLUTION

$-5 < n - 3$
$-5 + 3 < n - 3 + 3$ ← Addition property of $\neq$
$-2 < n$
$n > -2$

$(-2, \infty)$

-5 -4 -3 -2 -1 0 1 2

It is impossible to check every solution to inequalities like those in Examples 6 and 7. However, you can usually detect an error by checking one number from each region of the graph. For example, here is how you might verify that $n > -2$ is a reasonable solution to $-5 < n - 3$.

You should obtain a *true* statement when you replace n with any number greater than -2.

Try -1: $-5 < n - 3$ → $-5 < -1 - 3$ *true*

You should obtain a *false* statement when you replace n with any number less than -2.

Try -3: $-5 < n - 3$ → $-5 < -3 - 3$ *false*

Summary: Multiplying or dividing each side of an inequality by the same *positive* number *preserves* the order of the inequality. Multiplying or dividing each side of an inequality by the same *negative* number *changes* the order of the inequality.

EXAMPLES 8 and 9   Solving inequalities by using multiplication or division

Solve each inequality and graph the solution on a number line.

8 $\dfrac{a}{4} < -1$

■ SOLUTION

$\dfrac{a}{4} < -1$

$4\left(\dfrac{a}{4}\right) < 4(-1)$ ← **Multiplication property of $\neq$** Positive number → preserve order

$a < -4$

All numbers less than -4 are solutions.

 $(-\infty, -4)$
$-7\ -6\ -5\ -4\ -3\ -2\ -1\ \ 0$

9 $-4w \le 20$

■ SOLUTION

$-4w \le 20$

$\dfrac{-4w}{-4} \ge \dfrac{20}{-4}$ ← **Division property of $\neq$** Negative number → change order

$w \ge -5$

All numbers greater than or equal to -5 are solutions.

$-7\ -6\ -5\ -4\ -3\ -2\ -1\ \ 0$ $[-5, \infty)$

You may need to apply the properties of inequality several times to isolate the variable and solve the inequality.

EXAMPLE 10   Solving an inequality in multiple steps

10 Solve the inequality $-2(p - 5) \le -5$ and graph the solution on a number line.

■ SOLUTION 1

$-2(p - 5) \le -5$
$-2p + 10 \le -5$ ← **Distributive property**
$-2p \le -15$ ← **Subtraction property of $\neq$**
$p \ge 7.5$ ← **Division property of $\neq$. Negative number → change order**

All numbers greater than or equal to 7.5 are solutions. The graph is shown at the right.

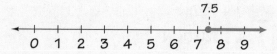
7.5
$0\ 1\ 2\ 3\ 4\ 5\ 6\ 7\ 8\ 9$

Two inequalities joined by the word *and* or the word *or* form a **compound inequality.**

$h > -2$ and $h < 4$

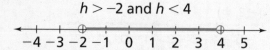
$-4\ -3\ -2\ -1\ \ 0\ \ 1\ \ 2\ \ 3\ \ 4\ \ 5$

The word *and* signals a conjunction. The solutions are all numbers that are solutions to both inequalities.

$j < -2$ or $j > 4$

$-4\ -3\ -2\ -1\ \ 0\ \ 1\ \ 2\ \ 3\ \ 4\ \ 5$

The word *or* signals a disjunction. The solutions are all numbers that are in the union of *either* inequality.

EXAMPLE 11 Solving a compound inequality

11 Solve $-3 < 2 - b \le 1$ and graph the solution on a number line.

▪ **SOLUTION**

Write two inequalities joined by *and*. Then solve each inequality.

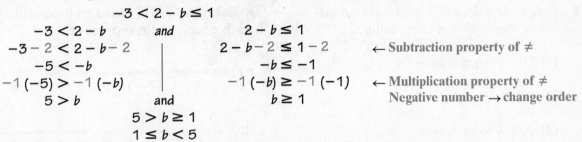

$$-3 < 2 - b \le 1$$

$-3 < 2 - b$	*and*	$2 - b \le 1$	
$-3 - 2 < 2 - b - 2$		$2 - b - 2 \le 1 - 2$	← **Subtraction property of ≠**
$-5 < -b$		$-b \le -1$	
$-1(-5) > -1(-b)$		$-1(-b) \ge -1(-1)$	← **Multiplication property of ≠**
$5 > b$	*and*	$b \ge 1$	**Negative number → change order**

$$5 > b \ge 1$$
$$1 \le b < 5$$

All numbers greater than or equal to 1 and less than 5 are solutions. The graph is at the right.

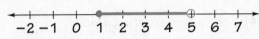

Just as with equations, some inequalities have no solution. For other inequalities, the solution set is the set of all real numbers.

$2(y - 3) > 2y + 8$	$5t + 1 \ge 6t - 1 - t$
$2y - 6 > 2y + 8$	$5t + 1 \ge 5t - 1$
$-6 > 8$ *false*	$1 \ge -1$ *true*

The inequality has no solution.   All real numbers are solutions.

Usually the replacement set for the variable in an inequality is the set of all real numbers. In some cases, however, the replacement set is restricted.

EXAMPLE 12 Solving an inequality given a restricted replacement set   (MP)

12 Given the set of integers as the replacement set for z, solve the following inequality. $2z < -1$ or $z + 3 > 5$

▪ **SOLUTION**

$2z < -1$	*or*	$z + 3 > 5$
$\dfrac{2z}{2} < \dfrac{-1}{2}$		$z + 3 - 3 > 5 - 3$
$z < -0.5$	*or*	$z > 2$

All *integers* less than -0.5 or greater than 2 are solutions. The graph is at the right.

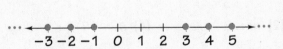

Practice

Choose the numeral preceding the word or expression that best completes the statement or answers the question.

1 Given $-4t < 28$, which step can be used to obtain the equivalent inequality $t > -7$?

   (1) Divide each side by -4.

   (2) Multiply each side by 4.

   (3) Add 4 to each side.

   (4) Subtract -4 from each side.

2 Which is not equivalent to $-3x < 15$?

   (1) $-x < 5$ **(3)** $x < -5$

   (2) $-5 < x$ **(4)** $5 > -x$

3 Which inequality is graphed below?

   (1) $4 < b \leq 9$ **(3)** $b \geq 4$ or $b < 9$

   (2) $4 \leq b < 9$ **(4)** $b \leq 4$ or $b > 9$

4 Which inequality is not equivalent to $-3 \leq k < 5$?

   (1) $5 < k \leq -3$ **(3)** $-3 \leq k$ and $k < 5$

   (2) $5 > k \geq -3$ **(4)** $k < 5$ and $k \geq -3$

5 Which inequality represents all of the solutions to $-3m + 8 \geq -13$?

   (1) $m \leq \dfrac{5}{3}$ **(3)** $m \geq 7$

   (2) $m \leq 7$ **(4)** $m \leq -7$

6 Suppose that m, n, r, and s are positive numbers, with $\frac{m}{n} < 1$ and $\frac{r}{s} > 1$. Which statement is always true?

   (1) $\dfrac{m}{n} \cdot \dfrac{r}{s} < 1$ **(3)** $\dfrac{m}{n} + \dfrac{r}{s} < 1$

   (2) $\dfrac{m}{n} \cdot \dfrac{r}{s} > 1$ **(4)** $\dfrac{m}{n} + \dfrac{r}{s} > 1$

In Exercises 7–10, write an inequality that each graph could represent.

7

8

9

10

In Exercises 11–18, graph each inequality on a number line.

11 $c > 5$ **12** $-2 > k$

13 $r < -1$ or $r \geq 3$ **14** $-7 < m < -2.5$

15 $x < 5$ and $x > 3$ **16** $g \geq 8$ or $g \leq -4$

17 $p \leq 12$ and $p \geq 1$ **18** $-5 \leq b \leq 2$

In Exercises 19–24, solve each inequality. State the solution in interval notation and graph it on the number line.

19 $n - 3 > -11$ **20** $-8x \geq -16$

21 $\dfrac{a}{6} \leq -3$ **22** $-y < 4$

23 $\dfrac{1}{3}w \geq 1$ **24** $3f - 12 \leq 15$

In Exercises 25–26, solve each inequality and justify each step with the algebraic property.

25 $45 > 3(6 - z)$

26 $5n + 3 - 4n < -5 - 3n$

In Exercises 27–29, given the set of real numbers as the replacement set, solve each inequality and graph the solution on a number line.

27 $5 - 2(4 - c) \le 9 - c$

28 $4d < -8$ or $6 < 2d$

29 $5 < x + 4 \le 8$

In Exercises 30–33, given the set of integers as the replacement set, solve each compound inequality and graph it on a number line.

30 $0 < a + 4 < 3$

31 $n - 6 \ge 4$

32 $s + 2 \le -2$ or $-2s \le -2$

33 $-2r \le 9$ and $7 > 3r$

In Exercises 34–35, solve the problem. Clearly show all necessary work.

34 Are there any integers that satisfy the following inequality? If so, what are they?

$0 \le 2c \le 9$ and $-4 < 3c - 5 < 13$

35 Is the statement below *true* or *false*? Explain your response.

The inequalities $2q + 5 \le 3$ and $q > 0$ taken together have no solution.

3.5 Problems Involving Linear Inequalities in One Variable

A.CED.1
A.CED.3
A.REI.3

When a verbal problem includes a verb such as *is, are, will be, were,* or *equals,* you often can translate it into an equation. The table below summarizes some ways to tell when an appropriate translation of a problem is an *inequality.*

English Sentence	Mathematical Statement
p is greater than q, p is more than q	$p > q$
p is greater than or equal to q, p is no less than q, p is at least q	$p \geq q$
p is less than q, p is fewer than q	$p < q$
p is less than or equal to q, p is no more than q, p is at most q	$p \leq q$
q is greater than p and less than r, q is between p and r	$p < q < r$
q is greater than or equal to p and less than or equal to r, q is between p and r, inclusive	$p \leq q \leq r$

EXAMPLES 1 and 2 — Translating and solving inequality problems

 Which inequality represents the following statement?

Five less than a number y is at most twenty.

(1) $y - 5 < 20$ (2) $y - 5 \leq 20$ (3) $y - 5 \geq 20$ (4) $5 < y < 20$

■ SOLUTION

Examine the choices and eliminate those that are inappropriate.

In (4), $5 < y < 20$ describes a number y between 5 and 20. *Eliminate choice (4).* In (3), the symbol $\geq$ means that $y - 5$ is 20 or more. *Eliminate choice (3).* In (1), the symbol $<$ means that $y - 5$ cannot equal 20. *Eliminate choice (1).*

The remaining choice is (2). Work backward to verify the translation.

$$
\underset{\substack{\downarrow \\ \text{five less than a number } y}}{y - 5} \quad \underset{\substack{\downarrow \\ \text{is at most}}}{\leq} \quad \underset{\substack{\downarrow \\ \text{twenty}}}{20}
$$

The correct choice is (2).

2 A real number c increased by six is more than four times c. Identify all possible values of c.

■ SOLUTION

Step 1 Translate the words into an inequality.

$$
\underset{\substack{\downarrow \\ c + 6}}{\text{a number } c \text{ increased by six}} \quad \underset{\substack{\downarrow \\ >}}{\text{is more than}} \quad \underset{\substack{\downarrow \\ 4c}}{\text{four times } c}
$$

Step 2 Solve the inequality.

$$c + 6 > 4c$$
$$6 > 3c$$
$$2 > c$$

All real numbers less than 2 can be values of c.

When you use an inequality to model a real-life problem, it is important to consider replacement sets. For instance, consider this situation.

The temperature t on Tuesday ranged from 25°F to 35°F, inclusive.

Temperature is a continuous measure. Therefore, the replacement set for t is the set of all real numbers, and the graph of the temperatures is the graph of all real-number solutions to $25 \leq t \leq 35$.

Now consider this situation.

The number n of students in a homeroom is between 25 and 35, inclusive.

The numbers of students in the homerooms form a discrete set of data. In this case, the replacement set for n is the set of whole numbers. So the graph is the graph of all whole-number solutions to $25 \leq n \leq 35$.

> **Note**
>
> The graph of a set of data that are **continuous** has no breaks in it. The set of real numbers would be a continuous graph.
>
> The graph of a set of data that are **discrete** consists of points that are not connected. The set of integers would be an example of a discrete graph.

EXAMPLES 3 and 4   Using an inequality to solve a real-life problem ⸺ **MP**

3 Nancy earns $6.50 per hour. How many hours must she work to earn $130? Solve and graph the solutions on a number line.

▪SOLUTION

Let h represent the number of hours Nancy must work. Then $6.50h$, or $6.5h$, represents the amount in dollars that she earns in h hours.

Step 1 Translate the words into an inequality.   **Step 2** Solve the inequality.

amount earned in dollars	is at least	130
↓	↓	↓
6.5h	≥	130

$$6.5h \geq 130$$
$$h \geq 20$$

Nancy must work at least 20 hours.

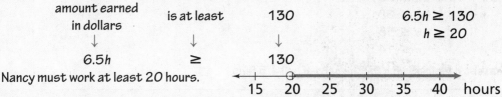

4 Stan has $55. He wants to buy a belt that costs $14 and some T-shirts that cost $9 each. How many T-shirts can he buy?

▪SOLUTION

Let n represent the number of T-shirts. Then $9n$ represents the cost in dollars of the T-shirts.

Step 1 Translate the words into an inequality.   **Step 2** Solve the inequality.

cost of belt in dollars	plus	cost of T-shirts in dollars	is no more than	55
↓	↓	↓	↓	↓
14	+	9n	≤	55

$$14 + 9n \leq 55$$
$$9n \leq 41$$
$$n \leq 4.\overline{5}$$

Stan can buy any whole number of T-shirts that is less than or equal to $4.\overline{5}$.

Stan can buy 0, 1, 2, 3, or 4 T-shirts.

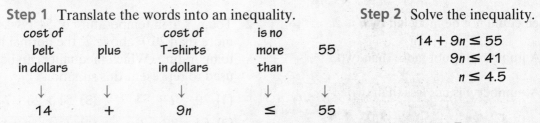

You can use a combined inequality to find a range of possible values.

EXAMPLE 5   **Using a combined inequality to solve a real-life problem**

5 To get a grade of A for the semester, you must earn between 540 and 600 points inclusive. Before the last test, you have a total of 503 points. How many points must you earn on the last test in order to get a grade of A for the semester?

■ SOLUTION

Let p represent the number of points you must score on the last test.
Then $503 + p$ represents your total points for the semester.

$$540 \leq 503 + p \leq 600$$
$$540 \leq 503 + p \quad \text{and} \quad 503 + p \leq 600$$
$$37 \leq p \quad \text{and} \quad p \leq 97$$
$$37 \leq p \leq 97$$

Your number of points on the last test must be between 37 and 97, inclusive.

Although formulas are equations, you may need to use a formula when solving a problem involving inequality.

EXAMPLE 6   **Using formulas when solving inequality problems**

6 Rosalita has 68 feet of fencing. She wants to use it to fence the perimeter of a rectangular garden so that it is 5 feet longer than it is wide. What is the greatest possible width for her garden?

■ SOLUTION

Let w represent the width of the garden. Then $w + 5$ represents the length.

$$2(w + 5) + 2w \leq 68$$
$$2w + 10 + 2w \leq 68$$
$$4w + 10 \leq 68$$
$$4w \leq 58$$
$$w \leq 14.5$$

The greatest possible width for the garden is 14.5 feet.

Practice

Choose the numeral preceding the word or expression that best completes the statement or answers the question.

1 Which could not be modeled by $n \leq 2$?

(1) A number n is not more than two.

(2) A number n is not less than two.

(3) A number n is less than or equal to two.

(4) A number n is not greater than two.

2 Today's high temperature of 54°F was more than 20°F above T, the normal high temperature. Which inequality can be used to represent this situation?

(1) $20 < T < 54$ **(3)** $54 > 20 - T$

(2) $54 > 20 + T$ **(4)** $T - 20 > 54$

3 In a certain equilateral triangle, the length of each side is a whole number of inches, and the perimeter is less than 15 inches. Which describes all possible values of s?

(1) $s < 5$

(2) $s \le 4$

(3) $s = 1, s = 2, s = 3,$ or $s = 4$

(4) $s = 1, s = 2, s = 3, s = 4,$ or $s = 5$

4 A bag contains some red marbles and some blue marbles. There are fewer than 63 marbles in all. The ratio of red marbles to blue marbles is 5 to 3. If b represents the number of blue marbles, which inequality represents this situation?

(1) $b + \dfrac{3}{5}b < 63$ **(3)** $b + \dfrac{5}{3}b \le 63$

(2) $b + \dfrac{3}{5}b \le 63$ **(4)** $b + \dfrac{5}{3}b < 63$

In Exercises 5–17, solve the problem. Clearly show all necessary work.

5 Ten more than 3 times a real number j is greater than negative 31. What are the possible values of j?

6 Twice the sum of a whole number w and 5 is at most 15. What are all possible values of w?

7 Find all sets of three consecutive odd whole numbers whose sum is less than 45.

8 The cost of a gallon container of orange juice is $3.50. What is the maximum number of containers you can buy for $15?

9 To rent a car for one day, you must pay a base fee of $19.50. There is an additional charge of $0.25 for each mile that you drive. You want to spend no more than $50 for the one-day rental. What is the greatest number of miles you can drive?

10 Jane is a salesperson at an automobile dealership. Each week she earns a base pay of $200, plus an 8% commission on her sales during the week. What must be the amount of her sales in one week if she wants her total earnings for the week to be at least $400?

11 A restaurant waiter earns a weekly base pay of $100, plus an average tip of $5 for each table served. In a five-day work week, how many tables must be served on average per day for the waiter to earn at least $450?

12 Ernest's job is to load shipping crates with cartons of merchandise. The weight of an empty shipping crate is 150 pounds. How many 35-pound cartons can Ernest load into a crate if the total weight of the crate and cartons may not exceed 850 pounds?

13 The perimeter of any triangle is the sum of the lengths of its sides. The lengths of the three sides of a certain triangle, in inches, are consecutive integers. The perimeter does not exceed 48 inches. What are all the possible measures for the longest side of this triangle?

14 The length and width of a rectangle are consecutive integers. The perimeter of this rectangle is at most 60 meters. What are the possible measures for the shorter side of this rectangle?

15 The Art Club is sponsoring a four-day art show. Their goal is for the average daily attendance to be between 100 and 120, inclusive. The attendance for the first three days of the show is 100, 105, and 91. What must be the attendance on the fourth day in order for the club to achieve its goal?

16 Two partners in a business share all profits in the ratio 4 to 5. They expect their profits for next month to be at least $1800 but no more than $3600. What amount of money might each partner expect to receive next month?

17 The formula $C = \frac{5}{9}(F - 32)$ gives the temperature C in degrees Celsius in terms of F degrees Fahrenheit. The temperature of a certain substance ranges from 20°C to 25°C inclusive. Find the corresponding range of temperatures in degrees Fahrenheit.

Preparing for the Assessment

Choose the numeral preceding the word or expression that best completes the statement or answers the question.

1 If $3(x + 2) = -12$, then $x =$

   (1) −6   **(2)** −2   **(3)** 2   **(4)** 6

2 If $-2d + 5 = -31$, then $3d - 9 =$

   (1) −63   **(2)** −54   **(3)** 18   **(4)** 45

3 If $-4t + 4 + 2a = 3a - 12 - 5t$, then $t =$

   (1) $a - 3$ **(3)** $a - 16$

   (2) $-a + 3$ **(4)** $a - 8$

4 Last week a company's income was \$530. From this, \$50 was withheld for expenses. The rest was shared by two partners in the ratio 3 to 5. How much did each receive?

   (1) \$180 and \$300

   (2) \$198.75 and \$331.25

   (3) \$72.50 and \$457.50

   (4) \$217.50 and \$362.50

5 Each situation below gives an original amount followed by a new amount. Which illustrates the greatest percent of increase?

   (1) 230 pencils; 253 pencils

   (2) 12 gallons; 15 gallons

   (3) 18 miles; 21 miles

   (4) \$12; \$3

6 The total value of a collection of 34 nickels and quarters is at least \$3.60. Let n represent the number of nickels. Which inequality models this situation?

   (1) $5n + 25(n - 34) \geq 360$

   (2) $5n + 25(34 - n) \geq 360$

   (3) $5n + 25(n - 34) \geq 3.60$

   (4) $5n + 25(34 - n) < 3.60$

7 A 14-ounce solution is made of water, salt, and sugar in the ratio 12 to 1 to 1. Which statement is false?

   (1) If x represents the number of ounces of sugar, then $12x + x + x = 14$.

   (2) Water, salt, and sugar are equal in amount.

   (3) The solution contains 12 ounces of water and 1 ounce each of salt and sugar.

   (4) The amount of water is 12 times the amount of salt.

8 Solve the proportion: $\dfrac{5.4}{8} = \dfrac{t}{6}$

   (1) $t = 4.05$ **(3)** $t = 1.43$

   (2) $t = 3.4$ **(4)** $t = 7.2$

9 Solve the inequality: $15c - 4 \leq 12c + 5$

   (1) $[3, \infty)$ **(3)** $(-\infty, 3]$

   (2) $(-\infty, \frac{1}{3}]$ **(4)** $(\frac{1}{3}, \infty)$

10 Which of the following includes all possible solutions of the inequality $-2 \leq -2m < 10$?

   (1) $1 \leq m < 5$ **(3)** $-5 > m$

   (2) $m \geq 1$ **(4)** $-5 < m \leq 1$

11 Which is the graph of the solution set of the inequality $p \leq -1.5$?

(1)
  -1.5

(2)
  -1.5

(3)
  -1.5

(4)
  -1.5

12 The graph matches the solution set of which of the following inequalities?

$-24\ -23\ -22\ -21\ -20\ -19\ -18\ -17$

(1) $-23 \leq k \leq -18$

(2) $-23 \geq k \geq -18$

(3) $-19 < k + 4 < -14$

(4) $-19 \geq k + 4 \geq -14$

13 Which of the following represents the set of all real numbers between -4 and 10 as a single inequality?

(1) $-4 < x < 10$

(2) $x < 10$

(3) $x > -4$

(4) $-4 > x > 10$

14 Which statement describes the set of all integers that satisfy $3(n-5) \geq 20$ and $n \leq 12$?

(1) $\{11.6, 11.7, \ldots, 12\}$

(2) all integers between 11.67 and 12

(3) no solution

(4) $\{12\}$

15 The ratio of right-handed students to left-handed students in a grade is $11:2$. There are 38 left-handed students in this class. How many right-handed students are there?

(1) 7   **(3)** 47

(2) 209   **(4)** 437

16 Greg bought a television on sale for $336. The regular price was $420. What was the percent of decrease in the price?

(1) 80%   **(3)** 25%

(2) 20%   **(4)** 16%

17 The formula for calculating simple interest is $I = prt$, where I is the amount of interest, p is the amount invested, r is the annual rate of interest, and t is the time in years. Suppose that you invested $1200 for a period of six years and earned $396 simple interest. What was the annual rate of interest?

(1) 0.055%   **(3)** 0.55%

(2) 18%   **(4)** 5.5%

In Exercises 18–29, solve the problem. Clearly show all necessary work.

18 Solve $5g = 3(h - 1)$ for h.

19 Find all integers that satisfy $6(y - 3) \leq 6$ and $y > 1$.

20 Explain how you know that $-5.5 \leq d \leq -2.5$ has no solutions greater than or equal to -1.

21 Solve $-4x + 3(x - 5) = 7$ for x.

22 On a trip to the mall, Mai Li spent half her money on clothes and one fourth of her money on a gift for a friend. She spent $24 in all. How much money did she have when she went to the mall?

23 The student council is sponsoring a concert fundraiser. The cost of a student ticket is $3, and the cost of an adult ticket is $5. The student council wants to raise over $1000, and they think, they will sell 200 student tickets. How many adult tickets must they sell to meet their goal?

24 Last month Ben's telephone bill was $96. It represented a base charge of $18.75, long-distance charges amounting to $47.25, and several local calls at $0.10 per call. How many local calls did Ben make?

25 The lengths of the sides of a certain triangle, in feet, are consecutive even numbers. The perimeter of this triangle is between 10 feet and 24 feet, inclusive. List all possible lengths for the longest side of the triangle.

26 Mr. Brown wants to make a rectangular pen for animals. He plans to use at least 120 feet of fencing, but no more than 200 feet. He wants the length of the pen to be three times the width, and the width to be at least 30 feet. Use an inequality to show that Mr. Brown cannot do what he plans to do.

27 For every serving of mashed potatoes, Maria boils $1\frac{1}{2}$ potatoes. How many servings can be made from 18 potatoes?

28 Sam just got a raise and now his hourly pay is $18 per hour. If the raise was a 20% increase, what was his previous hourly pay?

29 Given the compound inequality $3 - 2d \geq -5$ and $d - 1.5 > 2$, compare the solution if d were defined as an integer to the solution if d were defined as a real number.

In Exercises 30–32 the given equations / inequalities have been solved. On the lines next to each step write the letter of the algebraic property that justifies that step. (MP)

Properties:

A. Distributive Property   B. + of like terms

C. Transitive Property of =   D. + property of =

E. − property of =   F. x property of =

G. ÷ property of =   H. 1 property of $\neq$

J. − property of $\neq$ K. x property of $\neq$

M. ÷ property of $\neq$

---

30 Solve for h in terms of g,

$$5g = 3(h - 1) \qquad \text{Property}$$
$$5g = 3h - 3 \qquad \underline{\hspace{3cm}}$$
$$5g + 3 = 3h \qquad \underline{\hspace{3cm}}$$
$$\frac{5g + 3}{3} = h \qquad \underline{\hspace{3cm}}$$

31 Solve for y

$$6 - 5y = 2 - 4(y + 3) \qquad \text{Property}$$
$$6 - 5y = 2 - 4y - 12 \qquad \underline{\hspace{3cm}}$$
$$6 - 5y = -4y - 10 \qquad \underline{\hspace{3cm}}$$
$$6 = y - 10 \qquad \underline{\hspace{3cm}}$$
$$16 = y \qquad \underline{\hspace{3cm}}$$

32 Solve for x,

$$7 - 6x + 3 \geq 58 \qquad \text{Property}$$
$$10 - 6x \geq 58 \qquad \underline{\hspace{3cm}}$$
$$-6x \geq 48 \qquad \underline{\hspace{3cm}}$$
$$x \leq -8 \qquad \underline{\hspace{3cm}}$$

4 Linear Equations and Inequalities in Two Variables

Cryptanalyst

When most people think of code-breakers, they think of old-fashioned spy movies. But cryptanalysts hold important jobs today. Their job is still to decipher and write codes that cannot be cracked, but these days they work for software companies, banks, and online stores in addition to government agencies and the military.

Cryptanalysts use their knowledge of mathematics and data to create, set up, and implement security applications for ATM cards, computer passwords, and other information that must be encrypted. They decode and analyze messages for government agencies and businesses, and, in turn, help provide privacy for people by keeping hackers out of data systems that we use every day. Cryptanalysts must always change their methods to be sure that hackers can't figure out their codes.

S.ID.7
F.IF.6

MP

The **coordinate axes system** is created by two intersecting number lines, one **horizontal axis** called the *x*-axis and one **vertical axis** called the *y*-axis. The intersection point is called the **origin**. The axes system divides the plane into points on the axes and into four regions called **quadrants**. Points in the plane are named by using a capital letter and an **ordered pair, *P* (*a*, *b*)**. Point *P* has **abscissa**, or *x*-**coordinate**, *a*, and **ordinate**, or *y*-**coordinate**, *b*. Point $F(2, -4)$ has abscissa 2 and ordinate -4. Point *F* is in the fourth quadrant.

Just as the graph of a real number is the point on the number line representing that number, the **graph of an ordered pair** (a, b) of real numbers *a* and *b* is the point *P* in the coordinate plane whose *x*-coordinate is *a* and whose *y*-coordinate is *b*. As shown at the right, the ordered pairs $(-5, 5)$ and $(0, 3)$ are represented by points $B(-5, 5)$ and $C(0, 3)$, respectively.

(Diagram at right shows coordinate plane with Quadrant II, Quadrant I, y-axis, y-axis labeled; points $B(-5, 5)$, $C(0, 3)$, $A(3, 2)$, x-axis, origin O, $E(2, 0)$, $D(-5, -4)$, $F(2, -4)$, Quadrant III, Quadrant IV.)

EXAMPLES 1 and 2   Working with points in the coordinate plane

1   Which is true of all points in the second quadrant?

(1) positive *x*-coordinate; positive *y*-coordinate

(3) negative *x*-coordinate; positive *y*-coordinate

(2) negative *x*-coordinate; negative *y*-coordinate

(4) positive *x*-coordinate; negative *y*-coordinate

■ SOLUTION

To locate a point in the second quadrant, go left from the origin, and then go up.

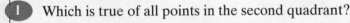

go left : negative *x*-coordinate
go up : positive *y*-coordinate

The correct choice is (3).

2   Which point lies in the third quadrant?

(1) $P(0, -5)$ (2) $Q(-5, -11)$ (3) $R(-5, 0)$ (4) $T(-5, 11)$

■ SOLUTION

Points in the third quadrant have a negative *x*-coordinate and a negative *y*-coordinate. The correct choice is (2). $Q(-5, -11) \rightarrow$ Quadrant III

Two points in the coordinate plane determine a line. The ratio of the vertical change to the horizontal change is the measure of the **slope of the line,** and the letter **m** is used to represent this measure. The horizontal change from point *A* to *B* is 5 units and the vertical change from *A* to *B* is 4 units.

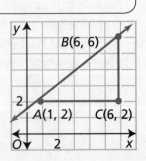

Slope of a Line

For any two points in the plane $P(x_1, y_1)$ and $Q(x_2, y_2)$ the slope can be represented in the following ways.

$$\text{slope} = m = \frac{\text{vertical change}}{\text{horizontal change}} = \frac{\text{rise}}{\text{run}} = \frac{\Delta y}{\Delta x} = \frac{y_1 - y_2}{x_1 - x_2} = \frac{y_2 - y_1}{x_2 - x_1}$$

These diagrams illustrate a line with positive slope, line m; a line with negative slope, line n; and a line with 0 slope, line z.

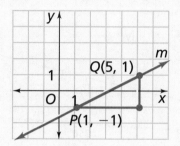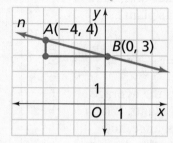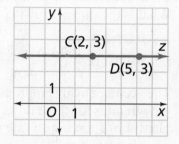

If the line is horizontal, then the vertical change $y_1 - y_2$, or rise, is equal to zero and the slope of the line is zero.

$$m = \frac{2 - 2}{1 - (-3)} = \frac{0}{4} = 0$$

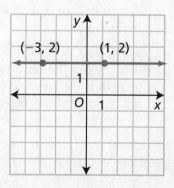

If the line is vertical, then the horizontal change, or run, is zero. A ratio is undefined when the denominator is zero and the numerator is nonzero. Therefore, **a vertical line has no slope.**

$$m = \frac{2 - 5}{1 - 1} = \frac{-3}{0} = \text{undefined}$$

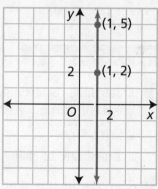

EXAMPLES 3 through 5   **Calculating the slope of a line**

Find the slope of the line containing the given points.

3 $P(1, -1)$ and $Q(5, 1)$

■ SOLUTION

$$m = \frac{1 - (-1)}{5 - 1} = \frac{2}{4} = \frac{1}{2}$$

4 $A(-4, 4)$ and $B(0, 3)$

■ SOLUTION

$$m = \frac{3 - 4}{0 - (-4)} = -\frac{1}{4}$$

5 $C(2, 3)$ and $D(5, 3)$

■ SOLUTION

$$m = \frac{3 - 3}{5 - 2} = 0$$

Slope can be thought of as the **rate of change** between two varying quantities. The rate of change shows the relationship between the two quantities where one depends upon the other.

$$\text{rate of change} = \frac{\text{change in the dependent variable}}{\text{change in the independent variable}}$$

EXAMPLES 6 and 7   **Determining the rate of change**

6 A gardener noted the height of a plant to be 2 inches on Monday and 14 inches on Friday. What is the rate of growth of this plant?

■ **SOLUTION**

$$\text{rate of change} = \frac{14\ in. - 2\ in.}{4\ days} = \frac{12\ in.}{4\ days} = \frac{3\ in.}{1\ day}$$

7 The accompanying graph shows the average growth rates for three different plants. Which plant shows the fastest rate of change, and how do you know? How tall was the slowest growing plant when the measurements began being taken?

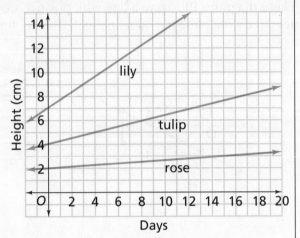

■ **SOLUTION**

The lily has the fastest growth rate because the slope of the line representing growth is the steepest for this plant. The rose was approximately 2 cm when the first measurement was taken.

In the case of non-linear functions, an *average rate of change* can be found between two points $(x_1, f(x_1))$ and $(x_2, f(x_2))$ by determining the ratio:

$$\text{average rate of change} = \frac{f(x_2) - f(x_1)}{x_2 - x_1}$$

EXAMPLES 8 and 9   **Using rate of change with data**

8 Determine the average rate of change over the interval from $x = 2$ to $x = 4$ for the data given in the table

■ **SOLUTION**

$$\text{average rate of change} = \frac{f(x_2) - f(x_1)}{x_2 - x_1} = \frac{60 - 30}{4 - 2} = \frac{30}{2} = \frac{15}{1}$$

x	y
1	0
2	30
3	47
4	60
5	69
6	77
7	84
8	90

9 The coordinates of points A and B are shown on the accompanying graph.

What is the average rate of change from A to B?

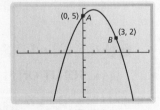

■ **SOLUTION**

$$\text{average rate of change} = \frac{f(x_2) - f(x_1)}{x_2 - x_1} = \frac{2 - 5}{3 - 0} = \frac{-3}{3} = -1$$

Practice

Choose the numeral preceding the word or expression that best completes the statement or answers the question.

1 Which statement best describes a line with positive slope?

(1) From left to right, the line falls.

(2) From left to right, the line rises.

(3) The line is parallel to the x-axis.

(4) The line is parallel to the y-axis.

2 Which line has negative slope?

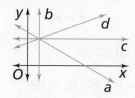

(1) a **(2)** b **(3)** c **(4)** d

3 The slope of the line containing $G(-7, 4)$ and $H(6, -2)$ is

(1) $\dfrac{6}{13}$ **(2)** $-\dfrac{13}{6}$ **(3)** $-\dfrac{6}{13}$ **(4)** $\dfrac{13}{6}$

4 Which ordered pairs represent X, Y, and Z?

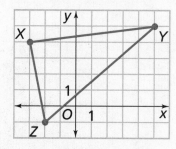

(1) $X(-3, 3)$, $Y(5, 4)$, and $Z(-2, -2)$

(2) $X(5, 5)$, $Y(-3, 4)$, and $Z(-2, -1)$

(3) $X(-3, 4)$, $Y(5, 5)$, and $Z(-2, 1)$

(4) $X(-3, 4)$, $Y(5, 5)$, and $Z(-2, -1)$

In Exercises 5–6, identify the figure determined by joining the points in the order given.

5 $A(-3, -5)$, $B(3, 5)$, and $C(10, -5)$

6 $C(0, 5)$, $D(-6, 0)$, $E(0, -5)$, and $F(6, 0)$

In Exercises 7–11, find the slope of the line containing each pair of points. If the line has no slope, so state.

7 $A(-3, -5)$, $B(3, 5)$ **8** $X(3, -7)$, $Y(-5, 11)$

9 $K(0, 5)$, $L(3, 0)$ **10** $P(4, 7)$, $Q(4, -7)$

11 $R(-3, -3)$, $S(3, 3)$

In Exercises 12–14, solve the problem. Clearly show all necessary work.

12 A line has slope -2 and contains $P(3, 4)$ and $Q(-4, a)$. Find the value of a.

13 Use this table to find the rate of change of distance (in miles) over time.

hour	1	2	3	4	5	6
distance	54	108	162	216	270	324

14 Which line is steeper, a line with slope 0.4 or a line with slope 0.6? Explain.

15 When an object is dropped from the roof of a house its distance (in feet) above the ground is given by the function $d(t) = -16t^2 + 50$ where t is in seconds. What is the average rate of change in the distance in the first 1.5 seconds?

16 Betty rode her bike at 6 miles per hour starting from a location that was 2 miles from her home. Which graph best represents her distance from home? *d* represents distance from home and *t* is time in hours since she started riding.

(1)

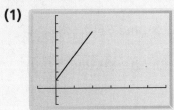

(2)

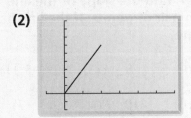

(3)

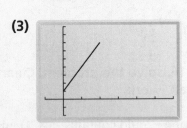

(4)

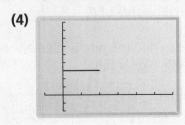

17 The table shows the numbers of two types of trees (in hundreds) in a forest reserve for five different years.

Year	2000	2004	2008	2010	2012
Spruce	53	63	73	83	93
Pine	85	80	75	70	65

(a) Calculate the rate of change for both the Spruce and Pine trees for 2000–2012.

(b) Explain the contextual meaning of each of these rates of change.

18 The slope of a line is $\frac{3}{2}$.

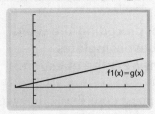

The accompanying figure shows the graph of a function. The table contains data that has been collected.

Variable 1	2	4	6	8	10
Variable 2	2	3	4	5	6

Three mathematical relationships are shown below:

(1) The equation of a line: $y = \frac{3}{2}x - 2$

(2) The given graph:

(3) The given table of values:

Which of these relationships has the smallest rate of change? Find each rate and compare.

Linear Equations
4.2 in Two Variables

A.CED.2
A.REI.10
F.IF.7
A.CED.4

MP

A **linear equation in two variables** is any equation that can be written in the form $ax + by = c$, where a, b, and c are real numbers. The equation $ax + by = c$ is called the **standard form** of a linear equation in two variables.

$$\text{Examples:}$$
$$y = 2x + 1$$
$$-3x + 2y = 6$$

A **solution to an equation in two variables** is any ordered pair (x, y) that makes the equation true.

The **graph of an equation in two variables** is the set of all points in the coordinate plane that correspond to solutions to the equation.

> ### Graph of a Linear Equation in Two Variables
>
> The graph of an equation of the form $ax + by = c$, where a, b, and c are real numbers and a, $b \neq 0$, is a line.

- A **y-intercept** of a graph is the y-coordinate of any point where the graph crosses the y-axis.

- An **x-intercept** of a graph is the x-coordinate of any point where the graph crosses the x-axis.

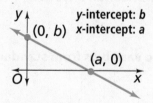

A linear equation in two variables can be written in **slope-intercept form,** $y = mx + b$, for real numbers m and b. The slope is m and the y-intercept is b.

EXAMPLE 1	**Writing a linear equation in two variables in slope-intercept form**

 Write $5x - 3y = 15$ in slope-intercept form. What are the slope and y-intercept?

- SOLUTION

$$5x - 3y = 15$$

$$y = \frac{5}{3}x + (-5), \text{ or } y = \frac{5}{3}x - 5 \leftarrow \text{slope-intercept form}$$

The slope is $\frac{5}{3}$ and the y-intercept is -5.

You can use a table of solutions to graph an equation in two variables.
You can also graph a line by plotting the *y*-intercept and using the definition
of slope $= \frac{\text{rise}}{\text{run}}$ to plot additional points of the line.

2 Graph $y = 2x + 1$.

- **SOLUTION**

Use a table of values.
Graph the points.

x	y
−1	$2(-1) + 1 = -1$
0	$2(0) + 1 = 1$
1	$2(1) + 1 = 3$

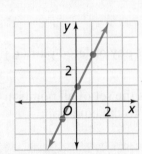

3 Graph $y = -\frac{2}{3}x + 3$.

- **SOLUTION**

Use slope $-\frac{2}{3}$ and *y*-intercept 3.

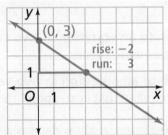

If *a* or *b* is zero in the equation $ax + by = c$, the resulting line is horizontal or
vertical, respectively. Recall that line *AB* is horizontal; therefore, its slope is
zero. $y = (0)x + 2$ or $y = 2$ is the equation of the line.

Line *BC* is vertical and has no slope; therefore, the slope-intercept form
is of no help in writing the equation. Every point on this line has an
x-value of 4; therefore, the equation of the line is $x = 4$.

Equations of **vertical lines** are of the form $x = k$ and **horizontal lines** are
$y = k$.

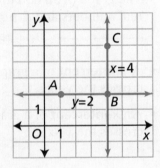

4 Graph $-3x + 2y = 6$, using any method.

- **SOLUTION 1**

using the intercepts of the graph

If $x = 0$, then $2y = 6$. So, $(0, 3)$ is a
solution.

If $y = 0$, then $-3x = 6$.
So, $(-2, 0)$ is a solution.

Graph $(0, 3)$ and $(-2, 0)$. Draw the line.

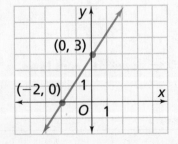

- **SOLUTION 2**

solving for y in terms of x

If $-3x + 2y = 6$, then $y = \frac{3}{2}x + 3$.

Plot the *y*-intercept $(0, 3)$.

Use the slope $= \frac{3}{2} = \frac{\text{rise}}{\text{run}}$ to plot
additional points of the line. Draw the line.

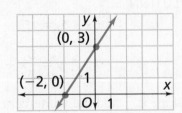

The amount of sales tax paid on a purchase depends on the value of the purchase. You can say that one variable, amount of purchase, is the **independent variable,** and a second variable, amount of tax, is the **dependent variable.** The amount of tax *varies directly* with amount of purchase.

In general, if the value of one variable y is found by multiplying the value of a second variable x by a constant nonzero real number k, the **constant of variation,** then the relationship is called a **direct variation.**

If $y = kx$, where $k \neq 0$, then y varies directly with x.

An important direct-variation relationship involves distance, rate, and time.

$$\text{Distance} = \text{rate} \times \text{time} \Rightarrow d = r \cdot t$$

EXAMPLE 5 **Solving problems involving distance, rate, and time**

5 During a 50-minute period, Frances and Dominic went out for a walk. The graph at the right shows distance traveled over time for each walker. In miles per hour, how much faster did Dominic walk than Frances?

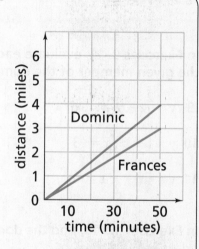

■ **SOLUTION**
In 50 minutes, $\frac{5}{6}$ of an hour, Dominic walked 4 miles and Frances walked 3 miles.

If $d = rt$, then $r = \dfrac{d}{t}$.

Dominic: $r = \dfrac{4}{\frac{5}{6}} = 4.8$ Frances: $r = \dfrac{3}{\frac{5}{6}} = 3.6$

Dominic walked 1.2 miles per hour faster than Frances.

Practice

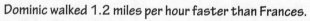

Choose the numeral preceding the word or expression that best completes the statement or answers the question.

1 Which of the following is not the equation of a line?

(1) $y = 4$

(2) $3x + 2y = 7$

(3) $y = x^2 - 6$

(4) $x = -5$

2 The equation of a line is $y = 3x - 7$. What is the y-intercept of the line?

(1) 3   **(3)** 7

(2) 4   **(4)** -7

3 Which equation represents variables that are related by direct variation?

(1) $y = 2x + 3$

(2) $F = 1.8C + 32$

(3) $zw = 6$

(4) $y = 3f$

4 Which ordered pair is a solution to the equation $5x - 3y = 9$?

(1) $(0, 0)$ **(3)** $(5, 5)$

(2) $(3, 2)$ **(4)** $(2, 3)$

101

In Exercises 5–8, the equation $F = \frac{9}{5}C + 32$ relates temperature in degrees Fahrenheit (F) to degrees Celsius (C). Rewrite this equation as a function C in terms of F. Use the appropriate equation to calculate, to the nearest tenth, the corresponding temperature for each of the following.

5 $9°C$

6 $-20°C$

7 $0°F$

8 $95°F$

In Exercises 9–11, evaluate each function for the given member of the domain.

9 $y = \frac{2}{3}x + 9;\ x = -6$

10 $y = 1 - x^2;\ x = -3$

11 $y = \frac{2}{3}x - \frac{1}{2};\ x = -6$

In Exercises 12–15, find the domain and range.

12 $y = 0.6x + 9$

13 $y = -0.25x$

14 $y = 1 - x^2$

15 $y = x^2 - 1$

In Exercises 16–27, graph each equation.

16 $y = -2x + 3$ **17** $y = 3x - 5$

18 $y = 2x - 1$ **19** $y = -3x$

20 $y = -\frac{1}{3}x - 2$ **21** $y = \frac{1}{2}x$

22 $-2x + y = 1$ **23** $x - y = 4$

24 $x + 3y = 3$ **25** $x + 2y = 2$

26 $-x + 2y = 3$ **27** $2x - 3y = 2$

28 During a 40-minute period, Dana and Li went out for a walk. The graph below shows the distance traveled over time for each walker. In miles per hour, how much faster did Dana walk than Li?

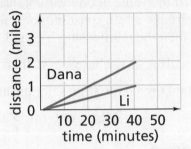

29 Marissa has $1.20 in nickels and dimes. Write an equation that represents this situation using n for the number of nickels and d for the number of dimes.

30 The sales tax in a certain area is 5%, or 5 cents on the dollar. Write an equation to represent the amount a of tax in terms of the cost c of a purchase.

31 Hank needs to algebraically represent 3 consecutive even integers whose sum is 126. Write an equation that represents this situation where n is the first even integer.

32 At a certain theater, an adult's ticket costs $9 and a child's ticket costs $5. The manager counted the receipts one night and determined that $2,250 was taken in. Write an equation to represent this situation, using a to represent the number of adults and c to represent the number of children.

33 A collection of 185 marbles consists of only red marbles, blue marbles, and 35 yellow marbles. Write an equation in r and b to represent the situation. List three possible solutions to the equation.

34 A choir sold fruit as represented below. Write an equation to represent this situation.

5-pound box	10-pound box	Total number of pounds
f boxes	t boxes	200

Determine two possible numbers of cartons of 5-pound boxes and 10-pound boxes that satisfy the given conditions.

Given sufficient information about a line in the coordinate plane, you can write a linear equation in two variables to represent it. Stated below are important forms for an equation of a line.

Slope-Intercept and Point-Slope Forms

A line with slope m and y-intercept b has **slope-intercept form:**

$$y = mx + b$$

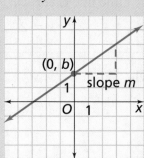

A line with slope m and containing $P(x_1, y_1)$ has **point-slope form:**

$$y - y_1 = m(x - x_1)$$

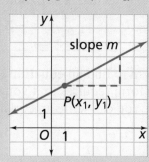

Any vertical line containing $P(x_1, y_1)$ has equation $x = x_1$. For example, if a vertical line contains the point $(5, 2)$, an equation for that line is $x = 5$.

Any horizontal line containing $P(x_1, y_1)$ has equation $y = y_1$. For example, if a horizontal line contains the point $(4, -8)$, an equation for that line is $y = -8$.

EXAMPLES 1 and 2   Using slope and y-intercept to identify an equation for a line

 Write an equation that represents the line with a slope of $-\frac{4}{5}$ and a y-intercept of 3?

■ SOLUTION

Use the slope-intercept form.

$$y = mx + b.$$
$$y = -\frac{4}{5}x + 3 \quad \leftarrow \text{Replace } m \text{ with } -\frac{4}{5} \text{ and } b \text{ with 3.}$$

 Which equation represents the line at the right?

(1) $y = \frac{1}{4}x + 3$ **(3)** $y = \frac{1}{4}x - 3$

(2) $y = -\frac{1}{4}x + 3$ **(4)** $y = -2x + 3$

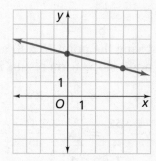

■ SOLUTION

The y-intercept is 3. The slope of the line is $-\frac{1}{4}$. Using the slope-intercept form, the correct choice is (2).

When you are given the slope and a point on a line, you can use the point-slope form to write an equation for that line.

EXAMPLES 3 through 5 **Writing an equation for a line by using slope and a point on the line**

Write an equation in slope-intercept form for each line, if possible.

3 the line with slope $\frac{3}{4}$ and containing $P(2,-3)$

■ SOLUTION

$$y - (-3) = \frac{3}{4}(x - 2)$$

$$y = \frac{3}{4}x - \frac{9}{2}$$

4 the line with slope 0 and containing $P(2,-3)$

■ SOLUTION

Because the slope is 0, the line is horizontal.

$$y = -3$$

5 the line with no slope and containing $P(2,-3)$

■ SOLUTION

Because there is no slope, the line is vertical.

$$x = 2$$

You can also use the point-slope form to find an equation of a line through two specific points. The point-slope form requires that you first find the slope. Recall that slope $= m = \frac{y_2 - y_1}{x_2 - x_1}$. You can write an equation of a line in slope-intercept or standard form.

EXAMPLES 6 through 9 **Writing an equation for a line given two points**

Write an equation for

6 the line containing $L(-5,-6)$ and $M(3,-6)$.

■ SOLUTION

The y-coordinates of L and M are equal. The line is horizontal.

$$y = -6$$

7 the line containing $R(4.2,-6)$ and $S(4.2,9)$.

■ SOLUTION

The x-coordinates of R and S are equal. The line is vertical.

$$x = 4.2$$

8 the line containing $A(-5,-6)$ and $B(3,8)$.

■ SOLUTION

First determine the slope.

$$m = \frac{y_2 - y_1}{x_2 - x_1} = \frac{-6 - 8}{-5 - 3}$$

$$= \frac{-14}{-8} = \frac{7}{4}$$

Using the point $B(3,8)$ and the point-slope form results in:

$$y - 8 = \frac{7}{4}(x - 3)$$

$$y - \frac{32}{4} = \frac{7}{4}x - \frac{21}{4}$$

$$y = \frac{7}{4}x + \frac{11}{4}$$

9 $\overleftrightarrow{DG}$ containing $D(2,3)$ and $G(8,11)$ in standard form.

■ SOLUTION

First determine the slope.

$$m = \frac{y_2 - y_1}{x_2 - x_1} = \frac{11 - 3}{8 - 2} = \frac{8}{6}$$

Using the point $D(2,3)$ and the point-slope form results in:

$$y - 3 = \frac{4}{3}(x - 2)$$

$$3y - 9 = 4x - 8$$

$$-4x + 3y = 1$$

The standard form for the equation is $-4x + 3y = 1$.

Use what you know to solve problems involving points on a line.

EXAMPLES 10 and 11   **Solving problems about points on a line**

10 The point $Z(3, w)$ is on the graph of $y = 2x + 5$. The value of w is

(1) -1 **(2)** $w - 5$ **(3)** 11 **(4)** $2w + 5$

■ **SOLUTION**

If $x = 3$ and $y = w$, then $w = 2(3) + 5$; that is, $w = 11$.
The correct choice is (**3**).

11 Which point lies on the line containing $P(-3, -1)$ and $Q(5, 6)$?

(1) $A(-3, 0)$ **(2)** $B(21, 19)$ **(3)** $C(21, 20)$ **(4)** $D(-3, -2)$

■ **SOLUTION**

$$m = \frac{6 - (-1)}{5 - (-3)} = \frac{7}{8} \quad \leftarrow \textbf{Determine the slope.}$$

$$y = \frac{7}{8}(x - 5) + 6 \quad \leftarrow \textbf{Write an equation for the line containing } P \text{ and } Q.$$

Because $\dfrac{7}{8}(21 - 5) + 6 = 20$, the correct choice is (**3**).

Two lines in a plane either intersect or do not intersect. If the lines never intersect, they are **parallel.** If the lines intersect at a right angle, the lines are **perpendicular.**

$m: \ y = \dfrac{1}{2}x + 3 \qquad n: \ y = \dfrac{1}{2}x - 1$ 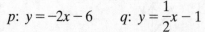 $p: \ y = -2x - 6 \qquad q: \ y = \dfrac{1}{2}x - 1$

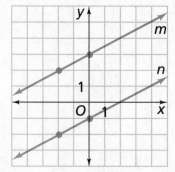   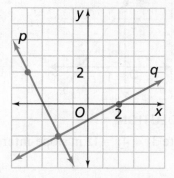

slope of m: $\dfrac{1}{2}$ slope of n: $\dfrac{1}{2}$

The lines are parallel lines.
The slopes of these lines are equal.

slope of p: -2 slope of q: $\dfrac{1}{2}$ Note: $-2 \cdot \dfrac{1}{2} = -1$

The lines are perpendicular lines.
The slopes are negative reciprocals of each other.

Parallel and Perpendicular Lines

■ Two lines with slopes m_1 and m_2 are parallel if and only if $m_1 = m_2$. (Any two vertical or horizontal lines are parallel.)

■ Two lines with slopes m_1 and m_2 are perpendicular if and only if $m_1 m_2 = -1$.
(Every vertical line is perpendicular to every horizontal line.)

12 Which line is parallel to the graph of $5x - 6y = 2$?

(1) the line with slope $-\frac{5}{6}$ and y-intercept $-\frac{1}{3}$ **(3)** the line with slope $-\frac{6}{5}$ and y-intercept $-\frac{1}{3}$

(2) the line with slope $\frac{5}{6}$ and y-intercept 3 **(4)** the line with slope $\frac{6}{5}$ and y-intercept 3

■ **SOLUTION**
Write $5x - 6y = 2$ in slope-intercept form.
$$5x - 6y = 2$$
$$-6y = -5x + 2$$
$$y = \frac{5}{6}x - \frac{1}{3}$$

A line parallel to the graph of $5x - 6y = 2$ must have slope $\frac{5}{6}$.
Therefore, eliminate choices (1), (3), and (4).
The correct choice is (2).

> **Note**
>
> To see whether two distinct nonvertical lines are parallel, check to see whether:
> - slopes are equal;
> - y-intercepts are unequal.

13 Which line is parallel to $3x + 4y = 12$?

(1)
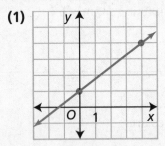

(3)
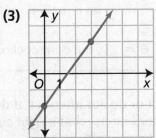

(2)
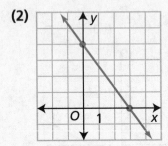

(4)
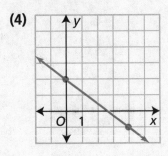

■ **SOLUTION**
Write $3x + 4y = 12$ in slope-intercept form.
$$y = -\frac{3}{4}x + 3$$

A line parallel to $3x + 4y = 12$ must have slope $-\frac{3}{4}$.
Therefore, eliminate choices (1) and (3).

Find the slope of the line in choice (2).
$$m = \frac{0 - 4}{3 - 0} = -\frac{4}{3}$$

The slope is not equal to $-\frac{3}{4}$; eliminate choice (2).
Verify the slope of the line in choice (4).
$$m = \frac{2 - (-1)}{0 - 4} = -\frac{3}{4}$$

The slope is equal to $-\frac{3}{4}$; the correct choice is **(4)**.

You can also use slope to identify perpendicular lines.

EXAMPLE 14   **Identifying a line perpendicular to a given line**

14 Which equation represents line q perpendicular to line p?

(1) $-x + 4y = -2$ (3) $-x + 4y = -7$

(2) $4x + y = 11$ (4) $4x + y = 2$

■ SOLUTION

Write each equation in slope-intercept form.

(1) $y = \frac{1}{4}x - \frac{1}{2}$ (3) $y = \frac{1}{4}x - \frac{7}{4}$

(2) $y = -4x + 11$ (4) $y = -4x + 2$

Because the slope of p is $\frac{1}{4}$, the slope of q is -4. Eliminate choices (1) and (3).
$C(3, -1)$ does not satisfy the equation in choice (4). The correct choice is **(2)**.

You can find an equation of a line parallel or perpendicular to a given line.

EXAMPLES 15 and 16   **Finding an equation for a line parallel or perpendicular to a given line**

Find an equation in slope-intercept form for the specified line.

15 line z containing $P(4, -3)$ and parallel to the graph of $y = \frac{1}{2}x + 3$

■ SOLUTION

Because z is parallel to the graph of $y = \frac{1}{2}x + 3$, the slope of z is $\frac{1}{2}$.
Also, z contains $P(4, -3)$.

$$y - (-3) = \frac{1}{2}(x - 4)$$

$$y = \frac{1}{2}x - 5$$

16 line n containing $Q(-2, 5)$ and perpendicular to the graph of $y = -\frac{1}{2}x + 5$

■ SOLUTION

Because n is perpendicular to the graph of $y = -\frac{1}{2}x + 5$, the slope of n is 2.
Also, n contains $Q(-2, 5)$.

$$y - 5 = 2(x - (-2))$$
$$y - 5 = 2(x + 2)$$
$$y = 2x + 9$$

Practice

Choose the numeral preceding the word or expression that best completes the statement or answers the question.

1 What is the slope of a line parallel to a line with slope -2?

(1) 2   (2) -2 (3) $\frac{1}{2}$ (4) $-\frac{1}{2}$

2 What is the slope of a line perpendicular to a line with slope -2?

(1) 2   (3) 0.5

(2) -2 (4) -0.5

3 Which describes the relationship between two distinct nonvertical parallel lines?

(1) equal slopes; unequal y-intercepts

(2) unequal slopes; unequal y-intercepts

(3) equal slopes; equal y-intercepts

(4) unequal slopes; equal y-intercepts

4 Find the slope of a line perpendicular to line *p*.

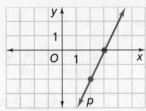

(1) 2 **(2)** 0.5 **(3)** −2 **(4)** −0.5

5 Which equation represents the line with slope −3 and *y*-intercept −7?

(1) $y = -3x + 7$ **(3)** $y = -3x - 7$

(2) $y = -7x + 3$ **(4)** $y = 7x - 3$

6 What is the slope of a line parallel to *m*?

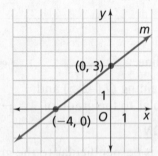

(1) $-\dfrac{4}{3}$ **(2)** $\dfrac{4}{3}$ **(3)** $-\dfrac{3}{4}$ **(4)** 0.75

7 Which equation could not represent a line parallel to the graph of $y = -2.5x + 1$?

(1) $y = -2.5x + 3$ **(3)** $y = -2.5x - 1$

(2) $y = 2.5x + 1$ **(4)** $y = -2.5x$

In Exercises 8–16, write an equation in slope-intercept form for the specified line, where possible.

8 the line containing $A(0, 7)$ and $B(7, 0)$

9 the line containing $C(3, -7)$ and $D(-3, 5)$

10 slope: 2; containing $P(4, 5)$

11 slope: −0.6; containing $Z(-1, 1)$

12 slope: 0; *y*-intercept −7

13 no slope; *x*-intercept −11

14 containing $H(2, 2)$ and parallel to the graph of $y = x - 3$

15 containing $A(-2, -2)$ and parallel to the graph of $y = 2x - 1$

16 containing $M(1, 4)$ and perpendicular to the graph of $y = -\frac{2}{3}x + 5$

In Exercises 17–22, solve the problem. Clearly show all necessary work.

17 What are the coordinates of the point where the line containing $K(-3, 5)$ and $L(5, -4)$ crosses the *y*-axis?

18 Is the relationship between *y* and *x* linear? Explain your answer.

x	0	4	8	12
y	2	5	8	11

19 Write an equation in standard form for this graph.

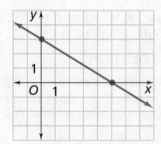

20 A student can work at a job that pays $4 an hour for 25 hours to earn $100 or can work at a second job that pays $5 per hour for 20 hours to earn $100. If the student spends time at each job, write an equation that uses a combined rate to earn $100. Show your work.

21 Is $S(93, 83)$ on the line containing $P(-3, -1)$ and $Q(5, 6)$? Justify your response.

22 Is $K(-90, -232)$ on the line shown below?

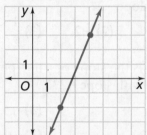

4.4 Graphs of Absolute Value Functions

You have learned that the **absolute value** of a number is its distance from zero on a number line. The definition of the absolute value is

$$abs(x) = |x| = \begin{cases} x \text{ if } x \geq 0 \\ -x \text{ if } x < 0 \end{cases} \quad or \quad abs(x) = |x| = \begin{cases} x \text{ if } x \text{ is positive or zero} \\ \text{the opposite of } x \text{ if } x \text{ is negative} \end{cases}$$

An alternate definition of the absolute value function is given by $|x| = \sqrt{x^2}$.

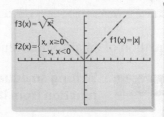

The accompanying figure shows the graphs of the absolute value function using these three definitions, Notice all three lie on top of each other. This provides strong visual evidence for the equivalence of these three definitions.

If you look at the table of values for this function, you will see that if x is negative, y is the opposite of x and if x is positive or zero, y is equal to x.

If the cofficient of the absolute value term of the function is positive, the **V** points down; if the coefficient is negative, the **V** points up.

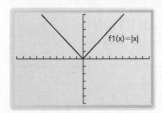 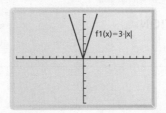 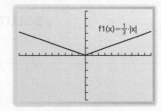

As you can see from the graphs above, if $y = a|x|$, the graph is narrower.

If $y = \left(\dfrac{1}{a}\right)|x|$, the graph is wider. In both of these equations a is an integer.

X	Y_1	
−3	3	
−2	2	
−1	1	
0	0	
2	2	
3	3	
X=3		

EXAMPLES I and 2   Graphing absolute value functions

Graph the following functions on a calculator.

1 $y = |x + 3|$

  ■ **SOLUTION**

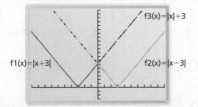

2 $y = |x - 3|$

  ■ **SOLUTION**

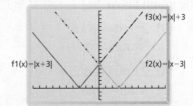

NOTE: Some technology tools allow for the use of color and the ability to change a function's graph to be dashed. In this way these three functions can be graphed on the same coordinate axis system which facilitates the comparison of these functions. Also, note that the functions are written in mathematically correct symbolism here.

A **translation** is a shift of a graph vertically, horizontally, or both. The resulting graph is the same size and shape as the original but is in a different position in the plane.

Graphs of Absolute Value Functions

- If $y = |x + a|$, the graph translates a units to the left.
- If $y = |x - a|$, the graph translates a units to the right.
- If $y = |x| + a$, the graph translates a units up.
- If $y = |x| - a$, the graph translates a units down.

You can also write an equation of an absolute value function from its graph.

EXAMPLES 3 through 5 **Writing an equation of an absolute value function from its graph**

Write an equation for each translation of $y = |x|$ shown below.

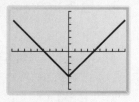 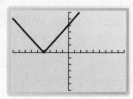 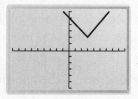

■ **SOLUTION**
$y = |x| - 4$

■ **SOLUTION**
$y = |x + 4|$

■ **SOLUTION**
$y = |x - 3| + 2$

Practice

In Exercises 1–2, use the graph below.

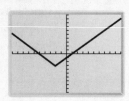

1 Which statement best describes the translation of $y = |x|$ shown in the graph above?

(1) 2 units up, 3 units left

(3) 2 units down, 3 units left

(2) 2 units left, 3 units down

(4) 2 units right, 3 units right

2 Which equation represents the graph?

(1) $y = |x + 2| - 3$ **(3)** $y = |x - 2| + 3$

(2) $y = |x + 3| - 2$ **(4)** $y = |x - 3| + 2$

In Exercises 3–6, graph each function and state its vertex.

3 $y = |x| + 2$ **4** $y = |x - 2|$

5 $y = |x| - 5$ **6** $y = |x - 1| + 3$

In Exercises 7–12, write an equation for each translation of $y = |x|$.

7 9 units up   **8** 6 units down

9 right 9 units   **10** left 0.5 units

11 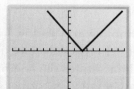 **12**

110

4.5 Systems of Linear Equations

A.REI.6
A.CED.2
N.VM.C.8
A.REI.C.9

A **system of equations in two variables** is a set of equations in the same two variables as illustrated at the right. You can use a single brace { to indicate that a collection of equations is a system.

$$\begin{cases} x + y = 30 \\ x - y = 8 \end{cases}$$

EXAMPLES 1 and 2 — Recognizing and representing a situation as a system of equations

1. The sum of two numbers x and y is 26. Twice x minus y equals 16. Which system could not represent this situation?

   (1) $\begin{cases} x + y = 26 \\ 2x - y = 16 \end{cases}$ **(2)** $\begin{cases} 2x - y = 16 \\ x + y = 26 \end{cases}$ **(3)** $\begin{cases} 26 = x + y \\ 16 = 2x - y \end{cases}$ **(4)** $\begin{cases} x + y = 16 \\ 2x - y = 26 \end{cases}$

   ■ **SOLUTION**

   The sum of two numbers is 26. $x + y = 26$
   Twice x minus y equals 16. $2x - y = 16$

   Only choice (4) does not contain these equations. The correct choice is (4).

2. Club members at the Bronx Video Game Store pay \$24 to be members and pay \$4 for each game rental. Those who are not members rent games for \$5.50 each. Represent total expense in terms of games rented as a system of equations.

   ■ **SOLUTION**

   Let n represent the number of games rented. Let c represent total cost.

Member expense c:	$4n + 24$	$c = 4n + 24$	$\begin{cases} c = 4n + 24 \\ c = 5.5n \end{cases}$
Nonmember expense c:	$5.5n$	$c = 5.5n$	

A **solution to a system of equations** in two variables x and y is any ordered pair (x, y) that makes each equation in the system true.

EXAMPLE 3 — Verifying a solution to a system of equations

3. Which ordered pair (a, b) is a solution to $\begin{cases} a + 2b = 12 \\ 2a - 3b = -25 \end{cases}$?

   (1) $(7, -2)$ **(2)** $(-2, 7)$ **(3)** $(4, 4)$ **(4)** $(-8, 3)$

   ■ **SOLUTION**

   Test each ordered pair in each equation.

   (1) $(7, -2)$ $\begin{cases} 7 + 2(-2) \neq 12 \\ 2(7) - 3(-2) \neq -25 \end{cases}$ ✗   **(3)** $(4, 4)$ $\begin{cases} 4 + 2(4) = 12 \\ 2(4) - 3(4) \neq -25 \end{cases}$ ✗

   (2) $(-2, 7)$ $\begin{cases} -2 + 2(7) = 12 \\ 2(-2) - 3(7) = -25 \end{cases}$ ✓   **(4)** $(-8, 3)$ $\begin{cases} -8 + 2(3) \neq 12 \\ 2(-8) - 3(3) = -25 \end{cases}$ ✗

   The correct choice is (2).

By graphing each equation in a system of equations, you can approximate the coordinates of any solution.

EXAMPLE 4 **Recognizing estimates of solutions to a system of equations**

4 Which best represents the coordinates of the point of intersection of these lines?

(1) x is between -2 and -1. **(3)** x is between -3 and -2.
     y is between 3 and 4. y is between 4 and 5.

(2) $x = -1.25$ **(4)** x is between -2 and -1.
     $y = 4.\overline{3}$ y is between 4 and 5.

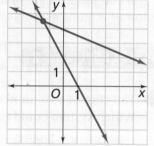

■ **SOLUTION**

The x-coordinate is more than 1 unit but less than 2 units left of the origin.
The y-coordinate is more than 4 units but less than 5 units above the origin.
No further claim can be made of the solution. The correct choice is **(4)**.

You can use a graphing calculator to find more accurate graphical solutions to systems of equations.

EXAMPLE 5 **Finding a solution to a system of equations by using a graphing calculator**

5 Solve the system $\begin{cases} y = 2x + 3 \\ y = -3x - 1 \end{cases}$.

■ **SOLUTION 1**

- Enter $y = 2x + 3$ and $y = -3x - 1$ into the function list.
- Set an appropriate window.
- Press **2nd** **CALC** #5Intersect.
- Choose the functions in response to the prompts.
- Enter a guess.
- The solution is displayed.

  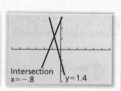

The solution is $(-0.8, 1.4)$.

■ **SOLUTION 2**

- Enter $f1(x) = 2x + 3$ and $f2(x) = -3x - 1$ into the function editor on a graphs page of the document.
- Press **MENU**, Geometry, Points and Lines, Points.
- Move the cursor to the point of intersection until you see the prompt "intersection point" and click symbol or delete.
- The intersection point will be marked and labeled.

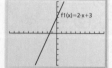  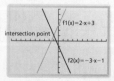 

You may have a system of equations in which y is not written in terms of x. To solve by graphing, first solve each equation for y.

$$\begin{cases} x + y = 8 \\ x - 2y = 2 \end{cases}$$

$$\begin{array}{ll} x + y = 8 & x - 2y = 2 \\ \quad y = -x + 8 & \quad y = 0.5x - 1 \end{array}$$

EXAMPLE 6 Solving systems by solving for the same variable

 Solve $\begin{cases} x + y = 8 \\ x - 2y = 2 \end{cases}$ graphically.

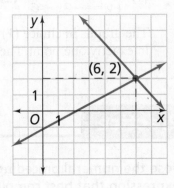

■ **SOLUTION 1**

Solve each equation for y in terms of x.

$$\begin{cases} x + y = 8 \\ x - 2y = 2 \end{cases} \rightarrow \begin{cases} y = -x + 8 \\ y = \frac{1}{2}x - 1 \end{cases}$$

Graph each equation on the same coordinate plane. Read the coordinates of the point of intersection. The solution is $(6, 2)$, or $x = 6$ and $y = 2$.

■ **SOLUTION 2**

Some graphing calculators have built-in features for solving systems of equations. In those cases the following method could be used for solving this system.

linSolve$\left(\begin{cases} x+y=8 \\ x-2y=2 \end{cases}, \{x, y\}\right)$

linSolve$\left(\begin{cases} x+y=8 \\ x-2\cdot y=2 \end{cases}, \{x, y\}\right)$ $\{6, 2\}$

Not every pair of equations in the same two variables has a solution.

* If the system has exactly one solution, it is called **independent**.

$$\begin{cases} y = x - 2 \\ y = -2x + 10 \end{cases}$$

* If the graphs of the equations are **distinct** and **intersect**, then the system is independent.

* If the system has infinitely many solutions, it is called **dependent**.

$$\begin{cases} y = x - 2 \\ x - y = 2 \end{cases}$$

* If the graphs of the equations **coincide**, then the system is dependent.

* If the system has no solution, it is called **inconsistent**.

$$\begin{cases} y = -x + 2 \\ y = -x \end{cases}$$

* If the graphs of the equations are parallel lines, then the system is inconsistent.

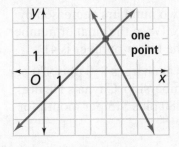

one point

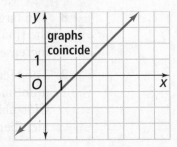

graphs coincide

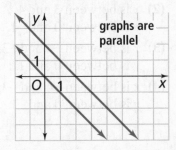

graphs are parallel

113

EXAMPLE 7   **Identifying independent, dependent, and inconsistent systems**

7 Which system of equations is independent?

  (1) $\begin{cases} x + y = 4 \\ 2x + y = 6 \end{cases}$ **(2)** $\begin{cases} 2x + y = 4 \\ 2x + y = 9 \end{cases}$ **(3)** $\begin{cases} x - y = 2 \\ 3x - 3y = 6 \end{cases}$ **(4)** $\begin{cases} x - y = 0 \\ 3x - 3y = 0 \end{cases}$

■ **SOLUTION**

In each system, solve for y. Read the slope and y-intercept.

  (1) $\begin{cases} y = -1x + 4 \\ y = -2x + 6 \end{cases}$ **(2)** $\begin{cases} y = -2x + 4 \\ y = -2x + 9 \end{cases}$ **(3)** $\begin{cases} y = 1x - 2 \\ y = 1x - 2 \end{cases}$ **(4)** $\begin{cases} y = 1x \\ y = 1x \end{cases}$

The graphs in choice (1) have unequal slopes and unequal y-intercepts. The graphs intersect in exactly one point. The correct choice is (1).

Practice

Choose the numeral preceding the word or expression that best completes the statement or answers the question.

1 Which ordered pair is the solution to $\begin{cases} 2x - 5y = -11 \\ 2x - y = 1 \end{cases}$?

  (1) $(-8, -1)$ **(3)** $(3, 2)$

  (2) $(3, 5)$ **(4)** $(2, 3)$

2 Which best describes the solution to the system whose graphs are shown here?

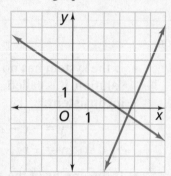

  (1) x is between 3 and 4; y is between 0 and 1.

  (2) x is between 3 and 4; y is between 0 and −1.

  (3) x is between −4 and −3; y is between 0 and 1.

  (4) x is between −4 and −3; y is between 0 and −1.

3 Which best describes $\begin{cases} y = 2x - 5 \\ y = 2x - 13 \end{cases}$?

  (1) No solution; the slopes are equal and the y-intercepts are unequal.

  (2) One solution; the slopes are equal and the y-intercepts are unequal.

  (3) Two solutions; the slopes are equal and the y-intercepts are unequal.

  (4) Infinite solutions; the slopes are equal and the y-intercepts are equal.

In Exercises 4–7, use graphs of the equations in each system to find the coordinates of any point of intersection.

4 $\begin{cases} x + y = 4 \\ -2x + y = 1 \end{cases}$ **5** $\begin{cases} y = 2x + 5 \\ y = 1 \end{cases}$

6 $\begin{cases} y = 3x + 1 \\ y = 4x + 2 \end{cases}$ **7** $\begin{cases} -7x + 5y = 10 \\ -2x + 5y = -15 \end{cases}$

In Exercises 8–11, represent each situation as a system of two equations in two variables. Identify the variables.

8 The larger of two numbers decreased by the smaller is 5. Twice the smaller number increased by the larger number is 41.

9 The Health Gym charges $50 plus $20 per month for membership. Chyna's Health Club charges $80 plus $15 per month for membership.

10 Kisha has $1.75 in nickels and dimes. She has 23 coins in all.

11 One number is twice another number. Their sum is 21.

In Exercises 12–16, solve the problem. Clearly show all necessary work.

12 Graph the equations in the system
$$\begin{cases} x + y = 7 \\ 3x - y = 7 \end{cases}$$ Find consecutive integers between which the x- and y-coordinates of the solution lie.

13 What are the coordinates of the solution to the system whose graph is shown here?

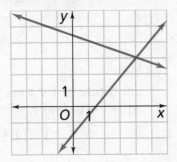

14 Is the system $\begin{cases} y = -2.5x - 3 \\ y = 2.2x - 10 \end{cases}$ independent, dependent, or inconsistent? Explain.

15 Is the system $\begin{cases} y = 3x + 5 \\ 4y = 12x + 20 \end{cases}$ independent, dependent, or inconsistent? Explain.

16 Graph $y = 1.5x - 1$, $x = 4$, and $y = -2$ on the same coordinate plane. Find the area of the triangle enclosed by the graphs.

4.6 Solving Systems of Equations

A.CED.3
A.REI.6

In the system of equations at the right, y is given in terms of x in each equation. Although you can solve this system graphically, there are several algebraic methods you can use. One of them is called the **substitution method.**

$$\begin{cases} y = -x + 4 \\ y = 2x + 7 \end{cases}$$

MP

When you use the substitution method, you transform a pair of equations in two variables into one equation in one variable.

If $y = -x + 4$ and $y = 2x + 7$, then $-x + 4 = 2x + 7$.

The solution to $-x + 4 = 2x + 7$ gives the value of x. The following example shows how to continue to get the complete solution.

> **Note**
> The *Transitive Property of Equality* states the following: If $a = b$ and $b = c$, then $a = c$.

EXAMPLE 1   Solving by simple substitution

1 Solve $\begin{cases} y = -x + 4 \\ y = 2x + 7 \end{cases}$ by substitution.

■ **SOLUTION**

Step 1

Equate the expressions for y.

$$-x + 4 = 2x + 7$$

Step 2

Solve $-x + 4 = 2x + 7$.

$$-x + 4 = 2x + 7$$
$$x = -1$$

Step 3

Substitute -1 for x in either equation to find y.

$$y = -(-1) + 4$$
$$= 5$$

The solution to the system is $(-1, 5)$.

Check: $\begin{cases} -(-1) + 4 = 5 \checkmark \\ 2(-1) + 7 = 5 \checkmark \end{cases}$

Sometimes you must first solve one of the equations for a specific value before you can use the substitution method.

EXAMPLES 2 and 3   Solving by isolating one variable and then using substitution

Solve each system of equations by substitution.

2 $\begin{cases} x + y = 7 \\ y = 2x - 3 \end{cases}$

3 $\begin{cases} x + y = -2 \\ 3x + y = 5 \end{cases}$

■ **SOLUTION**

$$x + (2x - 3) = 7$$
$$3x - 3 = 7$$
$$x = \frac{10}{3}$$

If $\frac{10}{3} + y = 7$, $y = \frac{11}{3}$. Solution: $\left(\frac{10}{3}, \frac{11}{3}\right)$

Check: $\begin{cases} \frac{10}{3} + \frac{11}{3} = \frac{21}{3} = 7 \qquad\qquad \checkmark \\ 2\left(\frac{10}{3}\right) - 3 = \frac{20}{3} - \frac{9}{3} = \frac{11}{3} \checkmark \end{cases}$

■ **SOLUTION**

Solve $3x + y = 5$ for y. $y = -3x + 5$.

$$x + (-3x + 5) = -2$$
$$-2x + 5 = -2$$
$$x = \frac{7}{2}$$

If $\frac{7}{2} + y = -2$, $y = -\frac{11}{2}$. Solution: $\left(\frac{7}{2}, -\frac{11}{2}\right)$

Check: $\begin{cases} \frac{7}{2} + \left(-\frac{11}{2}\right) = -\frac{4}{2} = -2 \qquad\qquad \checkmark \\ 3\left(\frac{7}{2}\right) + \left(-\frac{11}{2}\right) = \frac{21}{2} - \frac{11}{2} = \frac{10}{2} = 5 \checkmark \end{cases}$

You can use the substitution method to solve problems involving systems of equations.

4 Which system of equations has no solution?

(1) $\begin{cases} y = x - 3 \\ 2x - 3y = 5 \end{cases}$ (2) $\begin{cases} y = -5x - 3 \\ 2x - 2y = 5 \end{cases}$ (3) $\begin{cases} y = x - 2.5 \\ 2x - 2y = -5 \end{cases}$ (4) $\begin{cases} y = x - 3 \\ 2x - 2y = 5 \end{cases}$

■ SOLUTION

In choice (4), $2x - 2(x - 3) = 5$. So, $6 = 5$. Choice (4) has no solution.

5 Angela has 30 nickels and dimes totaling $2.40. How many of each has she?

■ SOLUTION

Let n and d represent the number of nickels and dimes, respectively.

   In all, she has 30 coins.   → $n + d = 30$

   In pennies, the total worth is 240 cents.   → $5n + 10d = 240$

Use substitution to eliminate d from $5n + 10d = 240$.

$$5n + 10(30 - n) = 240 \rightarrow \text{because } d = 30 - n$$
$$-5n = -60$$
$$n = 12$$

Therefore, $d = 30 - 12 = 18$. So, Angela has **12 nickels** and **18 dimes**.

The **addition-multiplication method,** or **elimination method,** is a useful solution method if the variables in a system have coefficients other than 1. Use the properties of equality to make an **equivalent system,** a system that has the same solution set.

To make an equivalent system you multiply each term of an equation by a value that results in coefficients of matching terms that are opposites of each other.

$$\begin{cases} 4x + 2y = 7 \\ 2x + 5y = 4 \end{cases}$$

$$\begin{aligned} -2(2x + 5y) &= (4)(-2) \\ -4y - 10y &= -8 \end{aligned} \quad \longrightarrow \quad \begin{cases} 4x + 2y = 7 \\ -4x - 10y = -8 \end{cases}$$

EXAMPLE 6   Identifying equivalent systems of equations

6 Which system of equations is equivalent to $\begin{cases} -3x - 5y = -3 \\ 5x - 15y = 7 \end{cases}$?

(1) $\begin{cases} -6x - 10y = -3 \\ 5x - 15y = 7 \end{cases}$ (2) $\begin{cases} -3x - 5y = -2 \\ 5x - 15y = 7 \end{cases}$ (3) $\begin{cases} -9x - 15y = -9 \\ 5x - 15y = 7 \end{cases}$ (4) $\begin{cases} 6x - 10y = -6 \\ 5x - 15y = 7 \end{cases}$

■ SOLUTION

The system in choice (3) is equivalent to the given system.

   $3(-3x - 5y) = -9x - 15y$ and $3(-3) = -9$ ✓

In the following example, the coefficients of each of the x-terms are opposites. When you add the terms of an equation, the x-term will be eliminated. Then you solve a simple one-variable equation.

EXAMPLE 7 **Solving a system with coefficients of one variable being opposites**

7 Solve $\begin{cases} -2x + 7y = 11 \\ 2x - 5y = -1 \end{cases}$ using the addition-multiplication method.

■ **SOLUTION**

Step 1 Use the Addition Property of Equality.

$$\begin{array}{rcr} -2x + 7y & = & 11 \\ + \ 2x - 5y & = & + \ -1 \\ \hline 2y & = & 10 \end{array}$$

$$y = 5$$

Step 2 If $y = 5$, then $-2x + 7(5) = 11$. So, $x = 12$.

The solution is $(12, 5)$.

You can carefully consider the equations of a system to determine which equation to rewrite.

EXAMPLE 8 **Using addition and one multiplier to solve a system**

8 Solve $\begin{cases} 4a + 2b = 7 \\ 2a + 5b = 4 \end{cases}$ by using addition and multiplication.

■ **SOLUTION**

Step 1 Multiply each side of $2a + 5b = 4$ by -2.

$$-4a - 10b = -8$$

Step 2 Add.

$$\begin{array}{rcr} 4a + \ 2b & = & 7 \\ + -4a - 10b & = & + -8 \\ \hline -8b & = & -1 \end{array}$$

$$b = \frac{1}{8}$$

Step 3 If $b = \frac{1}{8}$, then

$$2a + 5\left(\frac{1}{8}\right) = 4.$$

$$a = \frac{27}{16}$$

The solution to the system is $\left(\frac{27}{16}, \frac{1}{8}\right)$.

Sometimes you need to use the Multiplication Property of Equality twice to solve a system of equations.

118

EXAMPLE 9   **Using addition and two multipliers to solve a system**

9 Solve $\begin{cases} 2x + 3y = 15 \\ 5x - 2y = -29 \end{cases}$ by using the addition-multiplication method.

■ **SOLUTION**

$$\begin{cases} 2x + 3y = 15 \\ 5x - 2y = -29 \end{cases} \rightarrow \begin{cases} 2(2x + 3y) = 2(15) \\ 3(5x - 2y) = 3(-29) \end{cases} \rightarrow \begin{array}{r} 4x + 6y = \quad\; 30 \\ +15x - 6y = +\, -87 \\ \hline 19x \qquad\qquad -57 \end{array}$$

Therefore, $x = -3$. Substitute -3 for x in one of the given equations.
$$2(-3) + 3y = 15$$
$$y = 7$$

So, the solution is $(-3, 7)$.

Check: $\begin{cases} 2(-3) + 3(7) = -6 + 21 = 15 \quad \checkmark \\ 5(-3) - 2(7) = -15 - 14 = -29 \quad \checkmark \end{cases}$

Another solution method that can be implemented by using a calculator is a matrix solution. From the system below we can form a **coefficient matrix,** a **variable matrix,** and a **solution matrix.**

$$\begin{cases} 2x + 3y = 15 \\ 5x - 2y = -29 \end{cases}$$

$$A = \begin{bmatrix} 2 & 3 \\ 5 & -2 \end{bmatrix} \qquad\qquad \begin{bmatrix} x \\ y \end{bmatrix} \qquad\qquad B = \begin{bmatrix} 15 \\ -29 \end{bmatrix}$$

coefficient   variable   constant
matrix   matrix   matrix

You can enter these matrices into the calculator and multiply both sides of the equation by the inverse of [A], [A]$^{-1}$, to solve the following matrix equation:

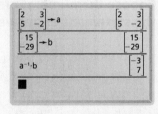

$$[A] \cdot \begin{bmatrix} x \\ y \end{bmatrix} = [B]$$

The solution is shown in the final matrix, $x = -3$ and $y = 7$.

A second matrix solution is to enter the augmented matrix C and execute a rref (row reduced echelon form) calculation. The solution is shown in the last column of the result $x = -3$ and $y = 7$.

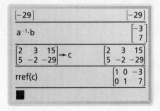

Note

The augmented matrix is formed by using the coefficients and the constants in one matrix.

You can use a system of equations to solve problems that describe two equations.

EXAMPLE 10

Using the addition-multiplication method to solve real-world problems

10 Twice one integer plus 3 times a second integer equals 9. Five times the first integer plus 4 times the second integer equals 5. What are the numbers?

■ **SOLUTION**

Step 1 Write a system of equations.

Twice one integer m plus 3 times a second integer n equals 9.   → $2m + 3n = 9$

Five times the first integer m plus 4 times the second integer n equals 5. → $5m + 4n = 5$

Step 2 Solve the system of equations.

Multiply by 5.
Multiply by −2.

$$\begin{cases} 2m + 3n = 9 \\ 5m + 4n = 5 \end{cases} \rightarrow \begin{cases} 10m + 15n = 45 \\ -10m - 8n = -10 \end{cases} \rightarrow$$

$$\begin{array}{r} 10m + 15n = 45 \\ +\ -10m - 8n = +\ -10 \\ \hline 7n = 35 \end{array}$$

Therefore, $n = 5$. Substitute 5 for n in $2m + 3n = 9$ to find m.

$$2m + 3(5) = 9$$
$$m = -3$$

Step 3 Answer the question. The first number is −3. The second number is 5.

Check: $\begin{cases} 2(-3) + 3(5) = -6 + 15 = 9 \quad \checkmark \\ 5(-3) + 4(5) = -15 + 20 = 5 \quad \checkmark \end{cases}$

Practice

Choose the numeral preceding the word or expression that best completes the statement or answers the question.

1 Which ordered pair (a, b) is the solution to $\begin{cases} b = 3.5a \\ b = 2a - 3 \end{cases}$?

(1) $(0, 0)$ **(3)** $(2, -3.5)$

(2) $(2, -8)$ **(4)** $(-2, -7)$

2 A line segment 15 inches long is separated into two smaller segments. The length y of the longer segment is 3 inches more than twice the length x of the shorter segment. Which system cannot represent this situation?

(1) $\begin{cases} x + y = 15 \\ y = 2x + 3 \end{cases}$ **(3)** $\begin{cases} x + y = 15 \\ x = 2y + 3 \end{cases}$

(2) $\begin{cases} y = 2x + 3 \\ x + y = 15 \end{cases}$ **(4)** $\begin{cases} y = 15 - x \\ y = 2x + 3 \end{cases}$

3 Which system of equations represents this situation?

Nikki has 20 dimes and quarters in all. Their total value is $3.80.

Let d represent the number of dimes and q represent the number of quarters.

(1) $\begin{cases} d + q = 20 \\ 25q + 10d = 3.80 \end{cases}$

(2) $\begin{cases} d + q = 20 \\ d + q = 3.80 \end{cases}$

(3) $\begin{cases} d + q = 20 \\ 10d + 25q = 3.80 \end{cases}$

(4) $\begin{cases} d + q = 20 \\ 0.1d + 0.25q = 3.80 \end{cases}$

120

4 Which system of equations has the same

solution as $\begin{cases} 5x - 3y = 24 \\ 2x - 7y = 11 \end{cases}$?

(1) $\begin{cases} 10x - 6y = 48 \\ 2x - 7y = 11 \end{cases}$

(2) $\begin{cases} 5x - 3y = 48 \\ 2x - 7y = 11 \end{cases}$

(3) $\begin{cases} 10x - 6y = 24 \\ 2x - 7y = 11 \end{cases}$

(4) $\begin{cases} 5x - 3y = 24 \\ 10x - 35y = 11 \end{cases}$

In Exercises 5–12, solve each system of equations.

5 $\begin{cases} x = 2y - 3 \\ 2x - 3y = -5 \end{cases}$ **6** $\begin{cases} y = 4 - 4x \\ 3x + y = 5 \end{cases}$

7 $\begin{cases} x = 3y + 5 \\ y = 2x + 1 \end{cases}$ **8** $\begin{cases} 2x + 3y = 0 \\ -2x + 5y = 8 \end{cases}$

9 $\begin{cases} 3x - 7y = 13 \\ 6x + 5y = 7 \end{cases}$ **10** $\begin{cases} 2x + 3y = 21 \\ 5x - 2y = -14 \end{cases}$

11 $\begin{cases} 2x = y + 12 \\ 3x + 2y = -3 \end{cases}$ **12** $\begin{cases} 5x = 4y + 15 \\ 6y = 3x - 9 \end{cases}$

In Exercises 13–20, use a system of equations to solve each problem.

13 The larger of two supplementary angles is 15° more than twice the measure of the smaller angle. Find each angle measure.

14 Top Tunes sells CDs for a single price and sells tapes for a single price. Bianna bought 3 CDs and 2 tapes for $58. Ramon bought 1 CD and 4 tapes for $46. Determine the selling price for 1 CD and for 1 tape.

15 The sum of two numbers is 70. The difference of the these numbers is 24. What are the numbers?

16 Tickets for the school play sell for $3 for a student and $5 for an adult. One night, 595 people bought tickets. The school took in $1951. How many adult tickets and how many student tickets were sold?

17 There are 250 students in the freshman class. The number of girls is 20 fewer than twice the number of boys. How many boys and how many girls are in the class?

18 The length of a rectangular flower garden is 6 feet more than three times the width. The perimeter of the garden is 32 feet. What is the area of the garden?

19 Stefan has a collection of nickels, dimes, and quarters. In all, he has 24 coins. Seven of the coins are quarters. The total value of the collection is $2.90. How many nickels and how many dimes does he have?

20 Delila has $1200 in a savings account and in a checking account. The ratio of money in savings to money in checking is 3 to 2. Use a system of equations to find how much money is in each account.

In Exercises 21–25, solve the problem. Clearly show all necessary work.

21 For what value of k will the system of equations below have no solution? Explain.

$$\begin{cases} 2x - 4y = 6 \\ kx - 4y = 9 \end{cases}$$

22 The graphs of $kx + 2y = 2$ and $2x + hy = 10$ intersect at $(2, -2)$. Find h and k.

23 What are the coordinates of the point where the graphs of the equations below intersect?

$$3x - 5y = 4 \text{ and } 4x + 7y = 19$$

24 Find the measures in degrees of the angles indicated by x and y. The measure of angle y is 15 degrees more than 3 times the measure of angle x.

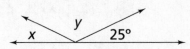

25 Find k such that the graphs of $y = 3x + 4$ and $y = kx - 5$ do not intersect.

4.7 Linear Inequalities in Two Variables

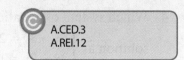
A.CED.3
A.REI.12

On a number line, the graph of $x \geq 3$ is a closed ray. In the coordinate plane, the graph of $x \geq 3$ is a **closed half-plane**. The graph of $x > 3$ is an **open half-plane**.

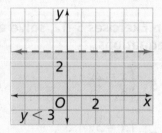

The **boundary** of the graph is the line separating it from the rest of the plane.

- If the inequality contains $\leq$ or $\geq$, the boundary is part of the solution.

$$\leq \text{ or } \geq \quad \text{solid line}$$

- If the inequality contains $>$ or $<$, the boundary is not part of the solution.

$$> \text{ or } < \quad \text{dashed line}$$

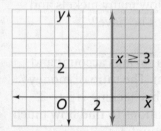 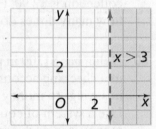 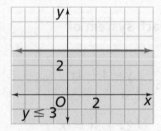 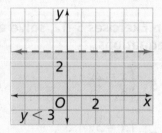

A **linear inequality in two variables** x and y is any inequality that can be written in one of these forms:

$$ax + by \geq c \qquad ax + by > c \qquad ax + by \leq c \qquad ax + by < c,$$

where a, b, and c are real numbers and not both a and b equal 0. A **solution to an inequality in two variables** is any ordered pair that makes the inequality true. The **graph of an inequality in two variables** is the graph of all solutions.

EXAMPLES 1 and 2 Graphing a linear inequality in two variables

Graph each linear inequality in two variables.

1 $y > x - 2$

■ SOLUTION

Graph $y = x - 2$ with a dashed line because the given inequality involves $>$. The solution region is all points above the graph of $y = x - 2$.

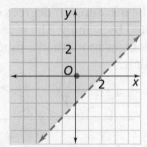

To check, test a point in the plane. For example, $(0, 0)$ satisfies $y > x - 2$. So, it is in the solution region.

2 $y \leq -2x - 2$

■ SOLUTION

Graph $y = -2x - 2$ with a solid line because the given inequality involves $\leq$. The solution region is all points on or below the graph of $y = -2x - 2$.

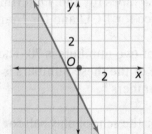

To check, test a point in the plane. For example, $(0, 0)$ does not satisfy $y \leq -2x - 2$. So, it is not in the solution region.

Sometimes it is easier to solve the inequality for y before graphing.

EXAMPLES 3 and 4 **Graphing a linear inequality in which y is not isolated**

Graph each linear inequality in two variables.

3 $2x + 3y < 9$

■ **SOLUTION**

Solve for y. $y < -\dfrac{2}{3}x + 3$

Graph $y = -\frac{2}{3}x + 3$ with a dashed line. Shade the region below the line.

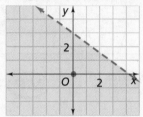

Because $(0, 0)$ satisfies $2x + 3y < 9$, the solution contains the origin.

4 $2x - 3y \geq 9$

■ **SOLUTION**

Solve for y. $y \leq \dfrac{2}{3}x - 3$

Graph $y = \frac{2}{3}x - 3$ with a solid line. Shade the line and the region below the line.

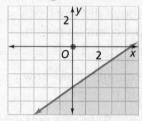

Because $(0, 0)$ does not satisfy $2x - 3y \geq 9$, the solution does not contain the origin.

A **system of inequalities in two variables** is a set of inequalities in those variables, as illustrated below. A **solution to a system of inequalities** is any ordered pair that makes all of the inequalities in the system true.

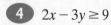
$$\begin{cases} y \geq -x + 2 \\ x \geq 0 \\ y \geq 0 \end{cases}$$

EXAMPLE 5 **Recognizing the correct solution region for a system**

5 Which system of inequalities represents the solution region shown here?

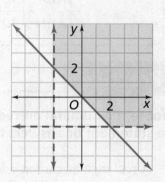

(1) $\begin{cases} y \geq -x \\ x > -2 \\ y > -2 \end{cases}$ **(2)** $\begin{cases} y \geq -x \\ x > -2 \\ y < -2 \end{cases}$ **(3)** $\begin{cases} y \geq -x \\ x < -2 \\ y < -2 \end{cases}$ **(4)** $\begin{cases} y \geq -x \\ x < -2 \\ y > -2 \end{cases}$

■ **SOLUTION**

The shaded region lies entirely to the right of $x = -2$ and above $y = -2$. It is also on and above the line $y = -x$. Only choice (1) meets all these conditions. The correct choice is **(1)**.

A system of linear inequalities can also consist of a pair of inequalities in two variables.

123

EXAMPLE 6 **Graphing systems of linear inequalities**

6 Graph this system of linear inequalities. $\begin{cases} 2x + 3y \le 6 \\ -5x + 2y > -4 \end{cases}$

■ **SOLUTION**

Solve for y. $\begin{cases} y \le -\frac{2}{3}x + 2 \\ y > \frac{5}{2}x - 2 \end{cases}$

Graph $y = -\frac{2}{3}x + 2$ with a solid line, and graph

$y = \frac{5}{2}x - 2$ with a dashed line.

Shade below the graph of $y = -\frac{2}{3}x + 2$. ▪

Shade above the graph of $y = \frac{5}{2}x - 2$. ▪
Shade the common region. ▪

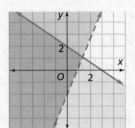

The following example shows how you can use a system of inequalities to solve a real-world problem.

EXAMPLE 7 **Solving a real-world problem by using a system of inequalities**

7 A gardener wants to use at least 40 feet and no more than 120 feet of fencing to enclose a rectangular garden. The length is equal to or greater than its width. What possible dimensions may the garden have if dimensions are multiples of 10 feet?

■ **SOLUTION**

Let L represent length in feet and W represent width in feet. Graph the solution to the system at the right. Mark points whose coordinates are multiples of 10. Keep in mind that length and width must be positive.

$\begin{cases} L + W \ge 20 \\ L + W \le 60 \\ L \ge W \end{cases}$

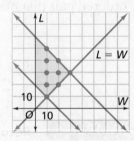

Make a table listing ordered pairs that satisfy all conditions.

Width	10	10	10	10	10	20	20	20	30
Length	10	20	30	40	50	20	30	40	30

Practice

Choose the numeral preceding the word or expression that best completes the statement or answers the question.

1 A rectangular garden is to have a perimeter no more than 66 feet. The length of the garden is to be at least twice the width. Which dimensions satisfy these conditions?

(1) length 20 feet and width 20 feet
(2) length 40 feet and width 20 feet
(3) length 30 feet and width 10 feet
(4) length 20 feet and width 8 feet

2 Sheila has nickels and dimes but not more than 25 coins. The value of the coins is between $2.00 and $3.00. Which combination of coins is not possible?

(1) 6 nickels and 18 dimes
(2) 8 nickels and 10 dimes
(3) 7 nickels and 18 dimes
(4) 1 nickel and 21 dimes

3 Which is a solution to $\begin{cases} y \le 3x + 5 \\ y \ge -x - 5 \end{cases}$?

(1) $x = 0, y = 5$ **(3)** $x = 4, y = -10$

(2) $x = -3, y = -7$ **(4)** $x = 0, y = -6$

4 Which system has the shaded region as its solution?

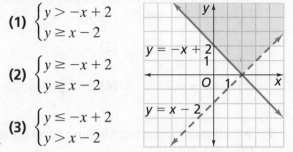

(1) $\begin{cases} y > -x + 2 \\ y \ge x - 2 \end{cases}$

(2) $\begin{cases} y \ge -x + 2 \\ y \ge x - 2 \end{cases}$

(3) $\begin{cases} y \le -x + 2 \\ y > x - 2 \end{cases}$

(4) $\begin{cases} y \ge -x + 2 \\ y > x - 2 \end{cases}$

5 Which accurately describes the solution region for $y \le -4x + 11$?

(1) all points on or below the graph of $y = -4x + 11$

(2) all points on or above the graph of $y = -4x + 11$

(3) all points below but not on the graph of $y = -4x + 11$

(4) all points above but not on the graph of $y = -4x + 11$

6 Which inequality symbol will make the solution region all points above but not on the graph of $y = 13x + 9$?

$$y \_\_\_\_\_ 13x + 9$$

(1) $\le$ **(2)** $\ge$ **(3)** $<$ **(4)** $>$

7 The length of a board in feet is between 14 and 16. The board is cut into two unequal pieces. Which pair of lengths is possible?

(1) 7 and 6   **(3)** 7 and 8

(2) 7.5 and 7.5   **(4)** 9 and 8

In Exercises 8–13, graph each linear inequality in two variables.

8 $y > x$ **9** $y \le x$

10 $y \ge 2x - 3$ **11** $y \le -x + 4$

12 $2x + y < 3$ **13** $2x + 3y \ge 6$

In Exercises 14–17, graph each system of linear inequalities in two variables.

14 $\begin{cases} y \le x + 2 \\ y \ge x - 2 \end{cases}$ **15** $\begin{cases} y \ge 3 \\ y > x \end{cases}$

16 $\begin{cases} y \le 3x + 2 \\ y < -2x + 1 \end{cases}$ **17** $\begin{cases} y < \frac{3}{5}x + 4 \\ -3x + 5y \ge -5 \end{cases}$

In Exercises 18–20, solve the problem. Clearly show all necessary work.

18 Today Jessica and Melissa are having a birthday. Both girls are at least 9 years old but not older than 16. If Melissa is 2 years older than Jessica, how old can they be? Show your work.

19 Graph the solution to $y \ge x$, $y \le 3$, and $y \ge -2x + 1.5$. Describe the solution region.

20 Jeremy is thinking of two positive integers. He says that their sum is less than 6 and both numbers are at least 2. What could the numbers be? Show your work and explain your reasoning.

21 Write a system of inequalities that define the shaded region in the accompanying figure.

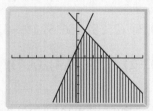

22 Write a system of inequalities that would create the shaded parallelogram shown in the accompanying figure.

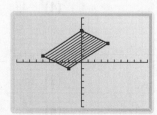

Preparing for the Assessment

Choose the numeral preceding the word or expression that best completes the statement or answers the question.

1 Which is the slope of the line containing $P(-5, 6)$ and $Q(3, -1)$?

(1) $-\dfrac{8}{7}$ **(3)** $\dfrac{7}{2}$

(2) $-\dfrac{7}{8}$ **(4)** $\dfrac{5}{2}$

2 Which is true of all points in the third quadrant?

(1) positive x-coordinate; positive y-coordinate

(2) negative x-coordinate; negative y-coordinate

(3) negative x-coordinate; positive y-coordinate

(4) positive x-coordinate; negative y-coordinate

3 Which list does not represent a function?

(1) $\{(0, 1), (1, 3), (2, 5), (3, 7)\}$

(2) $\{(-2, 2), (0, 3), (2, 4), (4, 5)\}$

(3) $\{(9, 3), (25, 5), (36, 6), (9, -3)\}$

(4) $\{(0, -2), (1, 1), (2, 4), (3, 7)\}$

4 Which of the following is not a value in the range of the function $\{(-2, 4), (0, -4), (1, -2), (3, 14)\}$?

(1) 1 **(3)** 14

(2) -2 **(4)** -4

5 If $y = \dfrac{2}{3}x - 4$ and $x = 15$, find y.

(1) 6 **(3)** 14

(2) 26 **(4)** $\dfrac{37}{2}$

6 Which of the following is the equation in slope-intercept form for the line containing $P(4, 1)$ with slope $\frac{3}{4}$?

(1) $y = \dfrac{3}{4}x + 1$ **(3)** $y = \dfrac{3}{4}x - \dfrac{13}{4}$

(2) $y = \dfrac{3}{4}x - 2$ **(4)** $y = \dfrac{3}{4}x + 4$

7 Which point lies along the line containing $P(-1, 2)$ and $Q(2, -4)$?

(1) $(-1, -2)$ **(3)** $(6, 12)$

(2) $(1, 2)$ **(4)** $(2, -4)$

8 The point $M(-2, t)$ is on the graph of $y = \frac{1}{4}x - 3$. What is the value of t?

(1) $-\dfrac{5}{2}$ **(3)** $-\dfrac{7}{2}$

(2) -1 **(4)** $-\dfrac{25}{8}$

9 Which ordered pair (a, b) is a solution to $\begin{cases} 3a + b = 5 \\ a - 5b = -9 \end{cases}$?

(1) $(4, -7)$ **(3)** $(3, -4)$

(2) $(1, 2)$ **(4)** $(-4, 1)$

10 The sum of two numbers x and y is 49. Twice one number less 14 is the other number. Which system could not represent this situation?

(1) $\begin{cases} x + y = 49 \\ 14 - 2x = 49 \end{cases}$

(2) $\begin{cases} x + y = 49 \\ 2x - 14 = y \end{cases}$

(3) $\begin{cases} 49 = x + y \\ y = 2x - 14 \end{cases}$

(4) $\begin{cases} 2x - 14 = y \\ x + y = 49 \end{cases}$

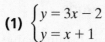

11 Which system of equations is dependent?

(1) $\begin{cases} y = 3x - 2 \\ y = x + 1 \end{cases}$ **(3)** $\begin{cases} x + y = 5 \\ y = x + 5 \end{cases}$

(2) $\begin{cases} y = x - 1 \\ y - 1 = x \end{cases}$ **(4)** $\begin{cases} y = \dfrac{2}{5}x - 4 \\ 5y = 2x - 20 \end{cases}$

12 Which system of equations has no solution?

(1) $\begin{cases} y = x + 4 \\ 3x - 2y = 10 \end{cases}$ **(3)** $\begin{cases} y = x - 2 \\ 3x + 3y = 12 \end{cases}$

(2) $\begin{cases} y = -3x - 5 \\ 2x - 2y = 50 \end{cases}$ **(4)** $\begin{cases} y = x - 4 \\ 3x - 3y = 15 \end{cases}$

13 Which system of equations is equivalent to $\begin{cases} -2x + 4y = -8 \\ 6x - 3y = 15 \end{cases}$?

(1) $\begin{cases} -4x + 8y = -16 \\ 6x - 3y = 15 \end{cases}$

(2) $\begin{cases} -2x + 4y = -8 \\ 18x - 9y = 15 \end{cases}$

(3) $\begin{cases} -x + 2y = -8 \\ 6x - 3y = 15 \end{cases}$

(4) $\begin{cases} -2x + 4y = -8 \\ 2x - y = 3 \end{cases}$

14 Which inequality symbol will make the solution region consist of all points below but not on the graph of $y = 7x - 3$?

(1) $\leq$ **(2)** $\geq$ **(3)** $<$ **(4)** $>$

15 Which accurately describes the solution region for the graph of $y \geq \frac{2}{3}x + 5$?

(1) all points on or below the graph of $y \geq \frac{2}{3}x + 5$

(2) all points on or above the graph of $y \geq \frac{2}{3}x + 5$

(3) all points below but not on the graph of $y \geq \frac{2}{3}x + 5$

(4) all points above but not on the graph of $y \geq \frac{2}{3}x + 5$

16 Brian and Lauren are at least 20 years old but not older than 30. If Lauren is 8 years younger than Brian, what could their ages be?

(1) 23 and 27

(2) 18 and 26

(3) 20 and 27

(4) 21 and 29

17 Which ordered pair (x, y) is the solution to this system? $\begin{cases} y = -2x + 7 \\ 2x + 5y = 19 \end{cases}$

(1) $(1, 5)$ **(3)** $(2, 3)$

(2) $(-3, 5)$ **(4)** $(3, 2)$

18 The vertex of $y + 3 = |x + 2|$ is

(1) $(2, 3)$.

(2) $(-2, 3)$.

(3) $(-2, -3)$.

(4) $(2, -3)$.

19 Which is the slope of a line perpendicular to the graph of $y = \frac{5}{4}x + 8$?

(1) -0.8 **(3)** 1.25

(2) 0.8 **(4)** -1.25

20 A collection of dimes and quarters has a value of \$4.60. The number of dimes is d and the number of quarters is q. Which equation represents this situation?

(1) $10d + 25q = 4.60$

(2) $25d + 10q = 460$

(3) $1.0d + 2.5q = 4.60$

(4) $0.1d + 0.25q = 4.60$

In Exercises 21–28, solve the problem. Clearly show all necessary work.

21 Write $-3x + 6y = 18$ in slope-intercept form and determine the slope and y-intercept.

22 If $\{-4, -2, 0, 2, 4\}$ is the domain, state the range of $y = 3x^2 - 2x$.

23 Find the vertex of $y = |x - 1| + 2$.

24 Write the equation for the translation of $y = |x|$ that is to the right three units and down two.

25 If Henry has 45 nickels and dimes totaling $2.90, write a system of equations that can be used to determine how many nickels (n) and dimes (d) Henry has.

26 Tara is thinking of two positive integers. She says their sum is less than 6. What could the numbers be if they are unequal?

27 What is a solution to $\begin{cases} y \leq 3x + 5 \\ y \geq -x - 5 \end{cases}$?

28 What is the slope of a line perpendicular to $y = \frac{2}{3}x + 10$? Explain your reasoning.

In Exercises 29–33, write an equation in slope-intercept form for each line.

29 slope -7 and y-intercept 4

30 containing $L(-3, 10)$ and $M(5, 6)$

31 slope -0.4 and containing $P(-6, 0)$

32 containing $Z(-2, -2)$ and parallel to the graph of $y = -x + 11$

33 containing $B(3, 7)$ and perpendicular to the graph of $y = -3x + 1.5$

In Exercises 34–35, solve the problem. Clearly show all necessary work.

34 Write the equation of the absolute value function that opens down and has a vertex at the point $(4, -2)$.

35 Is $(3, -4)$ a solution to the system at the right? Justify your response. $\begin{cases} y < x \\ y \geq -2x + 1 \end{cases}$

In Exercises 36–39, solve each system of equations.

36 $\begin{cases} y + 2x = -1 \\ y = 3x - 16 \end{cases}$

37 $\begin{cases} 3x - y = 9 \\ y = x + 1 \end{cases}$

38 $\begin{cases} 4a - 3b = 17 \\ 5a + 4b = 60 \end{cases}$

39 $\begin{cases} 6w - 4v = 11 \\ 3w = 23 - 5v \end{cases}$

In Exercises 40–43, graph each system of inequalities.

40 $\begin{cases} x + y \geq 6 \\ y \leq 4 \end{cases}$

41 $\begin{cases} 2x + 3y \leq 6 \\ y \geq x - 2 \end{cases}$

42 $\begin{cases} \frac{1}{3}x + y > 1 \\ x > 0 \end{cases}$

43 $\begin{cases} 3x + 2y \geq 2 \\ -2x + y \leq 1 \end{cases}$

In Exercises 44–45, solve the problem. Clearly show all necessary work.

44 Catlin has a total of $850 in her savings account and her checking account. The ratio of checking to savings is 3 to 7. How much does she have in each account?

45 A rectangular garden with perimeter 114 feet has length 3 feet more than twice width. Use a system of equations to find the dimensions of the garden.

5 Exponential Functions and Applications

Mathematician in the Spotlight

Shafi Goldwasser

Shafi Goldwasser was born in 1958 in New York City. As an Israeli-American, her dual citizenship would play an important role in her education and research. She moved to Tel Aviv with her family where, as a high school student, she became interested in physics, mathematics, and literature. Upon her return to the U.S., she enrolled in the mathematics department at Carnegie Mellon University. She then became interested in programming and computer science and pursued a graduate degree at University of California, Berkeley, followed by post-doctoral work at Massachusetts Institute of Technology (MIT).

Dr. Goldwasser is the RSA Professor of Electrical Engineering and Computer Science at MIT, a co-leader of the cryptography and information security group and a member of the complexity theory group within the Theory of Computation Group and the Computer Science and Artificial Intelligence Laboratory.

5.1 Exponential Functions

A.SSE.1a
F.LE.1a
F.LE.5
F.BF.2

Many teenagers would like to persuade their parents to pay them an allowance in the following way. One cent (1¢) is paid on the first day of the month and doubled each successive day. The table shows the amount to be paid each day for the month of February.

Day	Amount	Day	Amount
1	$0.01	15	$163.84
2	$0.02	16	$327.68
3	$0.04	17	$655.36
4	$0.08	18	$1,310.72
5	$0.16	19	$2,621.44
6	$0.32	20	$5,242.88
7	$0.64	21	$10,485.76
8	$1.28	22	$20,971.52
9	$2.56	23	$41,943.04
10	$5.12	24	$83,886.08
11	$10.24	25	$167,772.16
12	$20.48	26	$335,544.32
13	$40.96	27	$671,088.64
14	$81.92	28	$1,342,177.28

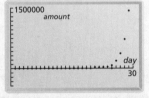

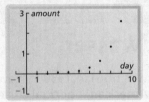

The amount paid on the last day in February is over one million dollars, and it all started with just one penny!

What pattern is in the table? Notice that each day the new amount is the previous amount multiplied by 2.

This is a **common ratio** for a geometric sequence!

The geometric sequence would be defined using the formula for the nth term: $a_n = a_1 \cdot r^{n-1}$

If $a_n = \$0.01$ and $r = 2$, then

$a_n = \$0.01 \cdot 2^{n-1}$ where n is the number of days expressed as an integer and $n \geq 1$.

Like a geometric sequence, if the dependent terms, $f(x)$, of the function have a common ratio, then this function is called an **Exponential Function**. The independent variable, x, is the exponent.

Exponential Functions

A function, f, defined by $f(x) = b^x$ where $b > 0$ and $b \neq 1$, is called an **Exponential Function**.

The Domain for Exponential functions is usually the set of real numbers. For work in Algebra I, the Domain will be **restricted** to the set of integers. Work with rational and irrational exponents will be addressed in Algebra 2.

EXAMPLE 1   Identifying exponential functions from tables

 Which of the tables below represent an exponential function?

A.

x	f(x)
−1	$\frac{1}{3}$
0	1
1	3
2	9
3	27

B.

n	f(n)
−1	2
0	3
1	4
2	5
3	6

C.

p	f(p)
−1	−1
0	0
1	1
2	8
3	27

D.

m	f(m)
−1	3
0	1
1	$\frac{1}{3}$
2	$\frac{1}{9}$
3	$\frac{1}{27}$

Note

The *b* value in an exponential function is the value of the common ratio.

■ **SOLUTION**

The exponential functions are A with a common ratio of 3 and D with a common ratio of $\frac{1}{3}$.

Examples of the exponential functions $y = 2^x$, $y = 3^x$, and $y = 5^x$ and their graphs are shown below.

x	2^x	3^x	5^x
1	$2^{-1} = \frac{1}{2}$	$3^{-1} = \frac{1}{3}$	$5^{-1} = \frac{1}{5}$
0	$2^0 = 1$	$3^0 = 1$	$5^0 = 1$
1	$2^1 = 2$	$3^1 = 3$	$5^1 = 5$
2	$2^2 = 4$	$3^2 = 9$	$5^2 = 25$
3	$2^3 = 8$	$3^3 = 27$	$5^3 = 125$

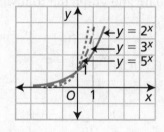

Notice that the point (0, 1) is the *y*-intercept for each of these graphs. Also notice that none of these graphs crosses the *x*-axis. There is no value of *x* for which *y* will be negative. The range of the exponential function is restricted to the set of positive real numbers, $(0, \infty)$.

EXAMPLE 2   Identifying the rule for an exponential function

 What would be the explicit function rule for Table A and D above?

■ **SOLUTION**

Table A: $f(x) = 3^x$ Table B: $f(m) = \left(\frac{1}{3}\right)^m$

Notice that the common ratio is the base of the exponential term.

Table and graph of an exponential function

3 Create a table of values for $x = \{-2, -1, 0, 1, 2\}$ and $y = f(x) = 5^x$.

■ **SOLUTION**

x	y
−2	0.04
−1	0.2
0	1
1	5
2	25

4 Create a graph of $y = f(x) = 5^x$

■ **SOLUTION**

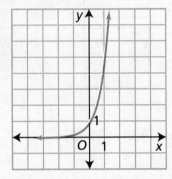

EXAMPLE 5   **Examining end behavior**

5 Evaluate and graph the following functions for $x = \{-2, -1, 0, 1, 2\}$.

$$f(x) = 4^x \quad \text{and} \quad f(x) = \left(\frac{1}{4}\right)^x = (0.25)^x$$

■ **SOLUTION** $f(x) = 4^x$

x	4^x
−2	$4^{-2} = \frac{1}{4^2} = \frac{1}{16}$
−1	$4^{-1} = \frac{1}{4}$
0	$4^0 = 1$
1	$4^1 = 4$
2	$4^2 = 16$

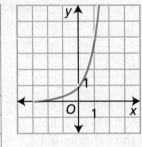

Notice that the curve of the function $f(x) = 4^x$ has a base that is greater than 1. The function is an increasing function rising from left to right and is unbounded.

$f(x) = \left(\frac{1}{4}\right)^x = (0.25)^x$

The function $f(x) = \left(\frac{1}{4}\right)^x = (0.25)^x$, has a base that is a value between 0 and 1. The function is decreasing from left to right and approaches the x-axis but never reaches it.

x	0.25^x
−2	$0.25^{-2} = 16$
−1	$0.25^{-1} = 4$
0	$0.25^0 = 1$
1	$0.25^1 = 0.25$
2	$0.25^2 = \frac{1}{16}$
3	$0.25^3 = \frac{1}{64}$

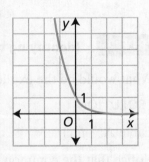

EXAMPLE 6 | **Examining exponential functions of the form**
$f(x) = ab^x$ **where a is non-zero**

MP

6 Evaluate and graph $f(x) = 3(4^x)$ for $x = \{-2, -1, 0, 1, 2\}$.

- **SOLUTION** $\quad f(x) = 3(4^x)$

x	$3(4^x)$
-2	$3(4^{-2}) = \dfrac{3}{16}$
-1	$3(4^{-1}) = \dfrac{3}{4}$
0	$3(4^0) = 3$
1	$3(4^1) = 12$
2	$3(4^2) = 48$
3	$3(4^3) = 192$

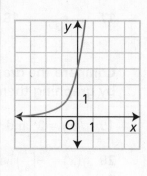

Notice that the common ratio of this exponential function is still 4 and the function is still increasing and has the expected positive end behavior.

Compare the table and graph of $f(x) = 3(4^x)$ to $f(x) = 4^x$ from example 5. The important change is that the y-intercept is no longer the expected $(0, 1)$. The coefficient of 3 is a factor of **each** exponential term and so changes the y-intercept from 1 to 3.

Practice

Choose the numeral preceding the word or expression that best completes the statement or answers the question.

1 Which function is shown in the graph?

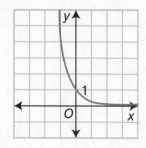

(1) $y = -0.5^x$ **(3)** $y = \left(\dfrac{1}{4}\right)^x$

(2) $y = 2(4^x)$ **(4)** $y = -(3)^x$

2 Which of the following is not an exponential function?

(1) $y = 0.2(8^x)$ **(3)** $y = 4x^2$

(2) $y = \left(\dfrac{1}{4}\right)^x + 2$ **(4)** $y = 2^x$

3 The graph of which function is shown below?

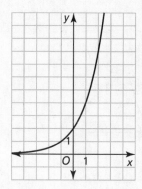

(1) $y = 2(2)^x$ **(3)** $y = 0.5^x$

(2) $y = 2\left(\dfrac{3}{4}\right)^x$ **(4)** $y = 2(0.5)^x$

In Exercises 4–7, solve the problem. Clearly show all necessary work.

4 When an exponential function has a base that is ≥ 1, does its graph rise or fall from left to right? Explain.

5 When an exponential function has a positive base that is ≤ 1, does its graph rise or fall from left to right? Explain.

6 Does the graph of an exponential function have an *x*-intercept? Explain.

7 Under what condition(s) does an exponential function have a *y*-intercept other than $(0, 1)$? Explain.

In Exercises 8–10, evaluate each function for $x = \{-2, -1, 0, 1, 2, 3\}$. Describe each function as increasing or decreasing and determine its end behavior.

8 $y = 2.5^x$ **9** $f(x) = 5(4^x)$ **10** $y = \left(\frac{2}{3}\right)^x$

In Exercises 11–13, match each of the following functions to its graph.

11 $y = 2^x$ **12** $y = \left(\frac{2}{3}\right)^x$ **13** $y = 5(2^x)$

(1)   **(3)**

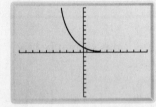   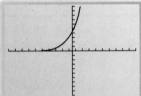

(2)

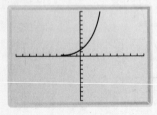

In Exercises 14–18, evaluate each function for $x = \{-2, -1, 0, 1, 2\}$ and graph the function.

14 $y = 2^x$ **15** $y = 0.5^x$ **16** $y = 2(3^x)$

17 $y = \left(\frac{1}{3}\right)^x$ **18** $f(x) = 0.4^x$

Compare the graphs of the functions below by graphing them on the same set if axis.

19 $f(x) = 2^x$ and $f(x) = -(2^x)$

20 $f(x) = -\left(\frac{3}{4}\right)^x$ and $f(x) = \left(\frac{3}{4}\right)^x$

21 Describe how the graphs of $f(x) = b^x$ and $f(x) = -b^x$ are related.

5.2 Exponential Growth and Decay

A.CED.1
F.LE.1a
F.LE.1c
F.LE.5

MP

Recall that an exponential function is of the form $y = a \cdot b^x$ where a is nonzero, $b > 0$, $b \neq 1$, and x is a real number. If the value of a is positive and the value of b is greater than 1, this function models growth.

Exponential Growth

Exponential growth can be modeled by the function
$$y = a \cdot b^x \text{ with } a > 0 \text{ and } b > 1.$$

a = the starting amount when $x = 0$.
b = is the growth factor and is greater than one.
x is the exponent.

EXAMPLE 1   **Solving problems involving exponential growth**

 If the population of Ontario County, New York, was 102,500 in 2003 and has been increasing at an average rate of 2.2% per year, find the projected population of the county in 2020. Round your answer to the nearest hundred.

■ **SOLUTION**

To determine the population of Ontario County, we can use the following formula.

Population in 2003
$\downarrow$

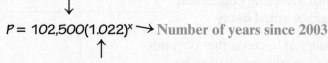

$P = 102{,}500(1.022)^x \rightarrow$ Number of years since 2003
$\uparrow$
Growth rate

$P = 102{,}500(1.022)^{17} = 102{,}500 \times 1.44766 \approx 148{,}400 \text{ people}$

Note

The growth rate is represented by $b = 1 + \%$ increase, where the 1 represents the whole amount before growth.

A function in the form $y = a \cdot b^x$ where a is greater than zero and b is between zero and one models exponential decay.

Exponential Decay

Exponential decay can be modeled by the function
$$y = a \cdot b^x \text{ with } a > 0 \text{ and } 0 < b < 1.$$

a = the starting amount when $x = 0$.
b = is the decay factor and is between zero and one.
x is the exponent.

The radioactive half-life of a substance is the length of time it takes for one half of the substance to decay.

 EXAMPLE 2 **Solving problems involving half-life with exponential decay**

2 Radioactive iodine is used to treat some medical conditions. The half-life of iodine-131 is 8 days. A doctor administers a 12-unit treatment to a patient. How much iodine-131 is left in the patient after 24 days?

■ SOLUTION

To write the decay function $f(x) = ab^x$ we need to define:
a, the initial amount = 12 unit treatment
b, the decay factor written as a fraction or decimal = 0.5 or $\frac{1}{2}$
and *x* is the number of 8 day cycles in 24 days or 24 ÷ 8 = 3.
The decay function is $f(x) = 12(0.5)^3 = 1.5$ units left.
This result can also be obtained in another way:

In 24 days, there are three 8-day half-lives.
After one half-life, there are 6 units.
After the second half-life, there are 3 units.
Finally, after the third half-life, there are 1.5 units.

Note

When a quantity is decreased by 10%, the result is 90% of the original quantity. When thinking of the decay factor, think of 100% minus the percent by which the quantity is decreasing.

You can also use exponential decay to model a decrease in population.

EXAMPLES 3 and 4 **Solving problems involving population decrease with exponential decay**

3 An antidote is introduced into a colony of bacteria that contains 1 million bacteria. If the antidote reduces the population by 25% every hour, what is the population after 24 hours?

■ SOLUTION

1,000,000	← This is the initial bacteria population.
1 − 0.25 = 0.75	← This is the decay factor.
$1,000,000(0.75)^x$	← This equation models the declining population.
$1,000,000(0.75)^{24}$	← This equation models the population after 24 hours.
$1,000,000(0.75)^{24} = 1,003.3913$	← This is the population after 24 hours.
≈ 1,003	

4 In 2000, the population of Someplace was 702,000 people. The population decreases about 1.7% per year. Predict the population of Someplace in 2015, rounded to the nearest thousand.

■ SOLUTION

702,000	← This is the initial number of people.
1 − 0.017 = 0.983	← This is the decay factor.
$y = 702,000(0.983)^x$	← This equation models the population since 2000.
$= 702,000(0.983)^{15}$	
= 542,800.05	
≈ 542,800 people	← This is the projected population in 2015.

Choose the numeral preceding the word or expression that best completes the statement or answers the question.

1 Which of the following is an exponential decay function with an initial amount of 2?

(1) $y = 5 \cdot 4^x$ **(3)** $y = 2(0.75)^x$

(2) $g(x) = \frac{1}{2}(3)^x$ **(4)** $f(t) = \frac{3}{4}\left(\frac{2}{3}\right)^t$

In Exercises 2–6, use the following information.
Suppose that the population of a city is 75,000 and is growing 2.5% per year.

2 What is the initial amount a?

3 What is the growth factor b?

4 What do you multiply 75,000 by to find the population after one year?

5 Write an equation to find the population after x years.

6 Use the equation to predict the population, rounded to the nearest thousand, after 25 years.

In Exercises 7–10, use the following information.
Suppose that the population of a large city was 8,000,000 six years ago, but since then it has been declining at an average rate of 1.75% per year.

7 What is the initial amount a?

8 What is the decay factor b?

9 Write an equation to find the population after x years.

10 Use the equation to predict the population, rounded to the nearest thousand, after 6 years.

11 The value of a new car decreases exponentially at a rate of 15% per year. A new car has an initial value of $24,000. What is the value of the car after 5 years?

In Exercises 12–15, identify the functions as *linear*, *exponential*, or *neither*.

12 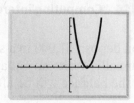   **13**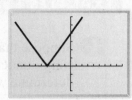

14 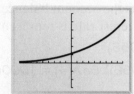   **15**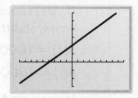

In Exercises 16–20, solve the problem. Clearly show all necessary work.

16 If the half-life of a certain compound is eight hours, how many half-lives occur in a two-day period?

17 The half-life of a certain substance is four days. If you have 100 grams of the substance, how much of it will remain after twelve days?

18 A common bacteria grows at a rate described by the function $B(t) = (3)^t$ where t is number of hours. How many bacteria are expected to have grown after 7 hours?

19 The amount in grams of a radioactive substance is given by the function $y = 50(1.7)^{-0.3t}$ where t is time in years. Find the number of grams of the substance after 20 years.

20 New vehicles lose value at a rate of 18.5% per year. Write an equation to calculate the value of a vehicle with an original value of $21,000 after t years.

5.3 More Exponential Applications

Interest earned or charged on your money is another situation treated as an exponential growth model.

EXAMPLES 1 and 2   **Computing interest earned**

 Suppose that you deposit $1,000 in a savings account that pays 5.6% interest compounded annually. Write an equation to model the account balance, and determine what the balance will be after 4 years.

■ **SOLUTION**

If A(t) represents the account balance, then t represents *time* measured in years, and the interest rate is represented as 1.056.

$A(t) = 1000(1.056)^t$

$A(t) = 1000(1.056)^t$. So $A(4) = 1000(1.056)^4 = 1243.528298 \approx \$1243.53$

Interest can be calculated more than once a year. The table below shows how the interest rate and time are effected by the number of compounding periods.

Compounding periods	Interest rate if r is the yearly rate	Times calculated if t is the number of years
Quarterly; 4 per year	$\frac{r}{4}$	$4t$
Monthly; 12 per year	$\frac{r}{12}$	$12t$
Daily; 365 per year	$\frac{r}{365}$	$365t$

 Determine the amount that a $5000 investment over 3 years at an annual interest rate of 7.25% is worth for each compounding period.

a. annually ■ SOLUTION $A = 5000(1.0725)^3 \approx \$6168.25$

b. quarterly ■ SOLUTION $A = 5000\left(1 + \dfrac{0.0725}{4}\right)^{12} \approx \$6202.73$

c. monthly ■ SOLUTION $A = 5000\left(1 + \dfrac{0.0725}{12}\right)^{36} \approx \$6210.76$

d. daily ■ SOLUTION $A = 5000\left(1 + \dfrac{0.0725}{365}\right)^{1095} \approx \$6214.69$

You can determine the equation of a function given a set of data.

EXAMPLE 3   Determining a function that models given data

③ The data from the table are shown in the accompanying scatter plot. Write an equation to model the data.

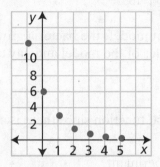

x	y
−1	12
0	6
1	3
2	1.5
3	0.75
4	0.375
5	0.1875

■ SOLUTION

The graph of the data suggests an exponential model. Test for a common ratio.

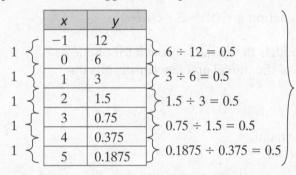

The common ratio is 0.5.

The value $y = 6$ when $x = 0$ determines the value of a.
The common ratio determines the decay factor. **Therefore, the equation that models these data is $y = 6(\frac{1}{2})^x = 6(0.5)^x$.**

Geometric sequences have a common ratio. They can be expressed and graphed as exponential functions.

EXAMPLE 4   Geometric sequences

④ Given the geometric sequence: 5, 12.5, 31.25, 78.125, ... write both the recursive and explicit function rules and graph the function.

Define all variables and any constraints on those variables.

■ SOLUTION

This geometric sequence has a common ratio of 2.5. If $n =$ the term position; n is an integer ≥ 1, then $G(n) =$ the value of each term of the sequence.

Explicit function rule: $G(n) = 5(2.5)^{n-1}$

Recursive function rule: $G(1) = 5$ and $G(n) = 2.5(G(n - 1))$

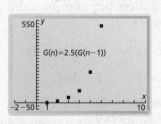

Note

An explicit function defines the function based on the term's position.

139

Note

A recursive function defines the function based on the previous term.

Shelley's biology experiment began with 5 bacteria in an agar medium. The table below shows the bacterial growth over the next four days.

Day	1	2	3	4
# Bacterial cells	5	15	45	135

5 Write a recursive function that models the bacteria growth for Shelley's experiment. Define all variables of the model and any constraints on those variables.

■SOLUTION

The data model an exponential function since there is a common ratio of 3.

d = the day number of the experiment.
Constraints: d is an integer and $d \geq 1$.

$G(d)$ = the number of bacteria cells on day d.

For $G(1) = 5$ and the recursive function is $G(d) = 3 \cdot G(d-1)$.

6 Write an explicit function that models the bacteria growth for Shelley's experiment. Define all variables of the model and any constraints on those variables.

■SOLUTION

d = the day number of the experiment.
Constraints: d is an integer and $d \geq 1$.

$G(d)$ = the number of bacteria cells on day d.

Since the model is exponential, use the formula $y = ab^x$ or $G(d) = ab^d$.

If $a = 5$ and $b = 3$, then $G(d) = 5 \cdot 3^{d-1}$.

Practice

1 Write an exponential equation to represent the value of an account with a $4000 principal that earns a rate of 4.5% compounded annually.

For Exercises 2–5: Find the value of a $4000 principal that earns a rate of 4.5% for each of the following compounding periods over 5 years.

2 annually   **3** quarterly

4 monthly   **5** daily

6 Find the value of a $500 investment that earns 3.5% for 7 years if compounded weekly.

7 If money can be invested at 8% interest, compounded quarterly, which would be worth more: $10,000 invested now for 5 years or a single payment of $12,500 in 5 years? Explain.

8 Determine whether the data in the accompanying table represent a linear, absolute value, or exponential function. Explain your reasoning.

x	y
1	3
2	9
3	27
4	81

For Exercises 9–11, use the data table from #8.

9 Write a function rule, $y = f(x)$ for the data.

10 If the pattern continued, find $f(10)$.

11 Predict a y-intercept value.

In Exercises 12–14, write the explicit or recursive function rule for each sequence.

12 Recursive function rule: $63, 42, 28, \frac{56}{3}, \frac{112}{9}, \frac{224}{27}$ … then graph the function.

13 Explicit function rule: $u_1 = 4$ and $r = \frac{1}{4}$ then write the first 4 terms.

14 $u_4 = -\frac{4}{5}$ and $r = \frac{2}{5}$. Find u_1 and the explicit function rule.

In Exercises 15–17, Clearly define variables, and state necessary constraints. Write the required function, then solve.

15 A ball is dropped from a height of 12 feet. Each time it hits the ground it rebounds to $\frac{3}{4}$ the height of the previous bounce. Write an explicit function rule and find the rebound height of the 5th bounce.

16 Mrs. Hamm shocks her pool with 5.4 gallons of chlorine. Each day 10% of the chlorine evaporates so she adds 0.2 gallon more chlorine. Write a recursive function rule and find how much chlorine will in her pool at the end of the sixth day?

17 The triangle pattern below show the first three Sierpinski's Triangles. The pattern creates a new triangle using the previous triangle pattern.

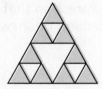

While there are many relationships in Sierpinski's Triangles, how are the perimeters of the triangles related? Write both an explicit and recursive function rule to find the perimeter of the 10th Sierpinski Triangle assuming the first triangle has a perimeter of 3 units.

18 When Anon solved exercise #13 in this Practice, he wrote the explicit function: $y = \left(\frac{1}{4}\right)^{n-2}$, also a correct form of the rule. Use the laws of negative exponents and exponent operations to show why it is equivalent to $y = 4\left(\frac{1}{4}\right)^{n-1}$.

Preparing for the Assessment

Choose the numeral preceding the word or expression that best completes the statement or answers the question.

1 Which of the following best describes the graph below?

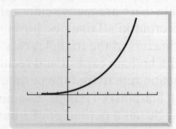

- **(1)** Linear growth
- **(2)** Exponential growth
- **(3)** Exponential decay
- **(4)** Quadratic growth

2 Which of the following best describes the graph below?

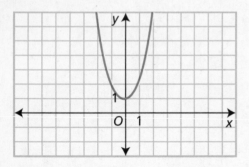

- **(1)** Linear growth
- **(2)** Exponential growth
- **(3)** Exponential decay
- **(4)** Quadratic relationship

In Exercises 3–6, match each of the following functions to its graph.

3 $y = \left(\dfrac{1}{4}\right)^x$

4 $y = -2(4^x)$

5 $y = 3^x$

6 $y = -(6^x)$

(1)

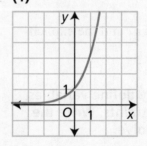

(3)

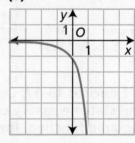

(2)

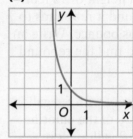

(4)

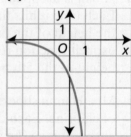

In Exercises 7 and 8, use the following information.

20% of a particular medicine is absorbed by the bloodstream every hour. A patient takes a 40 milligram dose of this medicine at 9 A.M.

7 Which function describes the amount of medicine absorbed in the bloodstream after x hours?

- **(1)** $y = 20(40)^x$
- **(2)** $\dfrac{1}{32}$
- **(3)** $y = 40(0.8)^x$
- **(4)** $y = 40(0.20)^x$

8 How many milligrams of medicine are absorbed in the bloodstream at 2 P.M.?

(1) 13.11 mg   **(3)** 0.0128 mg

(2) 160 mg   **(4)** 4,000 mg

9 Suppose that the population of a city is 22,500 and grows 3% per year. At this rate, what is the approximate projected population of this city in 8 years?

(1) 183,500   **(3)** 22,500

(2) 147,622,500   **(4)** 28,500

10 Which of the following is not an exponential function?

(1) $5^x - 3$ **(3)** $5x^3$

(2) $3\left(\dfrac{5}{2}\right)^x$ **(4)** $(0.25)^x$

11 Which exponential equation represents exponential decay?

(1) $y = 0.5(1.5)^x$

(2) $y = 1.5(3)^x$

(3) $y = \dfrac{7}{2}(2)^x$

(4) $y = 3\left(\dfrac{2}{7}\right)^x$

12 Explain when the function $y = ab^x$ shows exponential growth and when it shows exponential decay.

13 Construct a table of values for $y = \frac{1}{2} \cdot 2^x$, and graph this function, for $[-3, 3]$.

In Exercises 14–16, identify each sequence as arithmetic or geometric. Find the next term.

14 9, 6, 4, ...

15 9, 3, 1, ...

16 9, 6, 3, ...

In Exercises 17–19, graph each function to show its behavior for all real x.

17 $y = -\left(\dfrac{1}{2}\right)^x$

18 $y = 3.6^x$

19 $y = 7(0.5^x)$

In Exercises 20–22, for each of the functions graphed in 17–19 state the function's Domain, Range, Intercepts, End-behavior and if it is an increasing or decreasing function.

In Exercises 23–26, identify the initial amount a and the base b in each exponential function. Identify the function as growth or decay.

23 $y = \dfrac{1}{3}(5)^x$

24 $y = 4(0.25)^x$

25 $y = 6 \cdot 8^x$

26 $y = \dfrac{1}{3}\left(\dfrac{3}{4}\right)^x$

In Exercises 27–29, solve.

27 Suppose that you deposit $750 in a savings account that pays 4.8% interest compounded annually. Assuming no withdrawals or additional deposits, what is the balance after six years?

28 At the same time you deposited the $750 at 4.8% annually in Exercise 27, you deposited another $750 also at 4.8% but compounded monthly for the 6 years. How much more money did the account compounded monthly earn?

143

29 New vehicles lose value at a rate of 18.5% per year. Write an equation to calculate the value of a vehicle with an original value of $65,000 after t years.

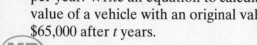

In Exercises 30–34, clearly define variables, and state necessary constraints. Write the required function, then solve.

30 You are asked to monitor the reproduction growth in a colony of bees over a 5 week period. The table below shows the bee populations at the end of each week.

Week	0	1	2	3	4	5
Population	64	96	144	216	324	?

Growth is known to be exponential. Define variables, state constraints, and write a function to model the observed bee growth.

31 According to your model, what would be the predicted bee population at the end of week 5?

32 Another observed colony of bees doubles its population each week. What would have been its initial population if there are 640 bees in the colony at the end of 5 weeks.

$A(n) = 2(3)^n$ and $B(n) = 2 + 3n$.

33 What type of function is $A(n)$ and $B(n)$?

34 In the interval $-2 \leq n \leq 2$, about how many time larger is the average rate of change of $A(n)$ compared to the average rate of change of $B(n)$.

In Exercises 35–37, write the explicit or recursive function rule for each sequence.

35 Recursive function rule: $64, 48, 36, 27, \frac{81}{4} \dots$ then graph the function.

36 Explicit function rule: $u_1 = 90$ and $r = \frac{5}{3}$ then write the first 4 terms.

37 $u_4 = -\frac{16}{25}$ and $r = \frac{2}{5}$. Find u_1 and the explicit function rule.

6 Transformations in the Plane

6.1 Vertical Shifts in Functions

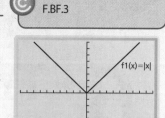

Fig. 6-1

There are a number of transformations that can be performed on functions. They can be stretched, shifted, and reflected. By transforming the function a new function is formed. Our investigation will begin with the transformation known as a translation. A **translation** does not change the shape of the graph of a function but only moves the graph to a different position in the coordinate plane (Fig. 6-1).

You have learned that the **absolute value** of a number is its distance from zero on a number line. The definition of the **absolute value function** can take a number of forms.

(MP)

$$abs(x) = |x| = \begin{cases} x \text{ if } x \ge 0 \\ -x \text{ if } x < 0 \end{cases} = \begin{cases} x \text{ if } x \text{ is positive or zero} \\ \text{the opposite of } x \text{ if } x \text{ is negative} \end{cases} = \sqrt{x^2}$$

Figure 6-2 shows the graphs of the absolute value function using these three definitions. Notice all three graphs lie on top of each other. This provides strong visual evidence for the equivalence of these three definitions.

Studying a table of values for the absolute value function, you will see that if x is negative, $f(x)$ is the opposite of x and if x is positive or zero, $f(x)$ is equal to x.

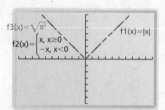

Fig. 6-2

x	$f(x) = |x|$
-3	3
-2	2
-1	1
0	0
1	1
2	2
3	3

Now imagine grabbing the graph of $f(x) = |x|$ and shifting it upward three units. What would the equation of the resulting function be? Let us first consider what the graph of the new function would look like. Moving the graph of $f(x) = |x|$ up three units would result in a graph like the one shown in Figure 6-3. Notice that every point on the original graph of $f(x) = |x|$ is shifted vertically three units resulting in the new function graph. Each new function value equals the old function value plus three. Writing this algebraically with N representing the new function we have:

$$N(x) = f(x) + 3 = |x| + 3.$$

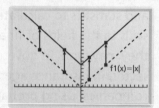

Fig. 6-3

EXAMPLE 1   Sketching a vertical shift

Sketch the result of shifting the function $g(x)$ shown in the graph down 5 units.
Write an expression for the new function k in terms of g.

■ SOLUTION

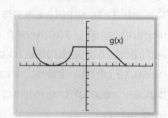

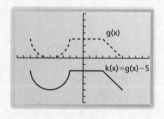

Vertical Shifts

If $y = f(x)$ is a function and k is a constant, then the graph of $y = f(x) + k$ is the graph of $f(x)$ shifted vertically k units. If k is positive the shift is up; if k is negative the shift is down. Because this shift is caused by a change in the output value it is called an **external change**.

EXAMPLE 2   **Writing an equation from a graph**

Write an equation for each of the translations of $y = |x|$ shown below.

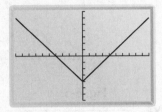   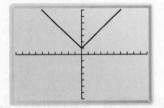

■ SOLUTION

$y = |x| - 4$

■ SOLUTION

$y = |x| + 1$

Practice

1 Under a translation 4 units up the point $(4, 0)$ would be located at

(1) $(4, 4)$ **(3)** $(0, 4)$

(2) $(4, -4)$ **(4)** $(-4, 4)$

2 The function $g(x)$ is to be translated three units down. The new function in terms of $g(x)$ would be

(1) $3g(x)$ **(3)** $g(x) - 3$

(2) $g(x - 3)$ **(4)** $g(3x)$

3 Two balls are thrown in the air at the same time and with the same initial velocity. For one, the height is given by $f(t)$. The second ball is thrown from a location 20 feet higher than the first ball. Its height is given by $h(t)$.

a. How does the graph of $h(t)$ compare with the graph of $f(t)$?

b. Write an expression for $h(t)$ in terms of $f(t)$.

4 A function table for $k(w)$ is given below. Complete the second table for the function $d(w) = k(w) + 3$.

w	−2	−1	1	3	5	8	10
k(w)	2	−1	−1	2	5	9	7

5 The graph of $g(x)$ is shown in the accompanying figure. Sketch the graph of $z(x) = g(x) + 3$.

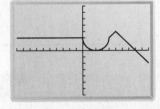

6 The point (x, y) is on the graph of $z(x)$ which point is on the graph of $z(x) + 4$?

(1) $(x, 4)$ **(3)** $(x, y + 4)$

(2) $(x + 4, y)$ **(4)** $(x + 4, y + 4)$

7 The graph of $f(x)$ is shown solid in the accompanying figure. Express in terms of $f(x)$ an equation for the function $s(x)$ shown dashed.

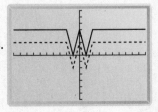

6.2 Horizontal Shifts

A manufacturing process, which runs 24 hours a day, causes the temperature of a machine to vary by three degrees as shown in Figure 6-4. If the machine must be shut down for 4 hours, what will the variation look like for this machine in the subsequent 24 hour period?

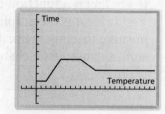

Fig. 6-4

With the machine shut down the process is shifted by 4 hours, so the new graph looks like the bold graph in Figure 6-5. The graph is shifted 4 units to the right because the process has been delayed by 4 hours. The temperature of the machine after the delay is equal to the temperature under the old process minus 4 hours. Written algebraically we would have $s(x) = f(x - 4)$.

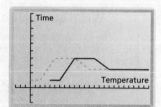

Fig. 6-5

EXAMPLES 1 and 2   **Interpreting horizontal shifts – Which way?**

1 Use a graphing calculator to graph $f(x) = |x|$. Now create a new function which is a transformation of $f(x)$ with a vertex at $(3, 0)$. What is the equation of the new function?

■ **SOLUTION**

The equation of the new function is shown. $f2(x) = |x - 3|$.

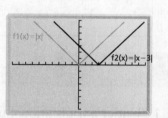

2 What if the point $(-5, 0)$ was to be the vertex? What would the equation be? Verify your answer using a graphing calculator.

■ **SOLUTION**

$f2(x) = |x + 5|$

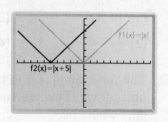

Horizontal Shifts

If $y = g(x)$ is a function and k is a constant, then the graph of $y = g(x + k)$ is the graph of $g(x)$ shifted horizontally k units. If k is **positive the shift is to the left. If k is negative the shift is to the right.** Because horizontal shifts involve a change in the input value x they are called an **internal change** to the function $g(x)$.

1 The graph of $f(x)$ is shown. Which of the following is the graph of $f(x-3)$?

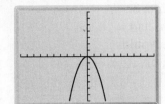

(1)

(2)

(3)

(4)

2 The point (a, b) is on the graph of $k(x)$. Which point is on the graph of $k(x+2)$?

(1) $(a, b+2)$

(2) $(a+2, b)$

(3) $(a, b-2)$

(4) $(a-2, b)$

3 How many fixed points are there when a graph in the coordinate plane is translated up three units?

(1) One (the origin)

(2) Infinitely many

(3) None

(4) All the points on the x-axis

4 Assume the height of high tide in NYC is given by the function $N(d)$ for a specific day, d, of the year. Find formulas, in terms of $N(d)$, for each of the following.

a. $A(d)$, the height of high tide in Atlantic City on day d given that high tide in Atlantic city is always two feet higher than in NYC.

b. $T(d)$, the height of high tide in Toms River on day d given that hight tide in Toms River is the same height as the previous day's tide in NYC.

5 The accompanying figure shows the graph of $f(x)$ as dashed and the graphs of $g(x)$ and $h(x)$. Which of the following is/are true?

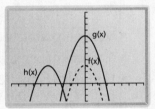

(1) $g(x) = f(x) + 5$

(2) $h(x) = f(x) - 5$

(3) $g(x) = f(x) + 8$

(4) $h(x) = f(x+5)$

Consider the graphs of $f(x) = x^2$, shown dashed, and $g(x) = 2\,f(x)$, shown solid, in Figure 6-6. Unlike the other transformations we have looked at, this one has a point that does not move as a result of the change. The origin is considered a **fixed point** in this transformation. All of the other points on the original parabola have been **vertically stretched** by 2 units. If we had multiplied the function $f(x)$ by a number between 0 and 1 the result would be a **vertical compression**. This can be seen in Figure 6.7, the graph of $g(x) = \frac{1}{3} f(x)$.

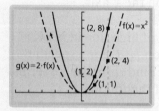

Fig. 6-6

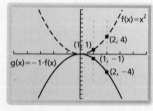

Fig. 6-7

Fig. 6-8

If $f(x)$ is multiplied by a factor of -1, the graph of the function is **reflected** over the x-axis (Fig. 6-8).

(MP)

Vertical Stretches or Compressions

If f is a function and k is a constant, then the graph of $y = kf(x)$ is the graph of $f(x)$:

- Vertically stretched by a factor of k if $k > 1$.
- Vertically compressed by a factor of k if $0 < k < 1$.
- Both vertically stretched or compressed by a factor of k and reflected over the x-axis if $k < 0$.

Note

Vertical stretches and compressions effect the output value of a function and therefore are considered external changes.

1 Let $s(h)$ represent the amount of snowfall in feet in h hours, and $g(n)$ the amount in inches. Find a formula for g in terms of s.

2 The amplifier in a headset takes a weak signal from an MP3 player and transform it into a stronger signal by amplifying it by a factor of 3. The weak signal is shown in the figure. Sketch the strong signal.

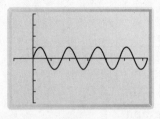

3 The function $N = p(A)$ represents the amount of paint, in gallons, needed to paint a room. A represents the surface area of the room. Match the following scenarios to the appropriate expression.

a) I decided to buy enough paint to give the room two coats of paint.

b) I figured out how much paint I needed and then bought two extra gallons to be safe.

c) I bought enough to cover the room and the DO NOT Disturb sign on the door which measures 2 ft^2.

(1) $2p(A)$

(2) $p(A + 2)$

(3) $p(A) + 2$

4 If (x, y) is on the graph of $f(x)$, which point is on the graph of $5f(x)$?

(1) $(5x, y)$

(2) $(x, 5y)$

(3) $(5x, 5y)$

(4) $(x + 5, y)$

5 The graph for $g(x)$ is shown as a dashed line. Graph #1 is a thick dotted graph, Graph #2 is thin and solid, and Graph #3 is thick and solid. Which graph represents the graph of $\frac{1}{2}g(x)$?

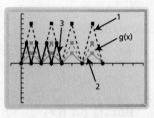

6.4 Horizontal Stretches

In Figure 6-9, $f(x)$ is graphed as dashed and $g(x) = f(2x)$ is graphed as solid. Observe what happens to select points on $f(x)$ under this transformation.

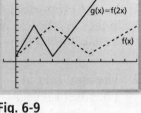

Fig. 6-9

Points on $f(x)$	Points on $g(x)$
$(2, 5)$	$(1, 5)$
$(4, 5)$	$(2, 5)$
$\left(8\frac{2}{3}, 5\right)$	$\left(4\frac{1}{3}, 5\right)$

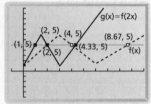

Fig. 6-10

Now the graph of $k(x) = f(\frac{1}{2}x)$ has been added to the graph (Fig. 6-10). Observe what happened to the points on the f under this transformation (Fig. 6-11).

Points on $f(x)$	Points on $k(x)$
$(2, 5)$	$(4, 5)$
$(4, 5)$	$(8, 5)$
$\left(8\frac{2}{3}, 5\right)$	$\left(17\frac{1}{3}, 5\right)$

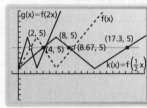

Fig. 6-11

The results of these internal changes, changes to the input of the function, result in either a horizontal compression or stretch.

Horizontal Stretch

If f is a function and k is a positive constant, then the graph of $y = f(kx)$ is the graph of f

- Horizontally compressed by a factor of $\frac{1}{k}$ if $k > 1$.
- Horizontally stretched by a factor of $\frac{1}{k}$ if $k < 1$
- If $k < 0$ then the graph of $y = f(kx)$ also includes a reflection about the y-axis.

EXAMPLE 1   Recognizing transformations

The graph of $y = f(x)$ is shown in the accompanying graph.
Match each of the following to the graphs below.

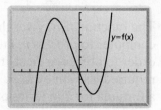

   a. $2f(x)$ c. $-f(x)$

   b. $-f(2x)$ d. $-\dfrac{1}{2}f(x)$

(1)

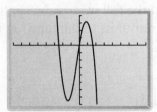

(3)

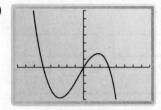

■ SOLUTION

a. to (2);
b. to (4);
c. to (3);
d. to (1).

(2)

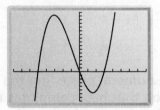

(4)

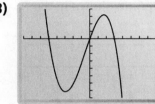

Transformations may be combined. For example, shift the graph of the absolute value function two units to the right and up four units. The horizontal shift is addressed internally and the vertical shift is addressed externally. The equation for the new function would be $d(x) = |x - 2| + 4$ and its graph is shown in the accompanying diagram.

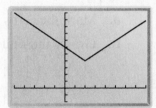

2   The graph of $y = |x - 2| + 3$ has a vertex at which of the following point?

   (1) $(2, 3)$ **(2)** $(3, 2)$ **(3)** $(-2, -3)$ **(4)** $(-2, 3)$

■ SOLUTION

This is the equation of the absolute value function translated two unit right and three units up. Therefore, the vertex is at the point $(2, 3)$.

3   The graph of a parabola is created by transforming the graph of $y = x^2$. What is the equation of the new function if the original is shifted three units to the left and down two units?

■ SOLUTION

$y = (x + 3)^2 - 2$

1 The function $f(m)$ gives the time it takes a computer to process m megabytes of data. In order to process g gigabytes of data, the time required is given by $k(g)$. If $1g = 1024m$ find a formula for k in terms of f.

2 A function contains the points shown in the table.

x	−3	−2	−1	0	1	2	3
f(x)	0	2	0	$-\frac{1}{4}$	0	−1	1

If $h(x) = f\left(\frac{1}{2}x\right)$, complete the table below and sketch $f(x)$ and $h(x)$.

x							
h(x)	0	2	0	$-\frac{1}{4}$	0	−1	1

3 Using a graphing calculator, graph $f(x) = 4 - x^2$.

  a. Mark the zeros of f on the graph.

  b. Graph and find a formula for $g(x) = f\left(\frac{1}{2}x\right)$. What are the zeros of $g(x)$?

  c. Graph and find a formula for $h(x) = f(2x)$. What are the zeros of $h(x)$?

  d. Without graphing what are the zeros of $f(10x)$?

4 The parabola $y = x^2$ is shifted down 3 units and to the left 2 units. Where is the vertex of the graph of the new parabola?

  (1) $(-3, 2)$

  (2) $(-3, -2)$

  (3) $(-2, -3)$

  (4) $(2, -3)$

5 Given $g(x) = |x + 3| + 2$, where is the vertex of the graph of this function?

6 The graph of $y = -x^2$ is translated to the right 4 units and up 3 units. The equation of the new function is?

  (1) $y = -(x + 4)^2 + 3$

  (2) $y = -(x + 3)^2 + 4$

  (3) $y = -(x - 4)^2 + 3$

  (4) $y = (-x + 4)^2 + 3$

Choose the numeral preceding the word or expression that best completes the statement or answers the question.

7 Which of the following represents a vertical shift of four units to the function $g(x)$?

  (1) $g(4x)$

  (2) $g(x) + 4$

  (3) $g(x + 4)$

  (4) $4g(x)$

8 The graph of $f(x)$ and $g(x)$ are shown. What is the relationship between $f(x)$ and $g(x)$?

  (1) $f(x) = g(x)$

  (2) $g(x) = f(x - 3)$

  (3) $g(x) = -f(x)$

  (4) $f(x) = g(-x)$

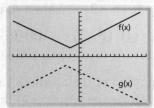

9 The equation of a parabola is given as $y = (x - 5)^2 - 3$. What is the vertex of this parabola?

  (1) $(-5, -3)$

  (2) $(5, -3)$

  (3) $(-5, 3)$

  (4) $(5, 3)$

10 The graph of $f(x) = \sqrt{x}$ is shown. Sketch the graph of $g(x) = 2f(x)$.

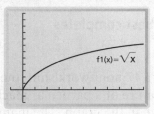

11 The point $(4, 8)$ is on the graph of $y = g(x)$. Which point is on the graph of $k(x) = g(x-3)$?

(1) $(4, 8)$

(2) $(8, 4)$

(3) $(1, 8)$

(4) $(7, 8)$

12 The graph of $z(x)$ is shown dashed in each graph. Which includes the graph of $y(x) = z(2x) + 1$?

(1)

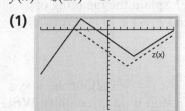

(2)

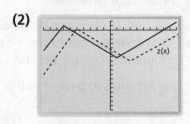

(3)

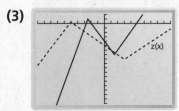

(4)

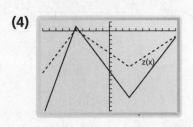

13 $f(x) = x + 5$. Which is (are) true about $f\left(\dfrac{1}{2}x\right)$?

(1) Its graph is the same as $f(x)$.

(2) Its graph is steeper than the graph of $f(x)$.

(3) Its graph is not as steep as the graph of $f(x)$.

(4) Their intercepts are the same.

14 g is a function in x. Explain the transformations that have taken place for the function $h(x) = g(x+2) - 1$.

15 State the coordinates of the vertex of the function $K(x) = -|x+2| + 3$.

16 The function $f(x)$ is to be transformed by a vertical stretch of s and horizontal shift of a units to the right and a vertical shift of b units down. The equation of the new function would be.

(1) $n(x) = s \cdot f(x-a) - b$

(2) $n(x) = a \cdot f(x-b) - s$

(3) $n(x) = s \cdot f(x+a) - b$

(4) $n(x) = s \cdot f(x+a) + b$

Preparing for the Assessment

Choose the numeral preceding the word or expression that best completes the statement or answers the question.

1 Which of the following would represent the function $y = \sqrt{x}$ when it is reflected in the y-axis?

(1) $y = -\sqrt{x}$

(2) $y = \dfrac{1}{\sqrt{x}}$

(3) $x = \sqrt{y}$

(4) $y = \sqrt{-x}$

2 The vertex of the function $f(x) = x^2$ is at the origin. Where is the vertex of the function $g(x) = 2 \cdot f(x+3) - 1$?

3 Which of the following represents a horizontal compression of $y = x^2$ by a factor of $\frac{1}{2}$?

(1) $y = \dfrac{1}{2}x^2$

(2) $y = 2x^2$

(3) $y = \left(\dfrac{1}{2}x\right)^2$

(4) $y = (2x)^2$

4 The graph of $f(x)$ is shown in the accompanying diagram. Sketch the graph of $2f(x-3) + 4$.

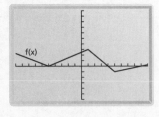

5 During a 12 hour work shift, the temperature of a particular machine varies as shown in the graph. The manufacturer wishes to start the shift two hours later and adjust the machine so the temperature decreases by half. Sketch the new graph and give its equation in terms of f.

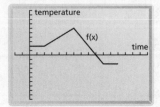

6 $P(A)$ gives the amount of paint, in gallons, needed to paint a room with an area of A square feet. Explain the meaning of $P(A + 10)$ and $P(A) + 10$ in terms of painting.

7 (a) Reflect $f(x) = \sqrt{x}$ about the y-axis and then shift it up three units. Write a formula for the new function.

(b) Shift the function $f(x) = \sqrt{x}$ up three units and then reflect it about the y-axis. Write a formula for the new function.

(c) Are the two function in parts a and b the same?

156

Use the given table to evaluate the expression in problems 8–15.

x	−4	−3	−2	−1	0	1	2	3	4
g(x)	25	16	9	4	1	0	1	4	9
h(x)	13	11	9	7	5	3	1	−1	−3

8 $g(2)$

9 $h(x) + 5$ for $x = -4$

10 $g(1) + h(2)$

11 $h(5 - 8)$

12 $g(1) \cdot \dfrac{12}{17}\sqrt{157}$

13 The product of $h(4)$ and $g(-1)$

14 The quotient of $g(-4)$ and $h(0)$.

15 $3h(-3)$

16 The graph of $f(x)$, in blue, and $k(x)$, in gray, are shown with the coordinates of the relative maximums and minimums labeled. If $k(x) = f(z \cdot x)$ what is the value of z?

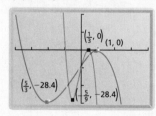

17 Explain the difference between $f(x + 3)$ and $f(x) + 3$.

18 The light blue circle is first transformed into the blue circle and then the blue circle is transformed into the gray circle. Which sequence of transformations best describes this action?

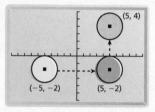

(1) Reflect about the x-axis and then reflect about the y-axis

(2) Reflect about the y-axis and then translate up 6 units.

(3) Translate right 10 units and then translate up 6 units.

(4) Reflect about the x-axis and then translate up 6 units.

7 Polynomials and Factoring

A.APR.1
A.SSE.1.a
A.SSE.2

A single-term algebraic expression is called a **monomial**. A monomial is the product of real numbers and variables with nonnegative integer exponents.

EXAMPLE 1 **Recognizing monomials**

 Which of the following are monomials?

(1) $-3abc$ (2) $\dfrac{4}{x}$ (3) $-2r^2s$ (4) $\dfrac{2}{3x}$ (5) xy^{-2}

■ SOLUTION

$-3abc$ and $-2r^2s$ are monomials. $\dfrac{4}{x}, \dfrac{2}{3x}$, and xy^{-2} are not because each has an unknown value in the denominator.

> **Note**
>
> No monomial may have a variable in the denominator because it may result in values for which the expression is undefined.

Recall that the number in front of the variable is called the **numerical coefficient** of the term, or **coefficient**.

Expression	Coefficient
$3x^2$	3
$-4y$	-4
$-\dfrac{5c}{6}$	$-\dfrac{5}{6}$

If no coefficient is indicated, then it is understood to be 1. For example, abc^2 has a numerical coefficient of 1.

Terms that have the same variable factors are **like terms**. Monomials with the same like terms can be combined.

EXAMPLES 2 and 3 **Combining monomials**

 Can the terms $7x^3y^2$ and $-3x^3y^2$ be combined? Explain why or why not and describe the resulting expression.

■ SOLUTION

$7x^3y^2$ and $-3x^3y^2$ can be combined because x^3 and y^2 are the same in both monomials. We apply the distributive property. So $7x^3y^2$ and $-3x^3y^2$ becomes $(7-3)x^3y^2$, or the monomial $4x^3y^2$.

Can the terms $2xy$ and y be combined?

■ SOLUTION

The monomials $2xy$ and y cannot be combined because one monomial has x and y as its variables and the second monomial has only y. Therefore, the monomials are not like terms. The resulting expression will remain $2xy + y$.

A **polynomial** is a monomial or a sum of monomials. Each of the monomials is a term of the polynomial. To write a polynomial in its simplest form, you must combine any like terms.

 EXAMPLES 4 and 5   Simplifying a polynomial

4   Simplify $3a - 2ab + 4a$.

■ SOLUTION

$$3a - 2ab + 4a$$
$$[3a + 4a] - 2ab \qquad \leftarrow \text{Group like terms.}$$
$$7a - 2ab \qquad \leftarrow \text{Add the coefficients of } a.$$

5   Simplify $5r^2s + 10rs^2 - 8r^2s$.

■ SOLUTION

$$5r^2s + 10rs^2 - 8r^2s$$
$$[5r^2s - 8r^2s] + 10rs^2 \qquad \leftarrow \text{Group like terms.}$$
$$-3r^2s + 10rs^2 \qquad \leftarrow \text{Subtract the coefficients of } r^2s.$$

Note

rs^2 is *not* like r^2s.

A polynomial in one variable is written in *descending order* when the powers of the variable decrease from left to right. It is written in *ascending order* when the powers of the variable increase from left to right. When a polynomial in one variable has no like terms, and the terms are written in descending order, the polynomial is said to be in **standard form**.

 EXAMPLE 6   Writing a polynomial in standard form

6   Write $-8 + 4x^2 + 5 - 3x^2 + 2x$ in standard form.

■ SOLUTION

$$-8 + 4x^2 + 5 - 3x^2 + 2x$$
$$(-8 + 5) + (4x^2 - 3x^2) + 2x \qquad \leftarrow \text{Group like terms.}$$
$$-3 \quad + \quad 1x^2 \quad + 2x \qquad \leftarrow \text{Simplify.}$$
$$x^2 + 2x - 3 \qquad \leftarrow \text{Use descending order: } x^2 + 2x^1 - 3x^0$$

Note

$x^1 = x$
$x^0 = 1$

You can classify some polynomials by their number of terms. Polynomials with one, two, or three terms have special names.

Classifying Polynomials by Number of Terms		
Number of Terms	**Classification**	**Examples**
one	monomial	m, n^5, xy, $-5ab^2$, r^2st^3, 9
two	binomial	$3x + 4y$, $jk - 3$, $a^2 + 7a$, $p^3qr - 5p^2q^4$
three	trinomial	$r + s - t$, $-4x^2 + 8xy - 5y^2$, $a^2 + 2a - 6$

 EXAMPLE 7   Classifying polynomials by number of terms

7   Classify $4x + 7$ as a monomial, binomial, or trinomial.

■ SOLUTION

$4x + 7$ has 2 terms; therefore, it is a binomial.

161

If a term of a polynomial has just one variable, the **degree of the term** is the exponent of the variable. A term that has no variable part is called a **constant term,** or simply a **constant.** The degree of a constant term is 0.

$$10k^4 \rightarrow \text{The degree is } 4.$$
$$-2t = -2t^1 \rightarrow \text{The degree is } 1.$$
$$6 = 6x^0 \rightarrow \text{The degree is } 0.$$

The **degree of a polynomial** is the greatest degree of any of its terms after it has been simplified. The term with the greatest degree is called the **leading term** of the polynomial. The coefficient of the leading term is called the **leading coefficient.**

Identifying the degree provides another means for classifying polynomials.

> **Note**
>
> When the term of a polynomial has more than one variable, the degree of the term is the sum of the exponents of the variables of the leading term.
>
> $5x^4y^2 \rightarrow$ The degree is 6.

Classifying Polynomials by Degree		
Degree of Polynomial	**Classification**	**Examples**
one	linear	$x,\ -6d,\ 5s - 3,\ 7 + 8y$
two	quadratic	$x^2,\ 3m^2,\ 9z^2 + 3z,\ k - k^2,\ 4 - 2g + 6g^2$
three	cubic	$x^3,\ -8b^3 + 5b,\ 4b^3 - b^2 + 7b + 6$

EXAMPLES 8 and 9 **Classifying polynomials by number of terms and degree**

8 Which phrase best describes $-z^3 + 3z^2 - 2z - 3z^2$?

(1) cubic trinomial (3) cubic monomial
(2) quadratic trinomial (4) cubic binomial

■ **SOLUTION**

First simplify the polynomial.
$$-z^3 + 3z^2 - 2z - 3z^2$$
$$-z^3 + (3z^2 - 3z^2) - 2z$$
$$-z^3 + 0 - 2z$$
$$-z^3 - 2z$$

The simplified polynomial has two terms, so it is a *binomial.*
The greatest degree of any of its terms is 3, so it is *cubic.*
The correct choice is (4).

9 Which phrase best describes $9x^2y + 3x^2 - 2x^2y - 5xy^2 - 4x^2$?

(1) quadratic binomial (3) cubic binomial
(2) quadratic trinomial (4) cubic trinomial

■ **SOLUTION**

First simplify the polynomial.
$$9x^2y + 3x^2 - 2x^2y - 5xy^2 - 4x^2$$
$$-5xy^2 + (9x^2y - 2x^2y) + (3x^2 - 4x^2)$$
$$-5xy^2 + 7x^2y - x^2$$

The simplified polynomial has 3 terms so it is a *trinomial.*
The greatest degree of any of its terms is 3, so it is *cubic.*
The correct choice is (4).

To find a sum of polynomials, you add the like terms from all the polynomials. You can do this using either a horizontal or vertical format.

EXAMPLES 10 and 11 **Adding polynomials**

Simplify each expression.

10 $(3x + x^2 - x^3) + (4x^3 + 2x^2 + 5x)$

■ **SOLUTION 1**

Group like terms.
Then add their coefficients.

$(3x + x^3 - x^3) + (4x^3 + 2x^2 + 5x)$
$(-x^3 + 4x^3) + (x^2 + 2x^2) + (3x + 5x)$
$= 3x^3 + 3x^2 + 8x$

■ **SOLUTION 2**

Line up like terms in columns.
Then add their coefficients.

$$\begin{array}{r} -x^3 + x^2 + 3x \\ +\ 4x^3 + 2x^2 + 5x \\ \hline 3x^3 + 3x^2 + 8x \end{array}$$

11 $(3n^2 - 2n) + (-5n^3 + n^2) + (2n - 5)$

■ **SOLUTION 1**

$(3n^2 - 2n) + (-5n^3 + n^2) + (2n - 5)$
$= -5n^3 + (3n^2 + n^2) + (-2n + 2n) - 5$
$= -5n^3 + 4n^2 - 5$

■ **SOLUTION 2**

$$\begin{array}{r} 3n^2 - 2n \\ -5n^3 + n^2 \\ +\ 2n - 5 \\ \hline -5n^3 + 4n^2 - 5 \end{array}$$

To subtract one polynomial from another, you add the opposite, or additive inverse. In order to do this, it will be helpful to first review the procedure for finding the additive inverse of a polynomial.

EXAMPLE 12 **Finding the additive inverse of a polynomial**

12 Find the additive inverse of $-6a^3 - 5a^2 + 3a + 1$.

■ **SOLUTION**

The sum of a number and its additive inverse is 0.
Find the polynomial that gives a sum of 0 when added to $-6a^3 - 5a^2 + 3a + 1$.

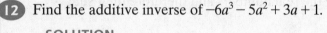

$$\begin{array}{r} -6a^3 - 5a^2 + 3a + 1 \\ + ? \\ \hline 0 \end{array} \quad \rightarrow \quad \begin{array}{r} -6a^3 - 5a^2 + 3a + 1 \\ +\ 6a^3 + 5a^2 - 3a - 1 \\ \hline 0 \end{array} \quad \begin{array}{l} \textbf{Write the opposite} \\ \leftarrow \textbf{of each term.} \end{array}$$

So the additive inverse of $-6a^3 - 5a^2 + 3a + 1$ is $6a^3 + 5a^2 - 3a - 1$.

You can find the additive inverse of a polynomial by finding the additive inverse of each term.

Opposites of Sums and Differences

For all real numbers a and b: $-(a + b) = -a + (-b) = -a - b$

$-(a - b) = -a + b$

Just as with addition, you can find a difference of polynomials using either a horizontal or vertical format.

EXAMPLES 13 and 14   **Subtracting polynomials**

13 Simplify $(3c^2 - 8c + 4) - (7 + c^2 - 8c)$.

■ SOLUTION 1

Change the subtraction to addition. Then write the opposite of each term of the polynomial being subtracted. Finally, combine like terms.

$$(3c^2 - 8c + 4) - (7 + c^2 - 8c)$$
$$= (3c^2 - 8c + 4) + (-7 - c^2 + 8c)$$
$$= (3c^2 - c^2) + (-8c + 8c) + (4 - 7)$$
$$= 2c^2 - 3$$

■ SOLUTION 2

Line up like terms in columns. Write the opposite of each term of the polynomial being subtracted. Finally, combine like terms.

$$\begin{array}{r} 3c^2 - 8c + 4 \\ + (-c^2 + 8c - 7) \\ \hline 2c^2 \qquad - 3 \end{array}$$

14 Simplify the result when $(5d^2 - 2d^3 + 3)$ is subtracted from $(d^2 + 8 - 5d)$.

■ SOLUTION 1

Subtract horizontally.

$$(d^2 + 8 - 5d) - (5d^2 - 2d^3 + 3)$$
$$= (d^2 + 8 - 5d) + (-5d^2 + 2d^3 - 3)$$
$$= 2d^3 + (d^2 - 5d^2) - 5d + (8 - 3)$$
$$= 2d^3 - 4d^2 - 5d + 5$$

■ SOLUTION 2

Subtract vertically.

$$\begin{array}{r} d^2 - 5d + 8 \\ + \ 2d^3 - 5d^2 \qquad - 3 \\ \hline 2d^3 - 4d^2 - 5d + 5 \end{array}$$

Recall that closure means the result of operating on two elements from a particular set results in an element from that same set.

- When adding or subtracting polynomials, the coefficients of like terms are added or subtracted. These coefficients are elements of the real numbers and therefore their sum and differences are also real numbers.

- The exponent of the sum or difference of like terms remains the same, a non-negative integer.

When adding or subtracting two polynomials, the result is a new polynomial.

Polynomials are closed under addition and subtraction.

Practice

Choose the numeral preceding the word or expression that best completes the statement or answers the question.

1 Which best describes $-3x^2 + 3 - x + 3x^2$?

(1) quadratic expression with four terms

(2) linear binomial

(3) polynomial with degree 2

(4) not a polynomial

2 Which is a quadratic binomial when written in simplest form?

(1) $(-z^2 + 3z) + (-z^2 - 3z)$

(2) $(-z^2 + 3z) + (z^2 - 3z)$

(3) $(-z^2 - 3z) + (-z^2 - 3z)$

(4) $(-z^2 + 3z) + (z^2 + 3z)$

3 Which polynomial added to $3d^2 - 3d + 1$ will result in a sum of 0?

(1) $-3d^2 - 3d + 1$

(2) $-3d^2 + 3d + 1$

(3) $-3d^2 + 3d - 1$

(4) $3d^2 - 3d + 1$

4 What is the result when $2c^2 - 3c + 6$ is subtracted from $c^2 + c - 2$?

(1) $c^2 - 4c + 8$

(2) $-c^2 - 2c + 4$

(3) $c^2 + 4c + 8$

(4) $-c^2 + 4c - 8$

5 The perimeter of a polygon is the sum of the lengths of its sides. Which does not represent the perimeter of the polygon below?

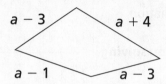

(1) $(a - 3) + (a - 3) + (a - 1) + (a + 4)$

(2) $2(a - 3) + (a - 1) + (a + 4)$

(3) $4a + 3$

(4) $4a - 3$

In Exercises 6–9, simplify each expression.

6 $yz^3 + 2y^3z - 4yz^3 - y^3z$

7 $5m^2n^2 - 4mn^2 - 9m^2n + 7mn^2$

8 $-4a^2b^2 + 3ab - a^3b - 8ba$

9 $2c^2d - 6d - 7d + 3cd^2 + c^4$

In Exercises 10–15, write each polynomial in standard form.

10 $y^2 - 7y - 3y^3$

11 $4b^3 + 1 - b + 9b^2$

12 $3x^2 - 2x + 5x - 6x^3$

13 $v^2 + v - 3v^3 - v^2$

14 $-7q^2 + 2q + 3q^2 - 2q + 5q^2$

15 $4w - 3w^2 + 7w^3 - w^3 - 7$

In Exercises 16–21, classify each polynomial by its degree and by its number of terms.

16 $3d^2$ **17** $y^2 - 3y - 7$

18 $-g - 4g^3 + 5g$ **19** $5d + 9$

20 $2m^2 + 3m^3 - 2m - 5m^2$

21 $b^3 - 2b - b^3 - 2b$

In Exercises 22–37, simplify each expression. Write answers in standard form.

22 $(n^3 + 8n^2 + 6n) + (8n^3 + 2n^2 - 6n)$

23 $(5s^2 + 7s - 11) + (4 + s - 5s^2)$

24 $(x^4 + x - 2) + (2x^4 + x^3 - 5)$

25 $(3a + 4a^3 - 8) + (a^2 + 2a - 7)$

26 $(3y^3 + 8y - 3) + (2y - 5y^2)$

27 $(-4r^3 + 2r - 3r^2 + 1) + (2r^3 - 5r + 1)$

28 $(5h^2 + 4h + 8) - (3h^2 + h + 3)$

29 $(-7z^3 + 2z - 7) - (2z^3 - z - 3)$

30 $(3c^2 + 4c - 6) - (3c - 8 + 5c^2)$

31 $(-a^2 - 3 + 7a) - (2a^3 - 7a)$

32 $(n^3 + n^2) - (2n^3 + 3n^2 - 2n)$

33 $(-2w^3 - 9 + 8w) - (2w^4 + 6w^3 - 11w^2)$

34 $(x^2 + 5) + (3x + 8) + (5x^2 + 3x)$

35 $(5j^2 + 3j) + (j^2 + 4j + 4) - (2j - 3)$

36 $(-5p^3 + 6p) - (2p^3 + 8p^2) + (6p + 2p^3)$

37 $(2z^2 - 4) - (z^2 - 4) - (-3z^2 - 2)$

In Exercises 38–42, solve the problem. Clearly show all necessary work.

38 Find the difference when $x^2 + 8 - 2x$ is subtracted from $2x - 10x^2 + 7$.

39 Is $2x^{-3} + x^2 + x - 4$ a polynomial? Explain your answer.

7.2 Multiplication and Division with Polynomials

A.APR.1
A.APR.7
A.SSE.2
A.APR.6

Recall that a polynomial is simply the sum of monomials; therefore, the same rules that apply for multiplication of monomials also apply when multiplying a polynomial by a monomial. Use the distributive property to multiply every term of the polynomial by the monomial.

EXAMPLES 1 through 3   **Multiplying a polynomial by a monomial: one variable**

Simplify each expression.

1 $3(5z - 6)$

■ SOLUTION

$3(5z - 6)$ **Use the distributive**
$3(5z) - 3(6)$ ← **property.**
$15z - 3(6)$ ← Simplify $3(5z)$.
$15z - 18$ ← Simplify $3(6)$.

2 $-7a(-2a + 9)$

■ SOLUTION

$-7a(-2a + 9)$
$(-7a)(-2a) + (-7a)(9)$
$14a^2 + (-63a)$
$14a^2 - 63a$

3 $2xy(-3x + 2y - 4)$

■ SOLUTION

$2xy(-3x + 2y - 4)$
$2xy(-3x) + 2xy(2y) + 2xy(-4)$
$-6x^2y + 4xy^2 - 8xy$

Sometimes you must multiply polynomials before solving an equation.

EXAMPLES 4 and 5   **Multiplying polynomials in equation solving**

4 Solve $(3b^2 + 2b - 1) - 3b(b + 5) = 12$.

■ SOLUTION

$$(3b^2 + 2b - 1) - 3b(b + 5) = 12$$
$(3b^2 + 2b - 1) + (-3b)(b + 5) = 12$ ← **Rewrite the subtraction as addition.**
$(3b^2 + 2b - 1) + (-3b)(b) + (-3b)(5) = 12$ ← **Apply the distributive property.**
$(3b^2 + 2b - 1) + (-3b^2) + (-15b) = 12$ ← **Simplify** $(-3b)(b)$ **and** $(-3b)(5)$.
$[3b^2 + (-3b^2)] + [2b + (-15b)] - 1 = 12$ ← **Combine like terms.**
$-13b - 1 = 12$ ← **Solve.**
$-13b = 13$
$b = -1$

5 Solve $3(2m^2 + 5) = 3m(2m + 7) - 3m - 3$.

■ SOLUTION

$$3(2m^2 + 5) = 3m(2m + 7) - 3m - 3$$
$3(2m^2) + 3(5) = 3m(2m) + 3m(7) - 3m - 3$ ← **Apply the distributive property.**
$6m^2 + 15 = 6m^2 + 21m - 3m - 3$ ← **Simplify.**
$6m^2 + 15 = 6m^2 + 18m - 3$ ← **Combine like terms.**
$6m^2 - 6m^2 + 15 = 6m^2 - 6m^2 + 18m - 3$ ← **Solve.**
$15 + 3 = 18m - 3 + 3$
$18 = 18m$
$1 = m$

166

To multiply a polynomial by a binomial, you must apply the distributive property more than once. You begin by distributing the first term in the binomial factor to each term in the polynomial, and then you distribute the second term in the binomial factor to each term in the polynomial.

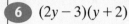 **EXAMPLES 6 and 7** **Multiplying by a binomial**

Simplify each expression.

6 $(2y - 3)(y + 2)$

■ SOLUTION 1

Multiply horizontally.

$(2y - 3)(y + 2)$
$(2y - 3)y + (2y - 3)2$ ← **Distribute $(2y - 3)$.**
$2y^2 - 3y + (2y - 3)2$ ← **Simplify $(2y - 3)y$.**
$2y^2 - 3y + 4y - 6$ ← **Simplify $(2y - 3)2$.**
$2y^2 + y - 6$ ← **Combine like terms.**

■ SOLUTION 2

Multiply vertically.

$$\begin{array}{r} 2y - 3 \\ \times \quad y + 2 \\ \hline 4y - 6 \\ 2y^2 - 3y \\ \hline 2y^2 + y - 6 \end{array}$$

← **Multiply $2(2y - 3)$.**
← **Multiply $y(2y - 3)$.**
← **Combine like terms.**

7 $(n + 4)(2n^2 - 3n + 3)$

■ SOLUTION 1

Multiply horizontally.

$(n + 4)(2n^2 - 3n + 3)$
$n(2n^2 - 3n + 3) + 4(2n^2 - 3n + 3)$
$2n^3 - 3n^2 + 3n + 4(2n^2 - 3n + 3)$
$2n^3 - 3n^2 + 3n + 8n^2 - 12n + 12$
$2n^3 + 5n^2 - 9n + 12$

■ SOLUTION 2

Multiply vertically.

$$\begin{array}{r} 2n^2 - 3n + 3 \\ \times \quad n + 4 \\ \hline 8n^2 - 12n + 12 \\ 2n^3 - 3n^2 + 3n \\ \hline 2n^2 + 5n^2 - 9n + 12 \end{array}$$

Recall that an area model is the visualization of any multiplication. It is a great model for polynomial multiplication as well.

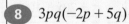 **EXAMPLES 8–10** **Using an area model**

Draw an area model to represent each product.

8 $3pq(-2p + 5q)$

■ SOLUTION

	$-2p$	$5q$
$3pq$	$-6p^2q$	$15pq^2$

$3pq(-2p + 5q) = -6p^2q + 15pq^2$

9 $(3x - 2)(4x + 5)$

■ SOLUTION

	$4x$	5
$3x$	$12x^2$	$15x$
-2	$-8x$	-10

$(3x - 2)(4x + 5) = 12x^2 + 15x - 8x - 10$
$= 12x^2 + 7x - 10$

10 $(y + 2)(5y^2 - 3y + 4)$

■ SOLUTION

	$5y^2$	$-3y$	4
y	$5y^3$	$-15y^2$	$4y$
2	$10y^2$	$-6y$	8

$(y + 2)(5y^2 - 3y + 4) = 5y^3 - 15y^2 + 4y + 10y^2 - 6y + 8$
$= 5y^3 - 5y^2 - 2y + 8$

You may also need to multiply polynomials before you can simplify an algebraic expression.

EXAMPLE 11 — **Using multiplication to simplify a polynomial**

 Simplify the expression $(b^2 + 2b - 1) - (b - 5)(b + 6)$.

■ SOLUTION

$(b^2 + 2b - 1) - (b - 5)(b + 6)$

$(b^2 + 2b - 1) - (b^2 + 1b - 30)$ → Multiply first.

$(b^2 + 2b - 1) + (-b^2) - 1b + 30$ → Subtract means to add the opposites.

$b + 29$ → Combine like terms.

Looking for a Pattern

Using a computer algebra system to compute the product of two binomials the accompanying table has been created. In each case the leading coefficient is one. Do you see a pattern between the constant terms of the binomials and the results in the product?

EXAMPLE 12 — **Identifying patterns**

 Write a statement for the pattern you see between the constants in the binomials and the constants in the product

■ SOLUTION

It appears that the constant term in the product is the product of the constant terms in the binomials. The coefficient of the linear term in the product is the sum of the constant terms of the binomials. **NOTE:** For this description of the patterns, both binomial factors must have a leading coefficient of one.

Binomial #1	Binomial #2	Product of Binomial #1 (Binomial #2)
$x + 1$	$x + 1$	$x^2 + 2x + 1$
$x + 1$	$x + 2$	$x^2 + 3x + 2$
$x + 3$	$x + 4$	$x^2 + 7x + 12$
$x + 4$	$x + 5$	$x^2 + 9x + 20$
$x + 6$	$x + 2$	$x^2 + 8x + 12$
$x - 2$	$x + 3$	$x^2 + x - 6$
$x + 8$	$x + 5$	$x^2 + 13x + 40$
$x - 3$	$x - 4$	$x^2 - 7x + 12$
$x - 4$	$x - 4$	$x^2 - 8x + 16$
$x + 10$	$x + 10$	$x^2 + 20x + 100$

EXAMPLE 13 — **Completing Expressions Based Upon the Pattern**

 Fill in the blank for each of the following expressions.

■ EXPRESSIONS

a. $(x + 4)(x + 3) = x^2 + \underline{\quad} x + 12$

b. $(x + 7)(x + 9) = x^2 + 16x + \underline{\quad}$

c. $(x + 3)(x + 3) = x^2 + 6x + \underline{\quad}$

d. $(x - 5)(x + 6) = x^2 + \underline{\quad} x - 30$

e. $(x + 2)(x + \underline{\quad}) = x^2 + 6x + 8$

f. $(x + \underline{\quad})(x + \underline{\quad}) = x^2 + 9x + 20$

■ SOLUTIONS

a. $(x + 4)(x + 3) = x^2 + \underline{7} x + 12$

b. $(x + 7)(x + 9) = x^2 + 16x + \underline{63}$

c. $(x + 3)(x + 3) = x^2 + 6x + \underline{9}$

d. $(x - 5)(x + 6) = x^2 + \underline{1} x - 30$

e. $(x + 2)(x + \underline{4}) = x^2 + 6x + 8$

f. $(x + \underline{4})(x + \underline{5}) = x^2 + 9x + 20$

A special product, called a **perfect square trinomial,** results when a binomial is squared. Look for the patterns in the following examples.

EXAMPLES 14 and 15   **Squaring a binomial**

Simplify each expression.

14 $(c+4)^2 = (c+4)(c+4)$

■ SOLUTION

$$c^2 + 4c + 4c + 4^2$$
$$c^2 + 2(4c) + 4^2$$
$$c^2 + 8c + 16$$

15 $(s-9)^2 = (s-9)(s-9)$

■ SOLUTION

$$s^2 + (-9s) + (-9s) + (-9)^2$$
$$s^2 + 2(-9s) + (-9)^2$$
$$s^2 - 18s + 81$$

These patterns are often generalized as follows.

Squares of Sums and Differences

For all real numbers a and b: $(a+b)^2 = a^2 + 2ab + b^2$

$$(a-b)^2 = a^2 - 2ab + b^2$$

Another pattern emerges when you multiply the sum of two terms by the difference of the same two terms. Study these two simplifications.

EXAMPLES 16 and 17   **Multiplying $(a+b)(a-b)$**

Simplify each expression.

16 $(m+5)(m-5)$

■ SOLUTION

$$m^2 + (-5m) + 5m + 5(-5)$$
$$m^2 + 0m + (-25)$$
$$m^2 - 25$$

17 $(3x-6)(3x+6)$

■ SOLUTION

$$(3x)^2 + (3x)(6) + (-6)(3x) + (-6)(6)$$
$$9x^2 + 18x + (-18x) + (-36)$$
$$9x^2 + 0x + (-36)$$
$$9x^2 - 36$$

This pattern is called the **difference of two squares** and can be generalized as follows.

Difference of Two Squares

For all real numbers a and b: $(a+b)(a-b) = a^2 - b^2$

Closure for multiplication of polynomials

- Using the distributive property when multiplying polynomials results in real coefficients being multiplied by real numbers. The real numbers are closed under multiplication and therefore each new coefficient is a real number.

- Using the properties of exponents when multiplying polynomials guarantees the exponents are nonnegative integers.

Therefore, when multiplying two polynomials the result is a new polynomial.

Polynomials are closed under multiplication.

The same rules that apply for division of monomials will apply for division of a polynomial by a monomial. Every term of the polynomial in the numerator will be divided by the monomial in the denominator.

For all real numbers a and b and all nonzero real numbers c,

$$\frac{a+b}{c} = \frac{a}{c} + \frac{b}{c} \quad \text{and} \quad \frac{a-b}{c} = \frac{a}{c} - \frac{b}{c}.$$

$$\frac{2+5}{9} = \frac{2}{9} + \frac{5}{9} = \frac{7}{9} \quad \text{and} \quad \frac{8-3}{7} = \frac{8}{7} - \frac{3}{7} = \frac{5}{7}$$

EXAMPLES 18 and 19	Dividing a polynomial by a monomial

Simplify each expression.

18 $\dfrac{8a^2 - 12a}{4a}$

■ SOLUTION

$\dfrac{8a^2 - 12a}{4a}$

$\dfrac{8a^2}{4a} - \dfrac{12a}{4a}$ ← **Divide each term by 4a.**

$2a - 3$

19 $\dfrac{16yz^2 - 8y^2z + 10yz}{-2yz}$

■ SOLUTION

$\dfrac{16yz^2 - 8y^2z + 10yz}{-2yz}$

$\dfrac{16yz^2}{-2yz} - \dfrac{8y^2z}{-2yz} + \dfrac{10yz}{-2yz}$ ← **Divide each term by −2yz.**

$-8z - (-4y) + (-5)$

$-8z + 4y - 5$

Choose the numeral preceding the word or expression that best completes the statement or answers the question.

1 The expression $(s-3)^2$ is equivalent to

(1) $s^2 + 9$ (3) $s^2 + 6s + 9$

(2) $s^2 - 9$ (4) $s^2 - 6s + 9$

2 The product of $4g^3 + 4g^2 + 2g$ and $2g$ is

(1) $2g^2 + 2g$ (3) $8g^2 + 8g + 4$

(2) $2g^2 + 2g + 1$ (4) $8g^4 + 8g^3 + 4g^2$

3 Which is equivalent to $23^2 - 13^2$?

(1) 10^2 (3) 36^2

(2) 10×36 (4) $2(23 - 13)$

4 Simplify $(5z - 9) - 4(-2z - 3)$.

(1) $13z - 3$ (3) $13z + 3$

(2) $-3z + 21$ (4) $3z - 8$

5 $4y^2 - 12y + 9$ is the perfect square of which binomial?

(1) $(-2y + 3)$ (3) $(y - 3)$

(2) $(-2y - 3)$ (4) $(2y + 3)$

For 6–9 represent the polynomial multiplication by an area model.

6 $(2x + y)(x - 3y)$ **7** $(5t + 2)(t^2 - 3t + 6)$

8 $(m - n)(m + n)$ **9** $(2x - 3)^2$

In Exercises 10–29, simplify each expression.

10 $6(4a - 2)$ **11** $(2r + 9)(-3)$

12 $-j(-6j + 1)$ **13** $(8v - 3)(-5v)$

14 $(2y + 3)(y - 2)$ **15** $(r + 4)(-4r + 1)$

16 $(2t - 5)(5t - 2)$ **17** $(3w + 7)(2w - 5)$

18 $(c + 7)^2$ **19** $(-3q - 4)^2$

20 $(v + 9)(v - 9)$ **21** $(5y - 2)(5y + 2)$

22 $\dfrac{6k^2 + 15k}{3k}$ **23** $\dfrac{4p^2 - 10p}{4p}$

24 $-5p^2(p^2 + 2p + 1)$

25 $(x^2 + 3x - 2)(x + 3)$

26 $(2n - 7)(n^2 - n + 3)$

27 $(3b^2 - b - 5)(4b - 1)$

28 $\dfrac{2w^3 + 6w^2 - 5w}{-2w}$

29 $\dfrac{12x^5 - 6x^4 + 6x^3 - 4x^2}{6x^2}$

In Exercises 30–35, solve each equation.

30 $2(3n + 2) = 5n - 4$

31 $-4g - 3 = (2g - 1)(-3)$

32 $8w - 5(2w + 7) = 2w - 9$

33 $2(3c + 2) = 1 - 3(4c - 3)$

34 Mark says that $(m + n)^2$ and $m^2 + n^2$ are equivalent expressions. Do you agree or disagree? Explain.

35 When $(x + a)$ is multiplied by $(x + b)$ the result is a trinomial $x^2 +$ _____ $x +$ _____. Fill in the Blanks with expressions in terms of a and b.

7.3 Factoring Polynomials

 A.SSE.2

When multiplying monomials, you write a simplified expression for their product. The reverse of this process, writing a product as factors, is called *factoring the monomial*.

To **factor** a monomial, you start with the simplified expression and find a multiplication equivalent of it. For instance, using whole number coefficients, there are five ways to factor $9x^2$. These are shown at the right. From these factorizations, you arrive at the following list of factors.

$$9x^2 = 1 \cdot 9x^2$$
$$9x^2 = 3 \cdot 3x^2$$
$$9x^2 = 9 \cdot x^2$$
$$9x^2 = x \cdot 9x$$
$$9x^2 = 3x \cdot 3x$$

factors of $9x^2$: 1, 3, 9, x, $3x$, $9x$, x^2, $3x^2$, $9x^2$

The **greatest common factor (GCF)** of two or more monomials is the product of the greatest common factor of their numerical coefficients and the greatest common factor of their variable parts.

EXAMPLE 1   Finding the GCF of monomials

 Find the GCF of $12x^3$, $30x^2$, and $42x$.

■ SOLUTION

Step 1

Write the factored form of each monomial. Circle the factors common to all the monomials.

$12x^3 = ②\cdot 2 \cdot ③\cdot Ⓧ\cdot x \cdot x$
$30x^2 = ②\cdot ③\cdot 5 \cdot Ⓧ\cdot x$
$42x = ②\cdot ③\cdot 7 \cdot Ⓧ$

Step 2

Multiply the circled factors.
$2 \cdot 3 \cdot x = 6x$

The GCF of $12x^3$, $30x^2$, and $42x$ is $6x$.

When the terms of a polynomial have a GCF other than 1, you can factor the polynomial by using the distributive property.

EXAMPLES 2 and 3   Finding common monomial factors with a numerical GCF

Factor each expression using the GCF of the terms.

2 $3a + 6$ ■ SOLUTION

$3a + 6$ ← The GCF of $3a$ and 6 is 3.
$3a + 3(2)$ ← Rewrite each term as a product.
$3(a + 2)$ ← Apply the distributive property.

3 $8x^2 - 12y + 20$ ■ SOLUTION

$8x^2 - 12y + 20$ ← The GCF of $8x^2$, $12y$, and 20 is 4.
$4(2x^2) - 4(3y) + 4(5)$ ← Rewrite each term as a product.
$4(2x^2 - 3y + 5)$ ← Apply the distributive property.

In Example 3, notice that it is also possible to factor $8x^2 - 12y + 20$ as $2(4x^2 - 6y + 10)$. However, the GCF was not used in this factoring. As a result, $4x^2 - 6y + 10$ can be factored further as $2(2x^2 - 3y + 5)$. This means that $2(4x^2 - 6y + 10)$ is considered only a *partial* factorization.

In general, your goal is to factor polynomials *completely*. A polynomial is factored completely when it is expressed as a product of one or more polynomials that cannot be factored further.

Factor each expression completely.

4 $6r^4 + 9r^2 + 4r$

■ SOLUTION

$6r^4 + 9r^2 + 4r$
$r(6r^3) + r(9r) + r(4)$
$r(6r^3 + 9r + 4)$

← The GCF of $6r^4$, $9r^2$, and $4r$ is r.

5 $4mn - 10m$

■ SOLUTION

$4mn - 10m$
$2m(2n) - 2m(5)$
$2m(2n - 5)$

← The GCF of $4mn$ and $10m$ is $2m$.

6 $8a^3b^2 + 16\,a^2b^2 - 4ab$

■ SOLUTION

$8a^3b^2 + 16\,a^2b^2 - 4ab$
$4ab(2a^2b) + 4ab(4ab) - 4ab(1)$
$4ab(2a^2b + 4ab - 1)$

← The GCF of $8a^3b^2$, $16a^2b^2$, and $4ab$ is $4ab$.

Many trinomials are the product of two binomial factors. The general form for a trinomial is $ax^2 + bx + c$, where c is a constant term. Study the products in the following table.

Factors		Distribute		Quadratic Term		Linear Term		Constant Term
$(x+2)\,(x+5)$	=	$x^2 + 5x + 2x + 10$	=	x^2	+	$7x$	+	10
$(x-3)\,(x-1)$	=	$x^2 - 1x - 3x + 3$	=	x^2	−	$4x$	+	3
$(x+6)\,(x-4)$	=	$x^2 - 4x + 6x - 24$	=	x^2	+	$2x$	−	24
$(x-8)\,(x+7)$	=	$x^2 + 7x - 8x - 56$	=	x^2	−	x	−	56

Notice that the terms of the trinomials are related to the terms of their binomial factors. The constant term is the product of the last terms of the factors. The coefficient of the linear term is the sum of the last terms of the factors. You can use these relationships to factor many quadratic trinomials.

Factor each expression completely.

 $h^2 + 8h + 15$

 $y^2 - 10y + 16$

■ SOLUTION

Look for factors of 15 whose sum is 8.

Factors of 15	Sum of Factors	
1, 15	16	← Both factors must be positive.
3, 5	8	

The numbers 3 and 5 have a product of 15 and a sum of 8.
So $h^2 + 8h + 15 = (h + 3)(h + 5)$.

■ SOLUTION

Look for factors of 16 whose sum is −10.

Factors of 16	Sum of Factors	
−1, −16	−17	← Both factors must be negative.
−2, −8	−10	
−4, −4	−8	

The numbers −2 and −8 have a product of 16 and a sum of −10.
So $y^2 - 10y + 16 = (y - 2)(y - 8)$.

If every term of a quadratic trinomial is positive, then the second term of each binomial will be positive. If the second term of the trinomial is negative and the last term is positive, then the second term of each binomial will be negative.

If the second term of a trinomial is positive and the third term is negative, then each binomial will be opposite in sign and the sign of the number with the largest absolute value will be positive. If the second and third terms of a trinomial are negative, then each binomial will be opposite in sign and the sign of the number with the largest absolute value will be negative.

EXAMPLES 9 and 10 **Factoring trinomials of the form $ax^2 + bx + c$ where $c < 0$**

Factor each expression completely.

 $n^2 + 3n - 10$

 (10) $n^2 - 3n - 10$

■ **SOLUTION**

Look for factors of -10 with sum 3.

Factors	Sum
$-1, 10$	9
$1, -10$	-9
$-2, 5$	3
$2, -5$	-3

← The factors must have opposite signs.

The numbers -2 and 5 have a product of -10 and a sum of 3.
So $n^2 + 3n - 10 = (n - 2)(n + 5)$.

■ **SOLUTION**

Look for factors of -10 with sum -3.

Factors	Sum
$-1, 10$	9
$1, -10$	-9
$-2, 5$	3
$2, -5$	-3

← The factors must have opposite signs.

The numbers 2 and -5 have a product of -10 and a sum of -3.
So $n^2 - 3n - 10 = (n + 2)(n - 5)$.

Sometimes you must factor a trinomial of the form $ax^2 + bx + c$ when a is a whole number greater than 1. In these cases you must consider not only the factors of the constant c, but also the factors of the leading coefficient a.

EXAMPLE 11 **Factoring trinomials of the form $ax^2 + bx + c$ where $a > 1$**

(11) Factor the expression $2w^2 - w - 6$.

■ **SOLUTION**

Step 1

List the factors of the leading coefficient, which is 2:

    1 and 2

List the factors of the constant, which is -6:

    1 and -6
    -1 and 6
    2 and -3
    -2 and 3

Step 2

Use the factors from Step 1 to write pairs of binomial factors. Look for $-1w$ as the middle term.

$(1w + 1)(2w - 6) \rightarrow -6w + 2w = -4w$
$(1w - 6)(2w + 1) \rightarrow 1w + (-12w) = -11w$
$(1w - 1)(2w + 6) \rightarrow 6w + (-2w) = 4w$
$(1w + 6)(2w - 1) \rightarrow -1w + 12w = 11w$
$(1w + 2)(2w - 3) \rightarrow -3w + 4w = 1w$
$(1w - 3)(2w + 2) \rightarrow 2w + (-6w) = -4w$
$(1w + 3)(2w - 2) \rightarrow -2w + 6w = 4w$
$(1w - 2)(2w + 3) \rightarrow 3w + (-4w) = -1w$ ✔

So $2w^2 - w - 6 = (w - 2)(2w + 3)$.

Note

Time Saver:
If the original trinomial had no common factor, its binomial factors cannot have common monomial factors. So, you do not have to test factors, such as $(2w - 6)$, that have a common factor of 2.

Recall that squares of sums and differences result in perfect square trinomials.

$$\text{For all real numbers } a \text{ and } b: \ (a+b)^2 = a^2 + 2ab + b^2$$
$$(a-b)^2 = a^2 - 2ab + b^2$$

You can use what you know about the squares of sums and differences to factor perfect square trinomials. The steps are described below.

To Factor a Perfect Square Trinomial

- Find the square root of the first and last terms.
- If the sign of the middle term is positive, then the second term of the factor is positive.
- If the sign of the middle term is negative, then the second term of the factor is negative.
- Check to make sure that twice the product of the first and last terms equals the middle term.

EXAMPLES 12 and 13   **Factoring perfect square trinomials**

 $x^2 + 6x + 9$

■ SOLUTION

$x^2 + 2(3)x + 3^2 = (x+3)^2$

13 $a^2 - 8ab + 16b^2$

■ SOLUTION

$a^2 - 4(2)b + (4b)^2 = (a-4b)^2$

Recall the rule for the product of the $a+b$ and $a-b$.

$$\text{For all real numbers } a \text{ and } b: \ (a-b)(a+b) = a^2 - b^2$$

You can use what you know about the product of $(a-b)(a+b)$ to factor the difference of two squares. The steps are described below.

To Factor the Difference of 2 Squares

- Find the square root of each term.
- Write two binomials that are the sum and difference of those square roots.

EXAMPLES 14 and 15   **Factoring the difference of 2 squares**

 $4x^4 - 9y^6$

■ SOLUTION

$(2x^2)^2 - (3y^3)^2 = (2x^2 - 3y^3)(2x^2 + 3y^3)$

15 $25a^2 - 49b^2$

■ SOLUTION

$(5a)^2 - (7b)^2 = (5a - 7b)(5a + 7b)$

You may be asked to determine the correctly factored form of a polynomial.

EXAMPLE 16   **Recognizing the correct factored form**

16 Which product is equivalent to $m^2 - 5m + 6$?

(1) $(m+3)(m-2)$ (3) $(m+3)(m+2)$
(2) $(m-3)(m-2)$ (4) $(m-3)(m+2)$

■ **SOLUTION**
Examine the choices.

(1) and (4) These products will each have a negative constant term.
(3)   This product will have a positive constant term, but the coefficient of the linear term will also be positive.
(2)   By a process of elimination, choice (2) must be the correct factorization. You can check any factorization by multiplying:

$$(m-3)(m-2) = m^2 - 2m - 3m + (-3)(-2) = m^2 - 5m + 6 \quad ✔$$

The correct choice is (2).

In some cases, factoring completely will involve two types of factorization. In general, you should always begin by looking for a common monomial factor.

EXAMPLES 17 and 18   **Factoring in two steps**

Factor each expression completely.

17 $5v^2 - 5$

■ **SOLUTION** $5v^2 - 5$ ← The GCF of $5v^2$ and 5 is 5.
$5(v^2 - 1)$ ← $v^2 - 1$ is a difference of two squares.
$5(v + 1)(v - 1)$

18 $6h^3 + 9h^2 - 6h$

■ **SOLUTION** $6h^3 + 9h^2 - 6h$ ← The GCF of $6h^3$, $9h^2$, and $6h$ is $3h$.
$3h(2h^2 + 3h - 2)$ ← $2h^2 + 3h - 2$ has two binomial factors.
$3h(2h - 1)(h + 2)$

Practice

Choose the numeral preceding the word or expression that best completes the statement or answers the question.

1 What is the greatest common factor of $24c^2d$, $18c^2d^2$, and $12cd^2$?

(1) $72c^2d^2$ (3) $6cd$
(2) $6c^2d$ (4) $2c^2d$

2 Which is a perfect square trinomial?

(1) $x^2 - 8x + 16x^2$ (3) $x^2 - 8x + 16$
(2) $x^2 + 8x - 16$ (4) $x^2 - 8x - 16$

3 Which is not a true statement?

(1) $a^2 + 2ab + b^2 = (a+b)^2$

(2) $a^2 - 2ab + b^2 = (a-b)^2$

(3) $a^2 + 2ab - b^2 = (b-a)^2$

(4) $a^2 - b^2 = (a+b)(a-b)$

4 Which expression is a factor of $9m^2 - 9m - 10$?

   (1) $3m - 5$ **(3)** $9m + 1$

   (2) $3m - 2$ **(4)** $9m - 1$

5 Which is equivalent to $9r^2 - 16s^2$?

   (1) $(3r + 4s)(3r - 4s)$

   (2) $(3r - 4s)^2$

   (3) $(9r + 16s)(9r - 16s)$

   (4) $(9r - 16s)^2$

6 Which expression cannot be factored?

   (1) $z^2 + 7z + 6$ **(3)** $z^2 + 5z - 6$

   (2) $z^2 + 7z - 6$ **(4)** $z^2 + 5z + 6$

In Exercises 7–10, find the GCF.

7 $9t^2, 15t, 12$ **8** $2y^3, 10y^2, 20y$

9 $4r^2s^2, 12rs^2, 9r^2s$ **10** a^3b^3, a^2b^3, a^2b

In Exercises 11–54, factor each expression completely. If it is not possible to factor over the integers, write *cannot be factored*.

11 $8n - 72$ **12** $9b^2 + 17b$

13 $12r^2 + 18r$ **14** $8v^3 - 36v$

15 $v^6 + v^3 + v$ **16** $3x^5 - 15x^3 + 9x^2$

17 $16j^2k^2 - 40jk$ **18** $4cd^2 + 2c^2d - 6cd$

19 $c^2 + 14c + 45$ **20** $a^2 - 16a + 28$

21 $x^2 - x - 30$ **22** $q^2 + 2q - 63$

23 $y^2 - 16y + 48$ **24** $b^2 - 14b - 72$

25 $h^2 + h - 42$ **26** $s^2 - 10s + 9$

27 $3d^2 + 8d + 5$ **28** $5m^2 - 11m + 2$

29 $3t^2 - 7t - 6$ **30** $3j^2 + 7j - 10$

31 $6x^2 - 19x + 15$ **32** $4y^2 - 4y - 15$

33 $w^2 - 10w + 25$ **34** $r^2 + 8r + 16$

35 $9z^2 + 30z + 25$ **36** $4c^2 - 60c + 225$

37 $4n^2 - 16$ **38** $12w^2 - 27$

39 $5z^2 + 25z + 30$ **40** $40d^2 - 10d - 15$

41 $50t^3 - 32t$ **42** $16y^3 + 48y^2 + 36y$

43 $k^6 - 9k^4$ **44** $b^4 - 1$

In Exercises 45–50, solve the problem. Clearly show all necessary work.

45 If $(x - 4)(x + w) = x^2 + 2x - 24$, what is the value of w?

46 What are all the possible values of n that make $x^2 + nx - 10$ a factorable expression over the integers?

47 For what value(s) of m is $x^2 + 2x + m$ a perfect square trinomial?

48 For what value(s) of p is $x^2 + px + 81$ a perfect square trinomial?

49 Explain why there is no integer value of q for which $x^2 + 7x + q$ is a perfect square.

50 Selena says that $(a - b)^2$ and $(b - a)^2$ are equivalent expressions. Do you agree or disagree? Explain.

Preparing for the Assessment

Choose the numeral preceding the word or expression that best completes the statement or answers the question.

1 What is the difference when $3r^2 + 5$ is subtracted from $3r^3 + 3r^2 + 2r$?

(1) $-3r^2 - 2r + 5$ **(3)** $3r^3 + 2r - 5$

(2) $3r^2 + 2r$ **(4)** $3r^3 + 6r^2 + 2r + 5$

2 Which is not equal to $5^2 \cdot 5^{-3}$?

(1) 5^{2-3} **(3)** $\dfrac{5^2}{5^3}$

(2) 5^{-1} **(4)** $(5^2)^{-3}$

3 Which is equivalent to the expression $(4w - 2)(3w - 5)$?

(1) $7w - 7$ **(3)** $7w^2 - 14w - 7$

(2) $-2w - 5$ **(4)** $12w^2 - 26w + 10$

4 Which of the following is a cubic binomial?

(1) $-6x^3$ **(3)** $5x^3 - 2x$

(2) $3x^2 + 3x$ **(4)** $-7x^3 + 4x + x^2$

5 What is the result when $2c^2 - 3c + 6$ is subtracted from $c^2 + c - 2$?

(1) $c^2 - 4c + 8$

(2) $-c^2 - 2c + 4$

(3) $c^2 - 4c + 8$

(4) $-c^2 + 4c - 8$

6 Which of the following is the product $(4x - 2)(5 - 3x)$?

(1) $-12x^2 + 14x - 10$

(2) $20x^2 + 12x - 10$

(3) $-12x^2 + 26x - 10$

(4) $-12x^2 + 20x$

7 Compare the degrees of the expressions $4x(x^2 + 5x)$ and $2x^2(4x + 10)$. Which has the greater degree?

(1) The degree of $4x(x^2 + 5x)$ is greater.

(2) The degree of $2x^2(4x + 10)$ is greater.

(3) The two degrees are equal.

(4) Cannot be determined

8 Which of the following is the factored form of $2x^2 - 5x - 12$?

(1) $(2x + 3)(x - 4)$ **(3)** $(2x - 5)(x - 7)$

(2) $(2x - 3)(x + 4)$ **(4)** $(2x - 2)(x - 6)$

9 Which is *not* equivalent to $-\dfrac{x + 5}{x - 1}$?

(1) $\dfrac{-x + 5}{x - 1}$ **(3)** $\dfrac{x + 5}{1 - x}$

(2) $\dfrac{-x - 5}{x - 1}$ **(4)** $\dfrac{x + 5}{-x + 1}$

10 What is equivalent to the expression $(6c^2 + 5c - 3) - (3c^2 + 8c - 1)$?

(1) $3c^2 + 13c - 4$ **(3)** $3c^2 - 3c - 2$

(2) $3c^2 - 3c - 4$ **(4)** $3c^2 + 13c - 2$

11 What is the product $(-3x^3y^2)(5xy^5)$?

(1) $-15x^4y^7$ **(3)** $-15x^3y^{10}$

(2) $2x^4y^7$ **(4)** $2x^3y^{10}$

12 Which is equivalent to the expression $(3xy)(2x^2y)^3$?

(1) $18x^6y^5$ **(3)** $216x^9y^6$

(2) $24x^7y^4$ **(4)** $18x^6y^3$

13 Which of the following expressions is equivalent to $\left(\dfrac{5x}{3y^2}\right)^{-1}$?

(1) $\dfrac{3y^2}{5x}$ **(2)** $\dfrac{3x}{5y^2}$ **(3)** $-\dfrac{5x}{3y^2}$ **(4)** $-\dfrac{3y^2}{5x}$

14 Simplify the expression $(w-8)+2(4w-1)$.

(1) $9w-10$ **(3)** $9w-9$

(2) $-23w+6$ **(4)** $10w-18$

15 What is the product $(2a-5)(3a+1)$?

(1) $6a^2-5$ **(3)** $6a^2-13a-5$

(2) $5a-4$ **(4)** $6a^2-17a-5$

16 Which trinomial is equivalent to $(2r-1)^2$?

(1) $4r^2+1$ **(3)** $4r^2+4r+1$

(2) $4r^2-4r+1$ **(4)** $4r-2$

17 Solve the equation $-4n+7=(n-1)(-3)$.

(1) $n=10$ **(3)** $n=4$

(2) $n=-\dfrac{10}{7}$ **(4)** $n=-4$

18 Which of the following is the solution for $5j-3(2j-1)=3j+8$?

(1) 10 **(2)** -3 **(3)** $-\dfrac{5}{4}$ **(4)** $-\dfrac{9}{4}$

19 Simplify the expression $(5j^2+3j)+(j^2+4j+4)-(2j-3)$.

(1) $11j^2-1$ **(3)** $6j^2+5j-1$

(2) $6j^2+5j+7$ **(4)** $11j^2-7$

20 Which of the following is equivalent to the expression $(2z^2-4)-(z^2-4)-(3z^2-2)$?

(1) $4z^2+2$ **(3)** $-2z^2+2$

(2) $-2z^2-10$ **(4)** $4z^2-10$

21 What is the GCF of the terms of the trinomial $3x^5-15x^3+9x^2$?

(1) 3 **(2)** x **(3)** $3x$ **(4)** $3x^2$

22 Which is the completely factored form of $5z^2+5z-30$?

(1) $(5z+15)(z-2)$ **(3)** $(5z-10)(z+3)$

(2) $5(z+3)(z-2)$ **(4)** $5(z-3)(z-2)$

23 The length of a triangular-shaped sail is represented by $2x+5$ and the height is represented by $2x-4$. Which expression represents the area of the sail?

(1) $4x+1$ **(3)** $2x^2+x-10$

(2) $4x^2-20$ **(4)** x^2+x-20

24 The length of a rug is represented by $x+6$, and the width is represented by $x-2$. Which expression represents the area of the rug?

(1) $2x+4$ **(3)** x^2-12

(2) $x^2+4x-12$ **(4)** $x^2-8x-12$

25 Two cars leave the same location at the same time. One car drives due east and the other travels south. The southbound car travels 12 mi less than the other. Which expression describes the distance between the two cars at that point?

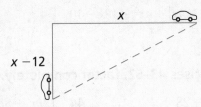

(1) $\sqrt{2x-12}$

(2) $\sqrt{x^2-12x}$

(3) $\sqrt{2x^2+144}$

(4) $\sqrt{2x^2-24x+144}$

26 Factor $2a^2+7a-4$ completely.

(1) $(2a+1)(a-4)$

(2) $2(a+4)(a-1)$

(3) $(a+4)(2a-1)$

(4) $(2a+4)(a-1)$

In Exercises 27–42, simplify each expression. Write answers in standard form.

27 $(6c^2 + 5c - 3) - (3c^2 + 8c - 1)$

28 $(4t + 7t^3 - t^2) + (3t - 2t^2 - 5t^3)$

29 $(4d - 6)(-3d)$

30 $5g(g^2 - 2g + 1)$

31 $(-2q^2 + q + 3) - 5(q^2 + 2q - 1)$

32 $(k + 9)(k - 2)$

33 $(y + 5)(y - 5)$

34 $(3y^3 + 8y - 3) + (2y - 5y^2)$

35 $(-4r^3 + 2r - 3r^2 + 1) + (2r^3 - 5r + 1)$

36 $(5h^2 + 4h + 8) - (3h^2 + h + 3)$

37 $(-7z^3 + 2z - 7) - (2z^3 - z - 3)$

38 $(3c^2 + 4c - 6) - (3c - 8 + 5c^2)$

39 $(x^2 + 5) + (3x + 8) + (5x^2 + 3x)$

40 $\dfrac{x^4 - 8x^3 + 15x^2 + 6x - 30}{x - 5}$

41 $\dfrac{3x^3 - 20x^2 - 63x}{x - 9}$

42 $\dfrac{8x^5 + 4x^4 + 4x^2 - 18x - 10}{4x + 2}$

In Exercises 43–52, factor completely.

43 $7z - 28$ **44** $12m^2 + 8m$

45 $a^2b^2 - ab^2 + a^2b$ **46** $t^2 + 6t - 55$

47 $w^2 + 16w + 64$ **48** $h^2 - 36$

49 $2p^2 + 9p + 7$ **50** $3d^2 - d - 10$

51 $32s^2 - 2$ **52** $6c^4 - 9c^3 - 15c^2$

In Exercises 53–56, solve the problem. Clearly show all necessary work.

53 The volume of a box is represented by the product $(x^2 + 5x + 6) \cdot (x + 4)$. Give the polynomial that represents the length of the base of the box.

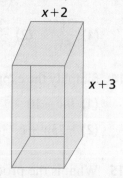

54 A rectangular pool is being constructed according to the plan shown below. A formula for the area A of a rectangle is $A = lw$, where l is the length of the rectangle and w is the width. Write a simplified expression for the total area in square feet of the pool and walkway.

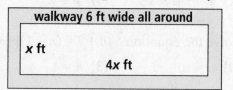

walkway 6 ft wide all around

x ft

$4x$ ft

55 The volume V of a rectangular prism is given by the formula $V = lwh$, where l is the length of the prism, w is its width, and h is its height. The length of a certain rectangular prism is three times its width w, and its height is 2 ft less than its width. Write a simplified expression that represents the volume in feet.

56 Suppose you deposit $1200 into an account that pays simple interest at an annual interest rate r. At the end of two years, the amount in the account in dollars is represented by $1200(1 + r)^2$. Simplify this expression and write the result in standard form.

8 Quadratic Equations and Functions

High School Mathematics Teacher

Being a high school mathematics teacher is a career that brings together a love of math, creativity, and a desire to work with young people. From creating lesson plans to teaching new material to writing tests, a teacher's day is never the same. Depending on state requirements, most mathematics teachers hold a bachelor's degree in their subject area, and must follow a training program that gives them fieldwork time in the classroom under the supervision of a master teacher. Their college coursework consists not only of upper-level math, but also educational practice and theory classes.

8.1 | Solving Quadratic Equations

A.CED.1
A.CED.3
A.REI.4

A **quadratic equation** is any equation that can be written in the form

$ax^2 + bx + c = 0$, where a, b, and c are real numbers and $a \neq 0$.

This is the **standard form of a quadratic equation** in x.

The following examples describe both quadratic and non-quadratic equations.

Equation	Degree	Description	Classification
$3x + 2 = 7x - 5$	1	Both expressions are linear in terms of x.	Linear equation
$n^2 = 25$	2	Not in standard form	Quadratic equation
$6x^2 + 5x - 7 = 0$	2	Standard form	Quadratic equation
$27a^3 = 9$	3	Degree > 2	Polynomial equation
$1 = 3^x$	x	Variable as exponent	Exponential equation

EXAMPLES 1 and 2   Writing quadratic equations in standard form

Write each quadratic equation in standard form.

1 $6 - n^2 = 5n$

- **SOLUTION**

$$6 - n^2 = 5n$$
$$6 - n^2 - 5n = 5n - 5n$$
$$6 - n^2 - 5n = 0$$
$$-n^2 - 5n + 6 = 0$$

2 $5x^2 = 3x - 2$

- **SOLUTION**

$$5x^2 = 3x - 2$$
$$5x^2 + 2 = 3x - 2 + 2$$
$$5x^2 + 2 = 3x$$
$$5x^2 + 2 - 3x = 0$$
$$5x^2 - 3x + 2 = 0$$

A **solution to a quadratic equation** in one variable is any number that makes the equation true. For example, if $g^2 + g = 6$, you can conclude that $g = 2$ and $g = -3$ are solutions since $(2)^2 + 2 = 4 + 2 = 6$ and $(-3)^2 + (-3) = 9 - 3 = 6$. Solutions are also called **roots.**

If the value of b (the coefficient of the linear term in a quadratic equation) is zero, the equation can be written as $x^2 = k$. If $k \geq 0$, this equation can be solved using square roots. There are no real solutions for the quadratic equation if k is negative ($k < 0$).

For example, you can solve the equation $x^2 = 64$ by finding the square root of each side of the equation. Therefore, $x = \pm\sqrt{64}$; $x = \pm 8$.

Solving quadratic equations in one variable

Solve each of the following quadratic equations.

3 $x^2 = 9$

■ SOLUTION
$x^2 = 9$
$x = \pm\sqrt{9}$
$x = \pm 3$

4 $5s^2 = 125$

■ SOLUTION
$5s^2 = 125$
$\dfrac{5s^2}{5} = \dfrac{125}{5}$
$s^2 = 25$
$s = \pm\sqrt{25} = \pm 5$

5 $x^2 - 61 = 20$

■ SOLUTION
$x^2 - 61 = 20$
$x^2 = 81$
$x = \pm\sqrt{81} = \pm 9$

6 $3m^2 - 24 = 2m^2 + 40$

■ SOLUTION
$3m^2 - 24 = 2m^2 + 40$
$3m^2 = 2m^2 + 64$
$m^2 = 64$
$m = \pm\sqrt{64} = \pm 8$

7 $x^2 + 40 = 15$

■ SOLUTION
$x^2 + 40 = 15$
$x^2 = -25$
$x = \pm\sqrt{-25}$
no real solution

8 $3(h + 5)^2 = 48$

■ SOLUTION
$3(h + 5)^2 = 48$
$(h + 5)^2 = 16$
$\sqrt{(h + 5)^2} = \pm\sqrt{16}$
$h + 5 = \pm 4$
$h + 5 = 4$ or $h + 5 = -4$
$h = -1$ or $h = -9$

If the value of k in the equation $x^2 = k$ is not a perfect square, then the roots are irrational. You can use a calculator to approximate the root to the desired degree of accuracy.

Solving quadratic equations with irrational roots

Solve each of the following equations and round your answers to the nearest hundredth.

9 $12n^2 = 60$

■ SOLUTION
$12n^2 = 60$
$n^2 = 5$
$n = \pm\sqrt{5}$
$n = \pm 2.24$

10 $3y^2 - 144 = 30$

■ SOLUTION
$3y^2 - 144 = 30$
$3y^2 = 174$
$y^2 = 58$
$y = \pm\sqrt{58}$
$y = \pm 7.62$

11 $2(x - 5)^2 - 10 = 24$

■ SOLUTION
$2(x - 5)^2 - 10 = 24$
$2(x - 5)^2 = 34$
$(x - 5)^2 = 17$
$x - 5 = \pm\sqrt{17}$
$x - 5 = \pm 4.12$
$x = 4.12 + 5$ or $x = -4.12 + 5$
$x = 9.12$ or $x = 0.88$

183

Certain verbal problems translate to quadratic equations. You can use what you know about quadratic equations to solve these types of equations.

 EXAMPLES 12 and 13 — **Using quadratic equations to solve verbal problems**

Solve the following problems using a quadratic equation.

12 The sum of a number and 5 is squared. The result is 81. What are the numbers that make this statement true?

■ **SOLUTION**

Let n represent the number.

$$(n + 5)^2 = 81$$
$$n + 5 = \pm\sqrt{81}$$
$$n + 5 = \pm 9$$
$$n + 5 = 9 \text{ or } n + 5 = -9$$
$$n = 4 \text{ or } n = -14$$

13 Five times the square of the sum of two and a number is equal to 45. What are the numbers that make this statement true?

■ **SOLUTION**

Let n represent the number.

$$5(n + 2)^2 = 45$$
$$n + 2 = \pm\sqrt{9}$$
$$n + 2 = \pm 3$$
$$n + 2 = 3 \text{ or } n + 2 = -3$$
$$n = 1 \text{ or } n = -5$$

Quadratic equations can be used to describe the area of some shapes algebraically. You can use these equations to find side lengths and areas.

It is important to check the solutions of equations with the information in the problem. Often a solution will be rejected because it does not make sense in the context of the problem. For example, if you are asked to find a side length, a negative solution does not make sense.

EXAMPLE 14 — **Using a quadratic equation to solve an area problem**

14 Write an expression in x for the area of the shaded region. Find x such that the area of the shaded region equals 75% of the full square.

■ **SOLUTION**

area of full square − area of small square

$$16^2 - x^2$$

Since 75% = 0.75, solve $16^2 - x^2 = 0.75 \times 16^2$.

$$16^2 - x^2 = 0.75 \times 256$$
$$256 - x^2 = 192$$
$$-x^2 = -64 \qquad \leftarrow \text{ Use the Addition Property of Equality.}$$
$$x = \pm 8$$
$$x = 8 \qquad \leftarrow \text{ Reject the negative solution.}$$

The desired value of x is 8 inches.

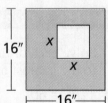

Note

Because the length of a square must be a positive number, keep 8 as a solution and reject −8 as a possible solution.

Choose the numeral preceding the word or expression that best completes the statement or answers the question.

1 Which is not a quadratic equation?

(1) $x^2 = 81$

(2) $3x^2 = 5x - 7$

(3) $4x + 5 = 9 - 2x$

(4) $5x - 7x^2 = 21$

2 Which equation has the same solutions as $2(b^2 - 5) = 18$?

(1) $b^2 = 14$ (3) $2b^2 = 23$

(2) $b^2 = 8$ (4) $b^2 = \dfrac{18}{2} - 5$

3 Which numbers are the solutions to $n^2 = 2.25$?

(1) $0.15; -0.15$ (3) $1.5; -1.5$

(2) $0.05; -0.05$ (4) $1.125; -1.125$

4 Suppose x represents a real number. Which statement is true?

(1) $\sqrt{x^2} = x$ for all x

(2) $\sqrt{x^2} = -x$ for all x

(3) $\sqrt{x^2} = \dfrac{1}{2}x$ for all x

(4) $\sqrt{x^2} = x$ for all x zero or more

In Exercises 5–14, solve each quadratic equation. Give exact solutions. If the equation has no solutions, so state.

5 $x^2 = 49$ **6** $-x^2 = -9$

7 $3a^2 = 48$ **8** $12x^2 = 3$

9 $3a^2 - 5 = 43$ **10** $12m^2 + 3 = 3$

11 $12m^2 - 23 = -11$

12 $5x^2 + 6x - 7 = 3x^2 + 6x - 5$

13 $5n^2 + n + 4 = 6n^2 + n - 5$

14 $5k^2 - 2k + 18 = 9k^2 - 2k - 82$

In Exercises 15–20, solve each quadratic equation. Give solutions rounded to the nearest hundredth. If the equation has no solutions, so state.

15 $-x^2 = -10$ **16** $-4t^2 = -48$

17 $3a^2 = 2a^2 + 2$ **18** $-3c^2 = 2c^2 - 10$

19 $3(x - 5)^2 = 120$

20 $5x^2 + x + 8 = 3x^2 + x + 30$

In Exercises 21–26, solve the problem. Clearly show all necessary work.

21 The ratio of 90 to some number is equal to the ratio of that number to 40. What is the number?

22 Suppose that you want to build a square garden whose area is to be 729 square feet. What should the length of one side be?

23 The area A of a circle with radius r is given by $A = \pi r^2$. If the area of a circular pond is 1156 square feet, what is the radius to the nearest tenth of a foot?

24 The length of a rectangular sign is three times its width. What are the dimensions of the sign if its area is 192 square feet?

25 Write an expression in m for the shaded region. For what m will the area of the shaded region be 175 square units?

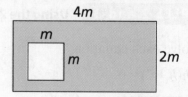

26 What are the lengths of the height and the base of this right triangle?

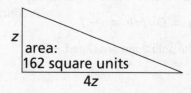

185

8.2 More Methods for Solving Quadratic Equations

Suppose that each card below has a number written on the reverse side. If you are told $ab = 0$, you must conclude that at least one of the cards has 0 written on it. For example, if card a has 2 written on it, then $2b = 0$. Therefore, b must equal 0.

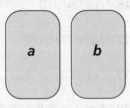

The *Zero-Product Property* is a generalization of this discussion.

Zero-Product Property

If a and b are real numbers and $ab = 0$, then either $a = 0$ or $b = 0$ (or both).

If $2x = 0$, then $x = 0$.   If $-3(x - 5) = 0$, then $x - 5 = 0$.   If $x(x - 2) = 0$, then $x = 0$ or $x - 2 = 0$.

EXAMPLE 1   **Reading solutions from a product equal to 0**

1. Which is true given that $(n - 5)(n + 4) = 0$?

    (1) $n - 5 = 0$ and $n + 4 = 0$ (3) $n - 5 = 0$ or $n + 4 = 0$
    (2) $n - 5 = 0$ and $n + 4 \neq 0$ (4) $n - 5 \neq 0$ and $n + 4 = 0$

    ■ **SOLUTION**

    By the Zero-Product Property, one or the other factor in $(n - 5)(n + 4)$ equals 0. Therefore, $n - 5 = 0$ or $n + 4 = 0$. The correct choice is **(3)**.

You can use the Zero-Product Property to solve a quadratic equation written in factored form.

EXAMPLES 2 and 3   **Using the Zero-Product Property with factored form**

Solve each equation.

2. $3h(h + 7) = 0$

    ■ **SOLUTION**

    $3h(h + 7) = 0$

    $3h = 0$ or $h + 7 = 0$ ← Apply the Zero-Product Property.

    $h = 0$ or $h = -7$

    The solutions are 0 and −7.

3. $(x + 5)(x + 6) = 0$

    ■ **SOLUTION**

    $(x + 5)(x + 6) = 0$

    $x + 5 = 0$ or $x + 6 = 0$ ← Apply the Zero-Product Property.

    $x = -5$ or $x = -6$

    The solutions are −5 and −6.

You can use the Zero-Product Property to solve quadratic equations not written in factored form like those shown below.

$$b^2 + 3b = 0 \qquad m^2 + m - 6 = 0 \qquad z^2 + 4z + 4 = 0$$

You can use these steps to solve quadratic equations by factoring.

Solving a Quadratic Equation by Factoring

Step 1 Write the given quadratic equation in standard form, if it is not already.

Step 2 Factor the quadratic expression into a pair of linear expressions.

Step 3 Use the Zero-Product Property to write a pair of linear equations.

Step 4 Solve the linear equations.

Step 5 The solutions to the linear equations are the solutions (roots) to the given equation.

EXAMPLES 4 through 6   **Solving a quadratic equation by factoring**

4   Solve $x^2 + 3x = 0$.

■ **SOLUTION**

$$x^2 + 3x = 0$$
$$x(x + 3) = 0 \qquad \leftarrow \text{Factor the quadratic expression.}$$
$$x = 0 \ or \ x = -3 \qquad \leftarrow \text{Apply the Zero-Product Property.}$$

5   Solve $\dfrac{z}{2} = \dfrac{z - 2}{z + 6}$.

■ **SOLUTION**

$$z(z + 6) = 2(z - 2) \qquad \leftarrow \text{Cross product.}$$
$$z^2 + 6z = 2z - 4$$
$$z^2 + 4z + 4 = 0$$
$$(z + 2)(z + 2) = 0 \qquad \leftarrow z^2 + 4z + 4 \text{ is a perfect square trinomial.}$$
$$z + 2 = 0 \ or \ z + 2 = 0 \qquad \leftarrow \text{Apply the Zero-Product Property.}$$
$$z = -2 \ or \ z = -2 \qquad \leftarrow -2 \text{ is called a double root.}$$

6   Find the roots of $6w^2 - 28 = 13w$.

■ **SOLUTION**

$$6w^2 - 28 = 13w$$
$$6w^2 - 13w - 28 = 0 \qquad \leftarrow \text{Write in standard form.}$$
$$(2w - 7)(3w + 4) = 0 \qquad \leftarrow \text{Apply the Zero-Product Property.}$$
$$2w - 7 = 0 \ or \ 3w + 4 = 0$$
$$w = \frac{7}{2} \ or \ w = -\frac{4}{3}$$

Note

A product must be equal to zero to use the Zero-Product Property.

187

EXAMPLES 7 and 8 **Using the Zero-Product Property to Write a Quadratic Equation**

7 Write a quadratic equation that would have roots of -5 and 3.

■ SOLUTION

Roots $\rightarrow$	-5 or 3
Solutions $\rightarrow$	$x = -5$ or $x = 3$
Set to 0 $\rightarrow$	$x + 5 = 0$ or $x - 3 = 0$
If $a = 0$ or $b = 0$, then $ab = 0 \rightarrow$	$(x + 5)(x - 3) = 0$ $\leftarrow$ **Zero-Property backwards**
Multiply binomials $\rightarrow$	$x^2 + 2x - 15 = 0$ $\leftarrow$ **Quadratic Equation**

8 Write a equation that would have roots of 0, -2 and $\dfrac{2}{3}$.

■ SOLUTION

$0, -2$ or $\dfrac{2}{3}$ $\leftarrow$ **Roots**

$x = 0$ or $x = -2$ or $x = \dfrac{2}{3}$ $\leftarrow$ **Solutions**

$x = 0$ or $x + 2 = 0$ or $3x - 2 = 0$ $\leftarrow$ **Set to 0**

$x(x + 2)(3x - 2) = 0$ $\leftarrow$ **Zero-Property backwards**

$x(3x^2 + 4x - 4) = 0$ $\leftarrow$ **Quadratic Equation**

$3x^3 + 4x^2 - 4x = 0$ $\leftarrow$ **Cubic or Polynomial Equation**

Notice that there are 3 roots and the polynomial equation's degree is 3.

Here is another way to solve a quadratic:

Solving a Quadratic Equation by Completing the Square

Step 1 Write the equation in Standard form.

Step 2 Divide all terms so $a = 1$.

Step 3 Isolate the constant term.

Step 4 Find the value that completes the quadratic and linear terms to a perfect square trinomial.

Step 5 Add the found value to both sides of the equation.

Step 6 Write the perfect square trinomial as a binomial squared.

Step 7 Use the square root method to solve the equation.

9   Solve $x^2 - 6x - 27 = 0$

■ **SOLUTION**

$x^2 - 6x - 27 = 0$ ← **Equation is in standard form with $a = 1$**

$x^2 - 6x = 27$ ← **Isolate the constant term.**

$\left[\dfrac{-6}{2}\right]^2 = [-3]^2 = 9$ ← **Find value to "complete the square"**

$x^2 - 6x + 9 = 27 + 9$ ← **Add value to both sides.**

$(x - 3)^2 = 36$ ← **Write the perfect trinomial as a binomial squared.**

$\sqrt{(x - 3)^2} = \pm 6$ ← **Square root both sides and solve.**

$x - 3 = 6$ or $x - 3 = -6$

$x = 9$ or $x = -3$

10   Solve $2x^2 = x + 6$

■ **SOLUTION**

$2x^2 = x + 6$

$2x^2 - x - 6 = 0$ ← **Equation is in standard form but $a \neq 1$**

$x^2 - \dfrac{1}{2}x - 3 = 0$ ← **Equation with $a = 1$**

$x^2 - \dfrac{1}{2}x = 3$ ← **Isolate the constant term.**

$\left[\dfrac{1}{2}\left(-\dfrac{1}{2}\right)\right]^2 = \left[-\dfrac{1}{4}\right]^2 = \dfrac{1}{16}$ ← **Find value to "complete the square"**

$x^2 - \dfrac{1}{2}x + \dfrac{1}{16} = 3 + \dfrac{1}{16}$ ← **Add value to both sides.**

$\left(x - \dfrac{1}{4}\right)^2 = \dfrac{49}{16}$ ← **Write the perfect trinomial as a binomial squared.**

$\sqrt{\left(x - \dfrac{1}{4}\right)^2} = \pm\dfrac{7}{4}$ ← **Square root both sides and solve.**

$x - \dfrac{1}{4} = \dfrac{7}{4}$ or $x - \dfrac{1}{4} = -\dfrac{7}{4}$

$x = \dfrac{8}{4} = 2$ or $x = -\dfrac{6}{4} = -\dfrac{3}{2}$

> **Note**
>
> Recall that the value that "completes the square" is $\left[\dfrac{b}{2}\right]^2$

A most important method to solve quadratic equations is a formula that is derived from $ax^2 + bx + c = 0$ using the completing the square method. You can use the **quadratic formula** to find the roots of any quadratic equation in standard form.

Solving a Quadratic Equation, Using the Quadratic Formula

If $ax^2 + bx + c = 0$, a, b, and c are real numbers, and $a \neq 0$,

$$x = \frac{-b \pm \sqrt{b^2 - 4ac}}{2a}.$$

- If $b^2 - 4ac \geq 0$, there are two distinct real solutions.
- If $b^2 - 4ac = 0$, there is one real solution.
- If $b^2 - 4ac \leq 0$, there are no real solutions.

EXAMPLES 11 and 12 **Using the quadratic formula to solve an equation**

11 Solve $n^2 + 5n - 7 = 0$. Approximate irrational solutions to the nearest hundredth.

■ SOLUTION

$n^2 + 5n - 7 = 0$

$$n = \frac{-5 \pm \sqrt{5^2 - 4(1)(-7)}}{2(1)} \leftarrow a = 1, b = 5, c = -7$$

$$n = \frac{-5 + \sqrt{53}}{2} \approx 1.14 \text{ or } n = \frac{-5 - \sqrt{53}}{2} \approx -6.14$$

12 Solve $y^2 - 3y = 9$ and express solution in simplified radical form.

■ SOLUTION

$y^2 - 3y = 9$ in standard form is $y^2 - 3y - 9 = 0$, so $a = 1$, $b = -3$, and $c = -9$.

$$y = \frac{3 \pm \sqrt{9 - 4(1)(-9)}}{2}$$

$$y = \frac{3 \pm \sqrt{9 + 36}}{2} = \frac{3 \pm \sqrt{45}}{2} = \frac{3 \pm 3\sqrt{5}}{2} = \frac{3}{2} \pm \frac{3\sqrt{5}}{2}$$

EXAMPLE 13   **Deriving the Quadratic Formula**

 Given $ax^2 + bx + c = 0$, use completing the square to derive the formula.

■ SOLUTION

$ax^2 + bx + c = 0$ ← Equation is in standard form but $a \neq 1$

$x^2 + \dfrac{b}{a}x + \dfrac{c}{a} = 0$ ← Divide by a . Equation with $a = 1$

$x^2 + \dfrac{b}{a}x = -\dfrac{c}{a}$ ← Isolate the constant term.

$\left[\dfrac{1}{2}\left(\dfrac{b}{a}\right)\right]^2 = \left[\dfrac{b}{2a}\right]^2 = \dfrac{b^2}{4a^2}$ ← Find value to "complete the square"

$x^2 + \dfrac{b}{a}x + \dfrac{b^2}{4a^2} = -\dfrac{c}{a} + \dfrac{b^2}{4a^2}$ ← Add value to both sides.

$\left(x + \dfrac{b}{2a}\right)^2 = \dfrac{-4ac \pm b^2}{4a^2}$ ← Write the perfect trinomial as a binomial squared.

$\sqrt{\left(x + \dfrac{b}{2a}\right)^2} = \pm\sqrt{\dfrac{b^2 - 4ac}{4a^2}}$ ← Square root both sides and solve.

$x + \dfrac{b}{2a} = \pm\dfrac{\sqrt{b^2 - 4ac}}{2a}$ ← Simplify square root both sides.

$x = -\dfrac{b}{2a} \pm \dfrac{\sqrt{b^2 - 4ac}}{2a}$ ← Solve for x.

$x = \dfrac{-b \pm \sqrt{b^2 - 4ac}}{2a}$

You can use the quadratic formula to solve quadratic equations that can also be solved by factoring. Consider $6x^2 + x = 12$.

$6x^2 + x = 12$

$6x^2 + x - 12 = 0$

$(2x + 3)(3x - 4) = 0$

$x = -\dfrac{3}{2}$ or $x = \dfrac{4}{3}$

$6x^2 + x - 12 = 0$

$x = \dfrac{-1 \pm \sqrt{1^2 - 4(6)(-12)}}{2(6)}$

$x = \dfrac{-1 \pm 17}{12} = -\dfrac{3}{2}$ or $x = \dfrac{4}{3}$

Choose the numeral preceding the word
or expression that best completes the
statement or answers the question.

1 The solutions to $(z + 1)(z + 2) = 0$ are

   (1) 1 and 2.   **(3)** −1 and −2.

   (2) 0 and −2.   **(4)** 0 and −1.

2 The solutions to $a^2 - 10a = 0$ are

   (1) 0 and −10.   **(3)** 1 and 10.

   (2) 0 and 10.   **(4)** 1 and −10.

3 The solutions to $n(n + 1)(n - 2) = 0$ are

   (1) 0, 1, and 2.   **(3)** −1 and −2.

   (2) 0 and −2.   **(4)** 0, −1, and 2.

**In Exercises 4–9, solve each equation using
the zero-product property.**

4 $x^2 + 5x + 6 = 0$ **5** $a^2 - 5a = 0$

6 $x^2 - 64 = 0$ **7** $18d - 81 = d^2$

8 $r^3 - 7r^2 - 18r = 0$ **9** $4x^3 - 100x = 0$

**For Exercises 10–12, write a equation in
standard form that has the given roots.**

10 −3 or 7   **11** 6 or $\dfrac{3}{4}$

12 0 or −1 or $\dfrac{5}{6}$

**For Exercises 13–15, solve each equation by
completing the square.**

13 $x^2 = 20 - 8x$ **14** $2b^2 - b = 21$

15 $x^2 + 7x = 8$

**In Exercises 16–23, solve the problem. Clearly
show all necessary work.**

16 The altitude of a model rocket is given by
$h = -16t^2 + 160t$ where h is the altitude in
feet and t is elapsed time in seconds. After
how many seconds of flight will the rocket
hit the ground?

17 The length and width of a rectangle are
represented by consecutive even integers.
The area of the rectangle is 224 square
inches. What are the length and the width?

18 A positive number is 5 more than another.
Their product is 36. What are the numbers?

19 A rectangle is 8 feet long and 6 feet wide. If
each side is increased by the same amount,
the area of the new rectangle is 72 square
feet more than the area of the original
rectangle. Find the length and width of the
new rectangle in feet.

20 The volume of a rectangular solid is the
product of its length, width, and height. The
volume of this solid is 440 cubic feet. What
are the dimensions of the base?

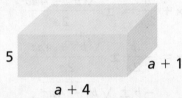

5                  $a + 1$

       $a + 4$

21 One number is 3 more than another. The sum
of their squares is 89. What are the numbers?

22 The figure below shows a square inside a
rectangle. If the area of the shaded region is
55 square units, determine the value of x.

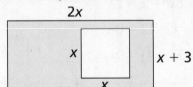

$2x$

x $x + 3$

x

23 The product of two consecutive integers is
132. What is the sum of the numbers?

In Exercises 24–26, solve by using the quadratic formula. Give solutions to the nearest tenth. If the equation has no real solutions, so state.

24 $n^2 + n - 1 = 0$

25 $p^2 + p - 3 = 0$

26 $-2h^2 + h + 1 = 0$

In Exercises 27–31, solve by using the quadratic formula. Give the solutions in simplified radical form.

27 $3d^2 - 8d + 3 = 0$

28 $-m^2 - m + 10 = 10m - 1$

29 $3z^2 - 3z - 1 = 2z^2 - z + 3$

30 $4x^2 + 13 = 16x$

31 $x^2 - 2x = 11$

8.3 Quadratic Functions: The Parabola

The equation $y = ax^2 + bx + c$, where a, b, and c are real numbers and $a \neq 0$ represents a **quadratic function.** Its graph is a **parabola,** a smooth, symmetric, U-shaped curve.

For example, a table of values for $y = x^2 - 2x - 4$ and its graph are shown here.

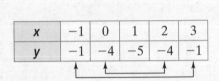

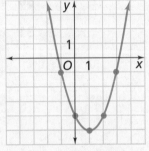

x	−1	0	1	2	3
y	−1	−4	−5	−4	−1

On the graph, imagine the vertical line of symmetry at $x = 1$. The table shows that symmetry numerically in the y-values about the point $(1,-5)$.

Characteristics of the Quadratic Function

Parabola with the equation form $y = ax^2 + bx + c$

- For a Quadratic Function, both the **Domain and Range** are subsets of the real numbers.

- The parabola has a **Vertex,** also called the *turning point*, which is the highest or lowest point. The x-coordinate of the vertex has a value of $-\frac{b}{2a}$.

- The parabola is symmetric about a vertical line called the **Axis of Symmetry.** This line passes through the vertex and has the equation: $x = -\frac{b}{2a}$.

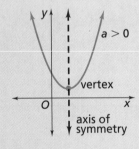

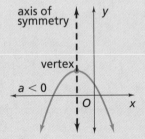

- If $a > 0$, the parabola opens upward and has positive end-behavior.

  If $a < 0$, the parabola opens downward and has negative end-behavior.

- If $a > 0$, the vertex is the lowest point on the parabola. The y-coordinate of the vertex is the **minimum** value of the function.

  If $a < 0$, the vertex is the highest point on the parabola. The y-coordinate of the vertex is the **maximum** value of the function.

- The parabola has a single y-intercept at $x = 0$.

Calculating a Vertex and Axis of Symmetry

  Given the quadratic function $f(x) = 2x^2 - 4x + 5$, find the equation of the parabola's axis of symmetry.

■ **SOLUTION**

The formula for a parabola's axis of symmetry is

$$x = -\frac{b}{2a}$$

The given function has $a = 2$ and $b = -4$

$$= -\frac{-4}{2(2)}$$

$$= -(-1)$$

Axis of symmetry is

$$x = 1$$

$$f(1) = 2(1)^2 - 4(1) = 5$$

$$= 2(1) - 4 + 5 = 3$$

Vertex is $(1, 3)$.

You can also identify the vertex and the axis of symmetry from the graph of a parabola.

Identifying the vertex and axis of symmetry of a parabola

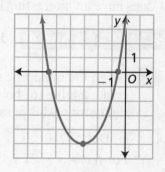

2 Find the vertex and the equation for the axis of symmetry of the parabola shown.

■ **SOLUTION**

Because the vertex is either the lowest or highest point of a parabola, the vertex of this parabola is $(-3, -5)$. The equation of the axis of symmetry is $x =$ 'the x-coordinate of the vertex'; therefore, the equation is $x = -3$.

You can use the characteristics of a parabola to match an equation to its graph.

Recognizing an equation for a parabola

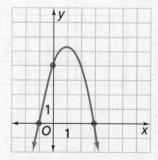

3 Which equation represents the graph shown here?

(1) $y = -\frac{4}{3}x^2 + \frac{8}{3}x + 4$ (3) $y = \frac{4}{3}x^2 - \frac{8}{3}x + 4$

(2) $y = -\frac{4}{3}x^2 - \frac{8}{3}x - 4$ (4) $y = \frac{4}{3}x^2 - \frac{8}{3}x - 4$

■ **SOLUTION**

Eliminate choices (3) and (4) because the parabola has negative end-behavior; $a < 0$. Because $y = 4$ when $x = 0$, the graph's y-intercept is $(0, 4)$. Eliminate choice (2). The correct choice is (1).

195

You can graph a quadratic function by making a table of values. Finding the coordinates of the vertex first can reduce the work involved.

EXAMPLE 4   **Using the vertex to help sketch a parabola**

4 Graph $y = -x^2 - 2x + 4$ using the vertex and a table of values. Label the axis of symmetry.

■ **SOLUTION**

Calculate the value of $-\dfrac{b}{2a} = x$. $-\dfrac{-2}{2(-1)} = -1 = x$

An equation for the axis of symmetry is $x = -1$. Make a table containing five x-values with -1 being the third x-value.

x	-3	-2	-1	0	1
y	1	4	5	4	1

Note

Notice the numerical symmetry around the ordered pair $(-1, 5)$, the parabola's vertex.

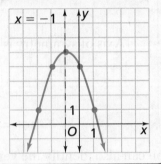

An important characteristic of a linear function is its constant rate of change or slope. The parabola as a smooth curve *does not* have a constant rate of change, but does have an interesting pattern of change between points.

EXAMPLES 5 and 6   **Investigating Change on a Parabola**   (MP)

5 Given the quadratic function $f(x) = x^2 - 2x + 1$, find its vertex, create a table to show the coordinates of the next four points on the right arm of this parabola, then graph the points.

■ **SOLUTION**

For $f(x) = x^2 - 2x + 1$, $a = 1$; $b = -2$ and $c = 1$. The parabola opens upward.

The equation of the axis of symmetry is $x = -\dfrac{b}{2a} = 1$

The coordinates of the vertex are $(x, f(x)) \rightarrow (1, 0)$

Note

The delta symbol Δ, means change or difference.

Table:

	Δx	1	1	1	1
x		1	2	3	4	5
$f(x)$		0	1	4	9	16
	Δy		1	3	5	7

→ The x values increase by 1 unit.

→ The $f(x)$ values increase by "odd number" units.

Graph:

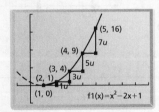

Given the quadratic function $f(x) = -x^2 + 4x - 3$, graph the parabola using vertex, axis of symmetry, the point change pattern, and line reflection.

■ **SOLUTION**

For $f(x) = -x^2 + 4x - 3$, $a = -1$; $b = 4$ and $c = -3$. The parabola has negative end-behavior.

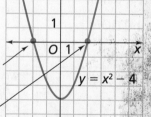

Axis: $x = 2$ Vertex: (2, 1)

Change pattern for 3 points on right arm:

$V(2, 1)$; $(3, 0)$; $(4, -3)$; $(5, -8)$ $\Delta x = +1$;

$$\Delta y = -1, -3, -5$$

Subtract "odd numbered" units since the parabola open downward.

The graph shows these points in blue. Reflect them over the axis of symmetry for their black image points:

$(3, 0) \rightarrow (1, 0)$; $(4, -3) \rightarrow (0, -3)$; $(5, -8) \rightarrow (-1, -8)$ to produce the left arm of the parabola.

The graph of a parabola can be used to find the solutions of its corresponding quadratic equation.

If $f(x) = ax^2 + bx + c$, where a, b, and c are real numbers and $a \neq 0$ represents the quadratic function, then $ax^2 + bx + c = 0$, with the same constraints, represents the quadratic equation.

The solutions to a quadratic equation are called the **roots**.

Look at how the x-intercepts of the parabola for $y = x^2 - 4$ are related to the roots of $x^2 - 4 = 0$.

The x-intercepts are $(-2, 0)$ and $(2, 0)$. Notice that when the point's x-values are substituted in

$$x^2 - 4 = 0$$

$x = -2 : 4 - 4 = 0$ is true and

$x = 2 : 4 - 4 = 0$ is also true.

x-intercept: -2

x-intercept: 2

The x-intercepts are both solutions or the roots of the equation.

197

In general, you can make the following statements relating solutions to quadratic equations and graphs of quadratic functions.

Solutions to Quadratic Equations and Graphs of Quadratic Functions

- The real numbers that are solutions to $ax^2 + bx + c = 0$ are the x-intercepts of the graph of $y = ax^2 + bx + c$.

- The x-intercepts of the graph of $y = ax^2 + bx + c$ are the real solutions to $ax^2 + bx + c = 0$.

- The x-intercepts of the graph are called the **zeros** of the function.

EXAMPLE 7   **Finding real solutions from the x-intercepts of a graph**

7 The diagram represents the graph of a quadratic function. Which are the solutions of the corresponding quadratic equation?

(1) −2 and −4   (2) −2 and 4   (3) 2 and −4   (4) 2 and 4

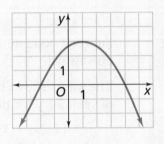

■ **SOLUTION**

The graph crosses the x-axis at $(-2, 0)$ and $(4, 0)$. Therefore, the x-intercepts are −2 and 4. The correct choice is **(2)**.

You can also use the capabilities of a graphing calculator to find the solutions of a quadratic equation.

EXAMPLE 8   **Finding real solutions of a quadratic equation from a graph**   (MP)

8 Solve $x^2 + 5x - 7 = 0$ graphically. Approximate the roots to the nearest tenth.

■ **SOLUTION**

Graph $y = x^2 + 5x - 7$.

To the nearest tenth, the *roots are $x = -6.1$ and $x = 1.1$.*

The nature of the roots of a quadratic equation can be determined by looking at its graph. One diagram below shows the graphs of three different quadratic equations. Equation A has one real root because it has one x-intercept. Equation B has two real roots because it has two x-intercepts. Finally, equation C has no real roots because it never crosses the x-axis. The other diagram shows the graph of a polynomial equation that has three real roots because it has three x-intercepts.

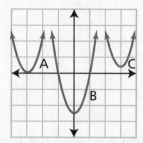
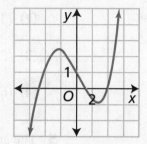

You can use the graph of a polynomial to determine the roots of a polynomial equation. You can solve the equation $x^3 - x^2 - 4x + 4 = 0$ by graphing $y = x^3 - x^2 - 4x + 4$, as shown below, and determining the x-intercepts. The roots are $x = 1$, $x = 2$, and $x = -2$.

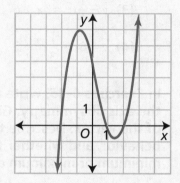

Note

The x-intercept is the point where the graph crosses the x-axis. A graph can have more than one x-intercept.

EXAMPLE 9   **Finding the number and type of roots of a quadratic equation**

9 Identify the number and type of solutions of the polynomial graphed at the right.

■ **SOLUTION**

Because the graph has three x-intercepts, the polynomial has **three real solutions.**

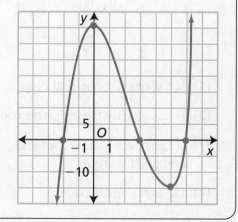

199

Practice

Choose the numeral preceding the word or expression that best completes the statement or answers the question.

1 The graph of an equation of the form $y = ax^2 + bx + c$ is shown. Which is true?

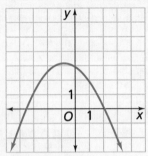

(1) $a > 0$ and $c > 0$

(2) $a > 0$ and $c < 0$

(3) $a < 0$ and $c < 0$

(4) $a < 0$ and $c > 0$

2 Which of the following statements is true of the equation graphed below?

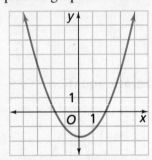

(1) It has exactly one real root.

(2) It has exactly two negative roots.

(3) It has one negative root and one positive root.

(4) It has no real roots.

3 Which is an equation of the axis of symmetry of the graph of $y = 3x^2 - 12x$?

(1) $x = 2$ (3) $x = -5$

(2) $x = \dfrac{1}{5}$ (4) $x = \dfrac{1}{2}$

4 Which represents the coordinates of the vertex of the graph of $y = x^2 - 6x - 10$?

(1) $(-6, 10)$

(2) $(3, -19)$

(3) $(3, -22)$

(4) $(6, 10)$

5 The graph of which equation has a maximum?

(1) $y = \dfrac{1}{3}x^2 - 3x + 2$

(2) $y = -5x + \dfrac{1}{2}x^2 - 5$

(3) $y - \dfrac{1}{2}x^2 = 4x + 6$

(4) $y = 6x - \dfrac{1}{3}x^2 + 2$

In Exercises 6–15, write an equation for the axis of symmetry. Give the coordinates of the vertex. Describe the graph's end behavior, and whether the vertex is the minimum or maximum of the graph.

6 $y = 2x^2$

7 $f(x) = -2x^2$

8 $y = -x^2 + 2$

9 $f(x) = 5 - 3x^2$

10 $f(x) = 1.5x^2 + 3x$

11 $y = 2.5x^2 - 3x$

12 $y = \dfrac{1}{2}x^2 + 4x$

13 $f(x) = -\dfrac{1}{2}x^2 + \dfrac{1}{3}x$

14 $y = 2x^2 + 4x - 5$

15 $f(x) = -x^2 + 6x - 1$

200

In Exercises 16–18, the graph of a quadratic function, $y = ax^2 + bx + c$, is given. Find the roots of the related equation $ax^2 + bx + c = 0$. Verify the solutions.

16
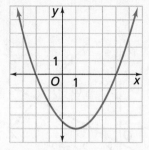

17
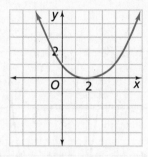

18
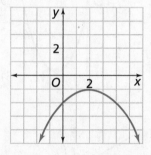

In Exercises 19–24, sketch each parabola.

19 $y = x^2 - 3x$

20 $y = x^2 - 2x + 2$

21 $y = x^2 - 3x + 2$

In Exercises 22–23, which of the given functions has a greater *average rate of change* over the defined interval?

22 $f(x) = 3x - 5$; $g(x) = 2x^2 - 8x + 3$; $0 \le x \le 4$

23 $h(x) = -3x^2 + 12x + 2$; $k(x) = 3\,(2)^x$

In Exercises 24–29, solve the problem. Clearly show all necessary work.

24 Profit P in dollars made by a manufacturing company that makes w units of a product is given by $P = w^2 - 25w + 5000$. Determine the minimum profit for this company.

25 Write an equation of a parabola that has a y-intercept 6 and x-intercepts -3 and 4. Explain how you arrived at your answer.

26 Write an equation for the set of all points in the coordinate plane whose y-coordinate is 2 less than half the square of the x-coordinate. Sketch that set of points.

27 Becky drops a coin into a well 64 feet deep. If the distance d in feet the coin falls is given by $d = 16t^2$, how many seconds t will it take the coin to hit the bottom?

28 Use a graph or an analysis of a graph to show that $x^2 + 5 = 4x$ has no real solutions.

29 Andre threw a ball into the air from the top of a building as shown. An equation for the altitude h of the ball in feet is given by $h = -16t^2 + 64t + 60$, where t is the elapsed time in seconds. What is the maximum altitude of the ball?

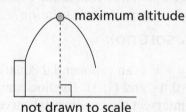
maximum altitude
not drawn to scale

In Exercises 30–33, Investigate the pattern of the "change" numbers for quadratic functions where $a \ne 1$. Find the vertex and 4 more points on one arm of each parabola. Based on the points, make a hypothesis of how the value of "a" effects the change.

30 $y = 3x^2 + 6x - 5$

31 $g(x) = (0.5)x^2 + 2x + 6$

32 $y = -2x^2 + 4x + 1$

33 $f(x) = -\dfrac{1}{4}x^2 + x + 1$

8.4 Reasoning with Multiple Functions

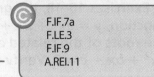
F.IF.7a
F.LE.3
F.IF.9
A.REI.11

You have already learned how to find solutions to a pair of linear equations in the same two variables. For example, the solution to the pair of equations $x + y = 8$ and $x - 2y = 2$ is the point with coordinates $(6, 2)$, the intersection of the graphs as shown at the right.

A system of equations may contain any type of equation, such as a linear, exponential, or a quadratic equation.

No matter what functions are in a system, the concept of the solution to the pair of equations remains the same, the point(s) at which the graphs intersect. To find the number of solutions of a system of equations, you can count the intersection points of the graphs.

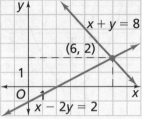

EXAMPLES 1 and 2   Counting points of intersection

1 In how many points does the graph of $y = x^2 - 4x - 1$ intersect the line $y = 3$?

■ SOLUTION

The graph of $y = x^2 - 4x - 1$ is a parabola opening up with vertex $(2, -5)$.

$$x = -\frac{b}{2a} \rightarrow x = -\frac{-4}{2(1)} = 2 \quad \text{So } y = (2)^2 - 4(2) - 1 = -5$$

Therefore, **the vertex** $= (2, -5)$.

The horizontal line $y = 3$ is above the vertex. This parabola intersects the horizontal line $y = 3$ in **two points**.

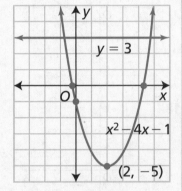

2 Graph a line containing $(-2, 3)$ and $(3, 0)$ and $y = 3^x$. How many points are in their solution?

■ SOLUTION

$y = 3^x$ is an exponential equation whose graph will pass through $(0, 1)$ and $(1, 3)$. The line connecting $(-2, 3)$ and $(3, 0)$ will intersect the exponential curve at *one point*.

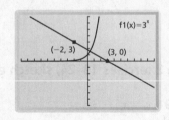

The graphs of a linear equation and a quadratic equation in two variables may intersect in two points, intersect in one point, or not intersect at all.

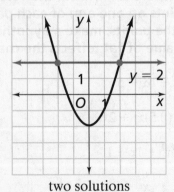

two solutions

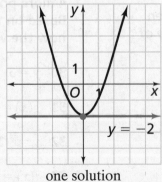

one solution

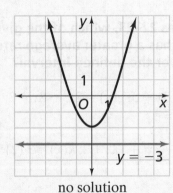

no solution

When given a function, you have learned that it has many identifying characteristics, such as its shape, end-behavior, intercepts, or vertex. These characteristics can help answer questions without graphs or calculations!

EXAMPLE 3   **Using reasoning to count solutions to a linear-quadratic system**

 A parabola has equation $y = x^2 + 2x + 4$. A line has equation $y + 2 = 2(x - 1)$. In how many points do the graphs intersect?

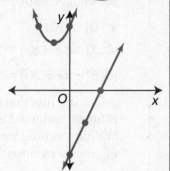

- **SOLUTION**

Step 1 $y = x^2 + 2x + 4 \rightarrow$ a parabola with vertex $(-1, 3)$ and y-intercept $(0, 4)$; $a > 0$, positive end-behavior.

$y - (-2) = 2(x - 1) \rightarrow$ a line containing $(1, -2)$, increasing function, $m = 2$.

Step 2 The slope of the line is not steep enough to cause an intersection higher in the first quadrant. Therefore, the parabola and the line do not intersect at any point.

You can use a graphing calculator to quickly find the intersection points of two or more equations.

EXAMPLE 4   **Using a graphing calculator to find points of intersection**

 Determine the coordinates of any points of intersection of the graphs of $y = x^2 + 3x - 5$ and $y = -2x + 3$.

- **SOLUTION**

Step 1 Graph the functions $y = x^2 + 3x - 5$ and $y = -2x + 3$.

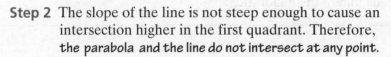

Step 2 After graphing the two functions, use the calculation feature to determine the points of intersection.

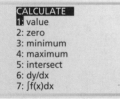 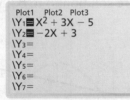 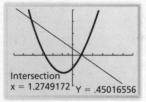

203

EXAMPLE 5   More reasoning with systems

5 Given the functions defined as $f(x) = 2^x$; $g(x) = x^2 + 1$; and $h(x) = x + 1$, order their *average rate of change* from least to greatest in the interval $[0, 2]$ and $[0, 5]$. Explain the change in order between the intervals.

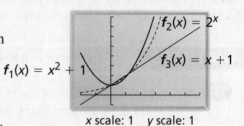

■ SOLUTION

$[0, 2]$: rate of $h(x) = 1 <$ rate of $f(x) = \dfrac{3}{2} <$ rate of $g(x) = 2$.

$[0, 5]$: rate of $h(x) = 1 <$ rate of $g(x) = 5 <$ rate of $f(x) = \dfrac{31}{5}$.

All of the functions are increasing functions in the given intervals. $h(x)$ is linear and will have a constant rate of change no matter what interval. Within the indicated interval, as x increases the exponential average rate of change eventually exceeds that of the quadratic.

Practice

Choose the numeral preceding the word or expression that best completes the statement or answers the question.

1 In how many points does the graph of $y = (x - 3)(x + 5)$ intersect the x-axis?

(1) none   **(3)** two

(2) one   **(4)** three

2 A parabola opens up with its vertex at the origin. For which equation will the parabola and the line not intersect?

(1) $x = 2$ **(3)** $y = 4$

(2) $y = 2$ **(4)** $y = -5$

3 For which equation will the graph of $y = x^2 + 1$ and the line intersect in two points?

(1) $y = -2x$ **(3)** $y = 2$

(2) $x = 1$ **(4)** $y = 2x$

4 For which equations will the graphs intersect in two points?

(1) $x = 0$; $y = x^2$ **(3)** $y = -1$; $y = x^2$

(2) $y = 2$; $y = x^2$ **(4)** $y = 0$; $y = x^2$

5 A linear and a quadratic function are graphed on the same coordinate plane. Which are solution(s) to both equations?

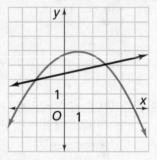

(1) $(-2, 2)$

(2) $(3, 3)$

(3) $(3, 3)$ and $(-2, 2)$

(4) $(-3, 3)$ and $(2, 2)$

6 An exponential function and a line lie in the same coordinate plane. Which situation is not possible?

(1) The graphs do not intersect.

(2) The graphs can intersect in one point.

(3) The graphs can intersect in two points.

(4) The graphs can intersect in three points.

In Exercises 7–8, use function characteristics to explain why the pair of equations has no solution.

7 $y = x - 10$
$y = x^2 + 2x - 5$

8 $y = x^2 + 1$
$y = -x^2 - 2$

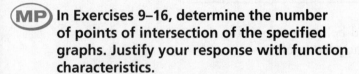

In Exercises 9–16, determine the number of points of intersection of the specified graphs. Justify your response with function characteristics.

9 A parabola opens up and has vertex $P(-2, 3)$. A line has equation $y = 3$.

10 A parabola opens down and has vertex $P(-2, 3)$. A line has equation $y = 3$.

11 A parabola opens up and has vertex $P(0, 0)$. A line has equation $y = 2x$.

12 Exponential function has positive end-behavior and y-intercept $(0, 4)$. Line has equation $y = 2x + 1$.

13 Exponential function has negative end-behavior and passes through $(0, -1)$. Line has equation $y = -3$.

14 Exponential function is $f(x) = 2^x$ and linear is $g(x) = x + 2$

15 $f(x) = -x + 3$ and $h(x) = x^2 - 2x$.

16 $f(x) = 3^x$ and $h(x) = x^2 - 6x + 8$.

In Exercises 17–19, compare the *average rate of change* of the given functions in the indicated interval.

17 $f(x) = x + 3$; $h(x) = x^2 - 2x$ in $[0, 3]$.

18 $f(x) = 3^x$ and $h(x) = x - 6x + 8$ in $[0, 3]$.

19 $f(x) = 3^x$ and $h(x) = x^2 - 6x + 8$ in $[-3, 0]$.

Another Form of the Quadratic Function

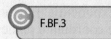
F.BF.3

You found when solving a quadratic that if it is factorable, then changing standard form into the zero-product form makes finding the roots easier.

$0 = 6x^2 + 11x - 10 = (3x - 2)(2x + 5)$, so the roots are $\frac{2}{3}$ and $-\frac{5}{2}$.

Similarly to solving for roots, there is another form of the quadratic function that is most useful for visualizing a parabola.

Vertex form

The quadratic function can be written in vertex form **$f(x) = a(x - h)^2 + k$**, where a, h, and k are real numbers and $a \neq 0$. The vertex of the parabola is the point with coordinates (h, k) and the equation of the Axis of symmetry is $x = h$. This form is also called A-H-K form.

Recall that the value of a determines the parabola's end-behavior as positive or negative and that it is also the factor of change for the pattern of the points on the arms of the parabola.

EXAMPLES 1 and 2   Using vertex form

MP

1 For the function $f(x) = (x + 3)^2 + 5$, find the vertex and axis of symmetry.

■ **SOLUTION**

In vertex form $f(x) = (x + 3)^2 + 5$

$$= 1(x - (-3))^2 + 5 \text{ and the value of}$$

$$a = 1, h = -3, \text{ and } k = 5$$

so, vertex $= (h, k) = (-3, 5)$ and the equation of the axis of symmetry is $x = -3$.

x	1	2	3	4
y	−6			

2 For the function $y = 2(x - 1)^2 - 6$, use the given vertex, the value of a, and the parabola's points pattern to complete the given table of values, then sketch the parabola.

x	1	2	3	4
y	−6	−4	2	12
Δy		2(1)	2(3)	2(5)

■ **SOLUTION**

Since **$a = 2$**, the parabola has positive end-behavior, So, as x increases by 1 unit, the y values increase by **2 •** $[1, 3, 5, 7...]$ units or **2 times the parabola's points pattern.**

Reflecting those points over the axis of symmetry for the left arm points, the sketch shows $y = 2(x - 1)^2 - 6$.

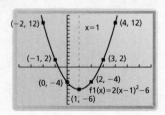

3   A parabola has a vertex of $(-4, 5)$ and passes through the point $(-2, 1)$. Write the equation of this parabola.

■ SOLUTION

Since the vertex $(-4, 5)$ is given, use the Vertex Form;

$$f(x) = a(x - h)^2 + k$$

$$f(x) = a(x - (-4))^2 + 5$$

$$1 = a(-2 + 4)^2 + 5 \quad \leftarrow \text{parabola contains}$$
$$\qquad\qquad\qquad\qquad\quad (-2, 1) = (x, f(x)),$$

$$1 = a(2)^2 + 5 \quad \leftarrow \text{Solving for } a:$$

$$1 = 4a + 5$$

$$-4 = 4a$$

$$-1 = a \qquad \text{Therefore the equation is } f(x) = -1(x + 4)^2 + 5.$$

Changing from one quadratic function form to another can make problem solving easier. The technique of Completing the Square is used to change Standard quadratic form to Vertex form.

4   Write $g(x) = x^2 + 2x - 3$ as a quadratic in Vertex form.

■ SOLUTION

$$g(x) = x^2 + 2x - 3 \qquad \leftarrow \textbf{Completing the Square requires } a = 1.$$

$$= (x^2 + 2x + \underline{\ \ }) - 3 \qquad \leftarrow \textbf{Isolate the quadratic and linear terms of the perfect square trinomial, make room for third term.}$$

$$= (x^2 + 2x + 1) - 1 - 3 \leftarrow \textbf{Add } [\tfrac{b}{2}]^2 \textbf{ to complete the perfect square trinomial as the third term but also subtract the same value outside the parentheses to keep the equation in balance.} \\ \textbf{+1 + (−1) = 0 change.}$$

$$g(x) = (x + 1)^2 - 4 \qquad \leftarrow \textbf{Write the perfect square trinomial as a binomial squared.}$$

$$g(x) = (x + 1)^2 - 4 \qquad \leftarrow \textbf{Vertex form; } a = 1, h = -1, \text{ and } k = -4.$$

5   Write $h(x) = -2(x - 1)(x + 3)$ as a quadratic in Vertex form.

■ SOLUTION

$$h(x) = -3(x - 2)(x + 1)$$

$$= -3(x^2 - x - 2) \qquad \leftarrow \textbf{Multiply.}$$

$$= -3((x^2 - x + 0.25) - 0.25 - 2) \quad \leftarrow \textbf{Add and subtract } [\tfrac{b}{2}]^2 = \tfrac{1}{4}.$$

$$= -3((x - 0.5)^2 - 0.25) \qquad \leftarrow \textbf{Write trinomial as binomial squared, and combine like terms.}$$

$$h(x) = -3(x - 0.5)^2 + 6.75 \qquad \leftarrow \textbf{Distribute the } -3.$$

$$h(x) = -3(x - 0.5)^2 + 6.75 \qquad \leftarrow \textbf{Vertex form; } a = -3, h = \tfrac{1}{2}, \text{ and } k = 6\tfrac{3}{4}.$$

Once a quadratic is in vertex form, transformations on the parabola are easily done. The table below reviews the function transformations previously studied.

Transformations of $f(x)$		
Form and Effect	**Constraints on k**	**Change**
$y = f(x) + k$ Vertical shift	$k > 0$	Shift up
	$k < 0$	Shift down
$y = f(x + k)$ Horizontal shift	$k > 0$	Shift left
	$k < 0$	Shift right
$y = k\,f(x)$ Vertical stretch/compression	$k > 1$	Stretch...gets "skinny"
	$0 < k < 1$	Compresses...gets "fat"
	$k < 0$	Also reflects over x-axis
$y = f(kx)$ Horizontal stretch/compression	$k > 1$	Compresses left by $\frac{1}{k}$
	$k < 1$	Stretches right by $\frac{1}{k}$
	$k < 0$	Also reflects over y-axis

EXAMPLES 6 and 7   **Describing Transformations**

6 Describe the transformations on $f(x) = x^2$ represented by the function $g(x) = -\frac{1}{2}(x + 2)^2 - 5$. Graph both functions on the same axes.

■ **SOLUTION**

The parabola is reflected over the x-axis. The vertex of $f(x)$ was at $(0, 0)$ and has been shifted 2 units to the left and 5 units down to $(-2, -5)$. The vertical compression of factor $\frac{1}{2}$ then "fattened" up the parabola.

7 Describe the transformations on $f(x) = x^2$ represented by the function $h(x) = (-2x - 8)^2 + 3$. Graph both functions on the same axes.

■ **SOLUTION**

The vertex of $f(x)$ was at $(0, 0)$ and has been shifted 8 units to the right and 3 units up to $(8, 3)$ before the horizontal compression of factor $\frac{1}{2}$ located it to $(4, 3)$. Then the parabola was reflected over the y-axis.

Note

It is better to reflect across the x-axis first.

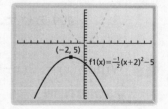

$(-2, 5)$

f1(x) = $-\frac{1}{2}(x+2)^2 - 5$

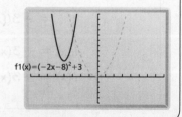

f1(x) = $(-2x-8)^2 + 3$

EXAMPLE 8   **Writing the Transformation Function**   MP

8 Write a rule for the function $g(x)$ obtained from the initial function $f(x) = x^2$, under the given transformations: shift the graph 4 units to the right, stretch it vertically by a factor of 3 and reflect it across the y-axis. Graph each step in building the function.

■ **SOLUTION**

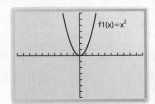 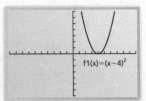 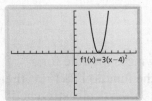 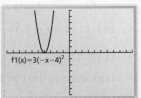

Initial function
$f(x) = x^2$

$\rightarrow$

shift the graph 4 units to the right
$g(x) = (x-4)^2$

$\rightarrow$

stretch it vertically by a factor of 3
$g(x) = 3(x-4)^2$

$\rightarrow$

reflect it across the y-axis
$g(x) = 3(-x-4)^2$

Practice

Choose the numeral preceding the word or expression that best completes the statement or answers the question.

1 What is the vertex of $g(x) = -(x-3)^2 - 4$?

(1) $(3, 4)$ (3) $(3, -4)$

(2) $(4, 3)$ (4) $(-3, 4)$

2 What is the axis of symmetry of $h(x) = -(x+2)^2 - 6$?

(1) $x = 2$ (3) $x = 6$

(2) $x = -2$ (4) $x = -6$

3 What number should be added to $x^2 - 10x$ to make a perfect square trinomial?

(1) 100   (3) 10

(2) 25   (4) 5

4 What number should be added to $x^2 - 7x$ to make a perfect square trinomial?

(1) 7   (3) $\dfrac{49}{2}$

(2) $\dfrac{7}{2}$ (4) $\dfrac{49}{4}$

5 Which of the following steps would be done first to use completing the square to change $y = 4x^2 - 6x + 9$ to Vertex form?

(1) divide the equation by 4

(2) add 9 to both sides

(3) add 9 to the trinomial

(4) factor the trinomial as a binomial squared

6 Which of the following is the rule for a transformation of the function $f(x) = x^2$ that is shifted five units to the right and up three units?

(1) $g(x) = (x + 5)^2 - 3$

(2) $g(x) = (x - 5)^2 + 3$

(3) $g(x) = (x + 5)^2 + 3$

(4) $g(x) = (x - 5)^2 - 3$

7 Which of the following is the rule for a transformation of the function $f(x) = x^2$ that has a vertex at $(-3, 7)$, vertically stretched by a factor of 2, and reflected over the x-axis?

(1) $h(x) = (-2x + 3)^2 - 7$

(2) $h(x) = 2(-x + 3)^2 - 7$

(3) $h(x) = -(2x + 3)^2 + 7$

(4) $h(x) = -2(x + 3)^2 + 7$

8 Which best describes the transformations on $f(x) = x^2$ that is represented by the function $h(x) = -(2x)^2$

(1) reflected over the x-axis with vertical stretch of factor 2.

(2) reflected over the x-axis with horizontal compression of factor $\frac{1}{2}$.

(3) reflected over the y-axis with horizontal stretch of factor 2.

(4) reflected over the y-axis with vertical compression of factor $\frac{1}{2}$.

9 Which best describes the transformations on $f(x) = x^2$ that is represented by the function $g(x) = 2(-x)^2$

(1) reflected over the x-axis with vertical stretch of factor $\frac{1}{2}$.

(2) reflected over the x-axis with horizontal compression of factor 2.

(3) reflected over the y-axis with vertical stretch of factor 2.

(4) reflected over the y-axis with horizontal compression of factor $\frac{1}{2}$.

10 Which graph shows the transformations on $f(x) = x^2$ that is represented by the function $h(x) = -(x + 1)^2 - 1$?

(1)
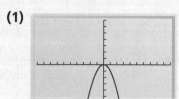

(2)
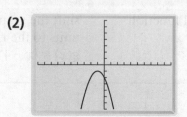

(3)
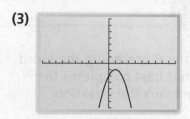

(4)
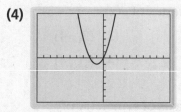

In Exercises 11–13, describe each transformation on $f(x) = x^2$ that is represented by the function $g(x)$.

11 $g(x) = -x^2$

12 $g(x) = (-x)^2$

13 $g(x) = -(-x)^2$

14 Of the three functions in 11–14 above, which two would show the same graph?

In Exercises 15–20, use Completing the Square to write each quadratic function in Vertex form.

15 $y = x^2 - 2x + 6$

16 $y = x^2 + 6x + 5$

17 $y + 4x = -x^2 - 5$

18 $y + 16x = 2x^2 + 35$

19 $y = 27 - 10x + x^2$

20 $y = 4x^2 + 4x - 3$

In Exercises 21–26, use the given transformations on $f(x) = x^2$ to write a rule, $g(x)$.

21 Transformations: shift 4 units to the right and 5 units down.

22 Transformations: reflect across the x-axis and shift up 1 unit.

23 Transformations: shift 3 units to the left and vertical stretch of factor 2.

24. Transformations: shift 1 unit down and horizontal compression of factor $\frac{1}{2}$.

25 Transformations: shift 4 units to the right, reflect over the x-axis, and horizontal stretch of factor 2.

26 Transformations: shift the 5 units down, reflect over the y-axis, and vertical stretch of factor 2.5.

In Exercises 27–30, determine the equation of the quadratic function in vertex form that passes through the points given in the table.

27

x	-2	-1	0	1	2
y	3	5	3	-3	-13

28

x	0	1	3	4	5
y	0	-3	-3	0	5

29 The height of a ball thrown straight up into the air is given by the function $h(t) = -16t^2 - 64t$, where h is the height of the ball in feet at time t seconds.

30 The farmer's rectangular pen uses the barn as the fourth side. The other three sides of the pen are enclosed with 200 feet of fencing. What is the area function of the pen in Vertex form? What is the maximum area of the pen?

Preparing for the Assessment

Choose the numeral preceding the word or expression that best completes the statement or answers the question.

1 Which is an equation of a parabola whose vertex is the origin and opens down?

(1) $y = 3x^2$ **(3)** $y - x^2 = 1$

(2) $y = -3x^2$ **(4)** $y + 1 = x^2$

2 In how many points does the parabola with vertex $(3, -4)$ that opens up intersect the line with equation $x = 3$?

(1) 1   **(2)** 3   **(3)** 2   **(4)** 0

3 Which is equivalent to $6x^2 + 19x + 10 = 0$?

(1) $(3x + 2)(2x + 5) = 0$

(2) $(3x - 2)(2x - 5) = 0$

(3) $(x + 2)(6x + 5) = 0$

(4) $(6x - 5)(x - 2) = 0$

4 Which are the solutions to $19n = 4n^2 + 19n - 9$?

(1) $\frac{3}{2}$ and $-\frac{3}{2}$ **(3)** $\frac{2}{3}$ and $-\frac{2}{3}$

(2) only $\frac{3}{2}$ **(4)** no solution

5 Which equation does not have the same solutions as $3x^2 = 6x - 9$?

(1) $3x^2 - 6x + 9 = 0$

(2) $3x^2 - 6x = -9$

(3) $3x^2 - 6x - 9 = 0$

(4) $x^2 - 2x + 3 = 0$

6 In how many points would $f(x) = x$ and $g(x) = x^2$ intersect?

(1) 0   **(3)** 2

(2) 1   **(4)** ∞

7 The solutions to $s(s - 3)(s + 8) = 0$ are

(1) 0, 3, and 8.   **(3)** 0, 3, and -8.

(2) -3 and 8.   **(4)** 0, -3, and 8.

8 What value should be added to $x^2 - 8x$ to make it a perfect square trinomial?

(1) -4 **(3)** -16

(2) 4   **(4)** 16

9 The roots of a quadratic are $x = -5$ and $x = 3$. Which of the following are possible factors of the quadratic?

(1) $(x - 5)$ and $(x + 3)$

(2) $(x + 5)$ and $(x - 3)$

(3) $x = -5$ and $x = 3$

(4) $(x - 5)$ and $(x - 3)$

In Exercises 10–12, solve the quadratic equation.

10 $4h^2 = 2h^2 + 32$

(1) 8 and -8 **(3)** -4 and 4

(2) 16   **(4)** 8

11 $4p^2 = -16$

(1) 4 and -4 **(3)** -2

(2) 2 and -2 **(4)** no real solution

12 $2a^2 = 13a + 7$

(1) -7 and $\frac{1}{2}$ **(3)** $-\frac{1}{2}$ and 7

(2) 1 and $\frac{7}{2}$ **(4)** -1 and $\frac{7}{2}$

13 Which points are the zeros of the equation $x^2 - 2x - 15 = 0$?

(1) $(-3, 0)$ and $(5, 0)$

(2) $(0, -3)$ and $(0, 5)$

(3) $(3, 0)$ and $(-5, 0)$

(4) $(0, -2)$ and $(0, -15)$

14 Which is not true of the parabola with equation $y = -3x^2 + 2x - 4$?

   (1) The parabola opens down.

   (2) The parabola has a minimum.

   (3) The parabola has vertex $\left(\dfrac{1}{3}, -\dfrac{11}{3}\right)$.

   (4) The axis of symmetry is $x = \dfrac{1}{3}$.

15 The graph of which equation has a maximum?

   (1) $y = \dfrac{1}{2}x^2 - 6x + 5$

   (2) $y = -2x + \dfrac{3}{4}x^2 - 1$

   (3) $y = 3x - \dfrac{7}{8}x^2 + 2$

   (4) $y - \dfrac{2}{3}x^2 = 7x + 5$

16 In how many points do the graphs of $y = \frac{1}{2}x + 3$ and $y = x^2 + 3x + 2$ intersect?

   (1) zero

   (2) one

   (3) two

   (4) three

In Exercises 17–27, solve. If solutions are irrational, approximate them to the nearest hundredth. If there is no real solution, so state.

17 $4k^2 + 2k = 2k + 1$

18 $-3d^2 + 5 = 22$

19 $0 = n^2 - 9$

20 $4h^2 - 25 = 0$

21 $x^2 - 12x + 36 = 0$

22 $y^2 - 10y + 25 = -1$

23 $3x^2 - 32x = -45$

24 $z^2 - 14z + 15 = 0$

25 $9m^2 - 36 = 0$

26 $6z^2 - 42 = 0$

27 $x^3 + 4x^2 + 4x = 0$

In Exercises 28–34, solve the problem. Clearly show all necessary work.

28 The area of a triangle is 36 square inches. The base is half the height. Find the height and base of the triangle.

29 The area of a rectangle is 108 square feet. The length is 3 feet more than the width. What are the length and width in feet?

30 The altitude of an object in feet is given by $h = -16t^2 + 8t + 48$. What is its maximum altitude? After how many seconds t will it strike the ground?

31 The shaded area is 324 square feet. Find x.

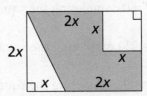

32 Compare the *average rate of change* for each function in the interval $[0, 3]$. $f(x) = 0.5x$; $g(x) = -x^2 - 5x + 3$ and $h(x) = -8x + 10$

33 The roots of a cubic are $x = -2$, $x = 3$, and $x = 5$. What are the possible factors of the cubic? Explain your reasoning.

34 The diagram below shows the graph of $y = x^3 + x^2 - 5x - 7$ and $y = x - 4$. How many solutions does this system of equations have? Explain your answer.

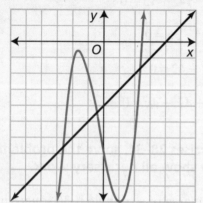

In Exercises 35–40, solve by the indicated method. If solutions are irrational, approximate them to the nearest hundredth. If there is no solution; so state.

35 $x^2 - 8x + 12 = 0$ by formula

36 $2x^2 + 1 = 5x$ by formula

37 $5x^2 = 2x - 3$ by formula

38 $x^2 - 4x - 7 = 0$ completing the square

39 $9x^2 + 12x = 21$ completing the square

40 $4x^2 - 12x = -9$ completing the square

41 What is the vertex of $g(x) = (x - 6)^2 - 7$?

    (1) $(6, -7)$ **(3)** $(-6, -7)$

    (2) $(7, -6)$ **(4)** $(-6, 7)$

42 What number should be added to $x^2 - 16x$ to make a perfect square trinomial?

    (1) -8 **(3)** 16

    (2) 8 **(4)** 64

43 Which best describes the transformations on $f(x) = x^2$ that is represented by the function $h(x) = -2(x)^2$

    (1) reflected over the x-axis with vertical stretch of factor 2.

    (2) reflected over the x-axis with horizontal compression of factor $\frac{1}{2}$.

    (3) reflected over the y-axis with horizontal stretch of factor 2.

    (4) reflected over the y-axis with vertical compression of factor $\frac{1}{2}$.

In Exercises 44–46, use Completing the Square to write each quadratic function in Vertex form.

44 $y = x^2 - 2x - 4$

45 $y = 2x^2 + 12x + 17$

46 $y + 3 = -x^2 + 4x$

In Exercises 47–49, use the given transformations on $f(x) = x^2$ to write a rule, $g(x)$.

47 Transformations: shift 1 unit to the right and 9 units up.

48 Transformations: reflect across the y-axis, vertical compression of $\frac{1}{2}$, and shift left 5 units.

49 Transformations: shift 3 units to the right, reflect over the x-axis, vertical stretch of factor 2, and down 4.

9 Statistics

Careers in Mathematics

Statistician

Statisticians use their understanding of math to analyze and interpret data, and use those data to draw conclusions. Their jobs may be in the public or private sector, in fields such as medicine, marketing, and the environment.

Statisticians often merge their interest in math with another field. Sports statisticians work with professional sports teams to assemble the numbers on each game. They must not only understand the game, but how to record and analyze data for all teams in a league. Environmental or ecological statisticians may work with research universities or government agencies, analyzing probabilities of floods or increasing wave heights, or changes in climate patterns. Their information may be used to help farmers plan their crops, or to help improve wildlife habitats.

Statistics is the study of the world in which we live. Random samples are used to gather information on a subset of the **population** called a **sample**. This information, or data, is organized and visualized, then analyzed by its shape, center, and spread. Finally, conclusions are drawn about the population as a whole.

Data may be of two general types, *qualitative* and *quantitative*. **Qualitative** data may be words or numbers. **Quantitative** data are represented by numerical values.

EXAMPLE 1   **Classifying data as qualitative or quantitative**

 Classify the following data as qualitative or quantitative: favorite band, gender, age, hair color, weight, test grade, zip code.

■ **SOLUTION**

Qualitative data	Quantitative data
Favorite band	Age
Gender	Weight
Hair color	Test grade
Zip code	

Quantitative data can be further classified as *discrete* or *continuous*. Discrete data are usually represented by integer values, while **continuous** data are represented by real number values.

EXAMPLE 2   **Classifying quantitative data as discrete or continuous**

 Classify the following quantitative data as discrete or continuous: time to complete homework, SAT score, blood pressure, weight, number of DVDs you own, height, number of children in a family.

■ **SOLUTION**

Quantitative Data

Discrete	Continuous
SAT score	Time to complete homework
Number of DVDs you own	Blood Pressure
Number of children in a family	Weight or Height

Univariate data are values collected for a single variable. For example, the ages of the first 50 students to arrive at school would create a univariate data set where age is the variable. **Bivariate data** are values collected for two different variables. If you ask the first 50 students who arrive at school how much time they spend doing homework per week and their GPA, a bivariate data set would be created where time on homework is one variable and GPA is the second variable.

The type of data determines the best type of graph, called a **distribution,** to visualize the data. The table below summarizes data types and choices of distribution.

Data Type		Distribution
Qualitative		Bar Graph; Pictograph; or Pie Chart
Quantitative	Discreet	Dot Plot; Stem Plot; Box & Whisker Plot; Histogram
	Continuous	Box & Whisker Plot; Histogram

EXAMPLES 3 through 5   **Describing univariate data distributions**

For each description of a statistical study, define the variable of study, and then classify it as qualitative or quantitative. If quantitative, whether the variable is discreet or continuous. What distribution(s) could be used to visualize the data?

3 To determine the age of an elephant, measure the length of its longest tusk.

■ SOLUTION

The variable is the length of each elephant's longest tusk. It is quantitative and continuous. The best distributions would be either a histogram or box & whisker plot.

4 50 students are asked whether they prefer courses scheduled for 45-minute classes every day for a year, or 90-minute classes every second day for a year, or 90-minute classes everyday for a semester.

■ SOLUTION

The variable is class meeting time. It is qualitative and the best distributions would be either a bar graph or pie chart.

5 A survey is taken to determine the number of pets in the typical American home.

■ SOLUTION

The variable is the number of pets. It is quantitative and discrete. The best distributions would also be dependent on how big the sample. If 30 or less then a dot plot or stem plot could be used. Otherwise, for large samples either a histogram or box & whisker plot could be used.

Data frequently need to be organized before creating any distribution. Good organizational tools are frequency tables, dot plots, histograms, and stem plots.

In many situations, a set of data will contain many of the same data values. Remember that the frequency of a data value is the number of times it occurs in the data set. In the data set below, the frequency of the data value **1.3** is 4.

$$\{1.1, 0.9, 0.8, 1.1, 1.1, 0.8, 1.5, \textbf{1.3}, \textbf{1.3}, 1.7, \textbf{1.3}, \textbf{1.3}\}$$

EXAMPLES 6 through 8   **Organizing data**

6 Construct a frequency table for the data below.

14	14	14	15	15	17	16	16	16	16
18	20	17	16	16	17	15	20	17	15
17	17	17	17	18	18	18	17	18	15

■ **SOLUTION**

Step 1 Enter the different data values in the left column of a three-column table.

Step 2 Write tally marks in the middle column of the table to count each different data value.

Step 3 Write the frequency from each tally in the right column.

Data value	Tally	Frequency
14	///	3
15	ℍℍ	5
16	ℍℍ /	6
17	ℍℍ ////	9
18	ℍℍ	5
20	//	2

7 The data below are the numbers of home runs made during 15 summer league baseball games. Construct a dot plot for the data.

3 5 0 1 2 2 3 4 5 9 3 2 1 5 2

■ **SOLUTION**

Step 1 Draw a number line that includes the values of the data elements.

Step 2 Place a dot • or x above each data value on the number line.

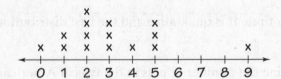

218

8 We will consider the scores on a mathematics test shown in the table below.

56	97	97	96	95	92	90	89
81	80	78	78	76	75	74	73
89	89	86	85	85	84	83	83
72	70	70	68	67	65	62	58

Construct a stem plot for the data.

■ **SOLUTION**

Step 1 Determine the lowest score, 56 and the highest score, 97.

Step 2 Draw a vertical line and to the left of the line, count by 10's from 50 to 90. Show only the 10's digit.

Step 3 To the right of the line, write the unit digit of each data element from low to high. Repeat unit digits to show multiple frequencies.

Step 4 Always include a Key.

Test scores

```
9 | 0 2 5 6 7 7
8 | 0 1 3 3 4 5 5 6 9 9 9
7 | 0 0 2 3 4 5 6 8 8
6 | 2 5 7 8
5 | 6 8
```

Key: 5 | 6 means 56

At times it is necessary to express each frequency as a part of the whole data set. If the frequency is divided by the total number of data elements, then the result is called **relative frequency** and can be expressed as a fraction, decimal, or percent.

EXAMPLE 9   Calculating relative frequency

9 The frequency table at the right shows completion times for the contestants in a race. What percentage of contestants finishing the race completed it in less than 23 minutes? 40 is the total of the frequencies. Dividing each frequency by 40 results in the percents shown.

Interval (min)	Frequency	Relative Frequency
14–16	2	5%
17–19	6	15%
20–22	10	25%
23–25	9	22.5%
26–28	8	20%
29–31	5	12.5%

■ **SOLUTION**

Two runners finished in 14–16 minutes, 6 in 17–19 minutes, and 10 finished in 20–22 minutes. Add the frequencies 2, 6, and 10.

$$2 + 6 + 10 = 18$$

Since 40 is the total of the frequencies, 18 runners of the 40 finished in less than 23 minutes.

$$18 \text{ out of } 40 \rightarrow \frac{18}{40} = 0.45$$

Thus, **45%** of the runners finished in less than 23 minutes.

A **histogram** is a univariate distribution used to represent continuous quantitative data. The horizontal scale shows all values of the variable in uniform intervals, while the vertical scale shows the frequencies of the data either as counts or as relative frequency.

10 In a study of 28 plants, their growth in centimeters over a 48-hour period represents continuous quantitative data. Construct a histogram of the data shown below.

4.0	1.2	6.0	4.9	3.2	1.3	2.8	6.9	5.3	4.4	3.3	2.0	5.7	3.5
2.0	3.4	5.3	5.6	2.1	4.8	5.6	3.5	4.5	5.4	5.6	5.3	4.8	4.6

■ **SOLUTION**

Step 1 Determine the lowest data value, 1.2 cm, and the highest value, 6.9 cm.

Step 2 Equally divide the distance between the lowest and highest values so that each data element is in **exactly** one of the equal intervals. For the plant data the intervals can be defined as: 1 cm < 2; 2 < 3; 3 < 4; 4 < 5; 5 < 6; and 6 < 7 cm.

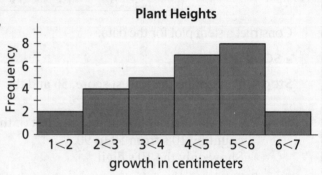

Step 3 Determine the frequencies for each defined interval.

Step 4 Draw and label the horizontal and vertical axis. Draw bars to show the frequencies. Title the histogram.

11 If the data are presented in a frequency table, the interval widths will have already been defined.

■ **SOLUTION**

Step 1 Draw and label the horizontal and vertical axis. Draw the bars to show the frequencies. Title the histogram.

ACT Scores	Frequency
0–5	1
6–10	7
11–15	14
16–20	22
21–25	8
26–30	1
31–35	1

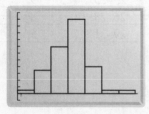
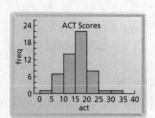

Note

Most graphing calculators will graph histograms. Some allow more options for labels than others. Two examples are shown.

In Exercises 1–6, determine whether the data are quantitative or qualitative. If they are quantitative, determine whether they are discrete or continuous.

1 The number of dollar bills in your wallet

2 Your favorite brand of jeans

3 Your waist size

4 Your area code

5 Number of students in each of your classes

6 Air pressure in your bike tire

In Exercises 7–10, determine whether the data being collected are univariate or bivariate.

7 A student's grade in mathematics

8 A car's weight and its miles per gallon rating

9 A person's age and the number of televisions in his or her home

10 A person's heart rate and the number of calories being burned

11 Data values of 14 are what percentage of the data shown?

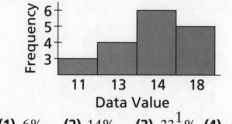

(1) 6%   (2) 14%   (3) $33\frac{1}{3}$% (4) 40%

12 Citizens monitored the number of random acts of kindness portrayed on TV in forty randomly selected hours in one week. Construct a cumulative frequency histogram for the data.

Number of random acts of kindness	Frequency
0–9	6
10–19	12
20–29	12
30–39	10

13 50 women took a gym class at 7 PM last Thursday. 20 took a spinning class, 14 did Zumba, 8 attended Kickboxing class, and 8 took Tai Chi. Find the relative frequencies for this data set.

14 The ages of 8 of 10 couples that were dining at the local restaurant between 4 PM and 5 PM on a weeknight are listed below. Create a dot plot to display this data set.

67,73; 60,63; 58,60; 63,66; 65,66;
71,73; 64,75; 59,66

In Exercises 15–18, use the given data set of dog weights.

17	16	16	18	17	18	22	22	19	21
17	18	20	20	21	19	19	20	21	17

15 Make a frequency table of the data set.

16 Make a relative frequency table of the data set expressed as percents.

17 What percentage of the dogs in the sample weigh more than 20 pounds?

   (1) 5%   **(2)** 25%   **(3)** 40%   **(4)** 60%

18 Make a dot plot of the data set.

19 Make a histogram of the data set.

In Exercises 20–22, use the given data set of test scores.

C	C	C	B	D	B	A	C	C	B
C	A	B	C	C	C	C	D	D	B

20 Make a relative frequency table of the data set.

21 The table represents test scores for one class of students on one mathematics test. Which statement is false?

   (1) Fifty percent of the students earned a **C** and 15% of the students earned a **D**.

   (2) Ten percent of the students earned an A.

   (3) The total number of students who earned a **B** is 25% of the total number of test scores.

   (4) The number of students earning **A**, **B**, or **D** was more than 50% of the class.

22 Make a dot plot of the data set.

23 Use the study of plants' growth data from Example 10 to make a stem plot using the key: **Key: 1 | 2** means **1.2 cm** growth.

24 Discuss the similarities and differences between the histogram is Example 10 to the stem-plot in exercise 23. Which is a better representation of the data and why?

25 Explain how the type of data variable affects how you label the intervals on the horizontal axis of a histogram. (MP)

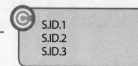

S.ID.1
S.ID.2
S.ID.3

An important characteristics of quantitative data is the **shape** of the data's distribution. A discussion of a distribution's shape includes gaps, clusters, and **outliers.** An **outlier** is a data value that is far removed from the body of the data.

To see shape, imagine a smooth curve over the distribution and then describe it based on the shapes below.

Shapes that Show Symmetry:

• **Uniform:**	**Bell Shaped:**	**Symmetric:**
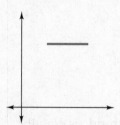	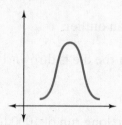	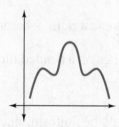
All data values have approximately the same frequency.	A vertical line of symmetry passes through the point of highest frequency.	The left and right sides of distribution show line symmetry.

Shapes that Are Not Symmetric:

• **Skewed Right:**	**Skewed Left:**
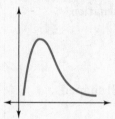	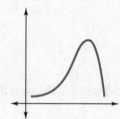
Data values at the right side of the number line have low frequency.	Data values at the left side of the number line have low frequency.

For each distribution, choose the most descriptive shape.

1 Dot plot of home runs during 15 baseball games

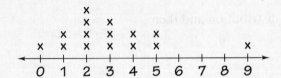

■ SOLUTION

The distribution is skewed right. 9 home runs is an outlier.

2 The times each number on a 6-sided die occurs if the die is thrown 1000 times.

■ SOLUTION

The distribution would be uniform, since over the long run of 1000 tosses, each side is equally likely to appear.

3 The stem plot shows 30 scores from an Algebra I midterm.

```
10 | 0
 9 | 0 2 3 4 5 7 7 8 9
 8 | 1 3 5 5 6 7 7 8 8 9
 7 | 0 1 2 4 5 6 7 7
 6 | 3 5
```

Note

No distribution is a "perfect" shape. Look for the "best" approximation.

■ SOLUTION

Look at the stem plot "sideways." The distribution appears symmetric and bell shaped.

4 The ages of the patients in a hip-replacement unit at the local hospital.

■ SOLUTION

The distribution would appear skewed to the left as most hip-replacement patients are on in years and few are younger.

In Exercises 1–6, for each data set defined below, state the most likely shape of the distribution.

(1) The scores on the SAT exams

(2) The salaries of the employees in a large corporation

(3) The last digit of your social security number

(4) The heights of women

(5) The housing costs in a wealthy suburban neighborhood

(6) The ages at which a woman gets married for the first time

In Exercises 7–10, for each data set defined below, create a statistical distribution of your choice, and discuss the distribution's shape including gaps, clusters or outliers.

7 The family got together for grandpa's birthday. The ages of the 20 party goers are given below.

23, 41, 65, 49, 33, 51, 67, 47, 27, 33,
54, 41, 47, 36, 42, 46, 58, 24, 45, 43

8 The office of the local candidate for mayor uses a 2 minute recorded phone message to promote the candidate. In a random sample of 30 calls, the times below show how much of the message was heard before the listener hung up.

2.0, 0.4, 1.6, 0.9, 0.3, 1.5, 0.6, 0.7, 2.0,
0.3, 0.2, 1.1, 0.8, 0.2, 1.5, 0.4, 1.4, 0.7,
0.6, 1.2, 0.6, 1.8, 2.0, 0.5, 0.3, 1.6, 0.3,
0.7, 1.0, 0.2

9 Miss Marra recorded the heights of her 16 fourth graders in September and then measured them in June. The data below represent the growth in inches over the school year.

2.0, 0.4, 1.6, 0.8, 1.5, 1.8, 0.7, 1.9,
0.5, 2.2, 1.1, 1.4, 5.1, 1.1, 1.3, 1.4

10 Math class data for June. Test scores for 25 students

84, 83, 98, 86, 76, 100, 87, 91, 56, 82, 81,
78, 92, 72, 85, 79, 100, 70, 91, 86, 99, 93, 90,
88, 86.

9.3 Measures of Central Tendency

S.ID.1
S.ID.2
S.ID.3

While the shape of the data distribution begins to give a picture of the sample, other numerical measures supply more information. A measure of "center" is always included in an analysis of sample data.

The mean, median, and mode are referred to as **measures of central tendency.** These statistics provide an idea of the value around which the set of data is centered.

The statistical formula for the mean uses the symbol $\bar{x}$, read x bar, to stand for the mean. x_i represents the individual data elements; $x_1, x_2, x_3, \ldots x_n$. Σ is the Greek letter sigma and means " the sum of", or add up the elements.

$$\textbf{Mean: } \bar{x} = \frac{\sum x_i}{n} = \frac{x_1 + x_2 + x_3 + \cdots + x_n}{n}$$

EXAMPLE 1   Calculating the mean of a data set

 Find the mean of the test scores below.

$$\{84, 80, 78, 73, 71, 95, 74, 93\}$$

■ SOLUTION

$$\bar{x} = \frac{\sum x_i}{n}$$

Step 1 Calculate the sum of the scores.
$$84 + 80 + 78 + 73 + 71 + 95 + 74 + 93 = 648$$

Step 2 Divide the total by 8.
$$\frac{648}{8} = 81 \qquad \bar{x} = 81$$

The mean of the test scores is 81. (A calculator solution is also shown.)

> 84+80+78+73+71+
> 95+74+93
>   648
> Ans/8
>   81

When values in a data set repeat, you can organize them in a *frequency table*. Recall, the **frequency** represents the number of times a particular value appears in the data set.

EXAMPLE 2   Using data frequencies to find the mean

 Find the mean of the data in this table.

Data value	3.5	3.4	3.7	3.8	4.0
Frequency	6	3	2	3	1

■ SOLUTION

Step 1 Calculate the sum of the products of data values and frequencies.
$$6(3.5) + 3(3.4) + 2(3.7) + 3(3.8) + 4.0 = 54$$

Step 2 Divide by the sum of the frequencies, which is 15.
$$\frac{54}{15} = 3.6 = \bar{x}$$

> **Note**
>
> The statistical symbol for mean is $\bar{x}$.

Sometimes it is helpful to write an equation to solve a problem involving the mean.

EXAMPLE 3 **Using an equation to solve a data problem with the mean**

3 Jasmine earns scores of 80, 78, 85, and 82 on four successive history tests. What score must she earn on her fifth test to have a mean (average) of 80?

■ **SOLUTION**

Let x represent the needed score. Solve the equation below.

$$\bar{x} = \frac{\sum x_i}{n} \rightarrow \frac{\text{sum of scores}}{\text{number of scores}} \rightarrow \frac{80 + 78 + 85 + 82 + x}{5} = 80 \leftarrow \text{mean}$$

$$325 + x = 400$$

$$x = 75$$

Jasmine needs to get a **75** to have a mean score of 80.

Check: $\dfrac{80 + 78 + 85 + 82 + 75}{5} = \dfrac{400}{5} = 80$ ✔

A second measure of center is the median. The **median** of a data set is the middle value in an ordered data set. If there is an even number of data values, the median is the average of the two middle values.

$$\text{Median} = \begin{cases} \text{If } n \text{ is odd, the median value is in the } \frac{n+1}{2} \text{ position.} \\ \text{If } n \text{ is even, the median value is the average of the} \\ \text{values in the } \frac{n}{2} \text{ and } \frac{n}{2} + 1 \text{ positions.} \end{cases}$$

EXAMPLES 4 and 5 **Finding the median of a data set**

Find the median of each data set.

4 {3, 6, 7, 2, 4, 8, 3}

■ **SOLUTION**

Arrange in order from least to greatest. Identify the middle number.

$$\frac{(n+1)}{2} = \text{4th value}$$

2 3 3 **4** 6 7 8

↑
middle number

The median is 4.

5 {3, 7, 8, 1, 3, 8, 4, 6}

■ **SOLUTION**

Arrange in order from least to greatest. Identify the middle numbers.

$$\frac{n}{2} \text{ and } \frac{n}{2} + 1 \text{ positions}$$

1 3 3 **4 6** 7 8 8

↑ ↑
middle numbers

The median is $\frac{4+6}{2}$, or 5.

The third measure of center is **mode.** The **mode** of a set of data is the value that has the greatest frequency.

{2, 3, 4, 5, 4, 5, 7, 8, 5, 9} The value 5 occurs three times. It has the greatest frequency. The mode is 5.

{5, 3, 6, 4, **8**, 6, **8**, 9, 7, 10, 11} Both 6 and 8 occur twice. There are two modes, 6 and 8.

The mode is more commonly used if the data are categorical/qualitative as a mean or median cannot be calculated.

If the data are quantitative, then either the mean or median will be the best measure of central tendency. How do you choose?

EXAMPLE 6   **Choosing the most appropriate measure of center**

 A real estate agent has listings for 5 houses for sale in Sometown, NY.

7 bedroom/6 bath mansion:	$1,999,000
4 bedroom/3 bath new contemporary:	$499,000
3 bedroom/3 bath new colonial:	$399,000
3 bedroom/2.5 bath older colonial:	$299,000
3 bedroom/2.5 bath older split level:	$259,000

Find the mean and median prices of the 5 houses that are for sale. Find the mean and median prices of the 4 remaining houses after the mansion is sold. Discuss your findings.

■ SOLUTION

For the 5 houses: mean = $691,000;   median = $399,000
After the mansion is sold: mean = $364,000;   median = $349,000

The prices of the 5 houses are a skewed data set because the mansion is an outlier which causes the mean to be much higher than the median. When the mansion is removed, the data set becomes more clustered and symmetric. The mean is no longer being affected by an extreme value and is much closer to the median.

Shape of the distribution determines the most appropriate measure of central tendency.

For **Symmetric** distributions, there are no outliers to affect the **mean**, so the Mean is best.

Shapes that show Symmetry:

• **Uniform:**   **Bell Shaped:**   **Symmetric:**

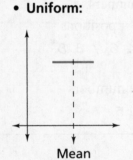
Mean
Median

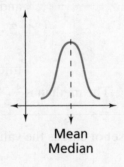
Mean
Median

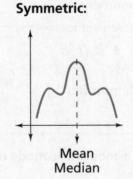
Mean
Median

For **Skewed** distributions, the **Median** is the best choice of center. The median is said to be a "robust" measure of center since it in not affected by outliers. The mean is pulled toward the tail of the distribution.

- **Skewed Right:**

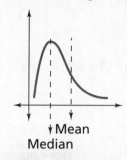

↓ Mean
Median

Skewed Left:

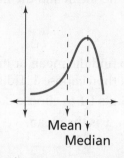

Mean ↓
Median

EXAMPLES 7 through 9   Describing shape and centers

For each given data set, define the shape of the data distribution, tell which measure of center would be most appropriate, and tell whether the mean is greater than, approximately equal to, or less than the median.

7 The ages when most people get their first driver's license

■ **SOLUTION**

The distribution would be skewed to the right; the median would be the best measure of central tendency; mean > median.

8 The scores of 10,000 randomly selected adults on an IQ test

■ **SOLUTION**

The distribution would be symmetric and bell shaped; the mean would be the best measure of central tendency; mean is approximately = to median.

9 The graph below shows the numbers of job applications completed by some people looking for a job.

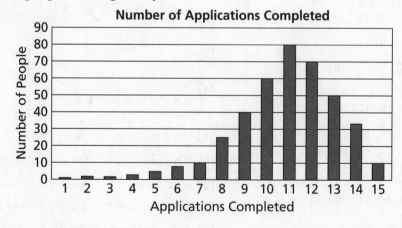

Number of Applications Completed

■ **SOLUTION**

The distribution is skewed left; the median would be the best measure of central tendency; mean < median.

EXAMPLE 10 **Using a calculator for centers**

10 Suppose that a basketball coach wants to determine the average weight of the members of the team. The players' weights, in pounds, are 125, 132, 128, 145, and 138. Find the mean and the median of the weights.

■ **SOLUTION 1**

You can use a graphing calculator to find the mean or median of a set of data. Enter the data by pressing STAT and then choose 1: Edit.

Next, press STAT, CALC, 1: 1 − Var Stats L1 to choose data list.

The statistics will show on the screen. $\bar{x}$ is the mean.

Practice

Choose the numeral preceding the word or expression that best completes the statement or answers the question.

1 Which value of x will make the mean of the data set below equal to 6?

$$\{3, 3, 4, 5, 6, 7, 8, x\}$$

(1) 8 **(2)** 12 **(3)** 40 **(4)** 48

2 Which value is the mean of the data set below?

$$\{1, 4, 4, 5, 6, 7, 8, 9\}$$

(1) 4 **(2)** 9 **(3)** 1 **(4)** 5.5

3 Which data set has 54 as its median?

(1) $\{10, 30, 40, 45, 50, 58, 60, 65, 75, 90\}$
(2) $\{25, 25, 30, 35, 50, 56, 65, 70, 75, 80\}$
(3) $\{30, 40, 45, 47, 54, 55, 60, 65, 75, 85\}$
(4) $\{10, 20, 30, 40, 50, 54, 60, 70, 80, 90\}$

4 Which expression does not represent the mean of the data set below?

$$\{2, 2, 5, 7, 8, 8, 8\}$$

(1) $\dfrac{2(2) + 5 + 7 + 3(8)}{7}$

(2) $\dfrac{2 + 2 + 5 + 7 + 8 + 8 + 8}{7}$

(3) $\dfrac{40}{7}$

(4) $\dfrac{7}{2 + 2 + 5 + 7 + 8 + 8 + 8}$

5 Which statement is always true?

(1) The median is a value in the data set.

(2) The median is also the maximum.

(3) The median and the mean are the same.

(4) Fifty percent of the data are at or below the median.

In Exercises 6–16, solve the following problems. Clearly show all necessary work.

6 Find the mean of the data set in this table.

Data Value	Frequency
6	//
4	////
8	///
11	/

7 Find the median of this data set.

Plant Height

9	3 6 7 8 9 9
8	2 4 6 8 9
7	4 6 8
6	2 5
5	3 6
4	4
3	3
2	1

Key: 2 | 1 means 2.1 cm

8 The mean of a number and 6 equals the mean of twice the number and 1. What is the number?

9 Which interval contains the median?

Interval	Frequency
14–16	2
17–19	6
20–22	9
23–25	8

10 Gina earns scores of 65, 78, 85, and 82 on four tests. What grade must she earn on the next test to have an average of 80?

11 If n represents the smallest of four consecutive integers, write an expression for the mean of the numbers.

12 For the data set {11, 13, 15, 15, 16, 17, 18, 19, 19, 20}, which is greater, the mean or the median?

13 Boxes weighing 12.5 pounds, 12.4 pounds, 12.5 pounds, and 13.6 pounds have the same average weight as 3 packages of equal weight. How much does each of the equal packages weigh?

14 A set of data contains 200 elements. Explain how to find the median of the data.

15 For which value of a will 2, 3, 5, a, 10, and 12, arranged in order from least to greatest, have a median of 5.5?

16 A survey taker forgot to write the frequency n for the data value 6 in the frequency table below, but noted a mean of 6.6. What was the frequency of the data value 6?

Data Value	Frequency
5	//
6	n
8	////

17 Mr. Jones teaches two sections of Algebra I. Both sections took the same Chapter 10 assessment. If the first section's 20 student's mean was 86, but the second section's 30 student's mean was 92, what was the combined mean for both sections.

18 In one local town, the mean housing sale price was $189,000, while the median housing sale price was $405,000. Sketch a possible distribution of housing sales.

19 In another class assessment, the mean score was 78 while the median score was 89. Sketch a possible distribution of the assessment scores.

20 In Example 10, the basketball coach weighted the players. Suppose the coach had inadvertently placed a foot on the scale resulting in the recorded weights being all 5 pounds higher. Find the true mean of the players. Compare and discuss the effect of the extra 5 pounds on the means and medians.

Measures of Spread

While the shape and center of the data distribution together give a good picture of the sample, one other numerical measure is yet needed. A measure of "spread" is always included in an analysis of a sample data.

Consider the three dot plots below.

Data Set A:

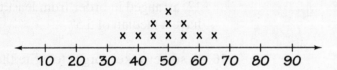

Data Set B:

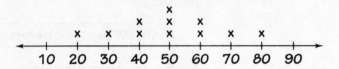

Data Set C:

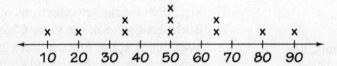

Each plot has the same symmetric shape, the same mean and median, yet they represent very different data sets because of the way the 11 data points are spread out. This characteristic of data distributions is called **variability**. Other terms used to describe variability are **dispersion** or **spread**.

The concept of variability is very simple:

- Data values that are relatively close together have lower measures of variability.

- Data values that are spread apart have higher measures of variability.

The **Range** is a first measure of variability. It should be found for all distributions as it is not affected by the distribution's shape.

Range

Range = (highest data value) − (lowest data value)

Find the range of Data Sets A–C above.

- **SOLUTION**

Data Set A: Highest value − Lowest value = Range

$$65 - 35 = 30$$

Data Set B: Highest value − Lowest value = Range

$$80 - 20 = 60$$

Data Set C: Highest value − Lowest value = Range

$$90 - 10 = 80$$

2 Explain how the value of the Range number affects the shape of a distribution.

- **SOLUTION**

The smaller the range value the less distance between the ends of the data. The data values are all clustered together. If the range value is large, then the data values are spread out. A large range value may also indicate the presence of an outlier.

Like centers, some measures of variability are affected by the distribution's shape. **MAD** or **Mean Absolute Deviation**, and **Standard Deviation** are measures of variability that are best used with symmetric data.

Mean Absolute Deviation

$$\textbf{MAD} = \frac{\sum |x_i - \bar{x}|}{n}.$$

 Find the MAD of Data Set B.

Data Set B:

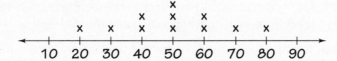

- **SOLUTION**

Step 1 Is the data set symmetric? Yes, so MAD is an appropriate measure of variability.

Step 2 Find $\bar{x}$, the mean. The mean is $\frac{\sum x_i}{n} = \frac{550}{11} = 50$

Step 3 Find $|x_i - \bar{x}|$, called the deviations. They are the absolute value of the difference between mean and each data element. The deviations are listed below.

$$30\ 20\ 10\ 10\ 0\ 0\ 0\ 10\ 10\ 20\ 30.$$

Step 4 Add up the deviations: $\sum |x_i - \bar{x}| = 140$

Step 5 Divide by *n* the number of data elements: $\frac{140}{11} \approx 12.7 = \text{MAD}$

4 Interpret Set B's MAD value in the context of the data set, then compare Set B's MAD to the MADs for Sets A and C.

- **SOLUTION**

Since MAD is a measure of variability, the value of B's MAD indicates that a majority of B's data elements are distributed in a range of about 13 units on either side of B's mean.

Most of B's data lie between approximately 37 and 43 units.

Since A's data points are more closely clustered about its mean, A's MAD will be less than B's. C's data points are much more spread out, so its MAD will be greater than B's MAD.

Standard deviation is another measure of variability that is even more specific about the shape of its distribution. Standard deviation is useful only if the symmetric distribution is bell-shaped.

Standard deviation is very similar to MAD as it also calculates a range about the mean in which most of the data elements are found. While there is difference is in their formulas, their values measure that same variability about the mean.

Standard Deviation of a Sample

$$\text{Standard deviation of a sample} = s = \sqrt{\frac{\sum (x_i - \bar{x})^2}{n-1}}$$

The formula is different from MAD in two ways:

- MAD uses absolute value to make the deviations positive to represent distance between the data elements and the mean. Standard deviation makes the deviations positive by squaring to make the difference positive. Since squaring changes the linear units to square units, the square root is then taken to keep distance positive and the units linear.

- MAD divides by n, the number of data elements. Standard deviation for a sample divides by $n - 1$.

This is done so that the standard deviation's value better represents the variability of the sample data.

5 Find the standard deviation, s, of a data set using the formula.

Data Set:

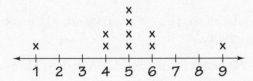

■ SOLUTION

Step 1 Is the data set symmetric and bell shaped? Yes, so standard deviation is an appropriate measure of variability.

$$\text{The formula: } s = \sqrt{\frac{\sum (x_i - \bar{x})^2}{n - 1}}$$

Step 2 Find $\bar{x}$, the mean. The mean is $\dfrac{\sum x_i}{n} = \dfrac{50}{10} = 5$

Step 3 Find $(x_i - \bar{x})^2$, the deviations squared. The deviations and their squares are listed below.

Deviations:	4	1	1	0	0	0	0	1	1	4
Squares:	16	1	1	0	0	0	0	1	1	16

Step 4 Add up the squared deviations: $\sum (x_i - \bar{x})^2 = 36$

Step 5 Divide the sum by $n - 1$: $\dfrac{\sum (x_i - \bar{x})^2}{n - 1} = \dfrac{36}{9} = 4$

Step 6 Find the square root of the quotient: $\sqrt{\dfrac{\sum (x_i - \bar{x})^2}{n - 1}} = 2 = s$

6 Find the standard deviation, *s*, of a data set from example 5 using a calculator.

▪ **SOLUTION**

Step 1 Is the data set symmetric and bell shaped? Yes, so standard deviation is an appropriate measure of variability.

Step 2 Enter the data, then use **1-Var Stats** for the appropriate list. Many calculators use the symbol S_x for the sample standard deviation.

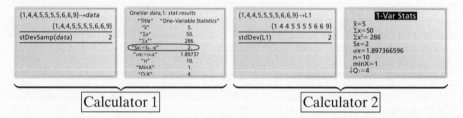

Calculator 1   Calculator 2

The study of the symmetric bell-shaped distribution using means and standard deviation found a pattern. The pattern was named the **Empirical Rule** and it states that for the symmetric bell-shaped distribution, often called a **normal distribution:** **MP**

• About 68% of all the data values lie within 1 standard deviation about the mean.

• About 95% of all the data values lie within 2 standard deviations about the mean.

• About 99.7% of all the data values lie within 3 standard deviations about the mean.

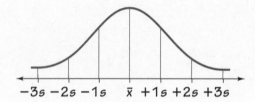

7 The distribution of the scores on a math exam was symmetric, bell-shaped, normal, with a mean of 85 and a standard deviation of 5 points. What percent of the class scored between 80 and 90 on the exam?

■ **SOLUTION**

Mean − 1 Standard deviation = $\bar{x} - 1s = 85 - 5 = 80$

Mean + 1 Standard deviation = $\bar{x} + 1s = 85 + 5 = 90$

According to the Empirical Rule, there should be 68% of the class in this interval.

8 Given $\bar{x} = 100$ and $s = 15$, label the horizontal axis on the sketch of a normal distribution shown below to show the data values from −3s to +3s.

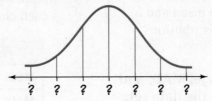

? ? ? ? ? ? ?

■ **SOLUTION**

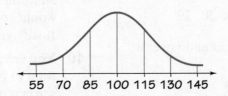

55 70 85 100 115 130 145

Mean ± 1s = 100 ± 15 = 85 and 115.

Mean ± 2s = 100 ± 2 • 15 = 100 ± 30 = 70 and 130.

Mean ± 3s = 100 ± 3 • 15 = 100 ± 45 = 55 and 145.

1 Find the MADs of Data Sets A and C. Explain how their values help define the shape of the distributions.

2 Distribution P has a range of 25 and 50 data items. Distribution Q has a range of 250 and 50 data items. Discuss the difference in the shapes of distributions P and Q.

3 In a symmetric bell-shaped normal distribution, it was found that 68% if the data elements are in the range 24 units to 40 units. What would be the mean and standard deviation of this distribution?

For Exercises 4–7, find the range, MAD, and sample Standard deviation of the data set.

4 The number of books read by a group of 10 year olds during a summer reading program:

17, 31, 27, 24, 19, 23, 25, 30, 29

5 The temperatures in a city at noon over a three-week period in July:

67, 91, 97, 74, 79, 63, 65,
80, 89, 60, 75, 83, 87, 82,
100, 86, 82, 79, 73, 101, 67

6 The top speeds of the winning cars at the race track:

198, 201, 187, 185, 199, 203, 205, 193, 197, 188, 192, 189

7 The prices ($) for the 15 most popular dishes at the dinner are listed below:

6.50, 11.75, 10.25, 11.50, 9.00, 13.00,
16.75, 17.75, 10.75, 12.25, 15.50,
17.95, 13.75, 14.50, 9.95

8 A survey was done in the ninth grade classes to determine the number of electronic devices in each student's home. The data were found to be symmetric and bell-shaped with $\bar{x} = 8$ and $s = 1.3$ devices. Label the horizontal axis on the sketch of a normal distribution below to show the data values from $-3s$ to $+3s$.

9 At the 5th grade field days, Ms. Smith's class challenged Mr. Jones class to bag races. The table shows some of the race statistics for each class.

	Smith	Jones
Mean Finishing Time	14.3 sec	14.5 sec
MAD	2.8 sec	2.3 sec

If the winning team was the first class with all its members across the finish-line, who would you predict won the bag races? Justify your answer.

10 You are planning a vacation and want to find a place with consistent warm temperatures. City X has a mean temperature of 72° with a standard deviation of 3°, while City Y has the same mean temperature of 72° but with a standard deviation of 7°. What city will you choose? Justify your choice.

(MP)

9.5 Box-and-Whisker Plots

S.ID.1
S.ID.2
S.ID.3

Recall that the median of a data set is the middle value.

Just as you can separate a set of numerical data into two equal parts by using the median, so you can separate a numerical data set into four equal parts by using the median, the **first quartile,** and the **third quartile.**

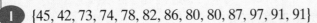

minimum   first quartile   median   third quartile   maximum
            median of   median of
            lower half   upper half

EXAMPLES 1 and 2   Finding the median, the first quartile, and the third quartile

For the data sets below, find the median, the first quartile, and the third quartile.

1 {45, 42, 73, 74, 78, 82, 86, 80, 80, 87, 97, 91, 91}

■ **SOLUTION**

Step 1   Arrange the data in order from least to greatest. Find the median.

42   45   73   74   78   80   80   82   86   87   91   91   97

The median is **80.**

Step 2   Find the median of the lower half of the data.

42   45   73   74   78   80

The first quartile is $\dfrac{73 + 74}{2}$, or **73.5.**

Step 3   Find the median of the upper half of the data.

82   86   87   91   91   97

The third quartile is $\dfrac{87 + 91}{2}$, or **89.**

2 {28, 12, 18, 27, 40, 32, 16}

■ **SOLUTION**

12,   16,   18,   27,   28,   32,   40

       1st   median   3rd
    quartile   quartile

The median is **27,** the first quartile is **16,** and the third quartile is **32.**

When you calculate the median, the first quartile, and the third quartile, you can construct and interpret a **box-and-whisker plot.**

In a box-and-whisker plot, one box is divided into two parts. The line segments to the left and to the right of the box are called the whiskers.

To make a box-and-whisker plot to display data, you need to use five important statistical measures. The measures are shown below.

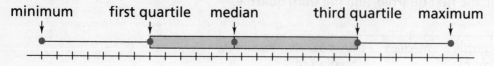

These five values are called a **Five Number Summary** of a data set.

EXAMPLE 3   **Constructing a box-and-whisker plot**

3   Construct a box-and-whisker plot for the data below.

99	97	95	92	90	88	88	87	86
85	82	80	78	74	74	73	72	71

■ **SOLUTION**

Step 1 Identify the minimum and the maximum.
minimum: 71 maximum: 99

Step 2 Find the median.
71 72 73 74 74 78 80 82 85 86 87 88 88 90 92 95 97 99
↑
85.5

Step 3 Find the first and third quartiles.
71 72 73 74 74 78 80 82 85|86 87 88 88 90 92 95 97 99
           ↑   ↑   ↑
   first quartile   median   third quartile

Step 4 Draw the box-and-whisker plot. Indicate the minimum, first quartile, median, third quartile, and maximum.

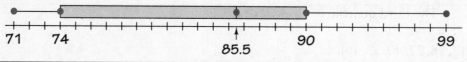

Since the first quartile, median, and third quartile divide the data into four equal groups of data, 50% of the data are between the first quartile and the third quartile. The difference between the third quartile and first quartile is called the **interquartile range,** IQR.

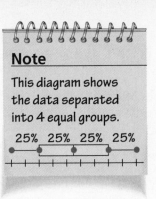
Box plots can be used to display both symmetric and non-symmetric data sets.

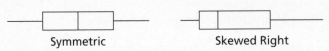

Symmetric   Skewed Right

The median is the measure of center while the data's range and the plot's interquartile range are the measures of variability. Box plots are often used to display and analyze non-symmetric data.

To interpret a box-and-whisker plot, remember the meaning of minimum, first quartile, median, third quartile, and maximum.

EXAMPLE 4   **Interpreting a box-and-whisker plot**

4 Describe the box-and-whisker plot below.

minimum   maximum

10 14 18 22 26 30 34 38 42 46

▪ **SOLUTION**
(1) The plot is skewed left.
(2) The median is 38.
(3) The data's range is 36.
(4) 50% of the data set is between 14 and 42.

You can also solve problems by using a box-and-whisker plot.

EXAMPLE 5   **Using a box-and-whisker plot to solve a problem**

5 The heights, in inches, of 20 high school students are shown in the table below. Use a box-and-whisker plot to determine which of the heights represent students who are taller than 75% of the others.

74	73	72	70	69	68	68	68	67	67
66	64	64	64	63	63	62	60	60	59

■ **SOLUTION**

Step 1 Identify the minimum and the maximum.
minimum: 59   maximum: 74

Step 2 Find the median and first and third quartiles.

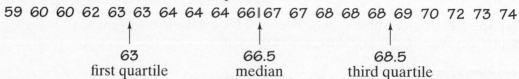

59 60 60 62 63 63 64 64 64 66 | 67 67 68 68 68 69 70 72 73 74

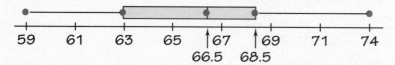

63   66.5   68.5
first quartile   median   third quartile

Step 3 Draw the box-and-whisker plot using the five-number summary values.

Since 25% of the data lie above the third quartile, the students whose heights are 69, 70, 72, 73, and 74 inches are taller than 75% of the others.

Box-and-whisker plots are helpful when comparing sets of data.

 EXAMPLE 6   **Using box-and-whisker plots to compare data**   **MP**

6 The set of data for Class 1 represents the test scores of 18 students and the set of data for Class 2 represents the scores of another class taking the same test. Construct a box-and-whisker plot for each set of data and compare the scores.

Class 1

99	97	95	92	90	88	88	87	86
85	82	80	78	74	74	73	72	71

Class 2

97	97	94	93	92	92	91	90	88
86	84	84	84	83	82	80	79	72

■ **SOLUTION 1**

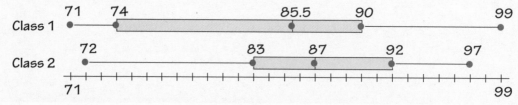

If the box-and-whisker plots for the two classes are placed one above the other, you can see that the medians are about equal, but that Class 2 scores have less variability and are more clustered about the median.

You can also use a graphing calculator to analyze and represent the data.

EXAMPLE 7 **Construct a box-and-whisker plot on a graphing calculator**

7 Use a graphing calculator to construct a box-and-whisker plot. Identify the 5 statistics used to construct the plot, and make a general statement about the data.

Heights of Children, in centimeters

120	122	125	119	123	121	120	132
140	145	147	120	149	160	110	150

▪ SOLUTION

Step 1
Enter the data.

Step 2
Analyze the data.

Step 3
Represent the data as a box-and-whisker plot.

Step 4
Summarize the data.

L1	L2	L3 1
120	-----	-----
122		
125		
119		
123		
121		
120		

L1(1)=120

1−Var Stats
≠n=16
minX=110
Q_1=120
Med=124
Q_3=146
maxX=160

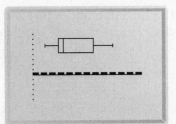

The distribution is skewed right. The range of the data is 50 cm. The data show large variability between the median at 124 cm and the 3rd quartile at 146 cm.

Practice

For Exercises 1–2, find the five-number summary values for the given data sets.

1 The ages of 30 teachers are shown.

24	25	22	54	55
35	38	29	37	46
43	49	38	45	26
27	48	37	47	40
36	44	49	48	50
56	54	53	52	51

2 The time in minutes that 24 random shoppers spent in the food store.

35	40	41	42	65	55	88	97
16	18	21	93	81	71	91	86
47	46	85	77	22	25	79	83

Choose the numeral preceding the word or expression that best completes the statement or answers the question.

3 Which statement best describes the box-and-whisker plot shown below?

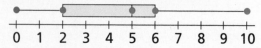

(1) All of the data values lie between 2 and 6 inclusive.

(2) Fifty percent of the data values are at or above 7.

(3) The number 5 is a data value.

(4) Fifty percent of the data values lie between 2 and 6 inclusive, and all data lie between 0 and 10 inclusive.

In Exercises 4–6, use the five-statistic summary given below.

$Min = 50$
$Q_1 = 70$
$Median = 83$
$Q_3 = 88$
$Max = 99$

4 What is the interquartile range?

(1) 18 **(2)** 49 **(3)** 83 **(4)** 20

5 What is the range of the data?

(1) 18 **(2)** 49 **(3)** 83 **(4)** 20

6 Which of the following scores would be an outlier for this data set?

(1) 83 **(2)** 120 **(3)** 40 **(4)** 100

In Exercises 7–10, represent each data set in a box-and-whisker-plot. Describe its shape.

7 {2, 2, 5, 5, 5, 6, 8, 5, 8, 9, 10, 11, 12, 7, 8}

8 {1.2, 1.2, 1.3, 1.1, 1.4, 1.5, 1.5, 1.5, 1.6}

9 {71, 81, 82, 80, 74, 76, 76, 76, 73, 73, 74}

10 minimum: 50; first quartile: 70; median: 83; third quartile: 88; maximum: 100

In Exercises 11–18, use the graph below, showing the box-and-whisker plots for data sets A and B.

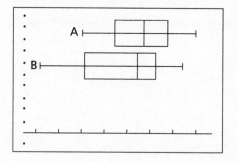

11 Which set of data has the greater range?

12 Which set of data has the lesser median?

13 Which set of data is a skewed distribution?

14 Which set of data has the greater variability about its median?

15 *True* or *False*. The minimum of set B is the lesser value in the two sets.

16 *True* or *False*. The third quartile of set B is less than the third quartile of set A.

17 *True* or *False*. The first quartile of set A is greater than the median of set B.

18 *True* or *False*. The mean of set B will be greater than its median.

For Exercises 19–20, use the information below.

I love hot coffee, but the two coffee machines in the kitchen seem to brew coffee at different temperatures each day. I tested the temperatures in each machine for a week. The data are shown below:

Coffee Temperature in °F						
Machine 1	150	155	145	140	165	170	160
Machine 2	157	167	160	162	165	159	164

19 Construct side-by-side Box plots for the data. Discuss their shapes, centers, and variability.

20 Explain which coffee machine is the better one to use if I want a cup of hot coffee.

Two-way tables are used in statistics to study categorical variables. The table organizes the variable's frequency data to show relationships or trends between the variables.

EXAMPLES 1 and 2   **Building a Two-Way Table**

 The prom planning committee took a survey of the Junior and Senior classes to find out how many were planning on attending the prom. They found that of the Juniors, 234 said yes and 126 said no, while 260 Seniors said yes and 140 said no.

Use these data to build a two-way table.

■ **SOLUTION**

Step 1 Identify the categorical variables.

Variable 1 is **Class** year. Variable 2 is yes or no on **Attending prom.**

Step 2 Create, label, and fill a table with the variables and their frequencies.

		Attending Prom?	
		Yes	**No**
Class	**Juniors**	234	126
	Seniors	260	140

The frequencies in the table are called the joint frequencies.

Step 3 Create a right column and a bottom row to hold the total frequencies.

		Attending Prom?		
		Yes	**No**	**Total**
Class	**Juniors**	234	126	**360**
	Seniors	260	140	**400**
	Total	**494**	**266**	**760**

Marginal Row frequencies

Marginal Column frequencies

Total of the Marginal frequencies

It is important to understand that the "two" in a two-way table refers to the number of categorical variables, not the number of rows and columns in the table. The rows and columns increase to represent the subcategories of each variable.

246

EXAMPLES 1 and 2 **continued**

2 To cut costs, the cafeteria is thinking of serving only cold entrees. The principal sends a survey to all students in grades 9–12 to choose Agree, Disagree, or No Opinion on the cafeteria issue.

The two-way table below is partially constructed. Fill in the 10 missing labels and frequencies shown with a ?.

		Grade Level				
		9th	**?**	**11th**	**12th**	**Total**
Choice	**Agree**	120	115	?	?	**375**
	?	5	?	60	75	**?**
	No Opinion	?	15	?	5	**55**
	?	**155**	**160**	**?**	**130**	**600**

▪ **SOLUTION**

The completed table is shown below.

		Grade Level				
		9th	**10th**	**11th**	**12th**	**Total**
Choice	**Agree**	120	115	90	50	**375**
	Disagree	5	30	60	75	**170**
	No Opinion	30	15	5	5	**55**
	Total	**155**	**160**	**155**	**130**	**600**

Many times it is impossible to see the relationships between the variables using only the frequencies as counts. Relationships become more visible when each joint value is expressed as a **relative frequency**, with respect to variable totals or total population.

3 Express the joint frequencies in the Prom table as relative frequencies with respect to the total population.

		Attending Prom?		
		Yes	No	Total
Class	Juniors	234	126	**360**
	Seniors	260	140	**400**
	Total	**494**	**266**	**760**

■ SOLUTION

The total population is 760 students. The joint relative frequencies would be found by dividing by each joint frequency by this total population.

Juniors-yes: $\dfrac{234}{760} \approx 31\%$ Juniors-no: $\dfrac{126}{760} \approx 17\%$

Seniors-yes: $\dfrac{260}{760} \approx 34\%$ Seniors-no: $\dfrac{140}{760} \approx 18\%$

The table now shows the joint relative frequencies with respect to total population. Note that the marginal totals are represented as percents as well.

		Attending Prom?		
		Yes	No	Total
Class	Juniors	31%	17%	**48%**
	Seniors	34%	18%	**52%**
	Total	**65%**	**35%**	**100%**

→ **Total Population**

4 Express the joint frequencies in the Prom table as relative frequencies with respect to the class totals.

■ SOLUTION

The class totals are the row marginal totals. Divide each joint frequency by their class total.

Juniors-yes: $\dfrac{234}{360} \approx 65\%$ Juniors-no: $\dfrac{126}{360} \approx 35\%$

Seniors-yes: $\dfrac{260}{400} \approx 65\%$ Seniors-no: $\dfrac{140}{400} \approx 35\%$

The table now shows the joint relative frequencies with respect to class totals. Again the row marginal totals have been adjusted.

		Attending Prom?		
		Yes	No	Total
Class	Juniors	65%	35%	**100%**
	Seniors	65%	35%	**100%**
	Total	-----	-----	**100%**

→ **Marginal Class Totals**

5 Express the joint frequencies in the Prom table in as relative frequencies with respect to the response totals.

▪ SOLUTION

The table now shows the joint relative frequencies with respect to response totals.

		Attending Prom?		
		Yes	No	Total
Class	Juniors	47%	47%	-----
	Seniors	53%	53%	-----
	Total	100%	100%	100%

↓

Marginal Response Totals

To interpret a two-way table, attention is paid to the variable of interest or to the whole population.

EXAMPLES 6 through 8   **Interpreting Two-way Tables**

For examples 6–10, use the Cold Entrée Survey table from Example 2.

		Grade Level				
		9th	10th	11th	12th	Total
Choice	Agree	120	115	90	50	375
	Disagree	5	30	60	75	170
	No Opinion	30	15	5	5	55
	Total	155	160	155	130	600

6 What percent of the total population are 9th graders who agree?

▪ SOLUTION

The total population is 600 students. The 9th graders who agree number 120:

$$\text{9th-Agree: } \frac{120}{600} = 20\%$$

7 Given that you are in 11th grade, what percent had No Opinion?

▪ SOLUTION

A condition has been set on the grade level variable. Only looking at the data for 11th grade, the column total is 155 with 5 having No Opinion.

$$\text{11th only-No Opinion: } \frac{5}{155} \approx 3\%$$

8 Given that you Disagree, what percent were Seniors?

▪ SOLUTION

A condition has been set on the choice variable. Only looking at the data for Disagree, the row total is 170 with 75 Seniors disagreeing.

$$\text{Disagree only-Senior: } \frac{75}{170} \approx 44\%$$

For exercises 1–5, use the following data.

325 male and female teenagers were asked if they had a TV in their bedroom. The survey results indicated that of the 150 males asked, 48 had a TV in their bedroom, while 49 of the female asked had a TV in their bedroom.

1 Create a two-way frequency table for this data, including marginal totals.

2 Create a two-way relative frequency table relative to the total population.

3 Create a two-way relative frequency table with respect to the gender totals.

4 Create a two-way relative frequency table with respect to the TV in bedroom response totals.

5 Which of the four two-way tables best helps you answer the question, "Who is more likely to have a TV in their bedroom, male or female teenagers?"

For Exercises 6–11, use the two-way table below.

6 What percent of the Cheese pizzas sold were Deep Dish?

7 Of all the pizzas sold, what percent were Thin Crust Meat only?

8 What percent of Thin Crust pizzas were the Works?

9 Veggie pizzas were what part of total pizzas sold?

10 What percent of all pizzas sold were Thin Crust?

11 What percent of Deep Dish pizzas sold were Veggie?

Pizza Sold at Sal's

		Toppings				
		Cheese	Veggie	Meat only	Works	Total
Type	Thin Crust	280	140	60	50	650
	Deep Dish	200	90	65	115	350
	Total	480	230	125	165	1000

9.7 Scatter Plots and Best Fit Models

S.ID.5
S.ID.8
S.ID.9

If both variables of interest are quantitative, **regression analysis** can be used to model the bivariate data. The data are represented with **ordered pairs,** and the pairs are then graphed with a **scatter plot.** The plot is first analyzed for its linear shape, and if appropriate, a **line of best fit** is found. The line acts as the center of the data and is used to predict values for the function variables.

Statistics often involves the study of relationships between two variables. These **bivariate data** are represented by **ordered pairs**. It is customary to have the first value be the **independent variable** and the second the **dependent variable**. The graph of the ordered pairs of bivariate data is called a **scatter diagram**.

EXAMPLE 1 **Drawing a scatter diagram**

 Mrs. Brown's physical education class recorded the following values for pull-ups and push-ups. Construct a scatter diagram for these data using pull-ups as the independent variable.

	Bob	Joe	Sam	Bill	Gene	Mary	Glenn	Beth	Jill	Sue
Pull-Ups	27	22	35	30	52	15	55	35	24	20
Push-Ups	30	26	42	38	40	25	54	32	30	29

■ **SOLUTION**

Graphing calculators offer a number of options for completing the scatter plot.

Calculator 1: Quick Graph

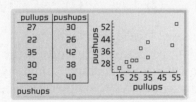

Calculator 2 Scatter Plot

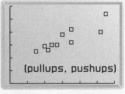

(pullups, pushups)

x scale: 10   *y* scale: 10

Calculator 3: Scatter Plot

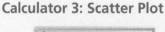
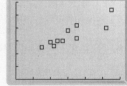

x scale: 10   *y* scale: 10

Examining a scatter plot can help determine the relationship between two variables. The scatter plots below show the various relationships between bivariate data.

No Association	Positive Association	High Positive Association
x scale: 5 *y* scale: 5	*x* scale: 5 *y* scale: 5	*x* scale: 5 *y* scale: 5
Negative Association	**High Negative Association**	**Perfect Positive Association**
x scale: 5 *y* scale: 5	*x* scale: 5 *y* scale: 5	*x* scale: 5 *y* scale: 5

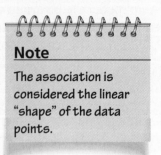

Note

The association is considered the linear "shape" of the data points.

Practice

In Exercises 1–5, choose the numeral preceding the word or expression that best completes the statement or answers the question.

1 What does a correlation coefficient value of −2 indicate?

   (1) Strong correlation

   (2) Weak correlation

   (3) No correlation

   (4) Computational error

2 Calculate the linear correlation for the following data. What does this value indicate about the data?

x	0	1	2	2.5
y	5	3	1	0

   (1) $r = 1$ no correlation

   (2) $r = -1$ points are collinear

   (3) $r = -1$ no correlation

   (4) $r = 1$ strong correlation

3 What is the slope of the least squares line of best fit for the following data?

x	0	2	1	4	1
y	2	10	4	18	6

   (1) 4.1   **(2)** 1.4   **(3)** .99   **(4)** −1

4 Jessica says, "Since the correlation coefficient is positive, the slope of the line of best fit will also be positive." Dale says, "the slope does not have to be positive when *r* is positive."

   (1) Jessica is correct.   **(3)** Both are correct.

   (2) Dale is correct.   **(4)** Both are wrong.

5 If the coefficient of correlation between two variables is 0.978, which of the following is not necessarily true?

   (1) The slope of the regression line is positive.

   (2) The scatter plot is tightly clustered.

   (3) One variable causes the other.

   (4) There is a positive correlation between the variables.

6 Calculate an exponential regression curve for the data in the accompanying table.

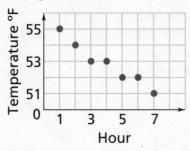

7 Which of the following statements is true of the scatter plot below?

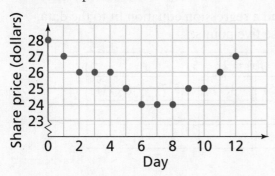

(1) The data have a negative correlation.

(2) The data have a positive correlation.

(3) The data have no correlation.

(4) The correlation cannot be determined.

8 Which of the following statements describes the scatter plot below?

(1) The data have a negative correlation.

(2) The data have a positive correlation.

(3) The data have no correlation.

(4) A quadratic model might be appropriate.

9 The weight and fuel consumption of different vehicles are given in the accompanying table. Construct a scatter plot of these data and find an equation of a linear model for the data. Use the equation to predict the fuel consumption for a vehicle that weighs 4,800 pounds. Also, predict the weight of a vehicle that gets 18 miles per gallon (mpg).

Weight (in 100 lbs)	27	45	30	47	22	40	34	50
mpg	30	16	24	15	29	20	22	13

10 The table below shows the respiration and heart rates for adult males. Construct a scatter plot of these data and determine a trend line. Use the equation of the line to predict the heart rate of a man with a respiration of 32 breaths per minute.

Respiration (breaths/min)	50	30	25	20	18	16	14
Heart Rate (beats/min)	200	150	140	130	120	110	100

9.8 Residual Analysis and Non-Linear Models

In the study of bivariate data, correlation (r) describes the linear shape of the data distribution while the regression line represents the center of those data points. **Residuals** are the measure of each data point's distance from the regression line, a deviation and a measure of variability. The residuals when plotted will also serve as test of the goodness of fit of the linear regression model. A good understanding of functions and a residual plot may indicate the need for a non-linear model. Residual analysis is the last step in modeling bivariate data.

The visual below shows the residual as distance from the regression line. (x_1, y_1) is a data point and $(x_1, f(x_1))$ is a point on the regression line. Since these two points are on the same vertical line $x = x_1$, the difference $y_1 - f(x_1)$ is the vertical distance between the points and is the residual.

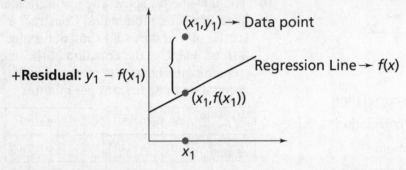

EXAMPLES 1 and 2 — Finding residuals

 The table below shows a data set of five points and a regression equation fit to the data. Complete the table and find the residuals for these five points.

Regression Equation	$f(x) = 2x - 5$				
Data Points (x, y)	$(1, -1)$	$(2, -5)$	$(4, 2)$	$(5, 7)$	$(7, 11)$
Regression Line Points					
Residuals					

■ SOLUTION

Since the residual is the distance between points with the same x-value, find the coordinates of the regression line points using the x-values of the data points. Find the difference $y - f(x)$.

Regression Equation	$f(x) = 2x - 5$				
Data Points (x, y)	$(1, -1)$	$(2, -5)$	$(4, 2)$	$(5, 7)$	$(7, 11)$
Regression Line Points	$(1, -3)$	$(2, -1)$	$(4, 3)$	$(5, 5)$	$(7, 9)$
Residuals	2	-4	-1	2	2

2 From example 1, some of the residuals are negative, positive, and zero. Explain what the sign of the residual tells about the position of the data point relative to the regression line.

■ **SOLUTION**

If the value of the residual is 0, the data point is on the regression line. The point is above the data line if the residual is positive and below the data line if negative.

Residual Plots

The residuals when plotted will serve as a test of the goodness of fit of the **linear** regression model.

EXAMPLES 3 and 4   Creating residual plots

3 At the wheel, you see a hazard and move your foot to the brake. How far did the car travel during the "see and react" time? It is dependent on speed. The screens below show the speed in miles per hour (L1) and the see/react distance in feet (L2). The data's scatter plot is fit with a linear regression defined by the equation: reaction distance = 2.175 speed + 2.

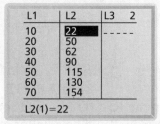

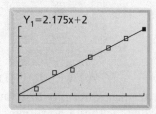

STAT   STAT PLOT with Y_1

Find the data's residuals and create a residual plot for these data points.

■ **SOLUTION**

Once the regression line is drawn, the residuals have been determined by the calculator and can be accessed from the Lists (2nd Stat) menu. The residuals are shown (L3 = RESID), a RESID plot set up and graphed.

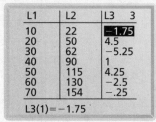   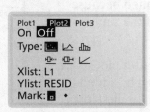   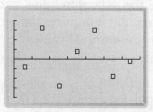

STATS   STAT PLOT   ZOOM-9 = RESID PLOT

The residuals are randomly distributed in the RESID PLOT, indicating that the linear regression is a good model for the data.

4 After reacting, then moving to the brake, what is the stopping distance relative to speed? The screens below show the speed (L1) and the stopping distance (L2). The data's scatter plot approximately fit with a linear regression is defined by the equation:

$$\text{Stopping distance} = 9.314\ \text{speed} - 108.7.$$

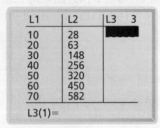

STAT

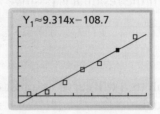

STAT PLOT with Y_1

Find the data's residuals and create a residual plot for these data points.

■ **SOLUTION**

The screens show the RESID values in L3 and the RESID Plot.

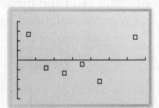

STAT with RESIDs

RESID PLOT

The residuals are not randomly distributed in the RESID PLOT. There seems to be a pattern that indicates that a non-linear regression would be a better model for the data.

Fitting a Model to Data

Two different terms are used with linear models. A **best fit model** usually refers to a line that is calculated manually using some but not all of the data points. The **least squares regression model** uses all of the data points and is so named because it is the line that minimizes the area of the squares formed by the residual values.

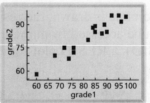

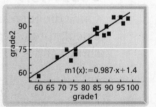

In the accompanying figure we see a scatter plot of two sets of grades. A movable line can be added and manipulated to find a best fit model for these data.

The residual plot may be added to confirm the appropriateness of a linear model. But how can we know which is the best linear model? The goal is to minimize the sum of the area of the residual squares.

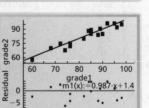

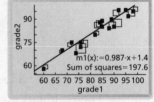

When a regression analysis is performed on these data the sum of the areas of the residual squares will be a minimum. In this case the sum of 181.439 is smaller than the sum 197.6 which had been obtained with the manual line of fit.

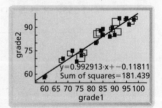

It is important to know that when you fit a linear model using a calculator, that model is always a least squares regression model.

After the residual values are used to determine the linear model, if the RESID PLOT shows a pattern, it is an indicator that the linear model is not a good fit. A non-linear model, exponential or quadratic, could be a better fit for the data.

EXAMPLE 5   **Using non-linear models** —————————————— (MP)

5 The RESID plot in Example 4 shows a non-random pattern, which appears to be a quadratic pattern. To find a better model for the stopping distance data, use QuadReg (CALC5). The screens below show the scatter of the data fit with the approximate Quad model, $y = 0.07x^2 + 3.4x - 20$ and its RESID plot.

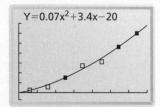 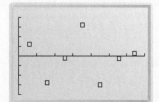

Explain how the RESID plot confirms that the Quadratic regression is the more appropriate model.

■ SOLUTION
The residuals are randomly distributed indicating that the Quadratic model is appropriate.

Practice

1 The screen below shows a data set of six points. Discuss the amount of linear shape in the data.

   Fit a linear model.

L1	L2	L3 2
2	4	- - - -
3	2	
4	1	
5	5	
6	7	
7	7	
- - - -	- - - -	

L2(1)=4

2 Show the residuals in L3. Create a RESID plot. Discuss the RESID plot.

3 Find a more appropriate non-linear model. Graph the data, the new model, and a new RESID plot.

For Exercises 4–5, use modeling to find a function to solve the problems. (MP)

4 The table below shows the amount of water vapor, w, that will saturate 1 cubic meter of air at different temperatures, t.

Temp in Celcius	−20	−10	0	10	20	30	40
Water Vapor (g)	1	2	5	9	17	29	50

Draw a scatter plot, determine a regression model, and use the model to predict the amount of water vapor that will saturate 1 cubic meter of air at 50°C.

5 An auto paint shop uses a drying agent to facilitate the paint drying process. Find the amount of agent that should be used if the desired drying time is 4.5 hours.

Additive (grams)	1	2	3	4	5	6	7	8
Time (hours)	7.2	6.7	4.7	3.7	4.7	4.2	5.2	5.7

Preparing for the Assessment

Choose the numeral preceding the word or expression that best completes the statement or answers the question.

1   A large advertising agency had advertising budgets of 8.9, 10.2, 11.4, 13.5 and 15.2 million dollars for the last five years. What was the mean for this period of time?

   (1) 59.2   **(2)** 11.84   **(3)** 51.6   **(4)** 2.53

2   Every value in a data set is increased by 25. What happens to the mean and standard deviation of this data?

   (1) The mean increases by 25 and the standard deviation remains the same.

   (2) The mean increases by 25 and the standard deviation increases by 5.

   (3) The mean remains the same and the standard deviation increases by 25.

   (4) The mean increases by 25 and the standard deviation increases by 25.

3   The salaries in a small company are $25,000, $25,000, $35,000, $40,000, $48,000, $50,000, and $100,000. Which measure of central tendency is the best to describe this set of data?

   (1) Range   **(3)** Median

   (2) Mode   **(4)** Variance

4   Which of the following represents a discrete variable?

   (1) The age of the oldest child in a family

   (2) The height of the youngest child in a family

   (3) The weight of the oldest child in a family

   (4) The number of children in a family

5   A list arranged in order from least to greatest is 25, 30, 44, x, 51, 60, 75, 80. If the median is 50, what does x equal?

   (1) 49   **(2)** 47.5   **(3)** 35   **(4)** 47

6   To be on the merit roll, Jerry must have an 85 average. If Jerry has grades of 78, 93, 88, 77, and 84, what must he earn on the next test in order to be on the merit roll?

   (1) 86   **(2)** 85   **(3)** 95   **(4)** 90

7   One number is represented by $3x + 5$ and another is represented by $7x - 3$. What is the average of these numbers in terms of x?

   (1) $10x + 1$ **(3)** $5x + 1$

   (2) $10x + \dfrac{8}{2}$ **(4)** $5x$

8   One week, Bob took 23, 25, 30, 20, and 32 minutes to get to work. What is the MAD of his travel times?

   (1) 130   **(2)** 26   **(3)** 20   **(4)** 4

9   One week, Bob took 23, 25, 30, 20, and 28 minutes to get to work. What is the sample standard deviation of his travel times?

   (1) 15.7   **(2)** 25.2   **(3)** 3.96   **(4)** 3.54

10   An aptitude test is known to have a mean score of 37.5 with a standard deviation of 3.6. A college requires an aptitude test score between ± 1.5 standard deviations about the mean as one of its entrance requirement. What must your score be in order to be considered for acceptance?

   (1) 32.1 to 37.5   **(2)** 32.1 to 42.9

   (3) 33.9 to 41.1   **(4)** 33.9 to 41.1

11 Write an expression for the mean of four consecutive even integers if the smallest is represented by $2n$, where n is an integer.

12 If the mean (average) of $3n - 1$, $4n + 2$, and $n - 7$ is 12, what are the numbers?

13 The expressions $2n - 1$ and $2n + 4$ represent the middle numbers in a set of data arranged from least to greatest. Write an expression for the median of the data set.

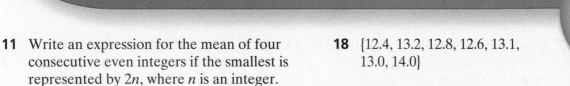

For exercises 14–15, compare the three distributions. Justify your answer using shape, center, and variability.

14 Distribution 1: mean = 50   median = 50
standard deviation = 10

Distribution 2: mean = 50   median = 50
standard deviation = 25

Distribution 3: mean = 50   median = 50
standard deviation = 5

15 Distribution 1: mean = 55   median = 50
IQR = 10

Distribution 2: mean = 50   median = 50
IQR = 25

Distribution 3: mean = 45   median = 50
IQR = 5

For exercises 16–20, do a statistical analysis of the data set. Remember to include the shape, appropriate center and an appropriate measure(s) of variability other than the range.

16 {1, 2, 4, 3, 5, 6, 3, 2, 8, 6, 8, 9}

17 Salaries of 12 teachers in Tennessee.

$25,500	$45,500	$46,800	$32,300
$34,000	$45,500	$56,000	$42,250
$52,000	$48,900	$44,600	$51,700

18 {12.4, 13.2, 12.8, 12.6, 13.1, 13.0, 14.0}

19 Ages of residents on one floor of a retirement home.

66	72	75	78	82	84	86
86	86	89	91	92	95	98

20 {12, 13, 14, 11, 12, 18, 19, 15, 17, 18, 11}

For exercises 21–22 use the two-way table shown below.

The Quick Bite food truck took a survey of 100 randomly selected customers and asked if they liked hot dogs or hamburgers. The two-way table below shows the results.

	Dogs	No Dogs
Burgers	64	12
No Burgers	15	9

21 Extend the table to show the marginal totals and then construct a two-way relative frequency table with respect to burger preference.

	Dogs	No Dogs	Total
Burgers	64	12	**76**
No Burgers	15	9	**24**
Total	**79**	**21**	**100**

22 According to the Quick Bite survey find the percent of customers who:

(a) Like hot dogs, but also like burgers.

(b) Do not like burgers, and do not like dogs.

(c) Like burgers.

23 Since 1990, fireworks usage nationwide has grown, as shown in the accompanying table, where t represents the number of years since 1990, and p represents the fireworks usage per year, in millions of pounds.

Years since 1990	0	2	4	6	7	8	9	11
Millions of lbs	67.6	88.8	119	120.1	132.5	118.3	159.2	161.6

(a) Find the equation of the linear regression model for this set of data, where t is the independent variable. Round values to the nearest tenth.

(b) Do a residual analysis of your linear model.

(c) Using this equation, determine in what year fireworks usage would have reached 99 million pounds.

(d) Based on your model, how many millions of pounds of fireworks would be used in the year 2008?

24 The table below shows the projected number of new shops in a Greek yogurt chain that opened in the past year.

Year	1	2	3	4	5	6	7	8	9
Number of New Stores	14	28	50	90	110	153	265	399	675

Find a model for the data. Show a residual analysis. Report all values to the *nearest tenth*.

25 The commuting traffic on the Interstate is not predictable. The set of data below shows the one-way commuting time in minutes for 20 days.

60.5	30.5	55.6	33.8	58.6	49.9	36	63.9	55.9	57.9
35	63.8	46.1	47.4	35.2	47.5	40.5	34.5	44.9	40.7

Do a statistical analysis of the data set. Remember to include the shape, appropriate center, and an appropriate measure(s) of variability other than the range.

Common Core Standards for Mathematics and Mathematics Practices in this Brief Review

*indicates modeling standards

GRADE 8		WHERE TO FIND
Functions		
Define, evaluate, and compare functions.		
8.F.1	Understand that a function is a rule that assigns to each input exactly one output. The graph of a function is the set of ordered pairs consisting of an input and the corresponding output.	2.1
Geometry		
Understand and apply the Pythagorean Theorem		
8.G.7	Apply the Pythagorean Theorem to determine unknown side lengths in right triangles in real-world and mathematical problems in two and three dimensions.	1.6
Statistics and Probability		
Investigate patterns of association in bivariate data		
8.SP.4	Understand that patterns of association can also be seen in bivariate categorical data by displaying frequencies and relative frequencies in a two-way table. Construct and interpret a two-way table summarizing data on two categorical variables collected from the same subjects. Use relative frequencies calculated for rows or columns to describe possible association between the two variables. *For example, collect data from students in your class on whether or not they have a curfew on school nights and whether or not they have assigned chores at home. Is there evidence that those who have a curfew also tend to have chores?*	1.1

NUMBER AND QUANTITY		WHERE TO FIND
The Real Number System		
Use properties of rational and irrational numbers.		
N.RN.3	Explain why the sum or product of two rational numbers is rational; that the sum of a rational number and an irrational number is irrational; and that the product of a nonzero rational number and an irrational number is irrational.	1.2, 1.5, 3.2, 5.1

NUMBER AND QUANTITY		WHERE TO FIND
Reason quantitatively and use units to solve problems.		
N.Q.1	Use units as a way to understand problems and to guide the solution of multi-step problems; choose and interpret units consistently in formulas; choose and interpret the scale and the origin in graphs and data displays.	1.8
N.Q.2	Define appropriate quantities for the purpose of descriptive modeling.	1.1, 1.3
N.Q.3	Choose a level of accuracy appropriate to limitations on measurement when reporting quantities.	1.1, 1.8

ALGEBRA		WHERE TO FIND
Seeing Structure in Expressions		
Interpret the structure of expressions		
A.SSE.1.a	Interpret parts of an expression, such as terms, factors, and coefficients.	7.1
A.SSE.1.b	Interpret complicated expressions by viewing one or more of their parts as a single entity. *For example, interpret P(1 + r)n as the product of P and a factor not depending on P.*	5.3
A.SSE.2	Use the structure of an expression to identify ways to rewrite it. *For example, see $x^4 - y^4$ as $(x^2)^2 - (y^2)^2$, thus recognizing it as a difference of squares that can be factored as $(x^2 - y^2)(x^2 + y^2)$.*	7.1, 7.2, 7.3
Write expressions in equivalent forms to solve problems		
A.SSE.3.a	Factor a quadratic expression to reveal the zeros of the function it defines.	8.2
A.SSE.3.b	Complete the square in a quadratic expression to reveal the maximum or minimum value of the function it defines.	8.2
A.SSE.3.c	Use the properties of exponents to transform expressions for exponential functions. *For example the expression 1.15t can be rewritten as (1.151/12)12t ≈ 1.01212t to reveal the approximate equivalent monthly interest rate if the annual rate is 15%.*	5.3
Arithmetic with Polynomials and Rational Expressions		
Perform arithmetic operations on polynomials		
A.APR.1	Understand that polynomials form a system analogous to the integers, namely, they are closed under the operations of addition, subtraction, and multiplication; add, subtract, and multiply polynomials.	7.1, 7.2
Understand the relationship between zeros and factors of polynomials		
A.APR.3	Identify zeros of polynomials when suitable factorizations are available, and use the zeros to construct a rough graph of the function defined by the polynomial.	8.2

Creating Equations*

Create equations that describe numbers or relationships

A.CED.1	Create equations and inequalities in one variable and use them to solve problems. Include equations arising from linear and quadratic functions, and simple rational and exponential functions.*	1.6, 1.9, 2.1, 3.1, 3.2, 3.3, 3.4, 3.5, 5.2, 5.3, 8.1
A.CED.2	Create equations in two or more variables to represent relationships between quantities; graph equations on coordinate axes with labels and scales.*	4.1, 4.5, 8.3
A.CED.3	Represent constraints by equations or inequalities, and by systems of equations and/or inequalities, and interpret solutions as viable or nonviable options in a modeling context. For example, represent inequalities describing nutritional and cost constraints on combinations of different foods.*	3.1, 3.4, 3.5, 4.6, 4.7, 8.1
A.CED.4	Rearrange formulas to highlight a quantity of interest, using the same reasoning as in solving equations. For example, rearrange Ohm's law $V = IR$ to highlight resistance R.*	3.3, 4.2

Reasoning with Equations and Inequalities

Understand solving equations as a process of reasoning and explain the reasoning

A.REI.1	Explain each step in solving a simple equation as following from the equality of numbers asserted at the previous step, starting from the assumption that the original equation has a solution. Construct a viable argument to justify a solution method.	3.1, 3.3, 3.4

Solve equations and inequalities in one variable

A.REI.3	Solve linear equations and inequalities in one variable, including equations with coefficients represented by letters.	3.1, 3.3, 3.5
A.REI.4	Solve quadratic equations in one variable.	8.1, 8.2
A.REI.4.a	Use the method of completing the square to transform any quadratic equation in x into an equation of the form $(x - p)^2 = q$ that has the same solutions. Derive the quadratic formula from this form.	8.1, 8.2
A.REI.4.b	Solve quadratic equations by inspection (e.g., for $x^2 = 49$), taking square roots, completing the square, the quadratic formula and factoring, as appropriate to the initial form of the equation. Recognize when the quadratic formula gives complex solutions and write them as $a \pm bi$ for real numbers a and b.	8.2

Solve systems of equations

A.REI.5	Prove that, given a system of two equations in two variables, replacing one equation by the sum of that equation and a multiple of the other produces a system with the same solutions.	4.6
A.REI.6	Solve systems of linear equations exactly and approximately (e.g., with graphs), focusing on pairs of linear equations in two variables.	4.5, 4.6

ALGEBRA		WHERE TO FIND
Represent and solve equations and inequalities graphically		
A.REI.10	Understand that the graph of an equation in two variables is the set of all its solutions plotted in the coordinate plane, often forming a curve (which could be a line).	4.2, 4.3
A.REI.11	Explain why the x-coordinates of the points where the graphs of the equations $y = f(x)$ and $y = g(x)$ intersect are the solutions of the equation $f(x) = g(x)$; find the solutions approximately, e.g., using technology to graph the functions, make tables of values, or find successive approximations. Include cases where $f(x)$ and/or $g(x)$ are linear, polynomial, rational, absolute value, exponential, and logarithmic functions.*	8.4
A.REI.12	Graph the solutions to a linear inequality in two variables as a halfplane (excluding the boundary in the case of a strict inequality), and graph the solution set to a system of linear inequalities in two variables as the intersection of the corresponding half-planes.	4.7

FUNCTIONS		WHERE TO FIND
Interpreting Functions		
Understand the concept of a function and use function notation		
F.IF.1	Understand that a function from one set (called the domain) to another set (called the range) assigns to each element of the domain exactly one element of the range. If f is a function and x is an element of its domain, then $f(x)$ denotes the output of f corresponding to the input x. The graph of f is the graph of the equation $y = f(x)$.	2.1
F.IF.2	Use function notation, evaluate functions for inputs in their domains, and interpret statements that use function notation in terms of a context.	2.1, 2.2, 2.3
F.IF.3	Recognize that sequences are functions, sometimes defined recursively, whose domain is a subset of the integers. For example, the Fibonacci sequence is defined recursively by $f(0) = f(1) = 1$, $f(n + 1) = f(n) + f(n - 1)$ for $n \geq 1$.	1.7, 2.1
Interpret functions that arise in applications in terms of the context		
F.IF.4	For a function that models a relationship between two quantities, interpret key features of graphs and tables in terms of the quantities, and sketch graphs showing key features given a verbal description of the relationship. Key features include: intercepts; intervals where the function is increasing, decreasing, positive, or negative; relative maximums and minimums; symmetries; end behavior; and periodicity.*	2.1, 8.3
F.IF.5	Relate the domain of a function to its graph and, where applicable, to the quantitative relationship it describes. For example, if the function $h(n)$ gives the number of person-hours it takes to assemble n engines in a factory, then the positive integers would be an appropriate domain for the function.*	2.2
F.IF.6	Calculate and interpret the average rate of change of a function (presented symbolically or as a table) over a specified interval. Estimate the rate of change from a graph.*	4.1, 8.3

Analyze functions using different representations

F.IF.7	Graph functions expressed symbolically and show key features of the graph, by hand in simple cases and using technology for more complicated cases.*	2.4
F.IF.7.a	Graph linear and quadratic functions and show intercepts, maxima, and minima.	4.2, 8.3, 8.4
F.IF.7.b	Graph square root, cube root, and piecewise-defined functions, including step functions and absolute value functions.	2.3, 4.4
F.IF.8	Write a function defined by an expression in different but equivalent forms to reveal and explain different properties of the function.	2.4
F.IF.8.a	Use the process of factoring and completing the square in a quadratic function to show zeros, extreme values, and symmetry of the graph, and interpret these in terms of a context.	8.3
F.IF.9	Compare properties of two functions each represented in a different way (algebraically, graphically, numerically in tables, or by verbal descriptions). For example, given a graph of one quadratic function and an algebraic expression for another, say which has the larger maximum.	8.4

Building Functions

Build a function that models a relationship between two quantities

F.BF.1	Write a function that describes a relationship between two quantities.*	2.1
F.BF.1.a	Determine an explicit expression, a recursive process, or steps for calculation from a context.	1.9
F.BF.2	Write arithmetic and geometric sequences both recursively and with an explicit formula, use them to model situations, and translate between the two forms.*	1.7, 3.2, 5.1

Build new functions from existing functions

F.BF.3	Identify the effect on the graph of replacing $f(x)$ by $f(x) + k$, $k\,f(x)$, $f(kx)$, and $f(x + k)$ for specific values of k (both positive and negative); find the value of k given the graphs. Experiment with cases and illustrate an explanation of the effects on the graph using technology. Include recognizing even and odd functions from their graphs and algebraic expressions for them.	4.4, 6.1, 8.5

Linear, Quadratic, and Exponential Models

Construct and compare linear, quadratic, and exponential models and solve problems

F.LE.1	Distinguish between situations that can be modeled with linear functions and with exponential functions.*	5.1
F.LE.1.a	Prove that linear functions grow by equal differences over equal intervals, and that exponential functions grow by equal factors over equal intervals.	5.2
F.LE.1.b	Recognize situations in which one quantity changes at a constant rate per unit interval relative to another.	4.1

FUNCTIONS		WHERE TO FIND
F.LE.1.c	Recognize situations in which a quantity grows or decays by a constant percent rate per unit interval relative to another.	5.2
F.LE.2	Construct linear and exponential functions, including arithmetic and geometric sequences, given a graph, a description of a relationship, or two input-output pairs (include reading these from a table).*	5.3
F.LE.3	Observe using graphs and tables that a quantity increasing exponentially eventually exceeds a quantity increasing linearly, quadratically, or (more generally) as a polynomial function.*	5.3, 8.4
Interpret expressions for functions in terms of the situation they model		
F.LE.5	Interpret the parameters in a linear or exponential function in terms of a context.*	5.1, 5.2, 5.3

GEOMETRY		WHERE TO FIND
Expressing Geometric Properties with Equations		
Use coordinates to prove simple geometric theorems algebraically		
G.GPE.5	Prove the slope criteria for parallel and perpendicular lines and use them to solve geometric problems (e.g., find the equation of a line parallel or perpendicular to a given line that passes through a given point).	4.1, 4.3

STATISTICS AND PROBABILITY		WHERE TO FIND
Interpreting Categorical and Quantitative Data		
Summarize, represent, and interpret data on a single count or measurement variable		
S.ID.1	Represent data with plots on the real number line (dot plots, histograms, and box plots).*	9.1, 9.2, 9.3, 9.4, 9.5
S.ID.2	Use statistics appropriate to the shape of the data distribution to compare center (median, mean) and spread (interquartile range, standard deviation) of two or more different data sets.*	9.2, 9.3, 9.4, 9.5
S.ID.3	Interpret differences in shape, center, and spread in the context of the data sets, accounting for possible effects of extreme data points (outliers).*	9.2, 9.3, 9.4, 9.5
Summarize, represent, and interpret data on two categorical and quantitative variables		
S.ID.5	Summarize categorical data for two categories in two-way frequency tables. Interpret relative frequencies in the context of the data (including joint, marginal, and conditional relative frequencies).*	9.6, 9.7
Recognize possible associations and trends in the data.		
S.ID.6	Represent data on two quantitative variables on a scatter plot, and describe how the variables are related.*	9.8

STATISTICS AND PROBABILITY		WHERE TO FIND
S.ID.6.a	Fit a function to the data; use functions fitted to data to solve problems in the context of the data. Use given functions or choose a function suggested by the context. Emphasize linear, quadratic, and exponential models.	9.7
S.ID.6.b	Informally assess the fit of a function by plotting and analyzing residuals.	9.8
S.ID.6.c	Fit a linear function for a scatter plot that suggests a linear association.	9.7
Interpret linear models		
S.ID.7	Interpret the slope (rate of change) and the intercept (constant term) of a linear model in the context of the data.*	4.1
S.ID.8	Compute (using technology) and interpret the correlation coefficient of a linear fit.*	9.7
S.ID.9	Distinguish between correlation and causation.*	9.7

STANDARDS FOR MATHEMATICAL PRACTICE		WHERE TO FIND
MP1	Make sense of problems and persevere in solving them.	Ch1 PA, 3.1, 3.2, 3.3, 4.7, 5.3, 7.1, 8.2, 9.4
MP2	Reason abstractly and quantitatively.	2.1, 4.4, 5.1, Ch5 PA, 7.1, 8.2, 8.4, 8.5, 9.1, 9.8
MP3	Construct viable arguments and critique the reasoning of others.	5.1, 5.3, 8.4, Ch9 PA
MP4	Model with mathematics.	3.3, 3.5, 5.2, 8.3, 9.1, 9.8
MP5	Use appropriate tools strategically.	1.3, 4.5, 8.3, 9.1, 9.3, 9.4
MP6	Attend to precision.	1.2, 3.2, 3.4, 4.1, 4.3, 4.6, 5.3, 6.1, 6.2, 6.3, 8.1, Ch9 PA
MP7	Look for and make use of structure.	1.6, 1.7, 2.2, 3.1, 3.3, Ch3 PA, 4.3, 5.1, 6.4, 8.2, 8.5, 9.3, 9.7
MP8	Look for and express regularity in repeated reasoning.	1.4, 4.2, 4.3, 4.6, 5.1, 5.2, 6.1, 7.3, 8.3, 8.5, 9.4

*PA = Preparing for the Assessment

Choosing a Movie-Rental Plan

Complete this performance task using as many response sheets as you need. Fully answer all parts of the performance task with detailed responses. You should provide sound mathematical reasoning to support your work.

You are considering three different ways to rent movies.

Plan A: Rent DVDs from a kiosk in a nearby grocery store for $1.50 each. The selection of movies is limited.

Plan B: Stream unlimited movies to your computer or TV for $10 per month. The selection of movies is good.

Plan C: Rent DVDs by mail for a $5 monthly fee plus $2 per movie. The selection of movies is outstanding.

Task Description

Choose the movie-rental plan that you think is best. Consider the cost of each plan, the selection offered, and how you like to receive and watch movies.

a. Write functions $A(x)$, $B(x)$, and $C(x)$ that give the cost to rent x movies per month for Plans A, B, and C, respectively.

b. If you consider only cost, under what condition does it make sense to choose Plan B over Plan A?

c. If you consider only cost, under what condition does it make sense to choose Plan C over Plan B?

d. Show that Plan A is always more cost-effective than Plan C. Does that mean that Plan A is a better choice than Plan C for everyone? Explain.

e. Which movie-rental plan would you choose? Justify your answer.

PERFORMANCE TASKS

Expanding a Parking Lot

Complete this performance task using as many response sheets as you need. Fully answer all parts of the performance task with detailed responses. You should provide sound mathematical reasoning to support your work.

A high school has a rectangular parking lot that measures 600 ft long by 400 ft wide. The school board wants to double the area of the lot by increasing both its length and width by the same amount, x ft. The board also wants to build a fence around the new lot. The cost to expand the lot is estimated to be $2 per square foot of new space. The cost to fence the lot is estimated to be $30 per foot of fencing. Costs include materials and labor.

Task Description

Estimate the total cost of expanding and fencing in the lot.

a. Draw a diagram of the situation. Your diagram should show both the original parking lot and what the lot will look like after it has been expanded. Label all dimensions.

b. Write an equation that you can use to find x. Solve the equation for x.

c. What is the area of the new portion of the parking lot that needs to be built? What is the perimeter of the new parking lot?

d. What is the estimated cost of expanding and fencing in the lot?

e. The school has only enough money to pay for half the estimated cost from part (d). The school board plans to raise the remaining funds by selling parking stickers for $100 to students and $200 to faculty. How many student stickers and how many faculty stickers must the school sell? Is there only one possible answer? Explain.

Projectile Motion

Complete this performance task using as many response sheets as you need. Fully answer all parts of the performance task with detailed responses. You should provide sound mathematical reasoning to support your work.

Suppose an object is launched at an angle of 45° with respect to horizontal. The object's height y (in feet) after it has traveled a horizontal distance of x feet is given by the equation

$$y = -\frac{g}{v^2}x^2 + x + y_0$$

where v is the object's initial speed (in feet per second), y_0 is the object's initial height (in feet), and $g \approx 32 \text{ ft/s}^2$ is the acceleration due to gravity.

Task Description

You throw a baseball at a 45° angle to your friend standing 100 ft away. Your friend holds her glove 5 ft above the ground to catch the ball. At what initial height, and with what initial speed, should you release the ball so that your friend can catch it without moving her glove?

a. Suppose you release the baseball with an initial height of 6 ft and an initial speed of 50 ft/s. Write and graph an equation that represents the ball's path. Does the ball land in your friend's glove? Explain.

b. If your friend catches the ball, what point must lie on the graph of the ball's path? (Assume you are standing at the point $(0, 0)$).

c. Use your answer to part (b) to write an equation that describes the initial heights and initial speeds for which your friend catches the ball. Explain why there is more than one initial height and initial speed that work.

d. Find an initial height and an initial speed for which your friend catches the ball. How can you check your answer?

PERFORMANCE TASKS

Calculating Inflation

Complete this performance task using as many response sheets as you need. Fully answer all parts of the performance task with detailed responses. You should provide sound mathematical reasoning to support your work.

The inflation rate for an item (such as a carton of eggs) measures how rapidly the price of the item has changed over time. If an item's price changes from p_1 to p_2 over a period of n years, then the annual inflation rate r (expressed as a decimal) is given by this equation:

$$r = \left(\frac{p_2}{p_1}\right)^{1/n} - 1$$

For example, if the price of an item increases from $2 to $3 over 5 years, then the annual inflation rate is:

$$r = \left(\frac{3}{2}\right)^{1/5} - 1 \approx 1.084 - 1 = 0.084 = 8.4\%$$

The table below shows the average retail prices of several foods in the United States for the years 2000 and 2009.

Task Description

Identify the foods in the table with the least and greatest annual rates of inflation for the period 2000–2009. Then predict the cost in 2015 of the groceries in a basket containing one of each food item from the table.

a. Find the annual inflation rate for each food in the table for the period 2000–2009. Round your answers to the nearest tenth of a percent.

b. Which food had the least inflation rate? Which had the greatest inflation rate?

c. Which foods, if any, had a negative annual inflation rate? What does a negative annual inflation rate mean?

d. Can you add the percentages of each item to determine the inflation rate for a basket of groceries? Explain.

e. What was the annual inflation rate for a basket of all the food items for the period 2000–2009?

Food	Price in 2000	Price in 2009
Bread (1 lb)	$0.99	$1.39
Butter (1 lb)	$2.80	$2.67
Cheddar cheese (1 lb)	$3.76	$4.55
Eggs, large (1 dozen)	$0.96	$1.77
Ground beef (1 lb)	$1.63	$2.19
Oranges (1 lb)	$0.62	$0.93
Peanut butter (1 lb)	$1.96	$2.10
Meat cutlets (1 lb)	$3.46	$3.29
Tomatoes (1 lb)	$1.57	$1.96

f. Predict the cost of the groceries in the basket in 2015. Explain how you determined your prediction.

Glossary

GLOSSARY

Abscissa The value of the *x*-coordinate in an ordered pair.

Absolute value The distance that a number is from zero on a number line. The symbol for the absolute value of a number *n* is $|n|$.

Absolute-value function A function whose graph is in the form $f(x) = |x|$.

Acute angle An angle whose measure is greater than 0° and less than 90°.

Acute triangle A triangle that has three acute angles.

Addend One of a set of numbers to be added. In the expression $a + b$, *a* and *b* are the addends.

Addition-multiplication method A method used to solve a system of equations in which the equations are added to eliminate one of the variables. In some cases, one or more of the equations must be multiplied by a nonzero constant before the addition can occur. Also called the *elimination method*.

Addition property of equality For all real numbers *a*, *b*, and *c*, if $a = b$, then $a + c = b + c$.

Addition property of inequality For all real numbers *a*, *b*, and *c*,

- If $a < b$, then $a + c < b + c$; and
- If $a > b$, then $a + c > b + c$.

Additive identity Zero. When 0 is added to any given number, the sum is identical to the given number. See also *identity property of addition*.

Additive inverse See *inverse property of addition*.

A-H-K form of a quadratic function See *Vertex form of a quadratic function*.

Algebraic expression See *variable expression*.

Angle of depression An angle whose vertex and horizontal side are level with an observer's eye and whose other side slopes downward from an observer's eye level to an object below.

Angle of elevation An angle whose vertex and horizontal side are level with an observer's eye and whose other side slopes upward from an observer's eye level to an object above.

Antecedent See *hypothesis*.

Area of a plane figure The number of nonoverlapping square units contained in its interior.

Arithmetic mean The sum of the values in a numerical set of data, divided by the number of data values in the set.

Also called *average*.

Arithmetic sequence A sequence in which each term differs by a common difference, *d*.

Associative property of addition For all real numbers *a*, *b*, and *c*, $a + b + c = (a + b) + c = a + (b + c)$.

Associative property of multiplication For all real numbers *a*, *b*, and *c*, $a \cdot b \cdot c = (a \cdot b) \cdot c = a \cdot (b \cdot c)$.

Asymptote A line that a curve approaches but never reaches.

Average See *Arithmetic mean*.

Average rate of change in non-linear functions, the rate of change between the endpoints of a defined interval.

Axis of symmetry of a parabola The line that divides the parabola into two matching parts. For a parabola with equation $y = ax^2 + bx + c$, $a \neq 0$, the equation of the axis of symmetry is $x = -\frac{b}{2a}$.

Bar graph A statistical display in which data are represented by bars that are determined by two axes; one of these axes is labeled with categories of data, and the other is labeled with a numerical scale.

Base The rate at which an exponential function will increase, given by the letter b in the exponential function $f(x) = a \cdot b^x + c$.

Base of a power When a number is written in the exponential form x^n, the number *x* is the base.

Bell shaped distribution a symmetric distribution where the line of symmetry passes through the point of highest frequency.

Bimodal *See mode.*

Binomial A polynomial with exactly two terms.

Bivariate data Data that are collected for two different variables.

Box-and-whisker plot A display of numerical data in which a *box* represents the data from the first to third quartiles, a vertical segment crosses the box at the median, and horizontal *whiskers* extend from the left and right of the box to represent the rest of the data.

Broken-line graph See *line graph*.

Cartesian coordinate system A system in which points on a plane are identified by ordered pairs.

Center of rotation See *rotation*.

Circle graph A statistical display in which a data set is represented by a circle, and distinct categories of the data are represented by distinct "slices" of the circle; the percent of the circle allotted to each slice is equal to the percent of the data set within that category.

Closed statement A statement that is either true or false.

Closure property of addition For all real numbers *a* and *b*, $a + b$ is a unique real number.

Closure property of multiplication For all real numbers a and b, $a \cdot b$ is a unique real number.

Coefficient of a term The numerical part of a term that contains variables. Also called the *numerical coefficient of a term*.

Column matrix An $n \cdot 1$ matrix, meaning there are n number of rows with only one element in each.

Common difference A fixed number by which all the terms in an arithmetic sequence will differ.

Common ratio A fixed number by which all the terms in a geometric sequence will vary.

Commutative property of addition For all real numbers a and b, $a + b = b + a$.

Commutative property of multiplication For all real numbers a and b, $a \cdot b = b \cdot a$.

Complete the square given the first two terms of a perfect square trinomial, $ax^2 + bx$, finding the trinomial's third term using the formula $\left[\!\left[\frac{b}{2}\right]\!\right]^2$.

Composite number A natural number greater than 1 that has more than two factors.

Composition When multiple transformations are applied to a figure.

Compound inequality Two inequalities joined by the word *and* or the word *or*.

Compound statement A statement formed by linking two or more simple statements.

Compression A transformation that changes a graph's size, shrinking it away from the x-axis.

Conditional probability The probability of an event occurring given that some other event has already occurred.

Conditional statement A statement formed by connecting two statements with the words *if* and *then*.

Conjunction A compound statement that is formed by linking simple statements with the word *and*.

Consecutive integers Integers that differ by 1.

Consequent See *conclusion*.

Constant term A term that has no variable part. Also called a *constant*.

Constant of variation See *direct variation*.

Constraints The inequalities making up an objective function.

Continued ratio A ratio that relates more than two numbers. Also called *extended ratio*.

Continuous data set A set of data that involves measurements such as length, weight, or temperature in which there is always another data value between any two given data values. The graph of a continuous data set is a line or a smooth curve with no holes or breaks.

Conversion factor A ratio of two measurements that is equal to one.

Coordinate plane A number plane formed by a horizontal number line and a vertical number line that intersect at their origins.

Coordinate(s) of a point The real number or numbers that correspond to the point. On a number line, the coordinate of each point is a single number. On a coordinate plane, each point has an ordered pair (x, y) of coordinates. The first number of the ordered pair is called the *x-coordinate* of the point, and the second is called the *y-coordinate*. See also *Ruler Postulate*.

Correlation A measure of the relationship between two sets of numerical data. If both sets of data generally increase or decrease together, there is a *positive correlation*. If one set generally increases as the other decreases, there is a *negative correlation*. If there is no apparent relationship, there is *no correlation*.

Counterexample A particular instance that shows a general statement is not true for all values in the replacement set.

Counting number See *natural number*.

Cross products property of proportions For real numbers a, b, c and d, where $b \neq 0$ and $d \neq 0$, if $\frac{a}{b} = \frac{c}{d}$, then $ad = bc$. Also stated as *In a proportion, the product of the means equals the product of the extremes*.

Cubic polynomial A polynomial of degree three.

Cumulative frequency histogram A histogram that displays the data from a cumulative frequency table.

Cumulative frequency table A summary of a data set in which each data value is paired with the sum of the frequencies of all values less than or equal to it.

D

Data A collection of information, usually numerical.

Decay function A negative exponential function used to model situations in real life.

Definition A statement of the meaning of a word or phrase.

Degree of a monomial The sum of the exponents of its variable(s).

Degree of a polynomial The greatest degree of any of its terms after it has been simplified.

Degree of a term of a polynomial The sum of the exponents of all the variables in the term. For a polynomial in one variable, the degree of each term is the exponent of the variable in that term. The degree of a constant term is 0.

Denominator In the fraction $\frac{a}{b}$, the number b is the denominator.

Dependent system of equations A system that has infinitely many solutions.

GLOSSARY

Dependent variable A variable whose value is affected by the value of another variable.

Difference The result of a subtraction.

Difference of two squares The product that results from multiplying two binomials that are the sum and difference of the same two terms. Algebraically, $(a + b)(a - b) = a^2 - b^2$.

Dimensional analysis A method for converting a measurement from one unit of measure to another by multiplying by a ratio representing the relationship between the units. The ratio is called a *conversion factor*.

Direct measurement See *indirect measurement*.

Direct variation A relationship described by an equation of the form $y = kx$, where k is a constant nonzero real number. The number k is called the *constant of variation*.

Discrete data set A set of data that involves a count, such as numbers of people or objects. The graph of a discrete data set consists of points that are not connected.

Discriminant of a quadratic equation For a quadratic equation of the form $ax^2 + bx + c = 0$, the discriminant is the expression $b^2 - 4ac$.

Disjunction A compound statement that is formed by linking simple statements with the word *or*.

Distance between two points (number line) The absolute value of the difference of the coordinates of the points. See also *Ruler Postulate*.

Distance formula (coordinate plane) The distance PQ between $P(x_1, y_1)$ and $Q(x_2, y_2)$ is given by the formula $PQ = \sqrt{(x_2 - x_1)^2 + (y_2 - y_1)^2}$.

Distribution any graph used to visualize the data.

Distributive property For all real numbers a, b, and c, $a \cdot (b + c) = a \cdot b + a \cdot c$ and $(b + c) \cdot a = b \cdot a + c \cdot a$.

Dividend In a division, the number that is being divided. In the expression $a \div b$, a is the dividend.

Divisible One number is divisible by another if the second number divides the first with remainder 0.

Division property of equality For all real numbers a and b and all nonzero real numbers c, if $a = b$, then $\frac{a}{c} = \frac{b}{c}$.

Division property of inequality For all real numbers a, b, and c,

1. If $a < b$ and $c > 0$, then $\frac{a}{c} < \frac{b}{c}$;

   If $a < b$ and $c < 0$, then $\frac{a}{c} > \frac{b}{c}$; and

2. If $a > b$ and $c > 0$, then $\frac{a}{c} > \frac{b}{c}$;

   If $a > b$ and $c < 0$, then $\frac{a}{c} < \frac{b}{c}$.

Divisor In a division, the number by which you divide. In the expression $a \div b$, b is the divisor.

Domain of a function See *function*.

Domain of a relation See *relation*.

Domain of a variable See *replacement set*.

Element of a set See *member of a set*.

Elimination method See *addition-multiplication method*.

Empirical Rule the pattern of standard deviation in which 68% of the data is ± 1 SD about the mean; 95% is ± 2 SD about the mean; and 99.7% is ± 3 SD about the mean.

End behavior That which happens to the graph as the line moves farther from the y-axis. This can be determined from the leading term.

Equation A statement that two mathematical expressions are equal.

Equilateral triangle A triangle that has three congruent sides.

Equivalent equations Equations that have the same solution set.

Equivalent expressions Expressions that name the same number.

Equivalent inequalities Inequalities that have the same solution set.

Equivalent systems Systems that have the same solution set.

Evaluate a variable expression To replace each variable in the expression with a value from its replacement set, then simplify the resulting numerical expression.

Even number A member of the set $\{\ldots, -4, -2, 0, 2, 4, \ldots\}$.

Excluded value Any value excluded from the domain of a variable because that value would result in a denominator of zero. The excluded values are said to be *restricted from the domain* of the variable.

Explicit sequence A sequence of terms in which subsequent terms are defined in relation to the number of the term without regard to the value of the preceding term or terms.

Exponent When a number is written in the exponential form x^n, the number n is the exponent.

Exponential form The expression x^n is the exponential form of the nth power of x. When n is a natural number, $x^n = x \cdot x \cdot x \cdot \ldots \cdot x$, with n factors of x.

Exponential function A function in the form $y = ab^x$ where the variable is an exponent; a function in the form of $y = a \cdot b^x$, where a is a nonzero constant and b is greater than zero but not equal to 1.

Extended ratio See *continued ratio*.

Extraneous root A root or solution that does not satisfy the original equation.

Extremes of a proportion In the proportion $\frac{a}{b} = \frac{c}{d}$, a and d are the extremes.

Factor of a multiplication One of a set of numbers to be multiplied. In the expression ab, a and b are the factors.

Factor a polynomial completely To express the polynomial as a product of one or more polynomials that cannot be factored further.

Factor of a whole number A natural number that divides the number with a remainder of 0.

First quartile In a numerical data set, the median of the data values that are less than the median of the entire set.

Formula A literal equation in which each variable represents a quantity.

Frequency of a data value The number of times the value occurs in the data set.

Frequency table A summary of a set of data in which each data value is matched with its frequency.

Function A relationship in which every member of one set, called the *domain*, is assigned exactly one member of a second set, called the *range*.

Geometric sequence When each term of the sequence varies by a constant quotient.

Graph of an equation or inequality in two variables The set of all points in the coordinate plane that correspond to solutions to the equation or inequality.

Graph of an inequality (number line) The set of the graphs of all solutions to the inequality.

Graph of a number The point that corresponds to the number on a number line.

Graph of an ordered pair The point that corresponds to the ordered pair on a coordinate plane.

Greatest common factor (GCF) of monomials The product of the greatest common factor of their numerical coefficients and the greatest common factor of their variable parts.

Greatest common factor (GCF) of natural numbers The greatest number that is a factor of each number in a set of two or more natural numbers.

Greatest integer function A step function that assigns to each real number the greatest integer that is less than or equal to that number.

Greatest possible error In a measurement, half the smallest unit on the measuring instrument.

Grouping symbol In a numerical or variable expression, a device that indicates certain operations are to be done before others. Common grouping symbols are parentheses, brackets, braces, fraction bars, radical signs, and absolute-value bars.

Growth function A positive exponential function used to model situations in real life.

Hexagon A polygon that has exactly six sides.

Histogram A vertical bar graph of a frequency distribution. The bars represent equal intervals of the data, and there is no space between the bars.

Hole in the graph A particular value on a graph which is not part of the domain of the function. Can occur in some rational functions.

Horizontal translation A shift of a graph along the x-axis.

Hypotenuse The side of a right triangle that is opposite the right angle.

Hypothesis In a conditional statement, the part that follows *if*. Also called the *antecedent*.

Identity An equation that is true for all values of the variable(s).

Identity property of addition For all real numbers a, $a + 0 = a$ and $0 + a = a$. See also *additive identity*.

Identity property of multiplication For all real numbers a, $a \cdot 1 = a$ and $1 \cdot a = a$. See also *multiplicative identity*.

Image See *transformation*.

Imaginary number A number whose squared value is a real number not greater than zero.

Inconsistent system of equations A system that has no solution.

Independent system of equations A system that has exactly one solution.

Independent variable A variable whose value is not affected by the value of another variable.

Index With a radical sign, the index indicates the degree of the root.

Indirect measurement Determining an unknown measurement by using mathematical relationships among known measurements rather than using a *direct measurement* tool such as a ruler or protractor.

Inequality A statement that consists of two expressions joined by an inequality symbol. Commonly used inequality symbols are $<, \leq, >, \geq$, and $\neq$.

Initial value variable The variable a in an exponential function where when $x = 0$, then $y = a$ in the function $y = a \cdot b^x + c$.

Integer A member of the set $\{\ldots, -3, -2, -1, 0, 1, 2, 3, \ldots\}$.

Intercepts The points on a graph where a function crosses each axis.

Interquartile range The difference when the first quartile of a data set is subtracted from the third quartile.

GLOSSARY

Interval The distance over which the data increases or decreases.

Inverse property of addition For every real number a, there is a unique real number $-a$ such that $a + (-a) = 0$ and $-a + a = 0$; $-a$ is the *additive inverse* of a, or the *opposite* of a.

Inverse property of multiplication For every nonzero real number a, there is a unique real number $\frac{1}{a}$ such that $a \cdot \frac{1}{a} = 1$ and $\frac{1}{a} \cdot a = 1$; $\frac{1}{a}$ is the *multiplicative inverse* of a, or the *reciprocal* of a.

Inverse variation When two quantities are related such that a change in one produces the opposite type of change in the other.

Irrational number A number represented by a decimal that does not terminate and does not repeat.

Isosceles trapezoid A trapezoid whose legs are congruent.

Isosceles triangle A triangle that has at least two congruent sides, called the *legs*. The third side is the *base*. The angles opposite the congruent sides are called the *base angles*. The third angle is the *vertex angle*.

Leading coefficient of a polynomial The coefficient of the leading term.

Leading term of a polynomial In a polynomial in one variable, the term with the greatest degree.

Least common denominator (LCD) The least common multiple of the denominators of a set of fractions.

Least common multiple (LCM) of numbers The least number that is a multiple of each number in a set of two or more numbers.

Legs of an isosceles triangle See *isosceles triangle*.

Legs of a right triangle The sides opposite the acute angles.

Legs of a trapezoid The nonparallel sides.

Length of a segment The distance between the endpoints of the segment.

Like radicals Radical expressions with exactly the same radicand.

Like terms Terms that have exactly the same variable parts.

Line graph A statistical display in which paired data are represented by points, the position of the points being determined by two axes labeled with numerical scales; the points are then connected in order with segments. Also called a *broken-line graph*.

Line Intersection Postulate If two lines intersect, then they intersect in exactly one point.

Line segment See *segment*.

Line symmetry A plane figure that has line symmetry is its own image after reflection across some line in the plane. The line is called a *line of symmetry* for the figure.

Linear equation in two variables For the variables x and y, any equation that can be written in the form $ax + by = c$, where a, b, and c are real numbers and a and b are not both 0. The equation $ax + by = c$ is called the *standard form* of a linear equation in two variables.

Linear inequality in two variables For the variables x and y, any inequality that can be written in the form $ax + by \geq c$, $ax + by > c$, $ax + by \leq c$, or $ax + by < c$, where a, b, and c are real numbers and a and b are not both 0.

Linear pair Adjacent angles whose noncommon sides are opposite rays.

Linear polynomial A polynomial of degree one.

Literal equation An equation that contains two or more variables.

Logically equivalent statements Statements that have the same truth values.

Lowest terms A fraction is in lowest terms if the GCF of its numerator and denominator is 1.

Mapping diagram A diagram that describes a relation by linking elements of the domain with elements of the range. In a mapping diagram, the domain is called the *pre-image* and the range is called the *image*.

Matrix A rectangular array of numbers.

Maximum data value The greatest data value in a set of numerical data.

Maximum value of a quadratic function The y-coordinate of the vertex of the graph of a quadratic function described by $y = ax^2 + bx + c$, where $a < 0$.

Mean The sum of the data values in a numerical set of data, divided by the number of data values in the set. Also called *average*.

Mean Absolute Deviation (MAD) In a symmetric distribution a measure of variability that indicates a average range about the mean.

Mean Absolute Deviation (MAD) formula
$$\text{MAD} = \frac{\sum |x_i - \bar{x}|}{n}.$$

Means of a proportion In the proportion $\frac{a}{b} = \frac{c}{d}$, b and c are the means.

Measure of central tendency A statistic that is in some way representative or typical of a set of data. Commonly used measures of central tendency are the *mean*, the *median*, and the *mode*.

Median of a data set The middle data value in a set of data that has been arranged in numerical order. If the number of data values in the set is even, then the median is the average of the *two* middle data values.

Member of a set Any object in the set. Also called *element of a set*.

Minimum data value The least data value in a set of numerical data.

Minimum value of a quadratic function The *y*-coordinate of the vertex of the graph of a quadratic function described by $y = ax^2 + bx + c$, where $a > 0$.

Mode In a data set, the data value(s) with the greatest frequency.

Monomial A number, a variable, or a product of a number and one or more variables with nonnegative exponents.

Multiple of a number The result when the number is multiplied by a whole number.

Multiplication property of equality For all real numbers a, b, and c, if $a = b$, then $ac = bc$.

Multiplication property of inequality For all real numbers a, b, and c,

1. If $a < b$ and $c > 0$, then $ac < bc$;
   If $a < b$ and $c < 0$, then $ac > bc$; and

2. If $a > b$ and $c > 0$, then $ac > bc$;
   If $a > b$ and $c < 0$, then $ac < bc$.

Multiplicative identity One. When any given number is multiplied by 1, the product is identical to the given number. See also *identity property of multiplication*.

Multiplicative inverse See *inverse property of multiplication*.

Multiplicity of factors The number of times that the same factor occurs in the complete factoring of a function.

Natural number A member of the set $\{1, 2, 3, 4, 5, 6, \ldots\}$. Also called *counting number*.

Negative correlation See *correlation*.

Negative number On a number line, a number that corresponds to a point on the negative side of zero. If the numbers increase in order from left to right, the negative side is to the left of zero.

Non-symmetric distribution the left and right sides of the distribution show no line of symmetry.

Normal distribution a bell shaped distribution whose standard deviation approximates the Empirical Rule.

Number line A line whose points have been placed in one-to-one correspondence with the set of real numbers.

Numerator In the fraction $\frac{a}{b}$, the number a is the numerator.

Numerical coefficient See *coefficient of a term*.

Numerical expression A name for a number.

Obtuse angle An angle whose measure is greater than 90° and less than 180°.

Obtuse triangle A triangle that has one obtuse angle.

Octagon A polygon that has exactly eight sides.

Odd number A member of the set $\{\ldots, -5, -3, -1, 1, 3, 5, \ldots\}$.

One-to-one function A function where each element in the domain is mapped to one and only one element in the range.

Open statement A statement that contains one or more variables.

Opposite(s) Numbers that are the same distance from zero on a number line, but on opposite sides of zero. The symbol for the opposite of a number n is $-n$. See also *inverse property of addition*.

Ordered pair In a coordinate plane, the pair of real numbers (x, y) that corresponds to a point.

Ordinate The value of the *y*-coordinate in an ordered pair.

Origin of a coordinate plane The point where the axes intersect.

Origin of a number line The point that corresponds to the number zero.

Outlier a data value that is far removed from the body of the data.

Parabola The U-shaped curve that is the graph of a quadratic function.

Parallel lines Coplanar lines that do not intersect. The symbol for parallel is ∥.

Parallelogram A quadrilateral that has two pairs of parallel sides. To calculate area, any of the sides may be considered the *base*, and the length of that side is also called the base. The *height* is then the length of any perpendicular segment drawn from a point on the side opposite the base to the line containing the base.

Parent function The most basic graph of each type of function.

Pearson correlation coefficient The Pearson correlation coefficient, r, is a number between -1 and 1, inclusive, that measures the linear relationship between a dependent and independent variable. When $r = 1$ or -1, the data is said to have a *perfect linear correlation*.

Pentagon A polygon that has exactly five sides.

GLOSSARY

Percent Percent means "per 100," "out of 100," or "divided by 100." The symbol for percent is %.

Percent of change The percent an amount changes from an original amount. The change may be a *percent of increase* or a *percent of decrease*.

Percentile rank If n percent of the data values in a set are less than or equal to a given data value, then n is the percentile rank of that data value.

Perfect square A number whose square roots are rational numbers.

Perfect square trinomial A trinomial that results from squaring a binomial. The form of the square of a binomial sum is $(a + b)^2 = a^2 + 2ab + b^2$. For a binomial difference, $(a - b)^2 = a^2 - 2ab + b^2$.

Perimeter of a plane figure The distance around the figure. The perimeter of a polygon is the sum of the lengths of its sides.

Perpendicular lines Lines that intersect to form right angles. The symbol for perpendicular is $\perp$.

Piecewise function A function with different function rules for different parts of the domain.

Point-slope form of an equation of a line For an equation in the variables x and y, the point-slope form is $y - y_1 = m(x - x_1)$, where $P(x_1, y_1)$ is a point on the line and m is the slope of the line.

Point symmetry A plane figure that has point symmetry is its own image after a half-turn in the plane.

Polygon A plane figure formed by three or more segments such that each segment intersects exactly two others, one at each endpoint, and no two segments with a common endpoint are collinear. Each segment is a *side* of the polygon. The common endpoint of two sides is a *vertex* of the polygon. A polygon completely encloses a region of the plane, called its *interior*.

Polynomial A monomial or a sum of monomials.

Population In a statistical study, the set of all individuals or objects being studied.

Positive correlation See *correlation*.

Positive number On a number line, a number that corresponds to a point on the positive side of zero. If the numbers increase in order from left to right, the positive side is to the right of zero.

Power The simplified form of x^n. For example, since $2^5 = 32$, 32 is the fifth power of 2.

Power of a power property of exponents For all integers m and n and all nonzero real numbers a, $(a^m)^n = a^{mn}$.

Power of a product property of exponents For all integers m and all nonzero real numbers a and b, $(ab)^m = a^m b^m$.

Power of a quotient property of exponents For all integers m and all nonzero real numbers a and b, $\left(\frac{a}{b}\right)^m = \frac{a^m}{b^m}$.

Precision The level of accuracy of a measurement.

Preimage See *transformation*.

Prime factorization An expression that shows a natural number as a product of prime numbers.

Prime number A natural number greater than 1 that has exactly two factors, 1 and the number itself.

Principal square root The positive square root of a number.

Prism A polyhedron with two parallel faces, called its *bases*, that are bounded by congruent polygons; and with *lateral faces* that are bounded by parallelograms connecting corresponding sides of the bases. The *height* of a prism is the length of any perpendicular segment drawn from a point on one base to the plane containing the other base.

Probability A number from 0 to 1, inclusive, that represents the likelihood an event will occur. If an event is *impossible*, its probability is 0. If an event is *certain*, its probability is 1. Events that are *possible but not certain* are assigned probabilities between 0 and 1.

Product The result of a multiplication.

Product of powers property of exponents For all integers m and n and all nonzero real numbers a, $a^m \cdot a^n = a^{m+n}$.

Product property of square roots If a and b are real numbers with $a \geq 0$ and $b \geq 0$, then $\sqrt{ab} = \sqrt{a} \cdot \sqrt{b}$.

Proportion A statement that two ratios are equal. The proportion that equates the ratios "a to b" and "c to d" can be written in three ways:

$$a \text{ is to } b \text{ as } c \text{ is to } d \qquad a : b = c : d \qquad \frac{a}{b} = \frac{c}{d}$$

Pyramid A polyhedron that consists of a face bounded by a polygon, called its *base*; a point called the *vertex* that is outside the plane of the base; and triangular *lateral faces* that connect the vertex to each side of the base. The *height* of a pyramid is the length of the perpendicular segment drawn from the vertex to the plane of the base.

Pythagorean Theorem If a triangle is a right triangle with legs of lengths a and b and hypotenuse of length c, then $a^2 + b^2 = c^2$.

Pythagorean triple Any set of three positive integers that satisfy the relationship $a^2 + b^2 = c^2$.

Quadrant One of the four regions into which a coordinate plane is divided by the x- and y-axes.

Quadratic equation An equation that can be written in the form $ax^2 + bx + c = 0$, where a, b, and c are real numbers and $a \neq 0$. The equation $ax^2 + bx + c = 0$ is called the *standard form* of a quadratic equation in x.

Quadratic formula A method for determining the solution set of a quadratic equation in one variable. If $ax^2 + bx + c = 0$, and a, b, and c are real numbers with $a \neq 0$, then $x = \frac{-b \pm \sqrt{b^2 - 4ac}}{2a}$.

Quadratic function A function that can be represented by an equation of the form $y = ax^2 + bx + c$, where a, b, and c are real numbers and $a \neq 0$.

Quadratic polynomial A polynomial of degree two.

Quadrilateral A polygon that has exactly four sides.

Quadrilateral Angle-Sum Theorem The sum of the measures of the interior angles of a quadrilateral is 360°.

Qualitative data Descriptive data that are represented by words.

Quantitative data Data that are represented by numbers.

Quartile See *first quartile, third quartile*.

Quotient The result of dividing one number by another.

Quotient of powers property of exponents For all integers m and n and all nonzero real numbers a, $\frac{a^m}{a^n} = a^{m-n}$.

Quotient property of square roots If a and b are real numbers with $a \geq 0$ and $b > 0$, then $\sqrt{\frac{a}{b}} = \frac{\sqrt{a}}{\sqrt{b}}$.

Radical equation An equation that contains one or more radical expressions with variables in the radicand.

Radical expression An expression that contains a radical sign. The square root symbol, $\sqrt{}$, is an example of a radical sign.

Radicand An expression under a radical sign.

Range of a data set In a set of numerical data, the difference when the minimum data value is subtracted from the maximum data value.

Range of a function See *function*.

Range of a relation See *relation*.

Rate A ratio that compares two different types of measures.

Ratio A comparison of two numbers by division. *The ratio of a to b can be written in three ways:*

$$a \text{ to } b \qquad a:b \qquad \frac{a}{b}$$

Rational equation An equation that contains one or more rational expressions.

Rational expression An expression that can be written in the form $\frac{P}{Q}$, where P and Q are polynomials and the value of Q is not zero.

Rational number A number that can be expressed in the form $\frac{a}{b}$, where a and b are integers and $b \neq 0$.

Rationalize the denominator A method in which the numerator and the denominator are multiplied by the conjugate of the denominator.

Rationalize the denominator Multiply the numerator and denominator by a given quantity.

Real number A number that is either a rational number or an irrational number.

Reciprocal Two numbers are reciprocals if their product is 1. See also *inverse property of multiplication*.

Rectangle A quadrilateral that has four right angles.

Recursive formula An algorithm used to identify terms in a recursive sequence.

Recursive sequence A sequence of terms in which subsequent terms are defined in relation to the preceding term or terms in the sequence.

Reflection A transformation that flips a graph *across* a line of symmetry without changing its size.

Reflection (or flip) The movement of a figure to a new position by flipping it over a line.

Reflexive property of equality For all real numbers a, $a = a$.

Regression A method to find the line of best fit for a set of points.

Regression analysis for bivariate data, the study of the scatterplot, the line of best fit, the residuals, and the goodness of fit.

Regular polygon A polygon that is both equilateral and equiangular.

Relation Any correspondence between two sets, called the *domain* and *range* of the relation.

Relatively prime Two natural numbers are relatively prime if their greatest common factor is 1.

Repeating decimal A decimal in which a digit or a block of digits repeats without end. The symbol for a repeating decimal is a bar over the repeating digit(s).

Replacement set The set of numbers that a variable may represent. Also called the *domain of a variable*.

Residual a measure of variability; the distance that each data point is from the regression line.

Residual plot a graph of a model's residuals; used as a test of the goodness of fit of the linear regression model.

Rhombus A quadrilateral that has four congruent sides.

Right angle An angle whose measure is 90°.

Right cone A cone in which the segment joining the center of the base to the vertex is perpendicular to the plane of the base. If a cone is not a right cone, then it is called *oblique*.

Right cylinder A cylinder in which the segment joining the centers of the bases is perpendicular to the planes of the bases. If a cylinder is not a right cylinder, then it is called *oblique*.

Right prism A prism in which the segments that connect corresponding vertices of the bases are perpendicular to the planes of the bases. The lateral faces of a right prism are bounded by rectangles. If a prism is not a right prism, then it is called *oblique*.

GLOSSARY

Right triangle A triangle with one right angle.

Root A solution to a quadratic equation; a zero of a function.

Sample In a statistical study, a subset of the population being studied.

Scalene triangle A triangle that has no congruent sides.

Scatter plot A statistical display of the relationship between two sets of data in which ordered pairs of the data are represented by points, the position of the points being determined by two axes labeled with numerical scales. See also *correlation*.

Scientific notation A number is written in scientific notation when it is written in the form $a \times 10^n$, where $1 \leq a < 10$ and n is an integer.

Segment Part of a line that begins at one point and ends at another. The points are called the *endpoints of the segment*. Also called *line segment*.

Sequence An ordered list of numbers. The *terms* of the sequence are the numbers in the sequence.

Set A group of objects.

Side of an equation One of two mathematical expressions that are joined by an equals sign.

Side of an inequality One of two mathematical expressions that are joined by an inequality symbol.

Significant digits Numbers that make a contribution to a value.

Similarity ratio The ratio of the lengths of corresponding sides of similar polygons. Also called the *scale factor*.

Simplest form of a radical expression The form of the expression in which the radicand contains no perfect-square factors other than 1; the radicand contains no fractions; and no denominator contains a radical.

Simplify a numerical expression To give the most common name for the number the expression represents.

Simplify a variable expression To perform as many of the indicated operations as possible.

Skewed left data values at the left side of the number line have low frequency.

Skewed right data values at the right side of the number line have low frequency.

Slope On a coordinate plane, the steepness of a nonvertical line, described informally as $\frac{\text{rise}}{\text{run}}$. Formally, if $P(x_1, y_1)$ and $Q(x_2, y_2)$ lie on $\overleftrightarrow{PQ}$, and $x_1 \neq x_2$, then the slope m of $\overleftrightarrow{PQ}$ is defined by $m = \frac{y_2 - y_1}{x_2 - x_1}$.

Slope-intercept form of an equation of a line For an equation in the variables x and y, $y = mx + b$, where m is the slope of the graph and b is the y-intercept.

Solution to an equation or inequality in two variables For an equation or inequality in the variables x and y, any ordered pair of numbers (x, y) that together make the equation or inequality a true statement.

Solution to an open statement Any value of the variable(s) that makes the statement true.

Solution set of an open statement The set of all solutions to the open statement.

Solution to a system of equations or inequalities in two variables For a system in the variables x and y, any ordered pair (x, y) that is a solution to each equation or inequality in the system.

Solve an equation or inequality To find the solution set of the equation or inequality.

Sphere The set of all points in space that are a fixed distance from a fixed point. The fixed point is called the *center of the sphere*. The fixed distance is called the *radius of the sphere*.

Spread See *variability*.

Square A quadrilateral that has four congruent sides and four right angles.

Square of a number The second power of the number.

Square root If $a^2 = b$, then a is a square root of b. The positive square root is denoted $\sqrt{b}$. The negative square root is denoted $-\sqrt{b}$.

Square root equation A radical equation where the index of the radical expression with the variable is 2.

Square root property If $x^2 = a$ where $a > 0$, then $x = \sqrt{a}$ or $x = -\sqrt{a}$, then $x^2 = a$ so $x = \pm\sqrt{a}$.

Standard deviation In a symmetric distribution a measure of variability that indicates an average deviation about the mean. The positive square root of the variance.

Standard deviation formula $s = \sqrt{\dfrac{\sum (x_i - \bar{x})^2}{n - 1}}$.

Standard form for a quadratic equation $ax^2 + bx + c = 0$

Standard form of a linear equation in two variables See *linear equation in two variables*.

Standard form of a polynomial A polynomial in one variable is in standard form when it has no like terms and the terms are written in descending order.

Standard form of a quadratic equation See *quadratic equation*.

Statement Any mathematical sentence.

Statistics The branch of mathematics that deals with the gathering, organization, analysis, representation, and interpretation of data.

Stem-and-leaf plot A display of data in which digits with higher place values are listed in a column as *stems*; digits with lower place values are listed in rows as *leaves* extending from the corresponding stems.

Step function Functions that result in graphs that are not continuous.

Straight angle An angle whose measure is 180°.

Stretch A transformation that changes a graph's size, widening it toward the *x*-axis.

Substitution method A method used to solve a system of equations in which one equation is solved for one variable in terms of the other. Then this expression is substituted for that variable in the other equation.

Substitution principle If $a = b$, then a may be replaced by b in any expression.

Subtraction property of equality For all real numbers a, b, and c, if $a = b$, then $a - c = b - c$.

Subtraction property of inequality For all real numbers a, b, and c,

- If $a < b$, then $a - c < b - c$; and
- If $a > b$, then $a - c > b - c$.

Sum The result of an addition.

Supplementary angles Two angles whose measures have a sum of 180°. Each angle is the *supplement* of the other.

Surface area The total area of all surfaces of a three-dimensional figure.

Symmetric distribution the left and right sides of the distribution show a line of symmetry.

Symmetric property of equality For all real numbers a and b, if $a = b$, then $b = a$.

System of equations or inequalities in two variables A set of equations or inequalities in the same two variables.

Term of an expression A number, a variable, or a product or quotient of numbers and variables.

Terminating decimal A decimal that stops, or terminates.

Terms of a proportion The numbers that form the proportion. In $\frac{a}{b} = \frac{c}{d}$, a, b, c, and d are the terms.

Theorem A statement that can be proved true.

Third quartile In a numerical data set, the median of the data values that are greater than the median of the entire set.

Transformation A correspondence between one figure, called a *preimage*, and a second figure, called its *image*, such that each point of the image is paired with exactly one point of the preimage, and each point of the preimage is paired with exactly one point of the image.

Transitive property of equality For all real numbers a, b, and c, if $a = b$ and $b = c$, then $a = c$.

Transitive property of inequality For all real numbers a, b, and c,

1. If $a < b$ and $b < c$, then $a < c$; and

2. If $a > b$ and $b > c$, then $a > c$.

Translation A transformation that shifts a graph vertically or horizontally without changing its size.

Translation (or slide) The movement of a figure along a straight line.

Trapezoid A quadrilateral that has exactly one pair of parallel sides. The parallel sides, and the lengths of the parallel sides, are called the *bases*. Two angles of the trapezoid whose vertices are the endpoints of a single base are a pair of *base angles*. The *height* is the length of any perpendicular segment drawn from a point on one base to the line containing the other base.

Trend line On a scatter plot, a line around which the data points seem to cluster. The trend line can be used to analyze the correlation between the data sets.

Triangle A polygon that has exactly three sides. To calculate area, any of the sides may be considered the *base*, and the length of that side is also called the base. The *height* is then the length of the altitude drawn to the base from the opposite vertex.

Triangle Angle-Sum Theorem The sum of the measures of the angles of a triangle is 180°.

Triangle Exterior-Angle Theorem The measure of each exterior angle of a triangle is equal to the sum of the measures of the remote interior angles.

Trinomial A polynomial with exactly three terms.

Truth value A closed statement is either *true* or *false*. These are its possible truth values.

Turning point of a parabola See *vertex of a parabola*.

Two-point form of an equation of a line For an equation in the variables x and y, $y - y_1 = \frac{y_2 - y_1}{x_2 - x_1}(x - x_1)$ where $P(x_1, y_1)$ and $Q(x_2, y_2)$ lie on a nonvertical line.

Two-way table organizes data for two categorical variables to show relationships between the variables

Uniform distribution all data values have approximately the same frequency.

Unit rate A rate per one unit of a measure. An example of a familiar unit rate is *miles per hour*.

Univariate data Data collected for a single variable.

GLOSSARY

Value of a function A member of the range of the function.

Value of a variable Any number in the replacement set of the variable.

Variability in a distribution the measure that indicates how close or far apart the data points are.

Variable A letter that represents a number.

Variable expression An expression that contains at least one variable. Also called *algebraic expression*.

Variance The average of the square of the difference between each value in a data set and the mean.

Vector A quantity that has magnitude and direction.

Venn diagram A diagram in which a rectangle represents all members of a set, with circles within it showing selected subsets and relationships among them.

Vertex form of a quadratic function A quadratic function of the form $y = ax^2 + bx + c$ that be written in the form $y = a(x - h)^2 + k$.

Vertex of a parabola For a parabola that opens upward, its vertex is its lowest point. For a parabola that opens downward, its vertex is its highest point. Also called the *turning point* of the parabola.

Vertical-line test If every vertical line that intersects a graph intersects that graph in exactly one point, then the graph represents a function.

Vertical translation A shift of a graph along the *y*-axis.

Volume of a three-dimensional figure The amount of space the figure encloses, measured by the number of nonoverlapping cubic units in its interior.

Whole number A member of the set $\{0, 1, 2, 3, 4, 5, 6, \ldots\}$.

x-**axis** The horizontal number line in a coordinate plane.

x-**coordinate** See *coordinate(s) of a point*.

x-**intercept of a graph** The *x*-coordinate of any point where the graph intersects the *x*-axis.

y-**axis** The vertical number line in a coordinate plane.

y-**coordinate** See *coordinate(s) of a point*.

y-**intercept of a graph** The *y*-coordinate of any point where the graph intersects the *y*-axis.

Zero of the function An input that makes the output of any function equal to 0, also referred to as a root.

Zero-product property If a and b are real numbers and $ab = 0$, then either $a = 0$ or $b = 0$.

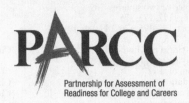

Partnership for Assessment of
Readiness for College and Careers

High School Assessment Reference Sheet

1 inch = 2.54 centimeters	1 kilometer = 0.62 mile	1 cup = 8 fluid ounces
1 meter = 39.37 inches	1 pound = 16 ounces	1 pint = 2 cups
1 mile = 5,280 feet	1 pound = 0.454 kilograms	1 quart = 2 pints
1 mile = 1,760 yards	1 kilogram = 2.2 pounds	1 gallon = 4 quarts
1 mile = 1.609 kilometers	1 ton = 2,000 pounds	1 gallon = 3.785 liters
		1 liter = 0.264 gallons
		1 liter = 1000 cubic centimeters

Triangle	$A = \dfrac{1}{2}bh$	Pythagorean Theorem	$a^2 + b^2 = c^2$
Parallelogram	$A = bh$	Quadratic Formula	$x = \dfrac{-b \pm \sqrt{b^2 - 4ac}}{2a}$
Circle	$A = \pi r^2$	Arithmetic Sequence	$a_n = a_1 + (n-1)d$
Circle	$C = \pi d$ or $C = 2\pi r$	Geometric Sequence	$a_n = a_1 r^{n-1}$
General Prisms	$V = Bh$	Geometric Series	$S_n = \dfrac{a_1 - a_1 r^n}{1 - r}$ where $r \neq 1$
Cylinder	$V = \pi r^2 h$	Radians	$1\ radian = \dfrac{180}{\pi}\ degrees$
Sphere	$V = \dfrac{4}{3}\pi r^3$	Degrees	$1\ degree = \dfrac{\pi}{180}\ radians$
Cone	$V = \dfrac{1}{3}\pi r^2 h$	Exponential Growth/Decay	$A = A_0\, e^{k(t-t_0)} + B_0$
Pyramid	$V = \dfrac{1}{3}Bh$		

INDEX

INDEX

INDEX

ACKNOWLEDGMENTS

Photographs

Every effort has been made to secure permission and provide appropriate credit for photographic material. The publisher deeply regrets any omission and pledges to correct errors called to its attention in subsequent editions.

Unless otherwise acknowledged, all photographs are the property of Pearson Education, Inc.

Photo locators denoted as follows: Top (T), Center (C), Bottom (B), Left (L), Right (R), Background (Bkgd)

Cover (L) JFreeman/Shutterstock, (R) Santhosh Kumar/Shutterstock.